£3-80

THE TECHNIQUE OF PIANO PLAYING

THE TECHNIQUE OF PIANO PLAYING

BY

JÓZSEF GÁT

Collet's
(PUBLISHERS) LTD.
LONDON AND WELLINGBOROUGH
1974

Title of the Hungarian original:
A zongorajáték technikája
Zeneműkiadó Budapest, 1964
Hungarian edition © József Gát, 1964

Translated by
István Kleszky

Binding and cover by
Tibor Szántó

Illustrations by
Jenő Szőts

Films by
Budapest Film Studio

SBN 569-00053-X

FOURTH EDITION
PUBLISHED IN COOPERATION WITH
CORVINA PRESS, BUDAPEST

© heirs of József Gát, 1965

COLLET'S (PUBLISHERS) LIMITED,
DENINGTON ESTATE,
WELLINGBOROUGH, NORTHANTS, U. K., 1974
PRINTED AND BOUND IN HUNGARY, 1974
RÉVAI PRINTING HOUSE, BUDAPEST

CONTENTS

PREFACE	9
PREFACE TO THE SECOND EDITION	10
TONE AND TONE-COLOURING POSSIBILITIES OF THE PIANO	11
OF THE SWING-STROKE	23
Can Touch Be Considered as the Smallest Element of Piano Technique?	23
The Two Kinds of Swing-Stroke	25
Control	26
Weight-Effect	26
Regulation of the Tone Volume	27
Proportion of Weight-Effect and Control in Shaping Dynamic Contours	29
THE SYNTHESIZING PROCESS AND THE ADAPTING MOVEMENTS	31
The Synthesizing Process	31
Adapting Movements	33
SEAT AND BODY POSTURE	49
LEGATO AND STACCATO	67
Legato	67
The Laws of Legato	69
Cantilena	70
Staccato	70
The Laws of Staccato	71
The Technique of Legato and Staccato	72
Legato and Staccato in Different Styles	73
ON FINDING CONTACT WITH THE INSTRUMENT	75
Consciousness and Inspiration	75
The Emotional Content	76
The Musical Concept	78
The Interrelation between Musical Imagination and Muscle Action	79

Expediency	81
Alterations of the Movements in the Interest of the Sound	86

ON THE NATURALNESS OF THE MOVEMENTS 89

Breathing	89
Participation of the Whole Body in the Piano Playing	90
Direction of the Eyes when Playing	91
Effect of the Emotional Content on the Body Position	92
The Connection of the Acoustic Spatial Reflex with the Musical Concept and through it with the Body Position	94
On Preserving the Naturalness of the Movements	97

ON PRACTISING 99

Repetition as a Means of Stabilizing New Conditioned Reflexes	99
The Attention	103

SLOW PRACTISING OF FAST PLAYING 105

Development of Velocity	107
Analysis of Velocity Playing	107
Application of Slow Practising	110
Rhythmic Variants	111
Synthesizing Movements in Slow Practising	114
Adapting Movements in Slow Practising	114

ON THE ROLE OF THE VARIOUS JOINTS 117

Hips	118
The Shoulder Joint	118
The Role of the Upper Arm in Synthesizing	119
Active Swing-Strokes of the Upper Arm	120
The Elbow and Radio-Ulnar Joint	122
The Wrist	125
The Finger Joints	127

STRUCTURE AND FORM OF THE HAND 131

Hand Structure	131
Form of the Hand	139

THE FUNDAMENTAL PLAYING FORMS AND THEIR VARIANTS 142

THE TECHNIQUE OF OCTAVES AND CHORDS 145

The Use of the Hand as a Unit	145
The Dynamic Shaping of the Chords	147
The Role of the Forearm in the Octave Technique	148

Complementary Wrist Motion	150
Vibrato	154
The Fingering of Octaves	156
The Preparation of Chord Practising	157
The Practising of Chords	157
The Practising of Octaves	160
Broken Chords	165
Arpeggio	167
THE TREMOLO	**170**
The Plain Forearm Tremolo	170
The Shaken Tremolo	171
Programme of Tremolo Teaching	172
Tremolo Practising	173
Broken Octaves	175
SKIPS	**177**
Even-Motion Skips	179
The Prepared Skip	182
Chord Skips	183
Reducing the Arm Movement with the Aid of Fingering	186
GLISSANDO	**188**
FINGER TECHNIQUE	**190**
Should We Raise the Fingers?	191
Positive Concentration	191
Anatomic Peculiarities of the Fingers	192
Correct Apportionment of the Work of the Joints	193
Prerequisites of Good Tone in Finger Technique	196
Application of Noise-Effects	197
The Joint Work of the Fingers and Forearm	197
Exercises for the Development of Finger Technique	198
THE PLAYING OF SCALES	**206**
Arm Movement in Scale Playing	206
The Changes of Position of the Hand in Scale Playing	207
Direction of the Thumb Stroke	209
Preparation of the Thumb Stroke	210
Slow Practising of Fast Scales	210
SCALES IN THIRDS	**215**
PASSAGES	**219**

TRILLS	225
Plain Finger Trills	227
Trills with Alternating Fingers	227
Tremolo Trills	227
The Practising of Trills	228
THE TECHNIQUE OF REPETITION	229
ON THE PLAYING OF ETUDES	233
FINGERING	236
The Special Role of the Thumb and the Little Finger	236
Passing the Fingers Over and Under	237
Role of the Fingering in the Synthesizing Movement	238
Crossing	239
Role of Fingering in Shifting the Centre of Gravity	241
Adapting Movements with the Aid of Fingering	242
Consideration of Peculiarities of the Individual Fingers	242
Repetition of the Same Fingering in Changing Octave Positions	242
Fingering in Sequences	243
Phrasing	243
Tremolo Fingering	244
Direction Fingering	245
COMPLEMENTARY GYMNASTIC EXERCISES	249
Recommendations concerning Rational Utilization of the Gymnastic Exercises	265
NOTES ON TEACHING THE TECHNICAL PROBLEMS OF BEGINNERS	266
Preparatory Schooling	266
Preparation of Technical Work	267
Legato	269
Playing to the Pupil	270
Improvisation	271
Rests, Counting	271
Tone Volume	272
Technical Exercises	273
Practising of Fundamental Playing Forms	273
The Use of the Pedal	275
Combining Musical and Technical Development	276
INDEX	277

PREFACE

Prefaces are usually apologies. I have the feeling that I have to apologize for having added one more book to the mass of – mostly unread – books on the method of piano playing.

This work was intended as a manual for pupils at teachers' conservatories. In order to preserve this handbook character of my work, I have mercilessly eliminated from the original manuscript everything which seemed to me unessential. As a result, the material of some chapters has become concentrated to such a degree that it is not enough to read them through superficially: they have to be studied.

The main fault of most books on piano playing is that they depend too much on the individual experiences of the authors gained in the course of teaching. These works are consequently often full of contradictions. The only solution is to search for the general laws. In order to reduce the errors to minimum, I endeavoured to arrange the book in such a manner as to present the general laws in the first chapters and to apply them in subsequent chapters as a means of control in dealing with the detailed technical problems. I hope that this method will enable the reader to find the fault I may have overlooked.

I did not strive to invent any new method of playing the piano. It is my belief that Bach, Beethoven, Mozart, Liszt and Chopin were not only outstanding composers but outstanding pianists, too. I believe in the piano as a prodigious, marvellous instrument – if the performer knows how to handle it. Two hundred years ago, Carl Philipp Emanuel Bach started a campaign to make the piano a singing instrument. He writes about the "thumping" pianists, who, by dint of ghastly effort finally succeeded in causing competent listeners to hate the piano.[1] If the reader will recollect how often, at the recitals of such piano-murderers, he wished that the piano were able to hit back, he will realize that even in our time we still have to fight against this kind of piano playing.

It is not a new, more modern method of piano playing we need, but good piano playing. The structure of the human organism has not undergone any changes since Beethoven's time and – in its essentials – the mechanism of the piano has also remained the same. Thus we have to find the common factors in the relation of the great artists to their instruments. This will reveal the right path which we, too, should follow. A superficial examination, however, will not prove sufficient. If a general law is not confirmed by everyday practice, it will thereby have been shown to be invalid save on paper. We will, therefore, accept only data which are adequate both from the point of view of anatomy and physics, that can be verified by physiology and are, at the same time, in conformity with the experiences gained in concert halls and in teaching.

---

[1] C. Ph. E. Bach: *Versuch über die wahre Art das Klavier zu spielen.* Einleitung, 2. §. "... so hat man mehrentheils Klavierspieler gehöret, welche nach einer abscheulichen Mühe endlich gelernet haben, verständigen Zuhörern, das Klavier durch ihr Spielen eckelhaft zu machen. Man hat in ihrem Spielen das runde, deutliche und natürliche vermisst, hingegen, an statt dessen lauter Gehacke, Poltern und Stolpern angetroffen. Indem alle andere Instrumente haben singen gelernt, so ist bloss das Klavier hierinnen zurück geblieben, und hat, an statt weniger unterhaltenen Noten, mit vielen bunten Figuren sich abgeben müssen, dergestalt dass man schon angefangen hat zu glauben, es würde einem angst, wenn man etwas langsames oder sangbares auf dem Klavier spielen soll..."

I have been working on this book for twenty years. During these years I have arrived at some new perceptions and results which made the use of new expressions inevitable. These will become intelligible for the reader only if he will take the trouble of thoroughly and carefully studying the book, chapter by chapter. His work will be facilitated by critical reading, as though engaged in a debate with the author.

I commend my book to those who are labouring to make the piano once more a singing instrument.

1958

The Author

PREFACE TO THE SECOND EDITION

The great interest, the numerous comments and letters received from pianists and teachers of music after the publication of the first edition of "The Technique of Piano Playing" has induced me to an enlargement, revision and reclassification of my work in the hope that in this new form it will serve as a further contribution to our common aim – musical education.

I am greatly indebted to Howard F. Gloyne, M.D. (U.S.A.) who, with his profound knowledge of the art of piano playing, has given help throughout the preparation of this new edition by suggesting corrections and improvements in the text. All my thanks are due also to Mrs. Márta Lukács-Szemes for making the acoustic measurement both to the previous and the present edition.

1965

The Author

TONE AND TONE-COLOURING POSSIBILITIES OF THE PIANO

For many decades polemics were written as to whether any change can be made in the colour of piano tones by different kinds of stroke. The debates flared up again and again, and in a certain form they continue even in our days.[1]

The controversy seems to be irreconcilable. The supporters of one believe that the change of the stroke cannot produce any difference whatsoever in the tone colour – provided that the tone volume remains the same – and thus only tones of different volumes can be produced on the piano but not tones of different colours. The most outstanding representative of this view is Tetzel.[2]

On the basis of their experiments executed repeatedly during the discussions the physicists came to the same result.[3] In the course of the debates even authorities like Max Planck were invited to express their opinion.

The supporters of the other side of the controversy – and the largest number of musicians belong to this side – felt that by the aid of different kinds of stroke an infinite series of tone colours can be produced.

[1] The so-called sinusoidal tones (e.g. those sounded on a tuning fork) differ from each other only in the frequency (number of oscillations). In other words this means that the individual tones of sound-generators with equal frequency cannot be distinguished from each other – if they are of equal tone volume and the generators are near to each other.

However, the tone of instruments, and of the human voice also, is much more complicated. A sound heard by us as a single musical tone is composed in reality of 10–18 tones. So, e.g., when sounding C we hear the following tones:

Example 1

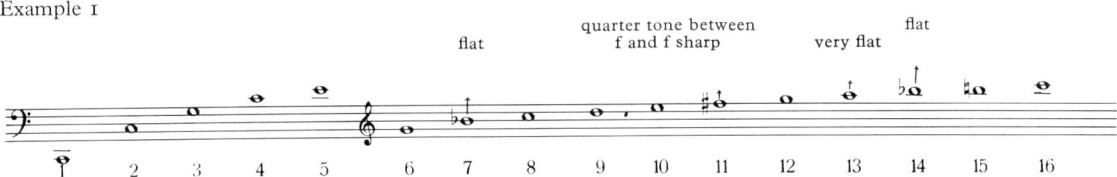

This is a series of harmonics; the first note fundamental. The frequencies of the harmonics are in the same proportion to each other as the integers (whole numbers); the frequency of the second harmonic is the double of the fundamental, that of the third is the threefold, etc.

This mass of tones is condensed into one sensation by our ears. The force (tone amount) of the overtones in relation to each other and to the key-note may show unlimited variations. If the high overtones are relatively strong we will have the sensation of a sharp, hard one. If the lower overtones are stronger we will have the sensation of a soft tone. Thus the tone colour depends solely on the number of the overtones and on the proportions of their intensity. If in two musical tones the number and proportions of the overtones are the same, their tone colour will also be felt as being the same.

[2] Eugen Tetzel: *Das Problem der modernen Klaviertechnik* (Leipzig, Breitkopf und Härtel, 1909).

"Der physikalische Ton kann... bei gleicher Tonstärke nicht durch den Anschlag eine verschiedene Klangfarbe erhalten." (With an identical tone amount the physical tone cannot obtain different tone colour, by the mere touch.)

[3] The Oct. 1934 issue of the Journal of Acoustical Society of America contains a paper by Hart, Filler and Lusby: *A Precision Study of Piano Touch and Tone* giving in addition to their own experiments also an account of repeating and checking of experiments made by different scientists.

There are teachers who are of the opinion that the statements of physicists – although true in themselves – cannot be accepted as explanations because piano playing cannot be explained on a rational basis.[4]

Is it possible that no explanation can be found that is based on the facts derived from physics experiments and yet that is still reconcilable with the conceptions of most musicians?

Let us try to summarize the facts found both by physicists in the course of their sound experiments, and those found in the piano manufacturer's practice.

1. An essential feature of the mechanism of the piano is the immediate rebounding of the hammer after having touched the string. If this were not true the vibration of the string would be impeded. Therefore the last part of the route of the hammer must be travelled entirely unhindered. This is known as "free travel." (The motion of the hammer resulting from the pianist's swing-stroke moving the key to the escapement level may be called the "driven travel.") The shorter the distance of free travel, the more the player will feel he is master of the motion of the hammer. However, at the moment of the striking of the string the hammer has to move entirely freely, independently of the key, in order to allow a free rebounding of the hammer.

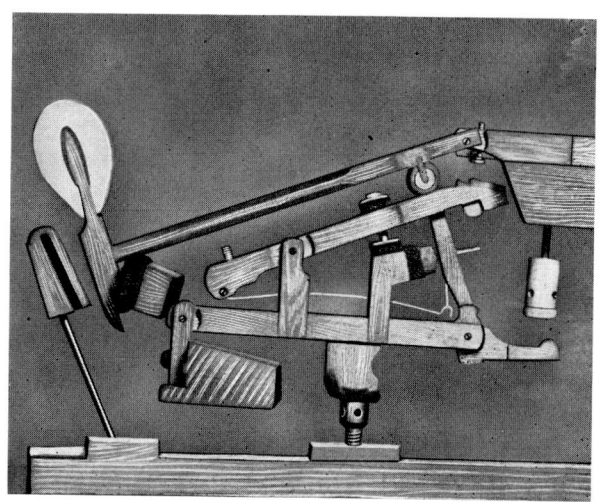

Phot. I
LANGER–ERARD MECHANISM

2. As the hammer moves freely at the moment of striking the string, the only variable component of this motion is the velocity of the hammer.[5]

3. The tone volume increases in direct proportion to the velocity of the hammer-stroke.

4. The velocity of the hammer at the moment of striking depends solely upon the velocity of the key attained at the escapement level. Thus, if the pianist wants to carry through alterations in the velocity of the hammer (and thus in the tone), he has to change the velocity of the key.[6]

5. The tone colour of the piano depends – apart from the construction of the piano (stringing, material and making of the sound-board, etc.) – mainly on the type of the coating of the hammer and on the quality of the felt.

It was found by Helmholtz[7] that the way the felt has been coated affects the length of time during which the hammer touches the string. An increase of the time of this contact will proportionally give prominence to the low overtones while a decrease will make the higher overtones dominate. A longer time of contact[8] will be more favourable for the sounding of the lower overtones and thus softer tone colours will be obtained as a result. If the contact time is a short one the higher overtones will become strong, and the tone will be felt hard and sharp.

To attain soft tone colours the piano manufacturers had to construct hammer heads permitting

[4] C. A. Martienssen: *Schöpferischer Klavierunterricht* (VEB Breitkopf und Härtel, 1954).

[5] H. Backhaus: *Nichtstationäre Schallvorgänge.*

[6] W. Lange: *Hochfr.-Technik und Elektroakustik.* P. 45, 120, 159. (1935).

[7] Helmholtz: *Lehre von den Tonempfindungen als physiologische Grundlage für die Theorie der Musik.*

[8] The time of the leather-coated wooden hammers (used in the age of the classics) in touching the string was too short and the endeavours to lengthen this time led to the use of the felt-coated hammers. Since having invented the felt-coating difficulties are now found by piano manufacturers in how to shorten the time of touch. If the hammer touches the string for a time longer than half of the frequency of the tone, it will oppress and also weaken the key tone. So e.g. in order to sound middle A the hammer should touch the string for only 1/880 sec.

a maximum contact period of hammer and string. This was realized by providing the hammer with layers of different degrees of hardness: progressively softer layers are applied over the hard centre. As a result, the hammer will recoil from the string only after the upper layers have been pressed to the string by the hard centre of the hammer.[9]

6. Higher overtones fade more slowly than lower ones.[10] The sustained tone thus alters, grows thinner.

7. The number of overtones increases in direct proportion to the velocity of the hammer stroke.[11] Within certain limits, alterations of the tone volume therefore bring about changes of the tone colour, too. (The changes of the tone colour are caused by the resonating elements of the instruments, mainly by the sound-board because – as proved by the experiments of R.N. Gosh[12] – the form of the vibration of the piano string is independent from the velocity of the hammer, i.e. from the tone volume. See Fig. 1.)

8. A forcefully struck note diminishes more rapidly than one struck with less energy.[13]

9. Higher notes fade away sooner than deep ones.[14] For this reason there is no need to have a damper on the upper octaves of the piano.

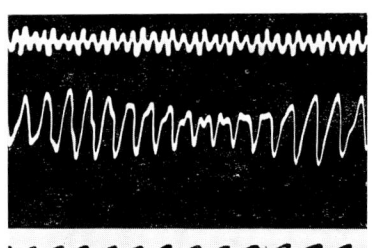

Fig. 1
OSCILLOGRAMS
OF A PIANO TONE

a) *Vibrations of string*, b) *Sound-board vibrations*, c) *Aerial vibrations*

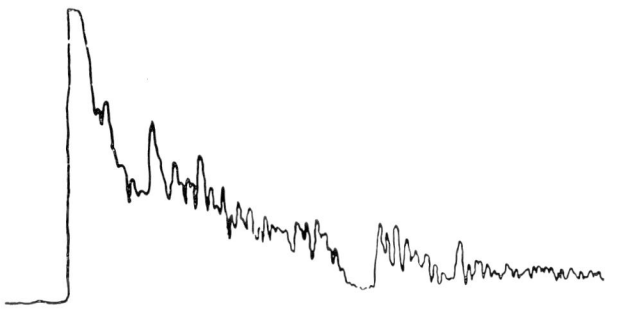

Fig. 2
A¹ SOUNDED FORTE AND PIANO

*The level-recorder clearly shows that the tone volume diminishes abruptly to almost a half immediately after the forte is sounded, while it will die away evenly, when the note is sounded piano**

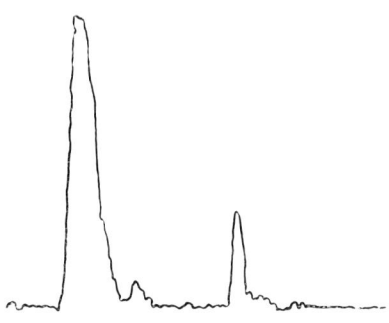

Fig. 3
A³ SOUNDED FORTE AND PIANO

The tone volume in both cases immediately diminishes to the minimum

[9] In the course of use the upper layer of the felt coat of the hammer becomes hardened and incised at the spot where it touches the key. A tuner "loosens" the upper layer by pinpricks (the so-called intonation). The unavoidable drawback of this method is that the felt will be torn by the pinpricks and so repeated intonations will be irreparably detrimental to the elasticity of the hammer.

[10] O. Vierling: *Diss. Univ.* Berlin, 1935.

[11] E. Meyer, G. Buchmann: *Berliner Bericht*, 735, 1931.

[12] J. Acoust. Soc. Amer. 7, 127, 1935.

[13] O. Vierling: *Diss. Univ.* Berlin, 1935.

[14] F. Urbach u. H. Schlesinger: *Wiener Anz.* Nr. 21, 208, 1936.

* As the needle of the level-recorder deviates proportionately to the intensity of the tone volume, we obtain a precise graph of the tone volume on the waxed paper running evenly under the needle. The microphone conveys the musical tone and the accompanying noises to the needle through an amplifier and so the graph obtained also gives a *summary* picture of the effective tone volume and of the noise. (The recordings were made by Márta Karsai-Szemes, research worker of the Research Group for Acoustics of the Hungarian Academy of Sciences.)

On the basis of paragraphs *1, 2, 3, 4* it can be seen that any manner of moving the key can result only in an increase or decrease of the velocity of the hammer, i.e. – from the point of view of the sounding of the string – in an increase or decrease of the tone volume. From paragraph 7 it can be also seen that a change of the tone colour is possible only in direct proportion to changes of the tone volume. In addition to these, the tone colour does not depend upon the pianist but on the construction of the instrument, i.e. on the kind of the felt coating of the hammers and on their state. In our above investigations, however, only the strings and – as a strengthening factor of the vibrations of the string – the sound-board had been taken into consideration as a source of tone. Simultaneously with those tones other vibrations will also arise, other sources of tone will start sounding: different *noises* will be heard by us. (Noises are composed – exactly like the musical tones – of tones of different pitches, but their overtones do not fit into harmonic overtone series and the numbers of vibration are not in regular connection with each other.) As noises will always start simultaneously with the musical tones, they must be taken into consideration in the development of the sensation of tone colour because the tone colours are evidently produced by the whole complex of sound impressions affecting us.

From the point of view of tone colour three groups of noises should be taken into consideration:[15]

a. Noises caused by vibrations of the hammer and the string at the moment of striking the string. These gradually increase in the upper pitch registers and in the highest registers they become rather disturbing.[16]

b. Noises caused by the collision of the wood of the key and the key-bed. (Lower noise.)

c. Noises caused by the collision of hand and key. (Upper noise.)

The apportioning of the lower and upper noises and their mixing with the tone of the string depends upon our will: the amount of them can be varied according to our musical conception. The deep hollow sound of the lower noise is an indispensable requisite of representing a dark, heavy, depressed mood, while the upper noises are needed in sharp, light, fresh sounds. However, their "over-dosing" – unfortunately a most frequent occurence in concert halls – will spoil the tone quality because the less the noise-effect (compared with the tone volume) the more "carrying" and sonorous the tone will be.

Even the most beautiful and sonorous singing would not come to full display if it were accompanied by noises of a street or a machine. Sometimes such an amount of noise is sounded in piano playing that it can only be compared with someone's trying to recite a poem simultaneously with the throbbing and purring of a motorcycle.

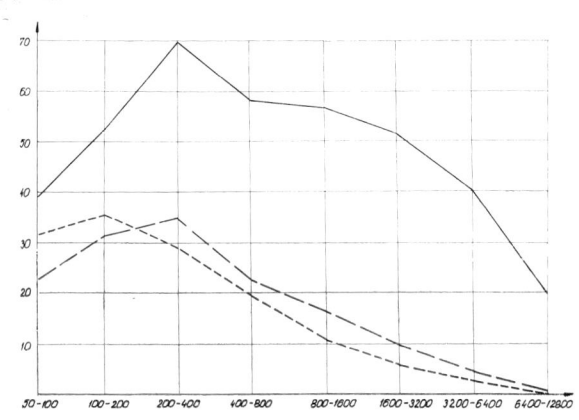

Fig. 4
NOISES OF THE KEY "g" ON A 274 CM STEINWAY PIANO

The values of the relative sound intensity are represented on the vertical axis while the frequency (in cps) on the horizontal one. The full line represents the complete sound together with the noises. The short-broken line represents the lower noises (dismounted hammer). The long-broken line represents the sound produced by a stroke with strong upper noises (dismounted hammer).

It is clearly visible that, compared to the total sound, the noises represent a considerable sound intensity. In the lower noises the largest force is found between 50 and 200 cps while in the upper noises the maximum force lies between 100 and 400 cps, and higher frequencies (up to 8,000 cps), too, will play a considerable role

---

[15] Among the noises arising during piano playing we will leave out of consideration the effect of the damper of the hammer mechanism and the noises arising when the keys are permitted to rebound. In slow, soft playing these latter noises may also be disturbing, if we let the key recoil abruptly. However, if our playing is adequately controlled they are so weak that they may be neglected.

The noise of the piano tone has been analyzed by Ludwig Riemann (*Das Wesen des Klavierklanges*, Leipzig, Breitkopf u. Härtel, 1911), but he did not recognize the role of noises in producing tone colour.

[16] E. Meyer, G. Buchmann: *Berliner Bericht*, 735, 1931.

This is also the explanation why with some pianists we will feel that their piano tone is "carrying" and why such a great difference is felt between piano tones of different players even when playing on the same instrument. Evidently not only the absolute dynamic grade is of importance because, if only that were the decisive factor, the listener would not feel that one pianist's tone "fills" the concert hall while, with another pianist, even his forte is felt to be poor in spite of his beating the piano with all his might. Thus the sensation of tone volume aroused in the listener depends not only upon the dynamic degree but also upon the pianist's ability to decrease the noise-effects in comparison with the tone volume. Although the importance of noise-effects in forming the tone colour is greater than generally believed (their relative tone volume is shown in Fig. 4.), it cannot be presumed that tone colours can be produced on the piano solely by the aid of noise-effects. In the playing of the outstanding pianists such an abundance and variety of tone-colour effects are to be found that it seems absurd to explain them exclusively by slight modifications of the tone colour, arising simultaneously with the variations of the tone volume, and from the colouring effect of the noises.

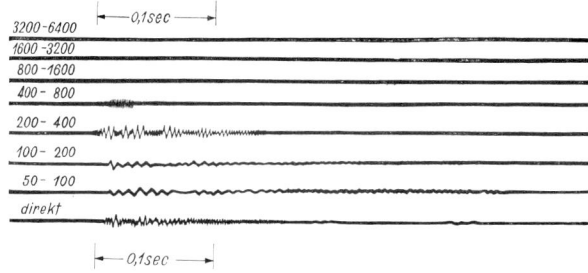

Fig. 5
LOWER NOISES OF d^3 ON A 221 CM STEINWAY PIANO WITH DISMOUNTED HAMMER
(Note the comparatively large tone amount even in the range of 200 – 400 cps.)

Up to this point single tones, sounding independently from each other, have been examined by us. With *single* piano tones very little if any change of tone colour is possible. This can offer no explanation of the extraordinary abundance of tone colours produced on the piano. Thus it must be supposed that, when several notes are sounded simultaneously or successively, certain factors may be found which will jointly give rise to certain tone colours. Although this sensation of tone colour does not correspond to requirements in their physical sense (because there is no change in the proportions of tone volume of overtones of the single tones), our investigations can be extended just the same. This can be done with good reason because when listening to music we never hear single independent tones but simultaneous or successive ones. In our further investigations the tone colour corresponding to the physical determination (i.e. the tone colour measurable in its overtone proportions) will be called an *objective tone colour*, while the tone-colour effect aroused in the individual listener by the interrelation of several tones will be called *subjective tone colour*.

The explanation is to be found mainly in the dynamic proportions of the tones. In the succession of several tones the agogics will also play their part, and in the different tone colours changing agogics can always be found in addition to changing dynamics.

The two components of the subjective tone colour are thus dynamics and agogics.

This statement is also confirmed by the fact that both the harpsichord and the organ, being incapable of dynamic alterations in the tones without changing the source of the sound, compensate for their lack of subjective tone colours through their objective colours, i.e. different registers (stops or pedals).[17] The piano does not need the use of complementary devices of this kind, and so the stops formerly used (harp and bassoon pedal, different p- and pp-pedals, carrillon) have been successively abandoned in the course of time.[18]

[17] The use of the stops causes objective changes in the tone colours. For instance, in organ playing different pipes or pipe-combinations are sounded.

[18] The only objective stop still possessed by the piano is the so-called "una corda". When the left pedal is depressed the hammer touches only two strings instead of three (or only one string instead of two), and so the tone volume diminishes. In addition there is also a change in the tone colour. In the course of using the piano the felt part of the hammer gets incised by the strings and hardens accordingly. When the left pedal is depressed, the row of hammers becomes displaced to the right, so that soft felt parts will again touch the string, instead of the hardened part, and this results in a softer tone.

Dynamics and agogics supplement each other in producing the subjective tone colour and may therefore, to a certain degree, replace each other. This is why the organist applies agogics in an increased degree. He marks the stresses by agogic alterations instead of changes in the tone volume.[19]

The performer attains the most varied effects of colouring by means of dynamic and agogic shading and with the aid of corresponding noise-effects.[20]

Within the concept of subjective tone colour we may distinguish between *generally valid* and *individual* subjective tone colour.

In the case of subjective tone colour of general validity the dynamic degree is fixed. (The concept *dolce* includes that of the *piano* while the concept *maestoso* covers that of *mezzoforte* or *meno forte*. Apparently this varies with the different countries. Upon questioning I had found that Hungarian musicians, teachers and pupils felt mezzoforte as the dynamic grade of the maestoso, while about 30 German musicians expressed the opinion that it is forte.) The corresponding apportionment of dynamics and agogics is superimposed. The dynamics and agogics of dolce, for instance, are equally extreme: its piano is characterized by great and sudden differences in tone volume, while at the same time the inner rhythm is extremely mobile and lively. The maestoso, on the other hand, requires even dynamics and strict, regular rhythm.

The *martellato* and *pomposo* are characterized by certain noise-effects. If we wish to imitate stringed instruments, we have to play as noiselessly as possible in order to obtain a soft smooth tone. In imitating wind instruments, characteristic colours may be obtained by a somewhat harder touch (united arm) and moderate noise-effects.

The individual subjective colour means the application of dynamics, agogics and noise-effects in a way characteristic of the respective player.[21] It does not depend upon dynamic degrees to the same extent as the general subjective colour does, because the accents, noise-effects, dynamic and agogic characteristics of the individual pianist assert themselves in all dynamic degrees.

The *crescendo* and *descrescendo* which accompany the melodic line vary individually with the pianist: there is an ever changing dynamic and agogic stress on particular notes.[22]

---

[19] The cylinders of the player (electric) piano are constructed on the basis of precise recording of the artist's playing, and so the agogics are reproduced perfectly. However, because the player piano is unable to reproduce the more subtle nuances of dynamics, it can only reproduce the subjective colours of the artist.

[20] The fact that dynamics and agogics play such a great part in our tone-colour concepts gives an explanation of the strange phenomenon that musicians attribute to a certain constant character and colour to the individual musical keys, despite the fact that the pitch of tuning changed during the course of the centuries. (So, e.g., in the last 50 years it has raised by nearly a semitone. The organ of Händel was with a third lower than the tuning of our organs, etc.) Why is the character of the keys felt exactly the same as 50–100 or even 150 years ago?

The feeling of a certain character of individual musical keys which arouses similar concepts – up to a certain degree – with many musicians has its real basis: the necessary changes of dynamics and agogics. Each of the keys does have its special character indeed but this is linked strictly to certain tone colours. With string instruments G major, D major and A major are clear, bright keys (also the easiest ones from the point of view of technique), but where is the radiant brightness of A major with a trombone? Here, on account of its difficult, uncomfortable grips, the A major becomes more suitable to express humorous or clumsy characters. The brilliant, bright tone colours will be performed by the trombone in B flat major because playing in this key is easiest on this instrument. With the piano one may also observe that a transposition with a semitone or a tone will entirely change the character of the composition, while if the piano is tuned a semitone higher or lower, those having no perfect pitch will hardly notice any difference. (See Helmholtz's quoted work, Engl. ed. 1875, p. 482.)

[21] Remember the characteristic tone of Bartók's playing.

[22] Besides dynamics, agogics and noise-effects, the use of the pedals, characteristic of each individual pianist, also contributes to tone-colouring. The right pedal complements the dynamic effect, and in addition it is also a special tone-colouring factor. Nevertheless, the manner of using the pedals cannot be considered as a constant factor in individual subjective colour, because the personal features will also assert themselves without use of the pedals. It is a well-known fact, too, that use of the pedals has to be adapted to the qualities of different concert halls. (Playing before a microphone requires a diminished use of the pedals.)

Fig. 6

The dynamic grade of both Beethoven's Funeral March and the Nocturne in D flat major by Chopin is the piano. But what a great difference between the two! The tone volume of the maestoso of the Funeral March almost attains the borders of the forte: the tones are perfectly even, not only dynamically but also agogically. Certain tones of the Nocturne attain the volume of the chords of the Funeral March, but others are hardly to be heard. Not only the individual values, but even the length of the bars will vary, and what strikes us most: Our ears not only fail to notice these unevennesses, they will accept as dolce only these dynamics and agogics, so rich in extremes

The distribution of the dynamic relationship between tones sounded simultaneously is also characteristic of individual colour. The same chord evokes different impressions if we apply different dynamic proportions. The dynamic "mixture" of the chords is one of the most perfect means at the pianist's disposal because he is able to indicate particular pitches and can transgress the limits of the tempered scale. To our ears the note that is struck somewhat more strongly sounds higher in pitch, while the note that is struck more softly sounds lower.

Now let us digress for a moment to consider the subjects of intonation and tempering. As to the concept of clear intonation a confusion of views is to be observed. The use of the tempered scales and intervals, as made necessary by reason of writing and instrumental technique, may give rise to the misconception that "tempered music" is also possible. In reality, the good musician has always thought in pure intervals. Delezenne observed in 1826 that the most outstanding violinists and cellists played pure thirds and sixths and not Pythagorean or tempered intervals. Helmholtz when listening to the playing of Joachim stated that he intoned regular pure intervals.

This was the actual situation, and with the best performers it never will be otherwise. The reason for this is that the musical imagination is unable to accept the 12-degree scale. Within the range of one octave even a man with no ear for music is capable of distinguishing many hundreds of tones, not to mention the musician with fine ears.

The necessity for thinking in pure intervals will instantly become evident if we take into consideration that with each musical tone we innervate pure intervals again and again, because in the overtone series we hear pure intervals. Thus everyone is capable of intoning clearly – at any rate, everyone should be able to do so – because the pure intervals become engraved in our memory with incredible intensity through many repetitions in everyday life. However, matters will go awry if we start teaching tempered intervals instead of the pure intonation taught us by nature. In this way, the very concept of the interval becomes confused in our minds. [In memorizing intervals nothing more harmful can be imagined than making a child sing tempered intervals instead of pure ones. This will cause confusion – i. e. the loss of sureness of intonation – in the same way as changing the pitch of the sound, signalling feeding-time (in Pavlov's well-known dog experiments), may cause nervous disorders.][23]

Tempered writing is a sort of abbreviation or simplification. The functions of the individual tones cannot be denoted. The tone called by the same name requires another pitch in its function of a fifth than in its function of a third and still another in its function as a seventh. The E as the fifth of A is higher than the corresponding tone of the tempered scale, but taken as a third of the tempered C it is considerably lower.

The importance of the pure interval is dual. On the one hand, the pureness of the simultaneously sounded tones will arouse an agreeable sensation and, on the other hand, the succession of tones will provide harmonic interrelations.

What is the solution? Are we to introduce (as suggested by Helmholtz) a more accurately tuned scale consisting of 53 tones within an octave, as the lesser evil? It would not give much help and cause immense complications both in music writing and in piano playing. There is definitely no need to do this. But temperation must not be considered as something more than it really is and then it will not disturb our thinking in clear harmonies but will arouse the impression of clear harmonies in our listeners.

As a matter of fact, performing in clear intervals is not as easy as it seems to be at first sight even when playing string instruments or when singing. If a chord sounds a longer time, only the mathematically exact sounding of the intervals is of importance. However, when playing melodies the single tones must be played higher or lower than is required by the pure tuning. The direction of the melody is made clearer by elevating or lowering the pitch and thus the function of the leading note and the dissonances are stressed. It cannot be determined how much the mathematically exact intervals must be modified in any given case. Emphasizing by raising or lowering the pitch is a question of artistic taste and affords, even individually, infinite possibilities of variation. This applies also to the case when, e. g., a violinist plays to the accompaniment of an organ or piano. The best possible adjustment of the tempered and pure intervals will be dictated by artistic taste.

Unlike the violinist or singer the pianist is not able to alter the pitch of the single tones but he is capable of giving a perfect illusion of playing pure intervals through dynamic differentiation. He will play the higher tones somewhat stronger and the lower ones somewhat softer. In this sense the pianist is also capable of correct or incorrect intonation, just like the violinist or singer. The only difference is that the singer produces real pitch differences while the pianist will make his listeners feel the same note higher or lower by the aid of appropriate dynamics.

In the first chord reproduced here (D major dominant seventh), we involuntarily sound the C sharp somewhat stronger in order to make it evoke the sensation of a higher pitch according to its function as a leading note. In the dominant seventh of

Example 2

---

[23] Teaching on the basis of temperation has unfortunately gained ground in recent years. Very often, even in solfeggio teaching a rigid 12-degree scale is practised and the pure intonation of melodies and chords is replaced by acrobatic feats of the throat and mechanical singing. This kind of solfeggio does more harm than good. The same rule is valid here as in every other field of music: Bad music is harmful. The singing of artificially concocted melodies, constructed only for the practising of difficult skips, will paralyze the musical imagination of the pupil.

A flat major, on the other hand, we want to hear the D flat of the soprano somewhat lower as the seventh, and so we play the tone softer.

Example 3

Thus the same tone – in harmony with its milieu – sounds higher or lower to us depending on the dynamic nuances.

If the pianist is guided in his playing by his musical imagination, the differences in dynamics will correspond exactly with those existing between the imagined pitch and the tempered tones of the piano, and thus the sensation of the same harmonies will be aroused in the listener as those imagined by the player.

The dynamic differences applied consequently (according to the imagined pitch) will provide a clear scale of evaluation for the listener and he will experience the dynamic differences as pitch differences without any difficulty. The only prerequisite for the pianist is – so to speak – to live within the harmonies in their fullest sense and to build them up in his imagination because only melodies felt in this way can be imagined in correct intonation. Only in the "fully felt," deeply experienced melody can the leading tone, the dissonances, etc. play part and on the other hand also the pure intervals.

Let us compare the most important intervals. The pure fifth of the natural overtone series (formed by the second and third harmonics) is somewhat larger than the tempered one. Conversely, its inversion to a fourth will be somewhat smaller.

The situation is more complicated with thirds. According to Helmholtz, the major third formed by the fourth and fifth tones of the overtone scale, and the minor third formed by the fifth and sixth members of the series, must be considered as regular. In practice, however, a more complicated solution is required. In the course of experiments made over many years I have come to the conclusion that the 4/5 major third and the 5/6 minor third are correct only as constituent parts of a major chord. Minor chords require another solution.

Now the problem is the following: Do we find any minor chord in the natural overtone series? The answer is yes, we do. The chord formed by the 6th, 7th and 9th overtones is an example. The 6/9 forms a pure fifth, the 6/7 a minor third, and the 7/9 a major third. This minor chord achieves a deeper, stronger innervation because it is nearer to the key-note than the other which is to be found as a full chord only in the 10/12/15 overtones. Even in the combinational tones this minor chord provides a better solution than that composed with the 5/6 minor third. The combination of the difference of the 5/6 minor third is c, which gives the impression of a seventh-chord of the first degree. The c sounding together with g and b is less disturbing.

The two different thirds can be distinguished most simply by reference to the basic major- and minor-key chords. Thus a major third – if it forms the basic third of a major-key chord – is lower than a tempered third. If the major third is the upper member of a minor-key chord, it is larger than if it were a tempered one. In the same way: a basic minor third will be smaller than the tempered minor third, and if a minor third is the upper member of a major-key chord, it will be larger than the tempered one.

This is also corroborated by practical experience. In this connection it is rewarding to observe the low basic thirds in a major or minor chord as intoned by choirs singing with pure intonation.

It is also worth noting that a minor seventh figuring as the 7th overtone (dominant seventh) is much lower than the tempered one. Thus, if we want to sound a seventh-chord harmoniously, smoothly, quietly, the seventh must be played softly, or else the chord sounds restless and will even lose its dominant character, arousing the impression of an augmented six-five chord.

The prerequisite of a pure major or minor chord played on the piano is the softly played third. But woe to him who tries to do this deliberately, who concentrates on playing this or any other tone softer or stronger. His playing will be as far from real music as even the best marionette figures are unable to reproduce the soft movements of a living body. The only way is to live in the melody as fully and as completely as possible, to imagine the pure harmonies in their full brilliancy of colours and to find these imagined colours on the piano.

Tetzel drew completely correct conclusions from the functioning of the mechanism of the piano, and his statement that the touch is not a technical but an artistic problem is in full conformity with the most up-to-date tendencies in the methodology.[24]

Tetzel was attacked by Martienssen but the latter was compelled to come to the same conclusions by saying that the player *has to play as if* the different touches really corresponded to different tone colours.[25] According to Martienssen's opinion, however, the process of instrumental tone arising from the imagined one is entirely irrational,[26] although he is quite well aware of the fact that dynamics and agogics have an influence on our sensations of tone colour. Thus if the performer makes himself believe that he is producing different tone colours by his "touch," he does nothing else than apply dynamics, agogics and noise-effects in a rational way according to certain rules. After all Martienssen is right when he states that the pianist's concentration on a mere playing softer or stronger tones results in a poor piano playing. However, this is not detrimental to the merits of Tetzel because the dethronement of the touch is of the utmost importance: the superstitious belief that different tone colours are produced by different ways of touching the piano allows of many bad, jerky movements.

Of course it is out of the question that we have to pay attention to our playing of stronger or softer tones or tones with more or less noise-effect. Once it is clearly understood that the keys must always be touched in the simplest way[27] it directly follows that there are no different kinds of touches clearly separable from each other, but rather an infinite variety or series of variants of a fundamental way of touching the piano. By applying ourselves to an intensive imagining of the tones our hands will be enabled to apportion dynamics, agogics and noise-effects in a way which will give a perfect illusion to the listeners. If the dynamics, agogics and noise-effects are employed in a regular way, i.e. in conformity with our musical concept, the whole process can be considered as a sort of coding our musical concepts for the instrument.

For the "player piano" the music must be translated into the language of the machine by the perforations of the cylinder. The music must also be translated into the language of the piano by the aid of different dynamic effects, agogics and noise-effects. If this coding is really logical and is consistently carried out on the basis of a uniform system, the listener – after a little practice – will be able to understand this code system, just like a telegraph operator who fluently reads the Morse signals consisting of dots and dashes. This is why a certain amount of practice is needed in order to be able to enjoy listening to piano playing. For the inexperienced listener fine solutions of

---

[24] Eugen Tetzel: *Das Problem der modernen Klaviertechnik*. 1909. "Ich weise logisch nach, dass die Bewegung des die Saite im freien Fluge erreichenden Hammers nur eine Verschiedenheit, nämlich die der *Schnelligkeitsgrade*, aufweisen kann, bei gleicher Schnelligkeit des Hammeranpralls also die Saite in gleicher Weise erschüttert werden muss. Der physikalische Ton kann daher bei gleicher Tonstärke nicht durch den Anschlag eine verschiedene Klangfarbe erhalten."

"Der Anschlag ist also mehr eine künstlerische als eine technische Angelegenheit."

(I can prove logically that the hammer, attaining the string with a free momentum, will show differences only with respect to the degree of velocity. Thus in case of equal velocities of the hammer strokes the string has to vibrate in the same way. The physical sound therefore, when produced with the same force, cannot obtain a different tone colour merely by the touch. Thus, the touch is more an artistic than a technical matter.)

[25] "Die psychologische Grundwahrheit für eine künstlerische Klavierpädagogik ist die Einstellung, als ob der Klavierton an sich durch eine besondere Art des Anschlages in der vielfältigsten Weise zu modifizieren sei." (In the same work, quoted above, p. 42.)

(One of the psychological basic principles of an artistic piano pedagogy is the approach as if the piano tone in itself could be modified in the most varied way by special kinds of touch.)

[26] (See p. 44 of the work quoted above:) "Nur auf irrationaler Basis, niemals auf rationaler beginnt das Klavier seine nie zu errechnenden letzten Klangwunder zu offenbaren."

(It is on an irrational basis and never on a rational one that the piano begins to reveal its never calculable final marvels.)

[27] See the striking analogy of A. B. Marx on p. 82.

detailed problems or beauty in detail are of no significance whatever. But this is also the reason why pianists have the most fanatical public. The pianist plays on the imagination of his listeners. The pianist's way of signalling tone colours arouses more beautiful tone-colour concepts in the listener than the real, objective tone colour of any other instrument, because the flight of fancy always transcends reality. So, a pianist when imitating the sound of a horn, or even when trying to reproduce the sound produced by the violinists of a whole orchestra is able to arouse emotions in his listeners which even the horn player or the violinists would be unable to do.

As Kalkbrenner said[28] the tone of the piano is not a ready or finished one, it can be better modified than the tone of any other instrument. The rules developed here concerning the tone-colouring possibilities of the piano corroborate the above statement.

The more sensitive our dynamic shading and agogic shaping, the more diversified and coloured our playing will be. Our aim is that our movements should reliably transmit even the smallest nuances in changes of tone volume – by conserving the most perfect agogic liberty.

---

[28] *Méthode pour apprendre le pianoforte à l'aide du guide-mains.* Paris, 1830.

Phot. 2
FRANZ LISZT
(*After a photograph taken in Weimar*)

OF THE SWING-STROKE

CAN TOUCH BE CONSIDERED AS THE SMALLEST ELEMENT OF PIANO TECHNIQUE?

According to the general opinion the smallest element of piano technique is the touch. The notion of touch includes many kinds of movements, and even tone-colour concepts are associated with it, so, e.g. we often speak about a dolce touch. However, in our investigations on the tone colour of the piano it has been stated that the tone colour depends primarily upon the mixture of dynamic and agogic elements. Therefore it is absolutely wrong to associate the tone colour with the notion of touch. But nothing is gained either, if only the motion elements are considered as parts of the touch because very many kinds of motion functions are needed to execute the touch. (It is evident to everyone that in the touch our feet and trunk, too, play an important role. But it is equally clear that this role is essentially different from that of the fingers.) It is absolutely hopeless to investigate motion elements, having differing tendencies, within one single unit, and this is probably why some methods are confusing because so many contradictions are mingled amongst each other and very frequently even within their own system.

First of all it should be cleared up which motion is required in order to make the mechanism of the piano bring the hammer to the string.

Swing-stroke or pressing the key?

It is a characteristic feature of the piano's hammer mechanism that the hammer falls back immediately after striking the string. The falling back of the hammer is made possible by the so-called escapement enabling the hammer to cover the last small part of its route completely freely. If the hammer could be pressed to the string, i.e. there were no release to cause the hammer to fall back, the latter would deaden the vibration of the string.

The hammer cannot be brought to the strings by a uniform motion and therefore a swinging motion has to be applied in order to give the hammer the required impetus.

The ability to perform a swinging motion is innate, up to a certain point, in all of us. Like the rest of our other natural abilities, it is capable of considerable development through practice. The greater part of our working movements consists of such swinging motions which, in the course of time, become entirely instinctive.

By pressing we mean a constant application of force. If instead of striking the key we push it down by a slow, even motion, no sound will result. (Mute sustaining.) If, on the other hand, we press the key to the bottom after the stroke, we perform unnecessary work, and this will detrimentally affect our other movements.

To speak about "pressure" in piano playing is to use a loose expression, giving rise to misunderstanding. This may lead to such faults as pressing down the key to the bottom of the key-bed, and even keeping it there with a display of force (vibrato).

If the pianist depresses the key he fails to take into consideration the laws of the operation of the piano's mechanism. As the release of the hammer takes place near the middle of the downward course of the key (at the escapement level), any further movement of the finger is merely supplementary.

In examining the sides of the keys of pianos used for at least four or five years, we find that the upper part of the wood of the key is of darker colour. This proves that keys do not as a rule touch the key-bed, otherwise their sides would have become uniformly dark.

Rapid tempo can be attained only through economy of movement so that even pianists who apply a veritable "key-massage" in slow tempi do not press the keys down completely in case of greater speed.

The factors of the swing-stroke

The swinging motion — to which we shall in the further course of this study apply the term "swing-stroke" — involves three factors:

1. a firm basis, *2.* an elastic support, *3.* an actively swinging unit for executing the swinging motion, subsequently referred to as "active unit."

1. A firm basis is attained by an appropriate position of the body; this involves a good music stool (or bench) and correct posture. (In some athletic sports a firm basis is of similar importance. The shot-putter, the discus-thrower or the boxer would be unable to give an adequate performance on loose, marshy ground, not to speak of an upholstered, springy mattress.)

2. In piano playing, the whole body functions as an elastic support. (Our body is always in an elastic state when working.) The rebound of the keys is unnoticeably absorbed by a series of elastic joints.

In striking a nail with a hammer, we do not hold the hammer down after the blow but rather let it rebound elastically. The key of the piano also rebounds, and this rebound has to be absorbed, otherwise it will hinder us in preparing for the next stroke.

Our whole body takes part in absorbing the rebound. It is therefore of great importance in piano playing to use the feet as a means of elastic support. Misinterpretation of this fact is at the root of the incorrect view that the feet play an *active* part in sounding a note.

3. In order to cause the hammer to strike, it is essential to execute an active swinging motion — the swing-stroke — starting from one of the joints. It is essential to emphasize this point because many players are unable to distinguish between their subjective impression while executing a movement, and what actually takes place. (This gives rise to such misconceptions as the following: to sound a tone it is sufficient to drop the hand on the keys or softly flex the fingers or even apply pressure in order to attain a more beautiful tone.) With the aid of certain analogies we may, it is true, create better psychological conditions for carrying out the stroke, but these must not be confused with the description of the actual movement.

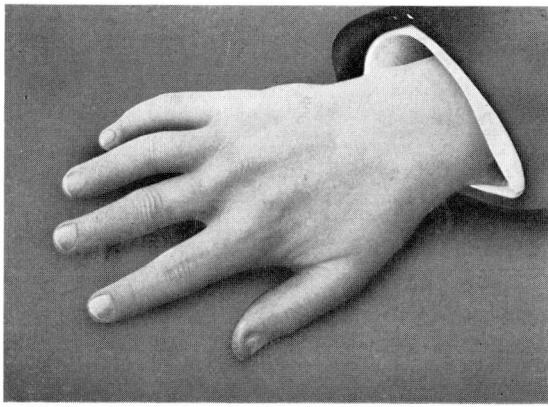

Phot. 3

THE HAND OF E. D'ALBERT

THE TWO KINDS OF SWING-STROKE

The hammer can be brought into motion by the
direct or
indirect swing-stroke.

In the direct swing-stroke, the finger clings to the key, which is brought into motion as an elongation of the arm. The pianist has the sensation of practically grasping the key and by means of this hold playing directly with the key.[1] This sensation of "grasping the key" is fully experienced only when playing from the shoulder joint.

The shoulder joint is, however, incapable of very fast movements for which we have to rely on the forearm or the fingers. Active work on the part of the fingers or the forearm, however, makes the direct swing-stroke inapplicable because the contact with the key becomes interrupted already at the beginning of the movement. The time-span of the contact will be abbreviated also by the fact that the fingers – in striving to display more energy – are forced to strike from a greater height. Thus – although the direct swing-stroke is the most perfect method of sounding the note – we have to apply (and even very often) the indirect swing-stroke also whenever our finger cannot "merge" with the key but strikes it.

In comparing the direct and indirect swing-strokes we may state the following:

Direct swing-stroke

1. The movement of the arm (active unit) accommodates itself to the movement of the key in order to keep the sensation of grasping and elongation.

2. The finger remains constantly in contact with the key.

3. The movement of the key is accelerated gradually, because it is in contact with the active unit from the very beginning of the movement.

Indirect swing-stroke

1. The finger or forearm (as active swinging unit) cannot accommodate itself to the fixed direction of the key's movement.

2. The finger has no contact with the key at the beginning of the movement.

3. The active swinging unit has already attained considerable speed at the moment of meeting the key. This will cause a sharp upper noise (on account of the inertia of the key). The collision will at the same time disturb the sureness of the strokes and therewith also the apportioning of the tone volume and the dynamic contours.

The most noteworthy drawback of the indirect swing-stroke is that the finger has no contact with the key at the beginning of the movement. Some methods try to eliminate this by restricting the active work of the fingers, which are made to touch the keys even when it is not their turn to strike. They thus give the impression of being able to execute a direct swing-stroke, too. As the finger is in contact with the key already at the beginning of the movement, the objections made under points *2* and *3* above are invalidated, but full accommodation to the direction of the key's rotation is impossible just the same. In addition, we also lose the extra energy gained by the increased movement and muscular activity of the fingers. The result may be loss of velocity and inability to maintain the tempo due to the comparative weakness of the finger muscles. Moreover, we

---

[1] Many of the faults arising later could be prevented by making the children during the first months of their beginners' course play the clavichord instead of the piano. This method would not only eliminate the contrast between the fragile little fingers of the child and the clumsily functioning piano keys, but would once and for all show the beginner the right way of handling the key. (As to the handling of the key, see more detailed instructions in the chapter "On Finding Contact with the Instrument.")

should not renounce the tone-colouring effects attained by raising the fingers to different levels. (Upper noises.)

Thus the use of the indirect swing-stroke proves to be unavoidable, but we have to find the means of bringing it as near as possible to the direct swing-stroke and of reducing its drawbacks to a minimum. For this purpose we should raise our fingers or arm only as much as is absolutely necessary for producing the desired tone colour. In addition, we should endeavour to make the active swinging unit accommodate itself as much as possible to the fixed rotation of the key; we should, therefore, slow down and brake its movement. This braking acquires special importance through the fact that to accomplish it more muscle work is required, necessitating more intense and resolute nerve impulses. The deeper the musical experiencing of the tones, the stronger the resulting nerve impulses will be, and thus appropriate braking is, in the last analysis, also a function of the musical concept.

CONTROL

Our movements are carried out by antagonistic muscles which counterbalance each other. Thus, in raising the finger, the greater part of the work is always done by the extensor but — depending on our will — the flexor carries out a counteracting movement of varying intensity, thus slowing down and controlling the initial movement. This braking (inhibiting) effect of the opposing muscle will therefore be called "control" in the further course of this work.

On account of the natural muscle tonus (see page 117) there is a minimal braking effect in all of our movements. For instance, when, in lifting a finger, we have the sensation of its being absolutely relaxed, the inhibition is imperceptible. In the case of controlled movements it will increase and, parallel with the intensity of control, become gradually more noticeable. When we raise our finger slowly with "held" finger-ends, the flexor already exercises a strong restraining activity. (This is how two tug-of-war groups counterbalance each other's force.)

The contrast between the direct and indirect swing-strokes is bridged by the aid of control, and it is by increasing the braking effect that the active unit is enabled to "cling" to the key. The energy affecting the key can be exactly apportioned by the control. This is why all our swing-strokes should be controlled.

The control of the opposing muscles, however, must never become conscious as muscular activity. When speaking about apportioning the force, we mean the production of a tone volume adequate to the melodic concept, whereby our fingers strike with greater or lesser strength as required by the volume of the individual tones of the melody. The more exactly we endeavour to follow the contours of the melody, *the more intensively we imagine the corresponding tone colour*, the more subtly and exactly will the control increase, and the more accurately detailed will the graduation of the tone volume become. This is a preliminary condition for the development of the expressive faculty.

WEIGHT-EFFECT

The greater the speed we give the key, the stronger will be its rebound. The rebound will displace the active swinging unit unless this rebound is counterbalanced, unless — that is — we increase the elastic resistance of the support simultaneously with the increase in the force of the stroke. In finger playing, the arm and — as its elongation — the whole body will serve to absorb the rebound of the keys, so that the hand does not move from the position required by the active function of the fingers.

The arm resistance must be increased in proportion not only to the force of the stroke but also to any increase in the tempo. In this event the arm has to counterbalance a growing number of key-rebounds per unit of time. This requires a gradual augmentation of muscle work. When playing in slow tempo only a small amount of muscle work is required for the purpose of resistance: the player practically "holds" his arms. In quick tempo the resistance must be increased and the player has the impression of being forced to press his arm to the keys.

The constant regulation of the resistance requires that the whole body functions as an elastic support. The sensation of absolute sureness felt by the pianist will be attained only if the whole body (from the fingers to the feet) takes part in absorbing the rebound of the key: only in this manner can the absorption become imperceptible. If, for instance, only the arm regulates the resistance, an occasional rebound of larger force may seriously impede the active swing-stroke starting at the same moment. This is why some pianists who fail to use their whole body as an elastic support (because of a wrong posture or some other reason) will play with an uncertain touch. The employment of the whole body requires that it be in a relaxed and elastic state. (This is confounded by many players with a slumping state of the body.)

The counterbalancing of the rebound of the key and the variation of the elasticity of the support in proportion to the force of the rebound complements the work of the active swinging unit and renders it more reliable. As the player has the sensation that this occurs with the aid of the weight of the arm or the body, respectively, it is called "weight-effect", or "weight-complement."

The term "weight-effect" is incorrect from the physical point of view, because there is no question of an actual weight-effect, but only of regulating the resistance of the elastic support. Any actual weight-effect would mean its constant operation not only at the moment of the swing-stroke but also during the interval between two consecutive swing-strokes. It is obvious that in this case the fingers would, for example, be pressed to the keys by ever so slight an additional weight. The miner working with his pressure-hammer counteracts its rebound by a continuous elastic resistance. If only a weight-effect were needed, the task could be accomplished by loading it with any sort of passive weight.

From a psychological point of view, however, the term "weight-effect" seems to be more serviceable than the word "resistance". To use the latter word may induce a strained, even cramped state of the body in some pianists while the word "weight-effect" brings about a state of relaxation. The expression "while letting the arm loose at the shoulder, support it with the fingers" is of course erroneous, but sometimes it helps the pianist to find the right way for the arm to function. However, we must be aware of the fact that the fingers must not become passive even for a single moment; hence it is absolutely wrong to bring any real weight – be it arm, shoulder or body – to bear and to apply pressure to the keys.

REGULATION OF THE TONE VOLUME

The tone volume increases in direct proportion with the speed of the hammer. In the last analysis the tone volume depends on the amount of kinetic energy which the player expends on swinging the key.

The kinetic energy is in direct proportion to the mass set in motion and the square of the velocity. Thus an increase in the energy may be attained either by increasing the mass or by increasing the velocity. In piano playing the tone volume produced by the individual swing-stroke may be increased in two ways:

1. by increasing the mass, i. e. actively swinging the forearm or the whole arm, instead of a smaller unit such as the finger;

2. by increasing the velocity of the active swinging unit and striking more quickly, i.e. with more force.

This raises the following question: What are the most favourable circumstances for utilizing the maximum amount of kinetic energy displayed by the active unit for producing the tone?

The velocity of the key has to attain its maximum at the escapement level, because beyond this its contact with the hammer ceases and the speed attained by the key beyond this point no longer influences the velocity of the hammer and consequently the tone volume. Only the amount of kinetic energy transmitted to the key down to the escapement level can be transformed into sound.

The velocity of the active unit undergoes changes even during the course of a single swing-stroke: it will increase up to a certain maximum and afterwards diminish again.

The maximum tone volume of a given swing-stroke may thus be produced if the active unit attains its maximum velocity at the escapement level.

However, the full amount of kinetic energy can be transmitted to the key only if the direction of the movement of the active swinging unit coincides with the direction of the movement of the key at the moment of escapement. In order to achieve this it is necessary that the active swinging unit be in a parallel position with the level of the key at its maximum velocity (in the medium position). The higher our hand is in relation to the key, the more the contrast of the rotation directions will increase and the less the amount of energy of the active swinging unit will be transmitted to the hammer.

The expressive ability of piano technique depends, on the one hand, on the player's ability to apportion exactly the finest force differences and, on the other, on the circumstance as to whether the differences of the velocity of the key are exactly adequate for the differences of force transmitted by us. Thus the prerequisite of a transmission of the force without loss is that the pianist exactly feels the escapement level of the key and is thus enabled to apportion the force required for the swinging of the key with the appropriate velocity. (This is why the pianist gets so disturbed by a wrongly adjusted, unevenly functioning piano.)

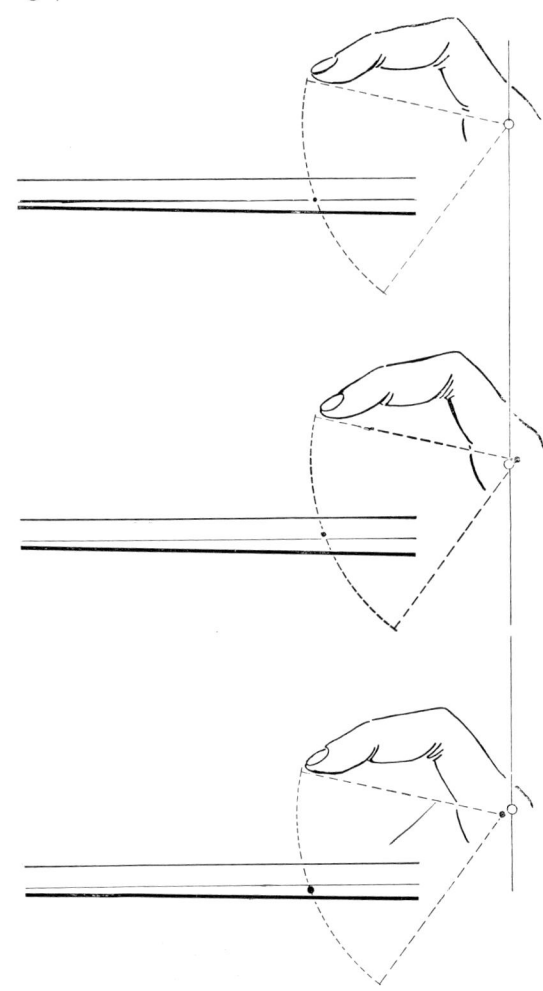

Fig. 7

As stated above, the maximum velocity must be attained at the moment of the escape, in order to transform the maximum of kinetic energy (engaged in the swing-stroke) into sound. If the active unit attains its maximum speed before the escapement level, only a part of the energy will reach the hammer, in spite of the fact that an equal amount of energy has been transmitted to the keys. This means in practice that we are able to increase or diminish the tone volume with strokes of equal force, if we approach or withdraw the axis of the fingers, that is, the whole hand, to or from the keyboard, respectively. When approaching it, the tone volume will increase only until the moment of maximum velocity coincides with the escapement level. Beyond this point the tone volume will diminish again and it will be useless to press the keys down any farther, because the instrument is unable to produce a larger tone volume and excessive pressing will only give rise to disagreeable lower noises.

——— Level of the escapement
——— Key in resting position
——— Key in lowest position

The approaching or withdrawing of the axis of the swinging motion is the most important means of regulating the tone volume. Since this approaching or withdrawing is brought about through increasing or diminishing the resistance, it follows that the weight-effect (the regulation of the resistance) is of great importance also in the shaping of the dynamic contours.

PROPORTION OF WEIGHT-EFFECT AND CONTROL IN SHAPING DYNAMIC CONTOURS

The role of weight-effect in the dynamic modelling increases proportionately to the increase of the tempo. In quick tempo there is barely any possibility of a precise "apportioning" of the individual strokes – and so even smaller details of contour-shaping are carried out with the aid of the weight-effect. (In velocity playing the number of strokes reaches 10 to 14 per second. At this speed it is impossible to concentrate on the individual strokes.)

With long tones such as occur in slow tempi, the dynamic contours can be properly shaped only with the aid of direct swing-strokes. In such cases, the role of the weight-effect is reduced to a minimum, in comparison with the control of the swing-strokes.

With slowing down of the tempo an increase of the role of swing-strokes in the modelling of dynamic contours will increase, but at the same time the apportioning of the weight-effect, too, needs great care. In slow tempo the dynamic contours can be observed much better and each fault thus becomes more conspicuous.

Since in quick tempo it is more difficult to notice the smaller deviations from the dynamic contours, it is generally assumed that attention in this case must be paid only to smooth, scintillating playing. This view must be firmly rejected. Mechanical playing, even when applied exclusively in quick tempi, leads unmistakably to an unmusical, lifeless performance. Precise, sensitive contour-shaping even in quick tempo is a preliminary condition for good musical expression.

We cannot determine metronomically when we should apply only weight-effect in shaping the dynamic contours. Neither can it be said exactly when the weight-effect should be relegated to the background and when the execution of the swing-stroke should become such a delicate task that it only can be carried out by the shoulder joint. The borderline between the two will vary with each style and performer.

The technical teaching has to enable the pupil – by starting from the music – to find the solution corresponding to his taste. Music must not be forced into the Procrustean bed of ready-made movement patterns.

Phot. 4
FRANZ LISZT

THE SYNTHESIZING PROCESS
AND THE ADAPTING MOVEMENTS

THE SYNTHESIZING PROCESS

The elastic resistance required for absorbing the rebound of the keys is given by the whole body. Thus our whole body participates in the dynamic regulation and the apportioning of the weight-effect.

The weight-effect increases or decreases according to the requirements of the dynamics. The more sensitively the weight-effect is apportioned according to the dynamic contours, the more colourful our playing will be.

Grave faults can be caused by the misconception that playing with uniform dynamics – where there is no dynamic fluctuation – the weight-effect must also be constantly kept on the same level. This misconception is the basis for making pupils practise scales played "from the fingers" or for the mechanical scintillating play of the passages of Mozart's sonatas, independently from the emotional content of the respective movement. The playing of absolutely equal, even, uniform notes does not mean uniform dynamics in the physical sense of the word. It means only a moderate, restricted dynamic fluctuation. Simultaneously with the melody the dynamic contours will also change and thus within the uniform dynamics an immense scale of fine dynamic alterations are needed for shaping the melody.

In the weight-effect constant changes would have to be carried out even if we strived for achieving an entirely uniform tone volume. Since high tones are weaker than low ones, different amounts of force would be required to give equal volume to tones of different pitch and therefore different grades of resistance would be needed to absorb the rebound of the keys.

The fluctuations and distribution of the dynamics are determined by the musical concept and by the requirements of the musical articulation. A coherent musical concept requires coherent dynamics and thus the weight-effect never changes in a jerky, staggered or stepwise way but always uniformly and evenly in the form of crescendo or decrescendo. Although the single tones sound with exactly measurable force differences, they are, nevertheless, details picked out from the increasing and decreasing changes of the force, the tone volume.

Musical concepts comprising wide interconnections can be realized by means of dynamics shaped in large dynamic units. Since the most important means of dynamic shaping is the alteration of the resistance, it follows that on the basis of the musical concept, the alteration of the weight effect must also be made by large units. *The apportioning of the weight-effect – which means the altering of the resistance by large musical units (e.g., a musical thought the size of a half-period) – is called the synthesizing process or in short: synthesizing.*

The movements required for the synthesizing are generally so small that they are not even noticeable. The differences of a few hundredths of millimeters required in order to approach or withdraw the axis of the fingers to the keys cannot be seen by the naked eye. But the apportioning of the weight-effect requires extraordinarily delicate muscular work and a cramp of any part of the body (even the clenching of one's lips) will hinder the appropriate functioning of the muscles.

The upper arm plays the most important role in the function of the body as an elastic support. Since constantly holding the upper arm in the same position will cause stiffness or cramping, one often has to execute plainly visible movements in order to avoid these difficulties. (This does not mean, however, that the synthesizing can only be realized through moving the arms. So, e.g., during the rests the synthesizing has to prevail as well as in the parts of the melody played before and after the rest although the arm will remain possibly completely unmoved.) *The movements executed by the upper arm with the aim of facilitating the apportioning of the weight-effect will be called synthesizing movements.*

The apportioning of the resistance, i.e. the approaching and withdrawing of the axis of the swinging motion of the fingers takes place always parallel with the keys, i.e. by movements to and fro by some 1/100 mm or even 1/1000 mm-s and always somewhat obliquely. (See Fig. 7.) This can be realized in practice only if the player is constantly feeling that his arms and even his body are constantly "behind" his fingers. Thus the synthesizing executed only by lateral or medial movements – so frequent with players – is nonsensical because it assures even at the best a general uniformity of the dynamics but no high-grade dynamic sensibility when even during velocity playing one has the feeling of being capable of altering dynamics almost with every tone.

It is to be repeatedly emphasized that since the whole body functions as an elastic support, the whole body has also to take part in the synthesizing. It is also evident that in the technique of octaves or in the active swing-strokes executed by the upper arm the role of the trunk will be of increased importance in the synthesizing. Any further analysis of the extent of its role, however, seems to us *superfluous*. It is evident that a stiff, rigidly held trunk will hinder the delicate alterations of the resistance as much as – if not more than – a stiffly held arm. But let us be careful: the rhythmic bowing and bending, so frequently used by pianists, is just as much an enemy of the musical expression as the rigid trunk. The rhythmic bowing and bending diminishes or increases the weight-effect independently from the musical concept and thus it hinders the realization of the latter. One need not fear that without bowing and bending the trunk will become rigid because the trunk will have opportunity enough for moving in connection with the constant changes of the emotional content of the piece (see p. 92).

Therefore, in accordance with the dynamic concepts the weight-effect is always provided by movements comprising large musical units (e.g. a musical thought the size of a half-period). This synthesizing prevails even when the individual strokes are executed by the upper arm. A case in point is the subject of the first movement in Mozart's Sonata in C minor.

Example 4

According to the above, synthesizing is needed in staccato passages in the same way as in legato ones because the dynamic shaping is also mainly carried out in staccato playing by the aid of the synthesizing process.

ADAPTING MOVEMENTS

In order to find the most appropriate position for the work of the fingers, i.e. to enable them to attain the escapement level with a maximum force, the arm has to find the position in which the work of the fingers can be executed as easily and simply as possible. The importance of this is increased by the fact that at the moment of the finger's utilizing the maximum force, its movement, too, will become rather similar to the direct swing-stroke (see page 28). In the same way, the upper arm also aids in executing the active swing-stroke of the forearm under the most favourable conditions. In the first case the arm is subordinated to the fingers while in the second one the upper arm accommodates, adapts itself to the forearm, submits its work to the latter. *The movements which adjust the active swinging unit to the different key positions, which bring the fingers into proper striking position and which help to regulate the noise-effects will be called adapting movements.* There are many kinds of these movements but a common feature of all of them is that they are always decided by the momentary requirement as to what kind and to what extent they must be utilized.

While the synthesizing process depends only upon the musical concept, these movements function as part of the mechanical solutions. Their task is to facilitate the execution of the active swing-strokes by the fingers or the forearm, to bring the fingers into a suitable position for the swing-stroke, to accommodate for playing of different groups of white and black keys and for the different pitch registers, and to change the angle of the stroke to the extent required by the noise-effects.

The adapting movements also aid us in compensating for the differences in weight caused by the different lengths and positions of the fingers. Thus, e.g., in the case of uniformly, evenly played repeated broken chords the arm lends assistance by executing continuous vertical motion. This motion – directed downwards at the beginning and upwards at the end – facilitates the strokes of the shorter fingers by bringing them nearer to the keyboard.

Rotation also serves for the equalization of the force differences. The weight difference occurring at the expense of the short fingers cannot be compensated for if a uniform position is maintained and, therefore, the adaptation of the arm will be helped and complemented by supination when fingers 3–4–5 succeed each other and by pronation in the case of fingers 2–1.

The shifting of the centre of gravity achieved through rotation is of extreme importance in the active swing-strokes of the arm. If, for instance, a swing-stroke executed from the shoulder is transferred to the key by the fifth finger, we can, by means of intense supination, succeed in bringing the weight of the whole arm to the finger's assistance. Thus when the fifth finger strikes as an elongation of the arm it will touch the key with its outer side. (Much harm is caused by the superstition that the fingers should touch the key exclusively in *one* definite position.)

It is, of course, wrong for the pianist to "lay down" his little finger instead of engaging it actively. Active finger work, moreover, obviously requires a much smaller shifting than active arm work, where the fingers strike as elongations of the arm. In the latter case the movement becomes inept and stiff, if the necessary shift in the centre of gravity is not carried out.

The extent of the shift in the centre of gravity depends upon the movements required for the solution of the particular task; its degree is determined by the movements which the preceding or succeeding tones require. The finger strikes the initial note of Beethoven's Sonata in G major Op. 31, No. 1, in a different position from that in which it commences Mozart's Sonata in C major (K. 330).

Example 5   Example 6

Still another position is needed at the end of the subject of the third movement of Mozart's Sonata in C minor, where the F sharp following the E flat does not allow of any supination, and the arm instead assists through a vigorous lateral motion.

Example 7

The adapting movements also play an important part in the regulation of the noise-effects. The maintenance of the equilibrium is facilitated by the almost incessant motion of the arm, permitting a far more exactly apportioned resistance (weight-effect) than if the arm were to remain motionless. The absolutely indispensable striking motion of the fingers (and also the noises) can thereby be reduced to a minimum, because the resistance currently required for the swing-strokes is regulated by the arm with the utmost precision.

Even apparently simple figures may necessitate the application of complex adapting movements. A case in point is the succession of broken common chords in the transition of the first movement of the "Waldstein" Sonata.

Example 8   Beethoven: Sonata in C major, Op. 53

The upper arm performs considerable vertical movements to which are added the rotation of the forearm, the passive movement of the wrist and even a slight bending of the elbow joint. Simultaneously with these movements – but independently of them – the fingers perform their own work with precision. The proportions of the individual movement vary with the chords, because the weight-effect required by a tonic chord is quite different from that needed by a six-four chord, etc.

It is of interest to draw a parallel between the accompanying figure in the Coda of the last movement of Mozart's Sonata in A major (Köchel 331) and the similar figure in the development of the first movement of the Sonata in B flat major (Köchel 333).

In the Coda of the Alla Turca vertical motions prevail. We do not separate the individual tones, and even the accented third semiquavers melt into the whole.

Example 9

The Sonata in B flat major needs a noisier and extremely rhythmical effect, which brings out every tone. For this reason, the vertical motion diminishes and the rotation dominates. Thus both the first and the third semiquavers are more strongly stressed because they are sounded through a supinating motion.

Example 10

An exact analysis of the adapting movements is most difficult because of their complexity. As several kinds of adapting movements may be called for simultaneously, one must not prescribe special exercises for vertical adaptation, rotational adaptation, etc. We must encourage the pupil to deduce the correct application of the adapting movements from the musical task before him. The mechanical prerequisite is that the arm must possess full freedom of action enabling it to adapt itself easily and to bring the fingers almost unnoticeably into the proper striking position. Much careful pedagogical work is needed to induce the arm to find the most comfortable finger position and to insure simultaneously an extensive synthesizing movement.

A frequent error on the part of pianists is to attempt to confine the adapting movements within regular geometrical forms, such as circles or semicircles. It may happen that the adapting movement has the shape of a semicircle or ellipse, but this is less frequently the case. As a rule, the adapting movement is of a much more complicated form because, in most cases, the need for different kinds of adapting movement arises simultaneously. If we add to this the modifying effect of the synthesizing movement and of the active swing-strokes we obtain a line of movement so variegated as to make it impossible to squeeze it into a pattern without running the risk of entirely falsifying the movements.

In the course of playing we are continually making adapting movements. Although these depend on the mechanical solutions we are nevertheless able to establish many a direct interrelationship with the musical requirements. The importance of the adapting movements and the extent of their application varies according to the character and style of the particular piece of music. Thus, we may state in general that slow parts require more adapting movements than fast ones. The role of the adapting movements increases considerably from Bach up to the romanticists. Chopin's style (e.g., the Berceuse) demands the maximum use of adapting movements.

Phot. 5
SVIATOSLAV RICHTER

Sviatoslav Richter, playing the middle part of Schubert's Impromptu in E flat major (85–90 bars)

(Adapting movements carried out by rotation, 24 photos per sec.)

Example 11

The pictures show clearly that the sounding of the tones is always carried out in a way which can be considered as the closest to the direct swing-stroke. The fingers will therefore remain even during a certain part of the pauses on the keys. Thus, e.g., it is only in frame No. 8 that the thumb does not touch key e^1, while in frame No. 9 it already touches that key and in Nos. 10 and 11 the key is already pressed down.

The adapting movements come to display through the rotation but the sounding of the tones is carried out by the active swinging movements of the upper arm and the active work of the fingers respectively and not by rotation movements. This is why no rotation, sufficient to sounding the tone by a side-stroke, can be noticed in any of the pictures. Note also that, when playing broken chords, both hands "hold" them already in the air in their full extent.

7. It can be clearly seen that the rotational adapting is mixed with the vertical movement of the active swing-stroke of the arm. If the tone were sounded merely by the rotational movement a much greater amount of rotation would be required.

This picture, blurred on account of the great speed of the right hand, shows the right hand preparing to emphasize tone d^2. One of the means of this stressing is also the prolongation, to be noticeable only by the aid of the film. The tones are the same also in pictures 14, 15 and 16: in the bass the sounding of tone B, and in the upper voice that of d^2 is to be seen. However, in picture 16 it can already be noticed that we are at the stage immediately preceding the sounding of the tones d^1-f^1 sharp.

18. On account of the great velocity the picture of both hands is blurred. Due to the agogic accent of the preceding quarter-note the shifting is to be executed with a greater speed than usual, in order to avoid the beginning tones of the next bar coming late.

20. Immediately before setting off f sharp. The fifth finger of the left hand passed beyond the f sharp key in order to catch it by the aid of a small arc. (See page 179.)

21. The extent of the agogic accent is shown by the fact that the quaver (c sharp) is held through five pictures.

37. The agogic accent is again shown by the holding of the quaver through 5 frames.

68. The right hand, when sounding the tone d^1 of the third crotchet, is already preparing for tones b^1 and c^2 sharp which are sounded only in frame 75.

82. The blurred picture shows that the left hand, after sounding, is skipping with lightning speed to key E.

83. Here the clearness of the picture proves that the key will be brought into motion by a direct swing-stroke of the hand (and thus the hand will not strike the key from the side).

85. The reverse motion is the same as seen in picture 82. Now the arm speeds inwards (after sounding e) in order to bring into motion G already by a direct swing-stroke.

95. It is clearly noticeable that the two hands make preparation for the direct swing-stroke.

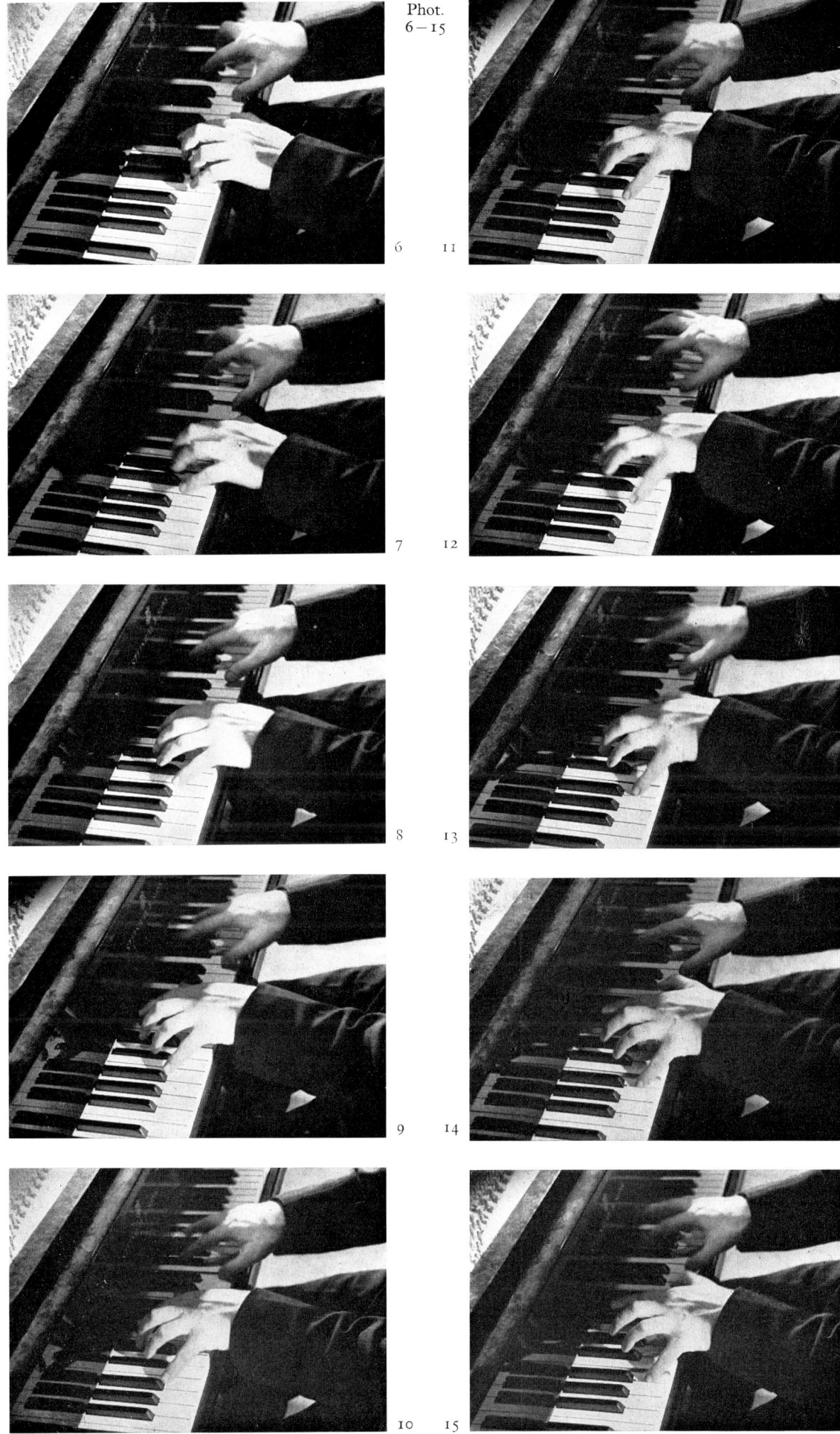

Phot. 6–15

Phot. 16–25

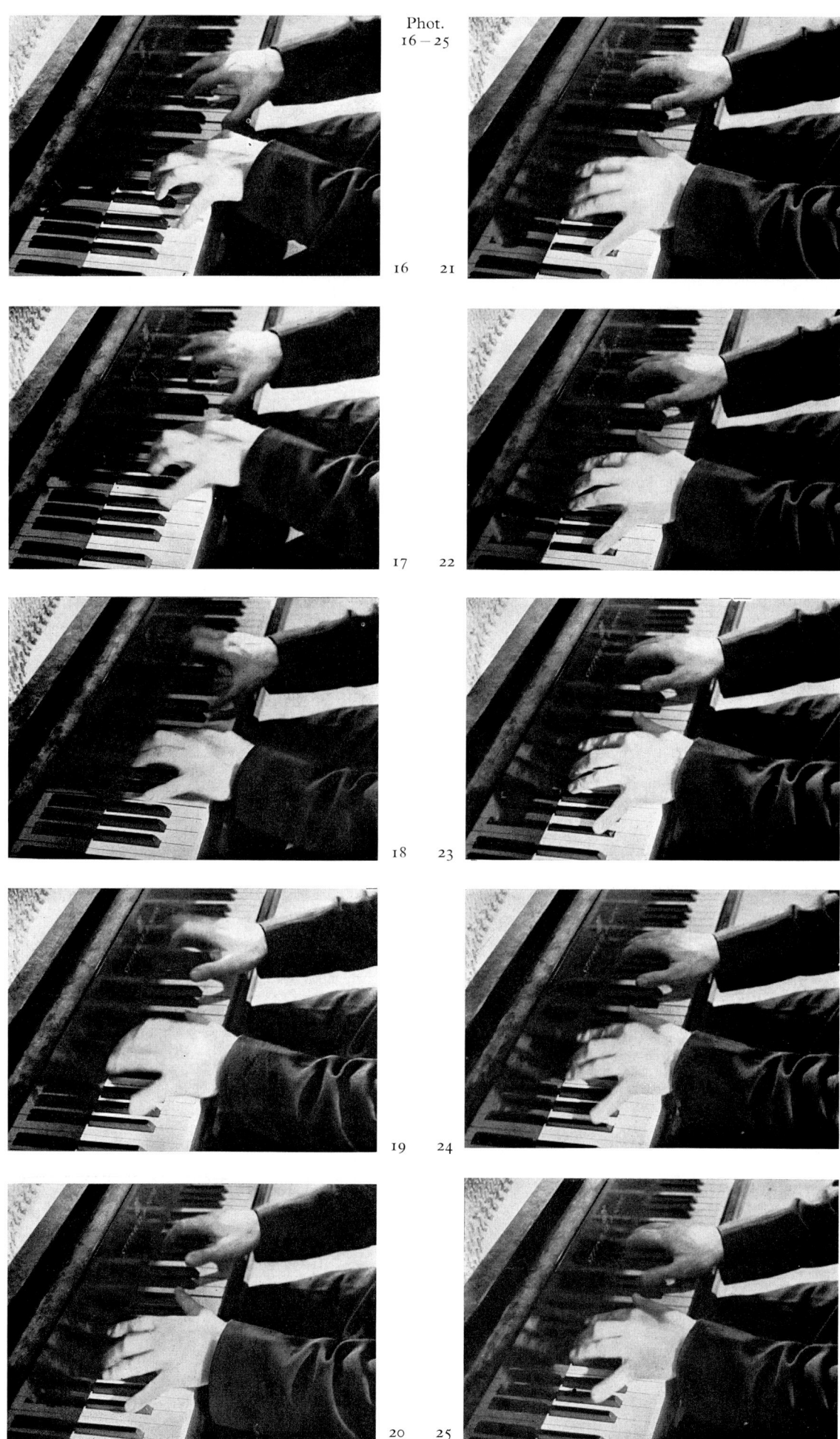

16 21
17 22
18 23
19 24
20 25

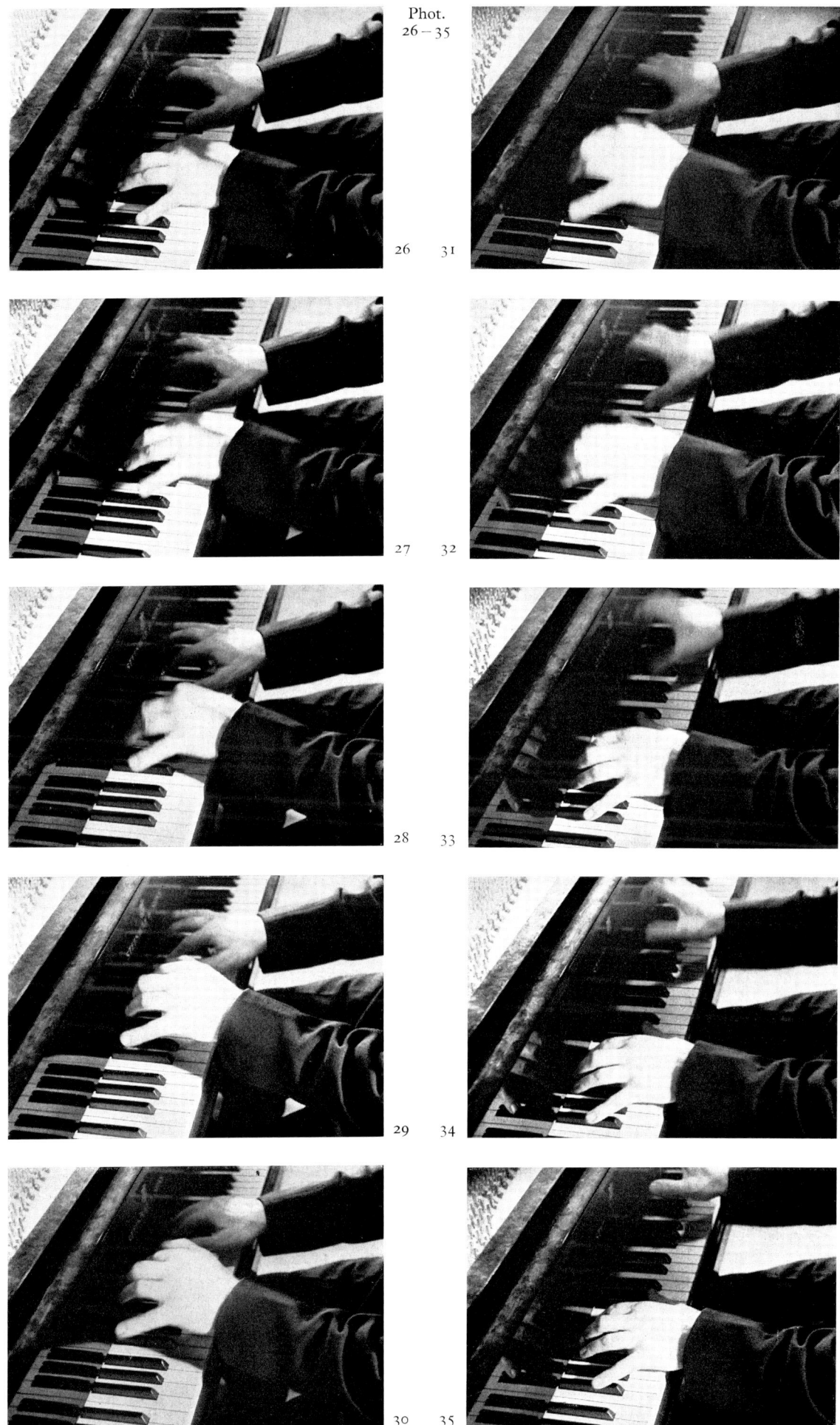

Phot. 26–35

41

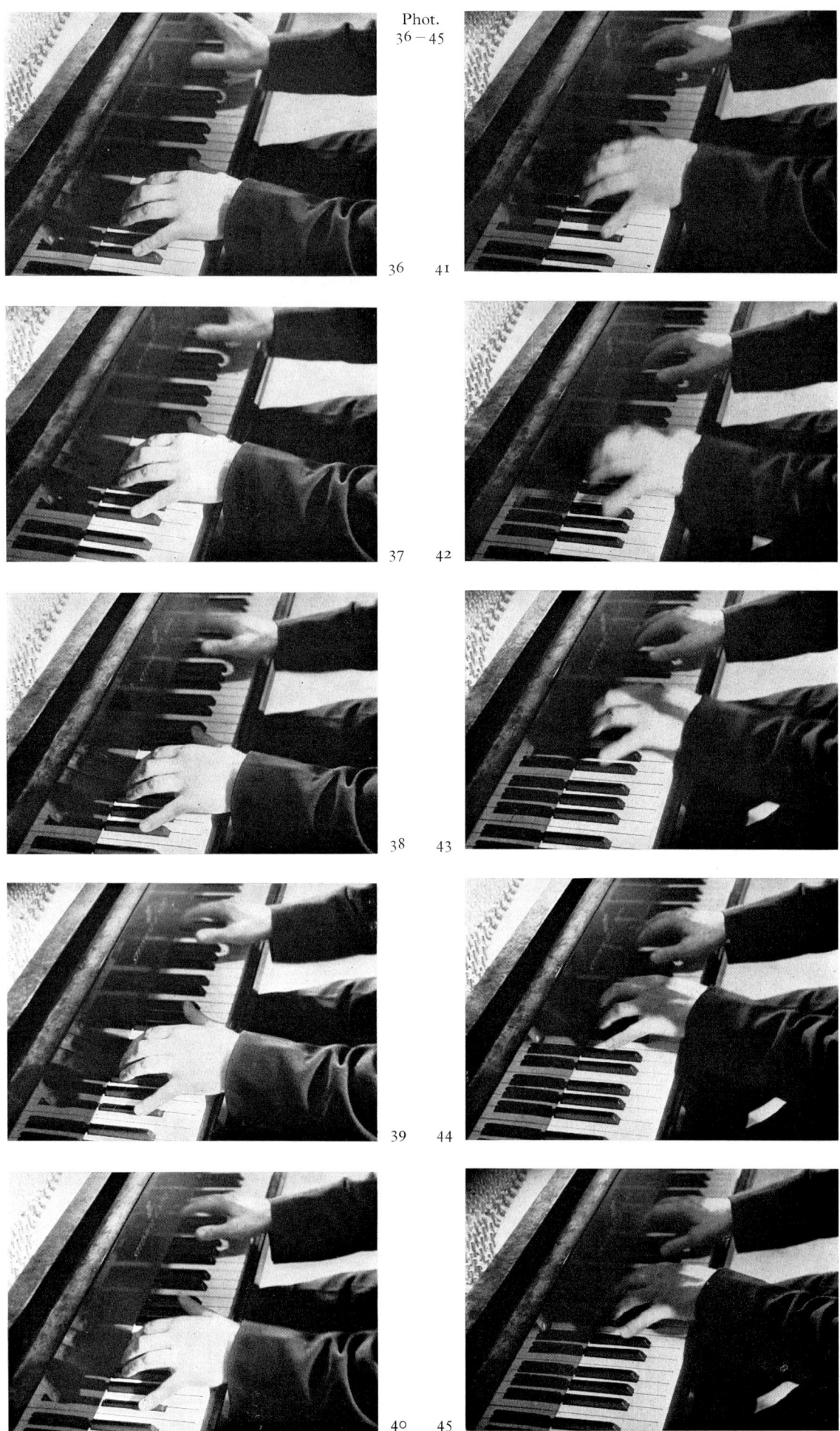

Phot. 36–45

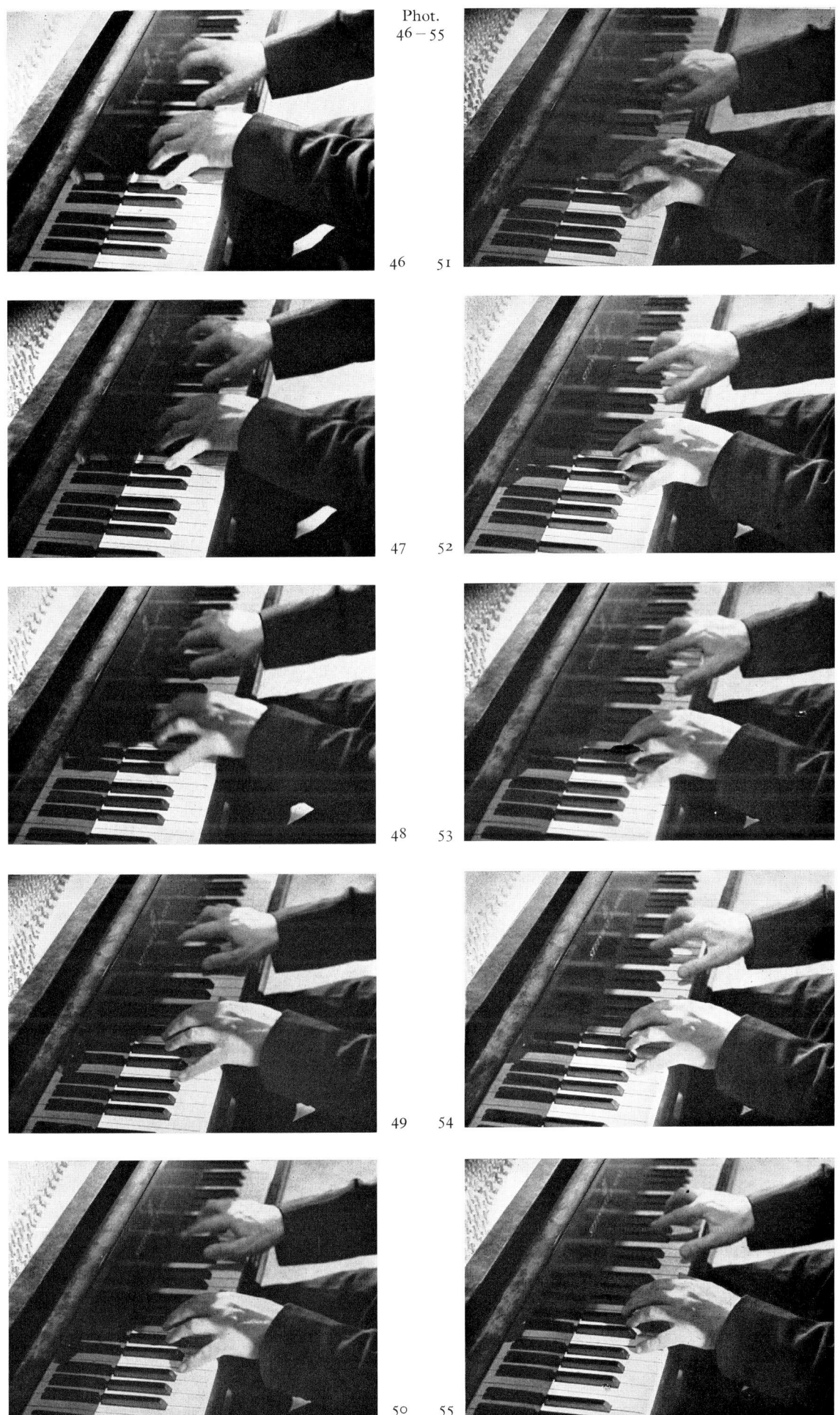

Phot. 46–55

Phot. 56–65

Phot. 66–75

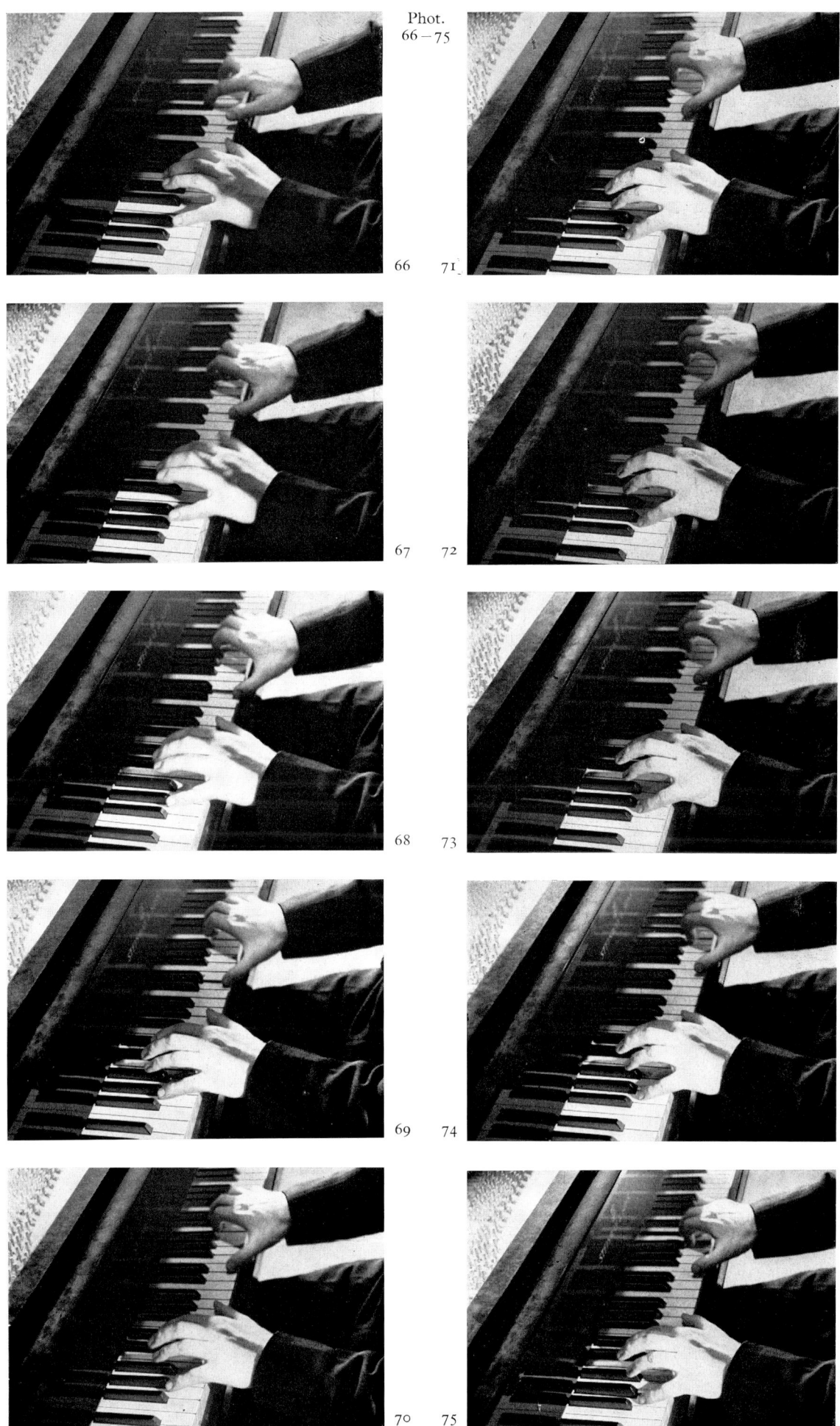

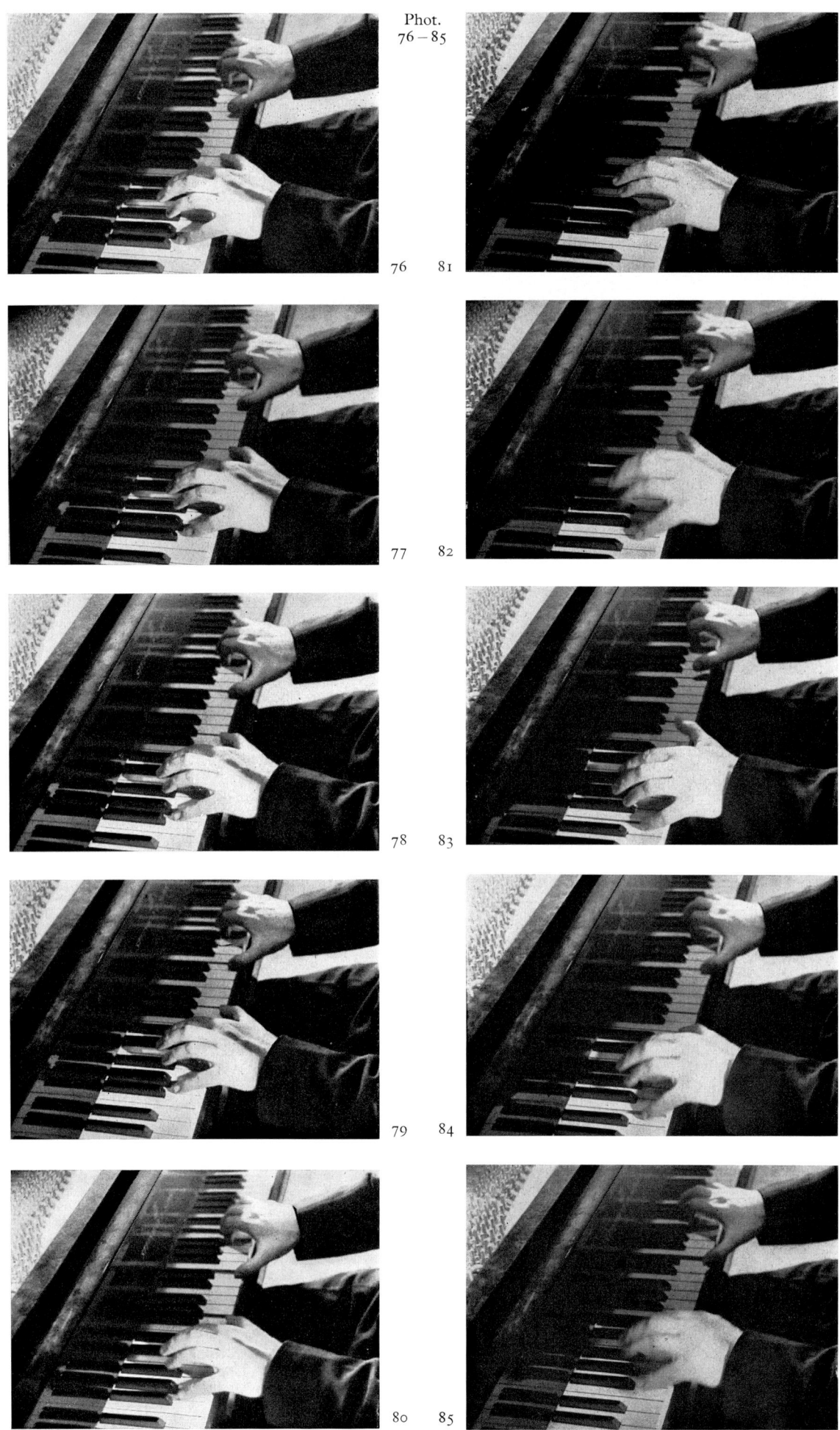

Phot. 76–85

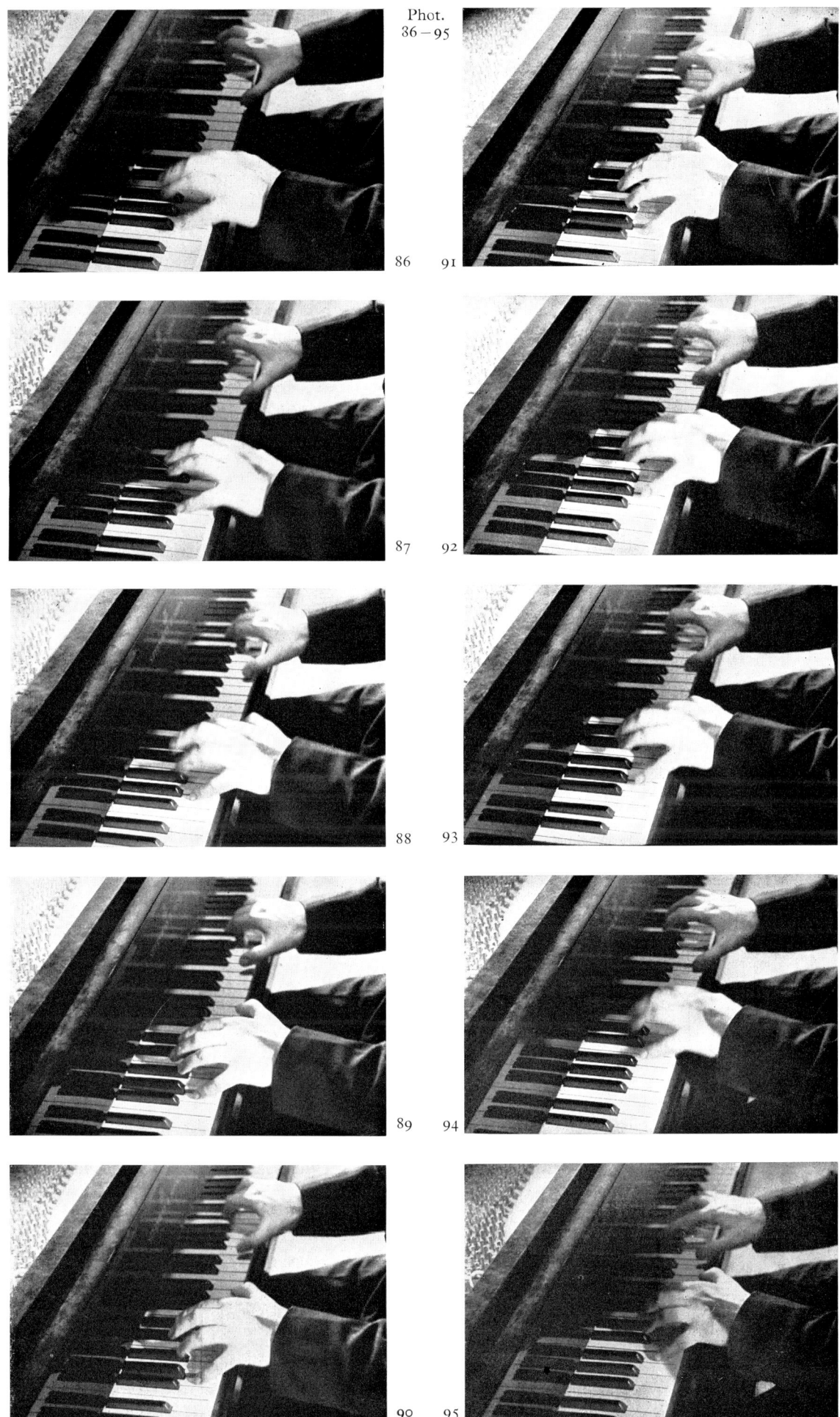

Phot. 36–95

Phot. 96
EMIL SAUER

SEAT AND BODY POSTURE

We have seen in the foregoing chapters that the primary condition of good piano playing is the execution of the swing-stroke up to an almost unimaginable preciseness. As the shifting[1] of the hand for 1/100 mm causes considerable dynamic differences, we are compelled to take a special care in investigating the most advantageous method of sitting before the piano in order to have the most favourable body posture.

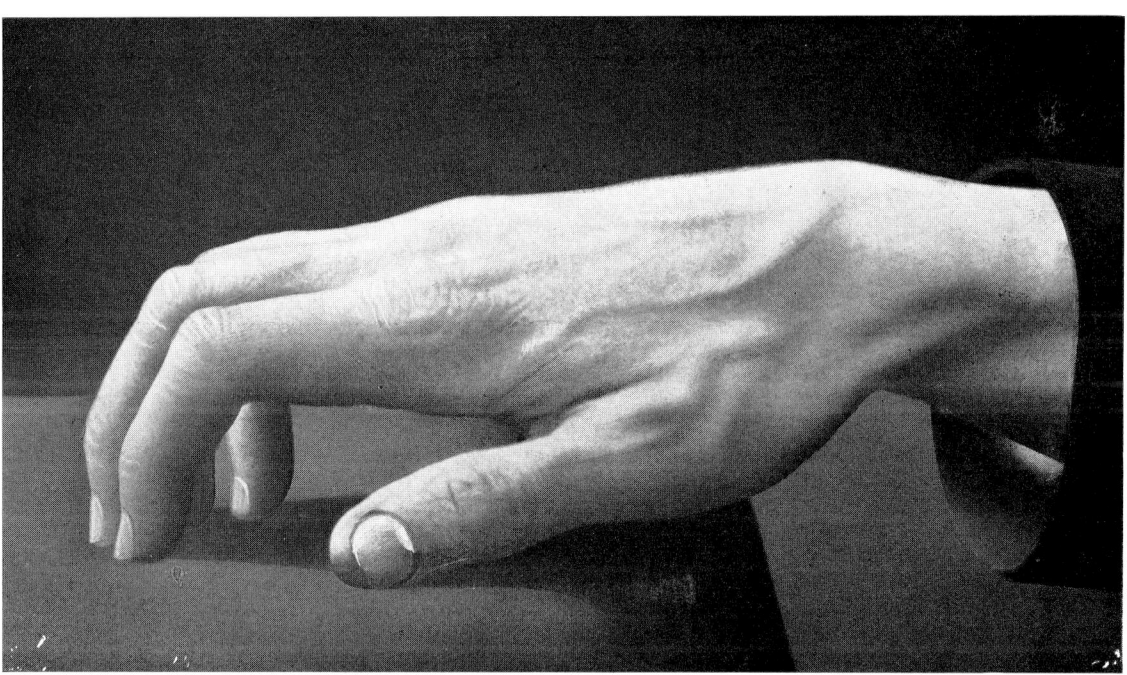

Phot. 97
THE HAND OF EMIL SAUER

What are the requirements of correct sitting from the point of view of the three components of the swing-stroke (firm basis, elastic support and active swinging unit)?

The firm basis necessitates that the piano bench or chair used be really firm allowing no swaying or shifting in any direction. The revolving music-stools are therefore entirely unfit for this purpose and the same applies to any cushioned or upholstered chair.

[1] With the shifting of the hand the axis of the fingers approach to or withdraw from the keyboard.

In piano playing the whole body functions as an elastic support and thus the freedom of the whole body must be ensured. However, the tasks of the single parts of the body are not of equal importance because the arm has the largest role in absorbing the rebound of the key, and the dynamic contours are also mainly formed by the aid of the action of the arm. The free unhindered motion of the arm is, however, impossible without the adaptability of the trunk. Mobility of the trunk is indispensable in order to permit the use of bent or streched arm positions in different forms of playing. If both arms move in the same direction, the trunk will also follow the level of the pitch registers by means of its horizontal movements.

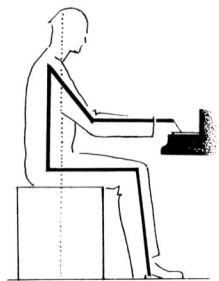

Fig. 8

The seat of the chair must be level and made of leather or textile cover which must be hard. A concave or soft chair will hinder the free movement of the trunk in any direction. We also have to care for a support given by the legs. If we sit too far backward on the chair the supporting action of our feet will diminish, and the motion of the trunk will become uncertain.

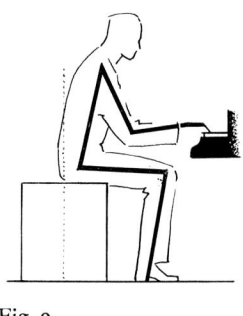

Fig. 9

If we sit on the edge of the chair, the preponderant part of our body's weight will rest on our feet. In this case the trunk is unable to move freely and thus the playing will become considerably stiffer than would be the case if the position were more adequate. If our main weight rests on the feet, the whole body is compelled to assume a strained position. We almost have to lean on the piano in order to keep our balance, thus putting a constant burden on the fingers. On account of the strained posture the arm is unable to provide a sufficiently differentiated resistance; this leads to constant exaggeration of the resistance. (By this method – and by constant and hard work – we may succeed in producing a "big tone" or a "balanced tone" but this will not be piano playing in the noblest sense of the word. Without sensitive dynamic and rhythmic shading, there can be no beatiful rendering. Striving after extreme tone volume paralyzes our sensitivity and overwhelms our inner musical conception with a uniform flood of sound.)

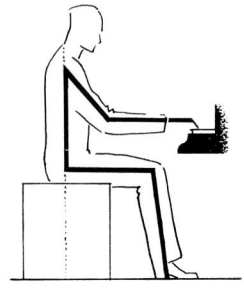

Fig. 10

When properly seated we lean on our feet, but the weight of our body mainly rests on the chair. Thus the trunk may move freely in any direction.

The motion of the trunk provides an aid to the position of the arms. Unnecessary bending or swaying prevents the arms from finding their suitable position. Thus unnecessary motion of our trunk is just as harmful as motionless rigidity. The "pendulum-motion" so frequently observed makes the dynamic contour-shaping independent from the musical concept because when bending forward a crescendo results, and a decrescendo when leaning backwards.

Adults of small stature or with short legs will find it necessary to sit farther forward on the chair in order to obtain comfortable support for their feet, but the pianist must strive in this case to place his weight as much as possible on the chair in order to ensure easy motion of his trunk and arms.

In choosing the height of the seat we have to take into consideration the position from which the active unit can function most easily.

Velocity of octave and chord playing will be facilitated if our arms assume a slightly stretched position, i.e. if they place themselves at a somewhat higher level than the keyboard.

(This may be confirmed by the following experiment: Make several quickly repeated movements in the air with your forearm, and you will be compelled to stretch your arms slightly. With your arms bent at a right angle or more, the execution of quick strokes will prove difficult and laborious.)

Velocity of finger playing, on the other hand, will be made easier if our forearms are held somewhat lower than the level of the keyboard. (Sitting too low, on the other hand, will hinder the motion of the thumb.)

In both cases we adapt ourselves to the medium position of the muscles because the strokes of the arm and of the fingers are most economical when they take place from the medium position of the respective muscles.

In high forearm position the strokes of the finger are carried out from a disadvantageous position – beyond the finger's medium position.

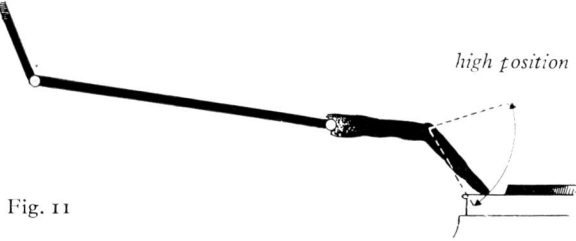

Fig. 11

In the high position (shown in Fig. 11), the key is swung by the finger only at the end of its course. At this moment only a fraction of the force is applied which would have been available at the centre of the arc. (See p. 28.) In addition, the stroke is not only weaker but also less reliable. The pianist is compelled to apply more force than is necessary in order to assure the sounding of the tones because it is unpredictable how much force of the finger-stroke he will be able to transmit to the key. Concomitantly with the increasing of the force the resistance has to be exaggerated and this will be at the expense of the velocity as well as that of the subtlety of the dynamic contours.

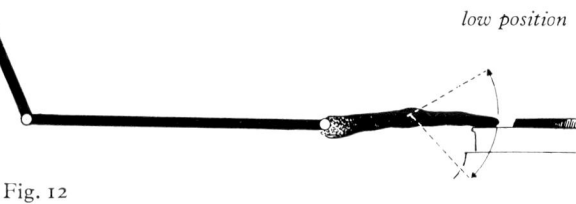

Fig. 12

With a low arm position (see Fig. 12) the escapement level can be reached at the moment of maximum display of force by the finger. *As the finger always attains maximum force at the same point along its course it is thereby able – so to speak – to aim at the escapement level.* This is most important both from the point of view of force and of velocity.

However, on deciding upon the height of the seat, the velocity must not be the most important or even the only aim. Our primary aim must be the exact calculation of the force of each swing-stroke and the dynamic sensitivity of playing. Only within their limits may we strive after attaining velocity.

Let us now analyse from the point of view of reliability the posture most favourable for the playing of octaves.

While executing the active swing-stroke the forearm moves away from the body along an arc-shaped trajectory until it reaches a horizontal position after which it again approaches the body. The key also describes a small part of a circle during which it moves away from the body.

Phot. 98
ANNIE FISCHER

Assuming that the forearm reaches a position parallel to the key at the moment of striking it (see Fig. 13), we will be able to control the force of the hammer-stroke exactly because the direction of the force approximately coincides with the direction of the key's motion. In this case the adequate apportioning of the force may be easily automatized with the musical concept.

On the other hand, the higher the position of the elbow above the keyboard at the moment of striking, the greater the divergence which may be observed between the direction of the force and the direction of the key's movement (Fig. 14). The exact apportioning of the force will also be much more difficult, thus diminishing the expressiveness of octave playing. From this it follows that the high position of the arms is of no real use even from the point of view of octave playing. The "over-dosing" of the force in consequence of the high arm position will diminish the velocity at least to the same extent that the somewhat more stretched position increased it.

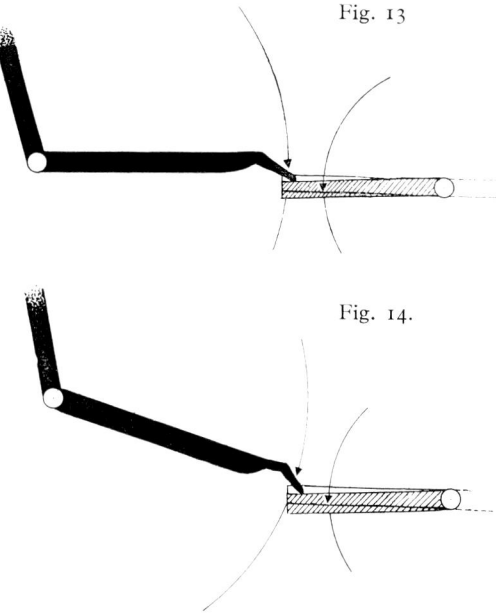

High arm position means an entire dynamic unreliability of the finger technique. In the position to be seen in Fig. 14 the functioning of the muscles is so unreliable that virtually none of the finger-strokes will be entirely exact. Pianists in general try to eliminate the faults arising from

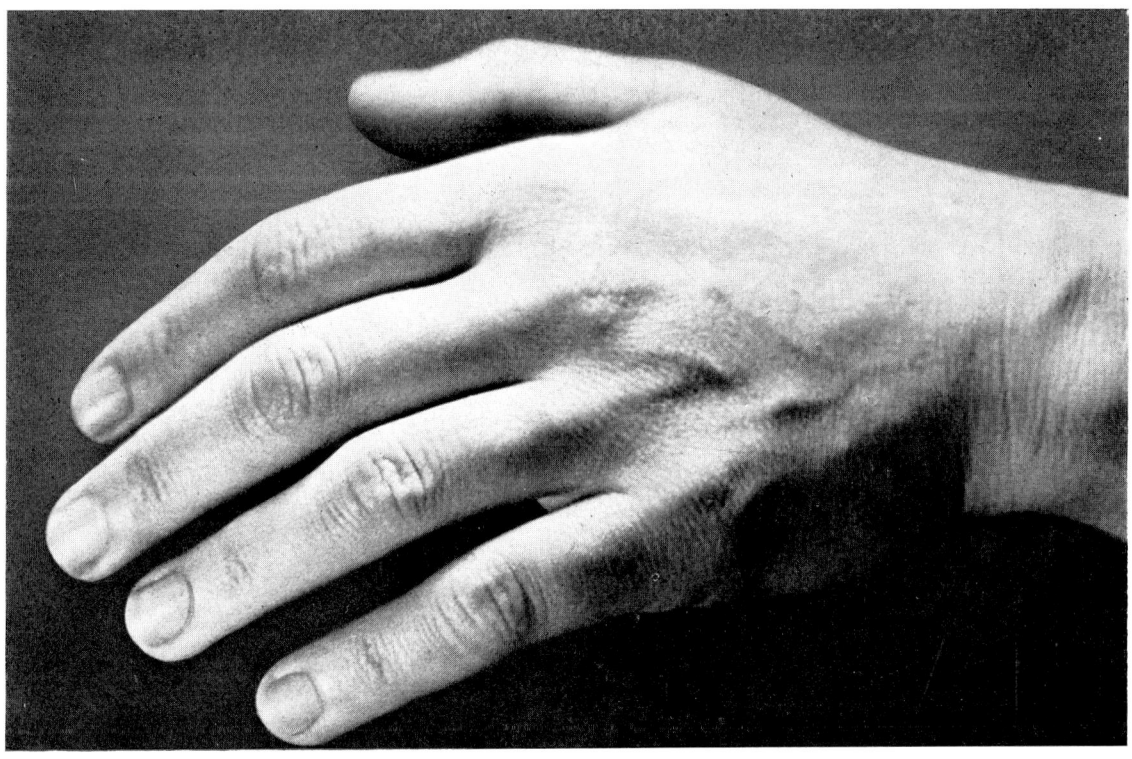

Phot. 99
THE HAND OF ANNIE FISCHER

this in two ways. Either they exaggerate and magnify the details of the dynamic contours or they strive after an even tone volume — even at the expense of the shading of the melody. The first solution is artifical while the second results in mechanical playing. Neither the exaggeration nor the mechanical playing will correspond with our musical concept and so in both cases the spontaneous character of the playing will suffer. Therefore it can be stated that a high seat will detrimentally affect the power of expression in the finger technique.

It follows from the above that the dynamic reliability of the finger technique definitely requires a low arm position, the low position of the fingers. This is instinctively felt by most pianists. This explains why the great majority of them will allow the first joint to sink when playing with bent fingers, and why they become stooped when playing difficult finger-technique passages.

Thus, the following method may be applied when determining the most suitable seat. If the player is of rather high stature, he must sit as far back on the chair as will allow him to move his trunk freely in any direction. The chair must be placed only so high as will permit the forearm to be level with the keys, i e. with the escapement level of the keys. This will facilitate solving the problems of finger technique and in addition will cause no difficulties in chord and octave technique.

A seat lower than that indicated makes the adapting and synthesizing movements of the upper arm difficult. However, it often occurs that the pianist "trying to find his tone" sits extremely low. The cause for this is that when doing so, he instinctively tries to bring his upper arm on one level with the escapement level. This indeed allows a great increase of the possibilities of delicate shaping of the swing-strokes of the upper arm but at the same time it also diminishes the sureness of the adapting movements and synthesizing process which are indispensable for the finger work.

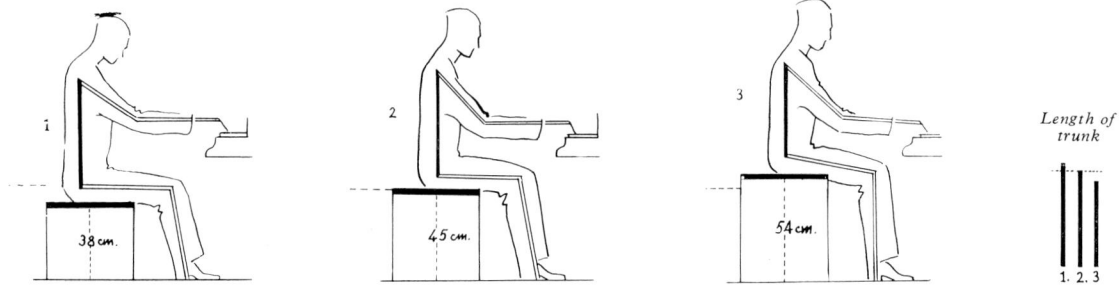

Figs. 15–17
The longer the trunk, the lower the stool should be

The sitting-height necessary for correct posture is mainly determined by the proportion of the trunk to the upper arm. A pianist with a long trunk and short upper arms has to sit on a very low chair, while a pianist with a short trunk and long upper arms is compelled to use a high chair.

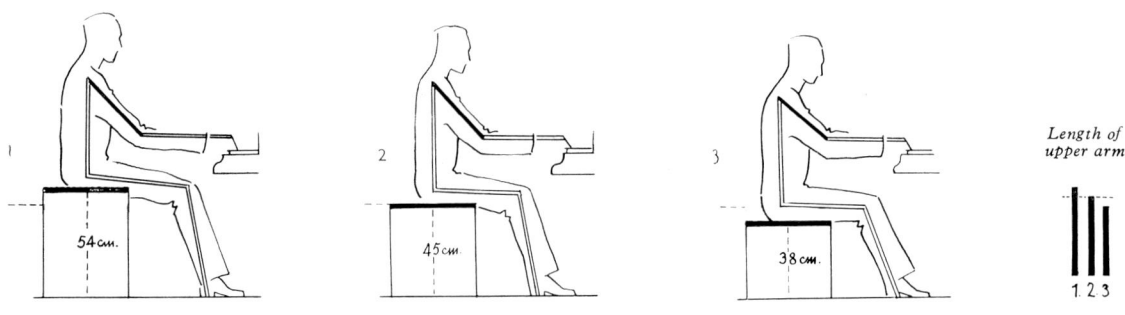

Figs. 18–20
The longer the upper arm, the higher the stool should be

Phot. 100
ANTON RUBINSTEIN

A generally valid distance of the chair from the piano cannot be even approximately determined. It may be influenced not only by the length of the forearm but also by that of the upper arm and their proportions. At best, the following rule can be applied: Seat yourself at such a distance from the piano as to be able to use the forearm and the upper arm with perfect freedom and to be able to move your trunk freely forward and backward.

A short forearm, while being most advantageous for the velocity of octave technique, renders the finding of the appropriate seat somewhat difficult. If the pianist takes into account the above-mentioned rules and brings his forearm to the level of the escapement, he is forced to sit too close to the piano. Thus pianists with short forearms are obliged to sit somewhat higher than the average height of the seat. This higher seat (provided that it is not excessively high) will not be harmful because pianists with short forearms execute the swing-strokes of the upper arms very easily and surely, and at the same time they very easily find the simplest way of carrying out the adapting and synthesizing movements.

The free movement of our trunk is best supported by the feet if the thighs are in horizontal position or bent slightly downwards. If we sit higher, our body becomes more stretched and tense, while if we sit lower — with our thighs bent towards the trunk — the supporting function of the feet is diminished which also increases body tension. From this it follows that not only the height of the chair but also the height of the feet of the piano has to be changed. The length of the pianist's legs does not change and thus the height of the chair ought to be constantly the same for the same pianist; instead the height of the piano legs ought to be adjustable to the needs of the individual player. As such pianos are, alas, not yet manufactured, pianists try to manage at home with supports (e.g., with glass coasters). To adapt the height of the chair to that of the piano is only a compulsory solution and so we are very often compelled to compromise by sitting too high or low (at the expense of the foot support) in order to enable our arm to assume a position best suited to the keyboard.

In our days the importance of regulating the sitting-height is still underrated by many people: "Talented pianists," they maintain, "cannot be influenced by such trifles." This amounts to saying, however, that adequate length of the arms and height of the trunk must also be considered as indispensable prerequisites of musical talent. The mechanical conditions of the pianist's playing are influenced in the same way by the sitting height as are those of the violinist by the manner of holding his instrument while playing. It is more comfortable to play the violin with the instrument supported against the chest, but this makes beautiful tone production impossible. The pianist also plays much more comfortably on a high seat but this comfort is obtained at the expense of musical expression.

In order to assure an appropriate sitting-height, many artists travelling all over the world find themselves compelled to carry their own music-chair with them (Emil Sauer, Wilhelm Backhaus, etc.). The necessity of doing this will remain so as the height of music-chairs is fixed by carpentry norms instead of by the requirements of piano playing. Tobias Matthay complained already in 1903: "Music-stools are often found insufficiently depressable."[2]

An examination of some of the photographs in the present work will help us to determine the proper sitting-height and distance. The reader will find no really high seat. (In Phot. 4 showing Liszt, the appearance of a high seat comes from his lifting his elbows.) In comparing the photographs it will be noted that by bending the trunk forward or backward the height of the forearm, too, will change. (See the film sequences of Sviatoslav Richter, Annie Fischer and Imre Ungár.)

The sitting-height is often confused with the height of the chair, whereas these two factors have nothing in common. (The photographs show Annie Fischer sitting lower than Imre Ungár. Yet she uses a music-stool 45 cm high, while the chair of Imre Ungár is unusually low: 40 cm.)

---

[2] Tobias Matthay: *The Act of Touch in All Its Diversity*. P. 134. (London, Longmans, Green and Co. 1903.)

Phot. 101
LOUIS KENTNER

In teaching children it is a particularly difficult task to find the proper sitting posture. The feet of the child can usually only find support with the aid of a footstool. In the first years of study pedalling has no important part yet and so the use of a footstool is not detrimental even from this point of view. However, faulty innervations, which will last his lifetime, may be caused by the child's not using a footstool. In such cases his feet will often "dangle" and he will be compelled to hold his trunk more stiffly or even to lean on the piano. The use of the footstool with beginners was required as early as in 1717 by Couperin[3] and since that time a great number of master pedagogues have been of the same opinion. On account of ignorance or irresponsibility, it still happens that no attention is paid by some teachers to the requirement that the pupil be seated correctly and in a natural posture. And still, if we want to attain a really durable result it is not sufficient to be concerned about all this only during the lesson. The teacher has to make the pupil use a hard piano-chair of adequate height and a footstool not only during the lessons but also when practising at home.

Phot. 102
SERGEI RACHMANINOFF

[3] François Couperin: *L'Art de toucher le Clavecin*. "On doit mettre quelque chose de plus, ou de moins hault sous les pieds des jeunes personnes, à mesure qu'elles croissent: afin que leurs pieds n'étant point en l'air; puissent soutenir le corps dans son juste équilibre."
(It will be necessary to place some additional support under the feet of young people, varying in height as they grow, so that their feet, not dangling in the air, may keep the body properly balanced.)

Phot. 103
FERRUCCIO BUSONI

Annie Fischer playing the middle portion of Chopin's Fantaisie Impromptu

Example 12

Phot. 104—108

Phot. 109—118

Sviatoslav Richter playing Schumann's "Warum?"

Example 13

Phot. 119–123

Imre Ungár playing Chopin's Nocturne in F major

Example 14

Phot. 124–128

István Antal plays the slow movement of Schubert's Sonata in A minor

Example 15

Andante poco moto

Phot. 129—133

Tamás Vásáry plays Chopin's Ballad in F minor

Example 16

Phot. 134–138

Phot. 139
LILI KRAUS

LEGATO AND STACCATO

LEGATO

Perfect legato is obtained when a vibrating body produces tones of different pitches without interruption. Thus the legato of the violin is not a perfect one. The continuity is assured by the bow stroke but the tones are always produced by the different strings (the strings, which may be shortened by the grips, can be considered as a series of strings of different length). With wind instruments the tone is also produced by several tubes of different length and only the blowing without interruption (corresponding to the uninterrupted bow stroke) gives a certain legato effect. Thus a perfect legato can be achieved only by singing, where the changes of pitch are created by the differences of tension of the vocal chords. This is why the legato of every instrument imitates singing.

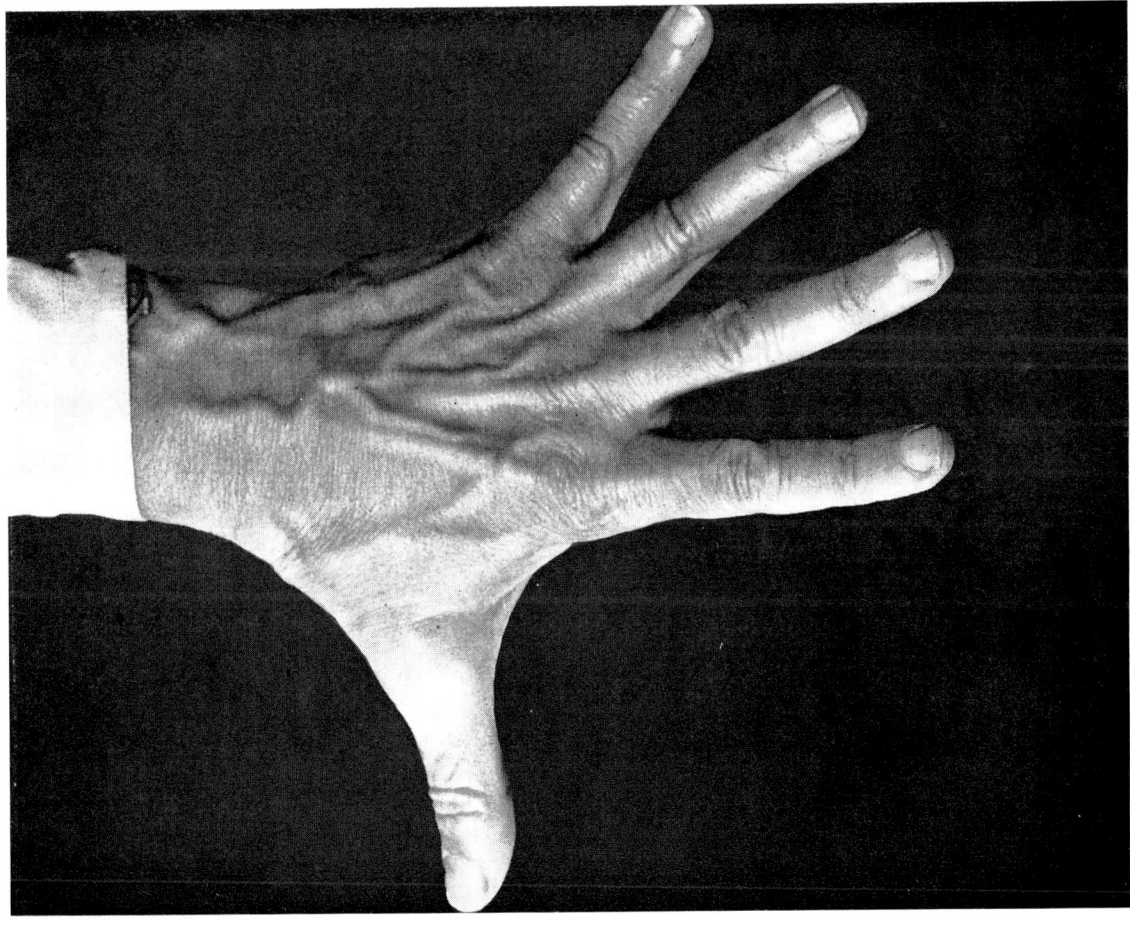

Phot. 140
THE HAND OF LILI KRAUS

The piano is even less able to meet the requirements of legato playing than a string or wind instrument. Every tone is sounded by a different chord, and, in addition to that, each of the strings is struck by a separate hammer. If one might say that legato is realized only partly by violin, the piano seems to be absolutely unable to attain a legato effect.

A good pianist, however, is able to make his public believe that he can perform a legato like the singer or violinist. Let us analyse by what means he will do that.

The prerequisite for the legato effect is that the tones should succeed each other without interruption, so that the start of a new tone should merely mean a change of pitch, i.e. of the number of vibrations. Since to change the pitch on the piano inevitably involves interruption of the preceding tone, the new tone must be sounded as imperceptibly as possible. In order to attain a legato effect, the new tone must be – as it were – "smuggled" into the melody without drawing attention to it.

What are the factors which tend to direct attention to the sounding of a new tone?

Gap between the notes

It is almost generally believed that the most important prerequisite of the legato is that no gap should occur between the notes. A gap between two notes is really most conspicuous and directs the attention to the sounding of the new tone. As an antithesis to that, an "over-holding" of the tones is advocated by many methods in order to attain a legatissimo effect. However, if the previous tone is still held when the new one is already sounding, a disturbing dissonance will result which is also conspicuous and does not give any legatissimo effect, nor even an acceptable legato effect.

Noises

As noises sound always at the beginning of the tone and soon fade away the noise-effect always brings the commencement of a new tone into prominence. (The noise-effect is associated with the beginning of the sound, one suggests the other.)

The hammer and string noises caused by the hammer stroke can only be diminished concurrently with a decrease in the dynamic degree. On the other hand, we are able to diminish both the key noise caused by the finger stroke and the noise arising from the impact between the wood of the key and the key-bed, without reducing the dynamic level.

The more noise-free our playing, the more beautiful our legato will be.

Sudden dynamic changes

Changes in dynamics, i.e. a conspicuous difference between the volume of two successive tones, will also draw attention to the sounding of the new tone. In the dynamic level of piano we have to be constantly prepared for the fact that (especially in slow tempi) the sound following the previous tone will sound with a surprising tone volume. It must also be taken into consideration that the fading away of the more strongly sounded tones takes place relatively quicker than that of the softly sounded tones. In order to attain a legato effect the performer has to strive for diminishing this difference of the tone volumes. This can be achieved e.g. in a very slow tempo only by sounding the second tone with a considerably weaker tone volume than the first one.

The inaccuracy of the dynamic contours

The commencing of the new tone is made conspicuous (and thus disturbing for the legato effect) if the volume of the sounded tone differs from that expected by us on the basis of the musical emotional content.

The most important requirement for arousing the sensation of legato in the listener is the exact shaping of the dynamic contours of the melodies. If the series of tones played by applying uniform force (uniform dynamics) is not in accordance with the concept of the musical piece it will not arouse any sensation of legato. This is why the notes of the organ, although not fading away and moving fluidly from one tone to the next, are at a disadvantage in comparison with those of the piano, with regard to legato effects, despite the fact that the fading tone volume and the noises reduce the piano's legato effects.

This role of the dynamic contours is also shown by the organist's and harpsichord player's endeavours to retrieve through stressed agogics what they are unable to express through dynamics. Up to a certain extent the agogic effect produces the impression of legato because it accentuates the melodic outlines. The non-legato is, therefore, almost free from agogics.

THE LAWS OF LEGATO

Although the piano is unable to reproduce real legato, a perfect legato effect can be obtained by
1. The gapless succession of tones;
2. The elimination, as far as possible, of noises;
3. The adaptation of the dynamic level and of the duration of the tones to the requirements of legato;
4. The choice of the most appropriate dynamic level;
5. The most precise observance of the dynamic contours required by the melody.

On the basis of the above, the following may be stated:

a. Because the noise-effects grow more and more disturbing with an increasing tempo, it is more difficult to arouse a legato sensation in the audience in a fast tempo than in a medium or slow tempo. The noises, fading away quickly, will disturb the long sounding tone at the beginning, because they are to be heard only for a short time. In a fast tempo, however, the duration of the tone is not very much longer than the sounding of the noise and so the noise-effect associated with the commencing of the tone is relatively strong.

b. With long tones the dynamic differences caused by the diminishing of the tone volume will hinder the legato effect.

c. Forte and fortissimo playing raises difficulties in creating the legato effect because of the considerable noise made by the strings. In the case of longer tones the rapid diminishing of the tone volume (taking place with forte tones) will also prove detrimental (see p. 13).

d. From the comparison of points *b.* and *c.* it will be seen that the more slowly the tones follow each other the more softly we have to play in order to attain a legato effect. In this way we can counterbalance the inevitable diminishing of the tone volume by the greatest possible elimination of the noises.

e. In slow playing the dynamic contours require a more careful elaboration than in fast tempo. Tones of longer duration involve larger changes in tone volume – even in the case of unaltered dynamic level – on account of the fading away of single tones. More careful dynamic elaboration is also called for because in slow tempo every detail of the dynamic contours is more perceptible.

f. Higher notes die away sooner than lower ones. Thus, in the lower pitch registers legato playing with sustained tones is possible, while in the upper registers a legato effect can be attained only through ever diminishing rhythmic values.

g. On account of the increasing hammer and string noises, it is difficult, in the upper pitch registers – and almost impossible in the highest octaves – to attain a legato effect. (In the upper registers the noises caused by the impact of the key-wood on the key-bed are also more audible because they are lower than the tone.)

CANTILENA

Cantilena is a singing, melodic form of tone production. It may also be considered as a special kind of legato because the qualities of both are nearly identical. (The legato also imitates the smooth, soft character of singing.)

When we compare the requirements of the legato with that of the cantilena (on the basis of the five above-mentioned elements of a perfect legato effect), we reach the following conclusions:

1. The postulate of gapless succession of tones is only of limited validity in the case of the cantilena, because in singing, portato is at least as frequent as simple legato. (As a matter of fact, the portato effect is produced by every consonant.)

2. The reduction of noises to a minimum is also an essential requirement of the cantilena because a sonorous, carrying tone may be obtained only in this way. This is why in the cantilena the upper-arm swing-strokes which produce noise-free, sonorous tones, are of such importance.

3. The cantilena is incompatible both with fast and with very slow tempo. Velocity and cantilena are antagonistic notions. Neither can a cantilena effect be attained in a very slow tempo, because the dying-away of the tones diminishes their singing quality.

4. Since a certain minimum tone volume is indispensable to the cantilena, it is very difficult — or even impossible — to achieve a cantilena effect in piano or pianissimo. Fortissimo, on the other hand, is unsuited to cantilena playing because of the excessive increase in noise-effects. The dynamic limits of the cantilena are mezzopiano and forte.

The cantilena character of playing is influenced, however, not only by the dynamic level of the melody but also by the tone volume of the accompaniment, i.e. by the surrounding voices. If the accompaniment is played more softly, the melody will stand out more radiantly against the grey background and will appear more sonorous.

This effect of the surrounding voices on the cantilena character of the melody applies also to point *3*. The cantilena effect may be produced more easily by a melody of larger rhythmical values than those of the accompaniment (e.g., melody in quavers, accompaniment in semiquavers). The cantilena character is similarly supported when a melody of larger rhythmical values follows a swift musical passage.

5. Indispensable components of the cantilena — the same as in legato — are the accuracy of the dynamic contours and the subtlety of the shading even in the smallest details. The dynamic contours of the cantilena, however, move between more extreme limits and are more vivid than those of the legato. (The dynamics of singing are also more lively than those of instrumental dynamics.)

STACCATO

Every kind of playing in which the tones are not sustained to their full value, but are separated from each other by pauses, is called staccato.

According to classical practice, staccato tones are sustained for only half their time value. Special importance to this rule is given by the fact that the classical composers employed staccato signs not only with fourth or eighth notes but also with half notes. Moreover, the sign of staccato occurred very frequently where tones had to be sustained even longer than the half of their values. So we meet with many kinds of staccato ranging from the sharp, short staccato to tones sustained to almost their full value. We may state that the tenuto coincides with the peripheral case of staccato where the tone is sustained to almost its full value. An important difference between tenuto and staccato is that in tenuto the tones are barely separated from each other, while the beginning of a staccato tone is stressed through a vigorous touch.

The sustaining of staccato tones up to the half of their value is not regarded as a general rule any more. The shortness of the staccato tones varies according to styles and even pieces and musical motives, but in the final analysis it should be determined by the pianist's feeling for style. The different variants of the staccato can be studied and mastered only by playing pieces of different style; their exact values can be determined only by their musical surroundings.

In legato playing we attemp to "smuggle" the new tone into the melody, while in staccato playing we seek to direct attention to the commencement of a new tone.

THE LAWS OF STACCATO

1. The longer the intervals between successive tones, i.e. the shorter the single tones, the more distinctly will the staccato character prevail.

2. The noise-effects reinforce the staccato character because they accentuate the introduction of the new tone. In slow tempo a short tone will of itself cause a staccato impression. With increasing tempo more noise-effects (mainly upper noises) are gradually needed in order to demarcate the tones. Excessively strong noise-effects, however, may efface – and to a certain extent even suppress – the initial sounding of the tone. In the upper pitch registers – where even the noises produced by the strings are also strongly noticeable – too noisy a playing will endanger the clarity of the melodic line.

3. Strange as it may seem, the staccato is more independent from the duration of the sound than the legato (at least in the highest three octaves of the piano). The only prerequisite is that the character of the tone be short which may be attained by the corresponding noise-effects. Thus the distinction made by the classics between the following two ways of playing is fully justified.

Example 17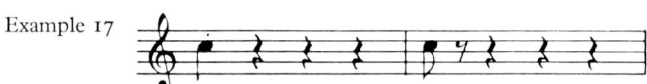

The staccato character requires a vigorous attack. Thus we commence the staccato crotchet (quarter-note) more strongly but it is not the same effect as if the composer had put an accent on the quaver (eighth-note).

Beethoven was guided by the same principle when he used crotchets with quarter rests and staccato half-notes immediately succeeding each other in Movement III of the Sonata in C minor (Op. 13, in bars 151–156). The difference lies here not so much in the duration of the tone but in the different mixing ratio of the noise-effect.

Example 18

In slow tempo, a staccato effect may be obtained in all kinds of soft playing because the fading of the tones and a correspondingly long gap will accentuate the new tone even in pianissimo. With the increasing of the tempo the gaps will shorten and the staccato can be separated from the non-legato only by its more energetic attack.

4. The dynamic level may be low in slow tempi but in a fast tempo a higher dynamic level is required in order to keep the staccato character. The more rapidly we repeat a staccato motive, the louder we have to play in order to insure the same staccato effect as in the previous slow tempo. Thus with the increasing of the metronome marks, the dynamic level should also be increased.

In the upper pitch registers an increase of the dynamic level will compensate for the insufficiently short sounding of the tones. The upper octaves are without dampers so the staccato effect has to be achieved through strengthening the touch. In this case, there is consequently no possibility whatever of producing a short, soft staccato.

5. The maintenance of the dynamic contours is necessary in the staccato, too, but does not require – and does not even allow – such detailed elaboration as in the case of the legato.

In slow tempo, where the tones are separated from each other by rather long pauses, even the most varied dynamic contours will not endanger the staccato character. Proportionately with the accelerated tempo, however, we have to apply more uniform dynamics. If we repeat a staccato motive (played previously in a lower pitch register) at the same speed in the highest octaves (which have no damper), a simplification of the dynamic contours will again become necessary.

THE TECHNIQUE OF LEGATO AND STACCATO

The swing-strokes of the upper arm are appropriate for legato playing only in slow tempo. Although the smooth flow of the tones will cause certain difficulties, these will be more than compensated for by the noise-free performance and superior shaping of the dynamic contours. The most productive use for the upper-arm swing-strokes is in cantilena playing.

Phot. 141
EMIL GILELS

The tones produced by forearm swing-strokes are accompanied by comparatively loud noise-effects. This is why legato playing in octave and chord technique always represents a difficult task.

The legato effect can be most easily obtained by applying finger technique, because here the task of carrying out smooth changes in the notes is easiest.

On the other hand, since staccato playing requires an increasing tone volume with increasing tempo, only upper-arm or forearm swing-strokes should be employed in staccato playing.

The swing-stroke of the upper arm does not necessarily imply that a large movement is required. The distance of the stroke is always determined by the required noise-effect. The "plucked" staccato is played by a direct swing-stroke with the addition of very slight lower noises, because the effect of the extremely short tone would be endangered by excessive noise.

Rapid staccatos should be played from the forearm. Such softening as may be needed is carried out by additional wrist motion which will also aid in apportioning the noise-effects (see chapter on "Octave Technique").

The fingers are not suitable for the execution of staccato technique, because they are not strong enough for it. Quick, short finger-strokes do not evoke any staccato impression, they are much more suited to leggiero playing. Employing the fingers for staccato playing only serves the purpose of producing special noise-effects. On such occasions the fingers will supplement the swing-strokes of the forearm.

In difficult staccato passages the finger motion must be reduced to a minimum. (The fingers have to execute only such motions as are imperatively required by the given key position. One has the sensation of their not moving at all.) In staccato playing the fingers participate in tone production only as elongations of the arm.

LEGATO AND STACCATO IN DIFFERENT STYLES

The performing of both legato and staccato varies according to the different styles. Clear determination of their specific use is almost impossible even within the particular styles because they both possess almost infinite possibilities of variation. At best we may set forth some general considerations.

The legato of Bach's style requires in most cases more definitely marked contours than the legato of Beethoven's style or even the romantic legato. The legato of Bach requires that the tones be coloured in many cases by adding a slight noise-effect, while the legato of Beethoven requires hardly any noise-effect. The technique of the impressionists calls for an even softer legato; here the tones have to melt into each other without any noise at all.

Since on the piano no real legato but only a legato effect can be produced, special technical solutions of the legato technique can be applied even when separated tones are played. Passages which would be played with bow changes (when the intention is to arouse the impression of a great orchestra) are played on the piano with legato technique. Real separation of the tones would deprive them of their character as tones of string instruments. The required effect is attained partly by adding a minimum noise-effect and partly by a certain simplification of the dynamic contours. (The execution of this is easier than the description of it, if the performer intensely imagines the sound of the orchestra.)

As regards the staccato, it is still more difficult to establish any concrete stylistic differences. One thing may be stated: In the style of Bach, a sharp staccato is hardly appropriate, and the kind of staccato most frequently used is what we now call half-staccato. With the romantics and still more in contemporary music, the short staccato occurs more frequently and even the sharp staccato is sometimes to be found.

Phot. 142
WILHELM BACKHAUS

ON FINDING CONTACT
WITH THE INSTRUMENT

The most ardent wish of every performer is to amalgamate, to become united with his instrument in such a way that it should no longer be felt by him to be some strange body but rather an organ of communication opening up wonderful vistas, an organ enabling him to talk more directly and more naturally about his feelings and emotions than he could have done in ordinary speech.

We must, therefore, dig down to the very roots of the question: how to transform the musical concept into a movement such as will produce an effect on the piano strictly corresponding to the cerebral image? Our task is to connect the necessary movements so thoroughly with the musical concept that almost all our attention may be turned to the music.

CONSCIOUSNESS AND INSPIRATION

As the first step, it must be made clear to what extent the *motion system* can be built up consciously. A certain degree of consciousness is a basic condition of all learning but it is important to determine what will be made conscious and to what degree.

Every artistic activity – e.g., painting, too – contains certain conscious elements. However, no painter would deliberately try to work with colour-blocks (as in a children's painting map) or drawing patterns in order to make his work conscious. In the same way it would be absurd for us to pre-determine the gestures which, in everyday life, we employ to enhance the intensity of what we wish to express. No rules can be determined as to how widely we should open our lips when smiling amiably, or as to precisely how we should frown to give vent to our anger. Every movement of our body is determined by the momentary intention to give expression to something. Even our words will acquire a false accent if we try to move our lips perfectly consciously. This kind of consciousness does harm in piano playing too. If we undertake to prescribe: "The F sharp is to be played stronger, the G somewhat softer, the D a little more briefly," etc., the tones will perhaps be precise but no music will be there.

The *full* consciousness of our movements is called "awkwardness" in everyday life. If somebody tries to walk consciously, i.e. if he concentrates on his walking, his movements will be clumsy.[1] The most obvious distinctive feature of a bad actor is that his movements and declamation on the stage are consciously built up: his playing will appear mannered. Could something possibly be good in piano playing which is bad in every other domain of life?

The human body is to be compared with an infinitely complicated electronic machine. Upon the appropriate impulsion, the brain will almost instantaneously send thousands of commands to

---

[1] Stanislavsky: *The Work of the Actor*. II. "How did I play? Badly, because all I did was to show myself in my role. That is to say, I cared only for my body and its movements. It is common knowledge that striving after an impressive appearance will result in straining our muscles and every tension causes stiffness, suffocates the voice and tethers the movements."

the body. Thus it is impossible to make piano playing conscious by separately sending partial commands. This would be as ridiculous as insisting on cranking a car with our hands in order to make driving more conscious and to disdainfully reject all cars with self-starters or with automatic gear-shifts.

The teacher has to know the whole mechanism of playing in order to repair possible defects in partial solutions of the individual movements. The advanced pupil also has to know the most important elements of his organism as a piano-playing machine in order to avoid impairing or destroying the homogeneous mechanism by faulty practising. However, during the playing he must not concentrate on the functioning of his organism, i.e. on watching the activity of his hands – just as we avoid concentrating on the operative details of our other everyday actions.

Does this mean that there is no need for any conscious element at all in piano playing? Of course not! We have to accommodate our movements to the mechanism of the piano and consequently many phases of our movements must be executed consciously. Memory also requires conscious aid.

But there can be no question of elaborating motion-patterns valid for particular types, and still less of always executing individual details of our movements consciously. The process in itself and not the partial solutions are to be made conscious and even more fundamentally the source of the process: the musical concept and its emotional content.[2]

THE EMOTIONAL CONTENT

Music – like any other manifestation of art – seeks to express human feelings, emotions, messages. The only difference is that by means of music we seek to express something we are unable to express in words or pictures. If the emotion we wish to reproduce is better expressed in a poem, it is useless to write it in music. Music makes sublime the emotional content and the performer's task is to reproduce this content.

A trill or a staccato passage cannot be good *per se* – just as, in reciting, the pronouncing of a word cannot be good in itself. No reciter would dream of practising the declamation of a poem by repeating the separate words as often as possible and without expression. So why should playing music without expression be considered practising? If in a certain piece the trill expresses joy, happiness, its playing will be good – also when practising – only if played as joyfully and naturally as birds sing. Music deprived of its emotional content will break up in meaningless tones which, however well sounding, arouse the impression of a recital, in a foreign language, of a poem by somebody having an agreeable voice but no idea of the language in question.

---

[2] As an example of how worthless isolated movements are in themselves, I recall a personal experience during the visit of the outstanding Soviet puppeteer, Obraztsov, at the Hungarian Academy of Dramatic Arts.

The pupils of the Academy showed us position exercises. One of them had the task of playing the role of a man crossing a street with a package in his hands. Suddenly a car sounds its horn, the man gets frightened and lets the package fall. The pupil played the role – and not even badly – but although he carried out all necessary movements, he made no deep impression on the audience.

Then Obraztsov asked him these questions: "Where are you coming from? (If you are coming from work, you are evidently more exhausted than if you are having a holiday.) Where are you going? What is in the package? Is it something fragile and valuable? Does dropping it mean a heavy material loss to you?" ...etc. In a few minutes a human fate arose before our eyes.

Likewise the tones of a Bach fugue are not characteristic in themselves. Here, too, we have to build up the whole picture, we have to uncover the human content hidden in the sounds. The same theme will sound different if sung by a wise bass than if sung by a buffo baritone. In the tenor voice we sometimes hear a romantic hero and sometimes even the Duke of Mantua. The alto can be the voice of a forgiving mother or of Carmen. Every motive expresses human fate, and a fugue is, as it were, a condensed opera.

The coherence of the tones of a melody is determined by the emotions. The mathematical interconnection – which is present in every case – means only that the tones of the melody are in a harmonic relation with each other, i.e. they have a certain balance.

The striving after a good tone only, after well-sounded or rippling tones, may cause a certain amount of pleasure. If the pianist derives satisfaction from this, he may communicate a sense of harmony and perfection, because it gives expression to a joyful emotion. The secret of the virtuoso's great success lies in the fact that he himself enjoys the scintillating beauty of his tones.

This feeling of rejoicing is the preliminary condition for the success of a performance which will lack, however, a deeper emotional connection with the composition played.

The really gifted performer is not content with this *l'art pour l'art* balance of the tones. He endeavours to find a deep, genuine harmony and if he does not succeed in finding it, he will sometimes be worried to such an extent that it will even become impossible for him to maintain the technical balance. This is why we see crises occurring more often in performers of outstanding talent than with those who make only slight pretensions to expressiveness and thus content themselves with superficial solutions.

Which is the main factor determining the artistic greatness of a performer? It is his striving to find and to reproduce deep interconnection, to find harmony even where it is inaudible to the average man.

This is the way followed also by the painter. He, too, reveals to us the abundance of colours and lines in the objects surrounding us, he practically teaches us to see.

Good musical performance goes even further: It teaches us not only to listen but to live.

A really good concert is one after which the listener feels he has become more human, a changed, well-balanced being. The performer – like a new Virgil – has shown him Heaven and Hell, made him a hero and a coward, Don Giovanni or Gilda, given him the impression of having made hundreds of journeys or listened to marvellous operas, and, above all, has convinced him that life, with all its exciting beauties and colours, is indeed wonderful. This was the impression aroused by the playing of Bach, and this was also the secret of Mozart and Liszt. And this is the only path for a performer striving to produce an abiding effect.

The deep interrelationships and truths revealed by a Bach fugue or a Beethoven sonata will be well reproduced only by a pianist who fully abandons himself to the emotional content of the piece he is playing.[3]

Thus the most important thing to be learned is that while playing he should let the sensations of the outside world fade away: the music should become the only reality. Do not imitate joy: be joyful yourself.[4] Do not imitate the expression of ultimate truths: become great yourself. A trill or cadence will sound well only if we succeed in arousing in ourselves the feeling of joy which prompts their use.

Stanislavsky insisted that the actor must transform himself instead of imitating others. How much more must this be kept in mind by the pianist, who is a whole theatrical company in one person. It is not enough merely to imitate the hero of the subject or the soubrette of the intermediate passage, or the romantic heroine of the second subject. If we only imitate the characters while maintaining our own dissenting opinion, the result will be an insincere, stereotyped playing. What we

---

[3] C. Ph. E. Bach: "Good performing means the ability of making musical conception audible according to their real contents..."

[4] Daniel Gottlob Türk (1750–1813): "The primary aim of the player is the characteristic expression. He has to endeavour to enter into the mood of the composition and to transmit its emotional contents to the public by means of sounds which speak." (*Klavierschule*, 1789).

István Gáti, the author of the first Hungarian school of piano playing, wrote the following in 1802: "If we want to play a composition, we have to arouse in ourselves the same feeling we find in it. If we notice that we are unable to feel the emotion prevailing in the piece, it will be better to give up the playing of it for the time being."

need here is a complete man who dares to live the life of the characters he re-creates, without any restrictions or reservations.

Unfortunately, it is still the fashion to insist on the principle that the performer has to observe himself critically while he is playing. This, however, can be carried out only if we do not identify ourselves with the roles we have to play, i. e. if we do not live the lives of the themes. Criticism is, of course, necessary. But in the theatre, too, this is the work of the director. Like him when practising we have to analyze the characters, we have to uncover the most hidden emotions and to create the equilibrium of the themes. Let us be inexorable in judging the slightest deviations of our performance from our concept. But what about a director criticizing the actors during the performance? This would paralyze the actors and prevent them from living their roles. In the "performance" of the pianist, too, it is only the prompter who has to remind the "player" of the order of succession in the "entry" of the themes, to call his attention to the beginning of a new direction, to the sounding of a certain chord in the intermediate part, etc. Incessant self-criticism during the performance is in contradiction with the most important requirement: the profundity and completeness of the inspiration. The complex task of a good performance – and as a preparation for this good practising – can be solved only by means of full and intensive inspiration, by the faultless reproduction of the emotional content of the piece.

If we avoid all insincerity, all artificiality, all petrified patterns, if we open a free path from the emotion to its realization, we shall find that there are many more good musicians than we expected. Every genuine sensation will arouse interest, provided the person who experienced it knows how to tell it sincerely. Only imitation and mannerism can be boring. The imitation of someone's performing – no matter how perfect the model – leads us far away from a real, effective performance, just as striving toward "decorative" effects will deflect us from good performance.

THE MUSICAL CONCEPT

The emotional content of a piece is set down by the composer by means of notes representing a kind of shorthand outline of his emotions. The skeleton formed by the notes has to be brought back to life, has to be re-created by the performer. This vitalizing process takes place with the aid of the artist's musical concept. It is not possible for the musical concept to take shape at the first reading, it will grow and ripen gradually.

Since emotional manifestations undergo considerable changes not only from person to person, but even within the same individual, the deep experiencing of the melodies will result in different interpretations.

The change in the emotional reaction is sometimes so intense that the composer has the feeling that all his solutions are insincere, and so he undertakes to re-write his earlier compositions. Bartók, for example, composed new harmonies to some of his pieces "For Children" at the end of his life. Under the impression of World War II and in the hurried, precipitate tempo of American life, he did not feel the old harmonies to be true any more. So he wrote new ones reflecting his state of mind at the time. These harmonies are more complicated, more bitter than the earlier ones.

There exists no such thing as *one single* ideal way of playing a piece. (Even that of the composer cannot be considered as an exclusive one. If for example some young girl reacts to a certain emotional content in the same way as say, Beethoven, we may be sure that the girl is abnormal.) It is impossible to determine exactly how a certain piece is to be played either as a whole or in certain of its details (for example how strong this or that note has to sound, etc.). All in all, the interpretations will, of course, resemble each other, and yet how many differences there will be!

The role of the musical concept in piano playing is even greater than in the case of other instruments, because the player of a string or wind instrument is still able to modify the tone after having sounded it. He may change the pitch or the tone colour, while the pianist has to concentrate entirely on the escapement level. He has no possibility of subsequently modifying the tone: the slightest uncertainty in the musical concept causes irremediable distortions because the sound quality, the subjective and objective tone colour, takes shape at the moment of escapement, i.e. in a hundredth of a second or even in a shorter time.

THE INTERRELATION BETWEEN MUSICAL IMAGINATION AND MUSCLE ACTION

From the fact that the pianist is unable to modify the tone once sounded, many theoreticians have drawn the conclusion that the pianist need be active only up to the escapement level, after which he may relax. Thus piano playing, in their view, is a constant alternation between activity and relaxation.

This would mean in practice that, in order to play a half-note in slow tempo, we would have to let our muscles work only for a moment and then we might rest up to the next note.

The apparent appeal of this solution lies in the possibility of saving muscle work. In reality, however, this method will ruin not only our technique but — sooner or later — even our musical imagination.

As there must be a close interrelation between musical imagination and physical motion, it is a prerequisite of good technique that the variations of the movements should exactly follow the modifications of the musical concept. To produce a stronger sound, the motion must be executed either with a larger mass or with a greater speed: in the same way, a shorter or longer tone requires a corresponding change in the movement.

What makes the piano tone last longer? The length depends not only on the time during which we hold the key down (i.e. lift the damper), but also on whether or not we succeed in making the listener believe that the quickly fading piano sound maintains its strength or even increases it.[5] This depends on whether we succeed in creating all those external circumstances which strengthen the listener's impression of hearing a long tone, and in avoiding those which tend to weaken this impression. The long and short tones differ even at the moment of their sounding in the amount of the accompanying noises.

The question arises whether we are capable of arousing the impression of a long tone by merely sticking to the rules of producing a noise-free tone. Is it possible to arouse the impression of a long tone by applying certain movements *independently of the tone conception?*

Indeed the illusion of a long tone can only be aroused with the aid of certain movements but these movements are not adequately realizable without an intensive tone imagination. We cannot cheat ourselves! Even a concluding chord has to be imagined at its full value, because at the moment of sounding the chord we have already intentionally determined how long we shall hold the chord, imagining the same duration of intensity as if we were singing or playing the violin.

It is evident that the commands directing the complicated work of the muscles have to precede the movements. If we have resolved to hold a chord intensively throughout its full value, we have to prepare for movements which will produce a long tone and thus these movements will exactly execute everything to ensure a noise-free sound thereby arousing the impression of a long tone.

If, on the other hand, we do not sound the chord intensively enough and, therefore, only hold the keys down sufficiently to avoid interrupting the tone, we shall — even before we sound the chord — have given the order to our muscles to produce a short tone — with a greater noise-effect.

This is a purely metrical conception which is very harmful. If we apply it, we content ourselves with registering the moment of sounding the single tones, but we do not fill their metric value with life, i.e. with dynamics. Here essentially two commands are received by the muscles at the

---

[5] See details in chapter on "Legato and Staccato."

same time. On the one hand, we have to hold down the key — because this is connected with the concept of a long tone indicated by the note, but on the other hand the intention arises within us to hold the tone with full intensity only for a short duration and this essentially requires muscle work corresponding to a short note. (It should not be forgotten that the musical concept and the motion commands connected with it necessarily precede the sounding of the tone.)

These contradictory motion commands will result in utter disorder and indifference. The tones — whether short or long — will be sounded by the hand in the same way and with the same noise content. The contradiction between the concept and its realization will sooner or later upset the sureness of the musical concept as a consequence of having applied the same muscle action and the same noise content to such radically different sounds as a long and a short tone.

In order to determine the correct action of the muscles, our only possible course is to start from the most intensive musical concepts possible. If we want to obtain a long tone, i.e. to make the listener believe he hears a long tone, we have to get the feeling of forming the tone even after actually sounding it, the same as we would expect from an outstanding singer or violinist.[6] Each tone must be played, even in quick tempo, as if it were of a certain duration. Even in prestissimo we must have the feeling of being capable of forming each single note. If we dare to imagine a crescendo in a chord, if we make ourselves believe that the tones grow stronger after they have been sounded, our movements will adjust themselves to this conception and the tones will produce the illusion of becoming stronger.

The strengthening of the tones is no mere illusion of the senses, because the application of the pedal will also change according to the pianist's musical concept.

If we have imagined a short sound, the pedal must be depressed very shortly after the sounding of the tone. Often the two actions will be carried out almost simultaneously. Thus the resonance produced by the pedal will strengthen the noise of the string and the hammer. These indeed will be increased comparatively to an even greater degree than the consonant elements of the tone itself: the harmonic overtones.

The components of the noises are sound elements having no harmonic connection with each other. The noises of the string or of the hammer have little disturbing effect because their duration is very short compared with that of the tone. However, if the pedal strengthens the noises of the string by means of the resonance of the other strings, the noises will become very strong and will produce a confused tone effect. Let us try it! Press down the pedal first and then play a note: the sound will be a confused and ugly one. Now press down the pedal somewhat later, after the noises have faded: the resonances will strengthen only the useful, harmonic elements of the tone.

If the pianist imagines a long tone, he will depress the pedal instinctively in such a way as not to strengthen the noise elements. The time within which pressing down the pedal has to follow the sounding of the tone varies, of course, according to the pitch. With bass notes the fading away of the noises takes more time, and, therefore, the pedal should also be pressed down later.

The correct muscle work will become proportionately more and more differentiated with the increase in intensity of the musical concept. The different tone volumes and colours of the tones

---

[6] It is not accidental that great performers and teachers always considered singing as the model of good performing on instruments.

Sigismund Thalberg (1812–1871): *L'art du chant appliqué au piano.* Op. 70. "For those who earnestly want to concern themselves with piano playing the best advice is to study the beautiful art of singing. Never miss the occasion to listen to great singers..."

"As for myself, I studied singing for five years under the guidance of one of the best teachers of the Italian school."

H. G. Neuhaus: *On the Art of Piano Playing.* 1958. P. 56. "I always most emphatically advise pupils to listen to good singers, violinists and violoncellists who are real artists of the cantilena, who are capable of bringing to the surface even from the tiniest notes the singing of the melody..."

A. B. Goldenweiser: *Soviet Masters of Piano Playing.* P. 146. (Ed. Nikolaev, 1954.) "If I play a long-sounding note I have to imagine that I am a singer or violinist and am singing or playing the melody with a bow."

of a melody require different muscle work, and as a melody must be imagined as continuous, the muscle activity, too, must be continuous. If the pianist – when sounding a long tone – were to remain active only up to the moment of sounding the tone and could relax after that, it would result in the fingers becoming passive and losing the feeling of balance which enables the pianist always to feel the keys as elongations of his fingers. The constant "holding," constant feeling of the keys requires a constant, active muscle work.

The degree of active muscle work varies also within the individual swing-strokes but the activity itself is continuous and enables the pianist to conserve his contact with the key, i.e. the feeling of balance. However, if he separates his individual impulses by periods of relaxation, the required feeling of balance will be disturbed, and the arm or the weight of the body, respectively, will press the key to the key-bed. (The result will be a pressed, forced tone and a mechanical playing.)

Holding a long tone is thus a special task also for the muscles. The muscle work has to follow exactly the conceptual changes and a shorter tone must be connected with shorter muscle work, while a longer tone must be linked with longer muscle work.

EXPEDIENCY

The overwhelming majority of our movements are innate unconditioned reflexes. These reflexes are, in the course of learning, complemented by the necessary new conditioned reflexes. During this process we draw up – so to speak – an inventory of our movements.

If learning to play the piano necessitated the innervation of entirely new movements, i.e. the formation of new conditioned reflexes, the attempt would be a hopeless venture. It would take hundred thousands (or perhaps millions) of years to learn to play. Thus, it is obvious that we have to select from among our innate movements those which can be utilized in piano playing, those by the aid of which we shall obtain tones corresponding to our musical conception, those which are practical and natural from the point of view of the task to be accomplished.

The fundamental prerequisite for the appropriateness of a movement is that it should be natural and correspond to our physiological endowments. The most simple and least laborious way of carrying out any kind of work is to do it with natural movements.

The most natural and least tiring way of piano playing must be found, but without permitting this to become a purpose in itself. Our aim should not be to find the most comfortable way to play, but rather to produce a musical concept most accurately in the most effortless way. Thus, although we carefully avoid all *superfluous* labour in piano playing, we must bear in mind that piano playing means carrying out a certain amount of work. Our aim is not to reduce this labour at all costs but rather to express our musical concepts through the most simple and natural movements.

In piano playing each movement must have its justification. One has to apply greater force only if a stronger tone is wanted. One's finger or arm should strike from a greater height only if this is required for the sake of the upper noises. The key should be forcefully swung against the key-bed only if one wants to produce lower noises.

In this way movement associations corresponding to all nuances of the musical concept will be built up. The series of associations becomes successively enlarged and stabilized in the process of learning. With the development of the motion system sooner or later a particular combination of muscle movements becomes directly associated with every frequently recurring musical element, with every tone relation. In accordance with the system of musical concepts a system of movements will be built up, and every changing nuance of the concept will be instantly reflected in a corresponding change in the movement.

The building up of a logical system of movements will be possible only if we adapt ourselves to the mechanism of the piano, in other words: if our movements are expedient.

When playing the piano, our movements are in the service of tone production. Only that movement will be expedient which serves to make the piano produce a tone adequate to our musical concept.

We have to concentrate on tone production and not on setting the key in motion. *Do not play on the keys but – with the aid of the keys – on the strings.*

Cold, dry playing of the piano is in many cases due to "shortness" of the swing-stroke. This means that the pianist measures his movements as if the keys were to produce the tones and not the strings. Since this is a mechanical idea not corresponding to reality, his movements will be inexpedient.

When playing with "short" swing-strokes, the performance will be accompanied by too many noises and the dynamic contours will also be poor and monotonous. Sensitive dynamic contours require full spontaneity of the movements. "Key-playing" permits only artificial, calculated dynamics and leads to "conscious" piano playing – but to consciousness in the wrong sense of the word.

The key has the same role in piano playing as the bow has in violin playing. We have to get the feeling that we grasp the key and play directly on the string with its aid.[7]

We have already mentioned that we have to make better use of the unconditioned reflexes if we wish to facilitate the linking of our movements with the musical imagination, with our musical concept. By reducing the mechanical functions of piano playing to their simplest foundation, i. e., to the *working process*, we will be able to attain a perfect spontaneity in our technique, because entire series of unconditioned reflexes are connected with the working process which man has developed over many thousands of years in the course of practical activity.

The key is a two-armed lever with the aid of which the hammer strikes the string from below. If the pianist is of the opinion that the work to be carried out consists of only moving the key, he will seek to use the key as a one-armed lever. This would be correct if the *keys* produced the sounds. In this case it would be right to strike the keys from above[8] and this would require entirely different movements from those called for by moving a two-armed lever, i. e. moving the key as an instrument to strike the strings with the hammer.

---

[7] Adolf Bernhard Marx (1795–1866): "By seizing the keys with gentleness and love instead of pressing, rubbing or striking them, we are capable of attaining much more than is generally believed and asserted...

"The keys must be felt and not pushed and hit by us: we must take hold of them just as when clasping the hand of a friend with compassion in moments of mighty and affectionate emotions–or else the poesy of Beethoven or Bach will never come to full expression."

Tobias Matthay: *The Act of Touch in All Its Diversity*. Part II, Chapter VII, Preamble, pp. 49–50 (London, Longmans, Green and Co. 1919).

"Realizing that our object must be to create key movement, we shall then neither attempt to hit or strike the key– as if it were a ball or a nail, nor shall we attempt to jam it down upon its 'bed'–as if it were a nut-cracker! We shall, on the contrary, project our minds as it were to the hammer-end of the key: and our purpose will be to move the string by means of that hammer-end. In a word, we shall not try to play on the keyboard, or at it: but shall instead try to play the strings by means of the key.

"Now we never dream of hitting or striking the Tennis racket or the Violin bow or the Billiard cue: instead, we take them up–take hold of them and use them. And that is precisely how we should treat the Pianoforte-key. When we wish to play a note, we must equip or 'arm' our finger-end with the implement we wish to employ–and that is the key. We must take hold of that key, by placing a finger-tip against its surface: and thus enable ourselves to realize its weight and resistance, through the muscular sense. Thus realizing the weight of the Tool we mean to employ, we must then proceed positively to aim with its opposite end–the hammer-end.

"It is of no use 'aiming' at the Key, we must aim with it: for the key is not to be regarded as a ball, but rather in the light of a racket, cue, or other speed-tool. With the finger thus equipped, the key will be felt but a mechanically-provided continuation of the finger itself–an intimate connection and elongation of our body, ending only with the hammer-tip: and we shall feel that it is with that end of the tool (thus under our immediate control) that we have to aim, and create speed in the string."

[8] Sigismund Thalberg: *L'art du chant appliqué au piano*. "The pupils should not strike the keys downwards."

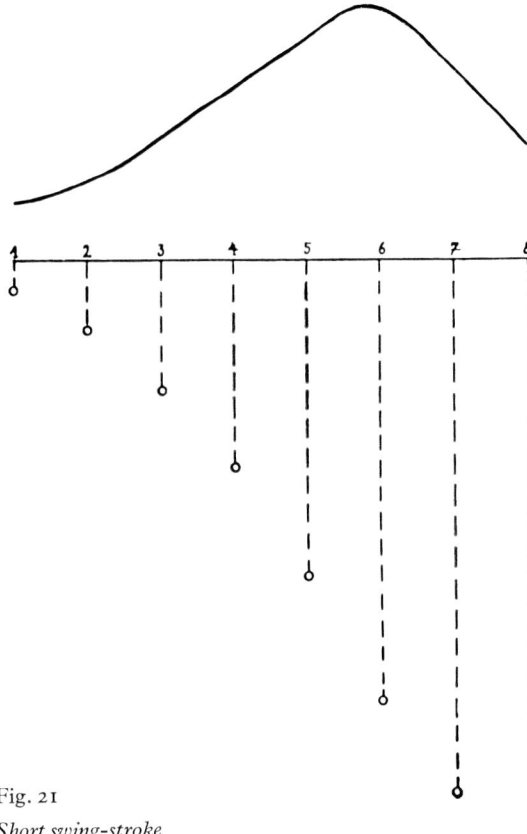

Fig. 21
Short swing-stroke

The difference between the correct swing-stroke (using the key as a two-armed lever) and the "short" swing-stroke can be proved also by slow-motion picture.

I have applied the most precise form of the direct swing-stroke, i.e. my finger did not relinquish the key. Although there were, of course, smaller deviations in the movements, the graphs made on the basis of the movements are very easily divisible into two characteristic groups, according to whether they record correct or short swing-strokes.

The course covered by the key is represented by the dotted line in the picture, thus the longest line corresponds to the full depth of the key-course (10 mm). The ciphers along the horizontal axis show the serial numbers of the recordings. Between each consecutive picture there is an interval of 1/120 of a second. In order to give a clearer impression of the changes in speed their values have been doubled on the graph above the axis.

In the correct swing-stroke, the speed increases gradually up to the escapement level, after which it decreases rapidly. (A comparatively slight lower noise will arise.)

In the short swing-stroke, the speed increases rapidly, but it will decrease already before reaching the escapement level. Thus if we want to attain a large enough speed at the escapement level – in spite of the decrease – we have to apply more force than would be necessary to attain the same tone volume by means of a correct swing-stroke. In view of the fact that the decrease of the speed is less than in the correct swing-stroke, the short swing-stroke produces a noisier tone – with the same tone volume – than the correct one.

In the short swing-stroke the sounding of the tone–i.e., the point of greatest speed–is imagined at the bottom of the key's course. This seems to be contradicted by the picture which, in the short swing-stroke, shows the speed as decreasing already before the escapement level.

This phenomenon may be explained by the following: the resistance of the mechanism of the piano increases abruptly before the escapement level. As the largest speed is to be attained–in the short swing-stroke–at the lowest position of the key, we are not yet able to apply the necessary force at the moment of abrupt increase in resistance. In a correct swing-stroke the muscle-force is so appointed that we apply the maximum force at the escapement level. Therefore, not even the abrupt increase in resistance can impede the augmentation of the speed.

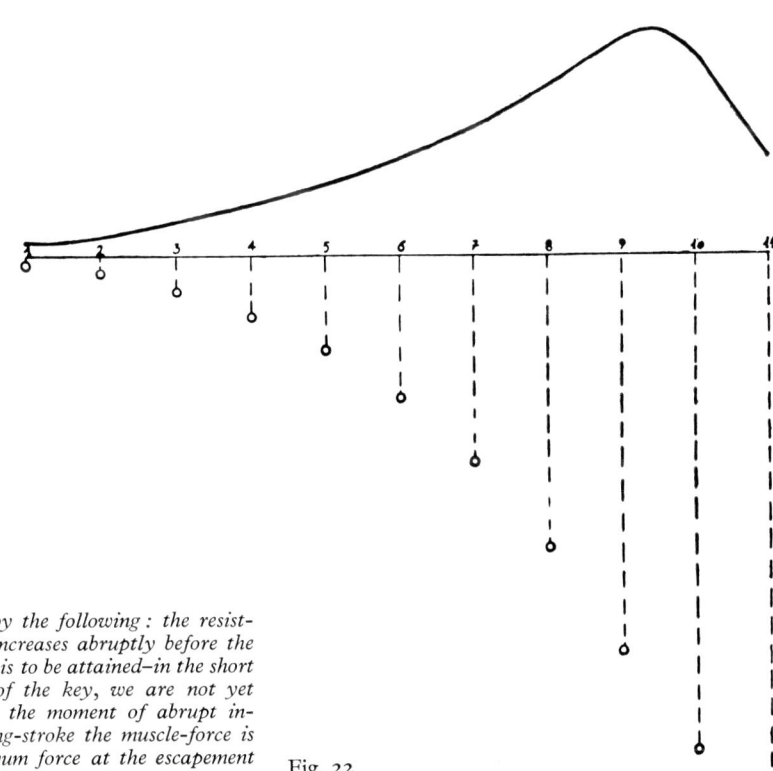

Fig. 22
Correct swing-stroke

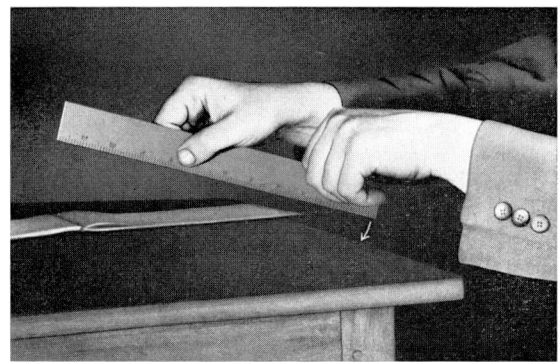

Phot. 143

Phot. 144

We may convince ourselves of the difference between using the key as a one-armed and as a two-armed lever by a simple experiment.

Try to make this experiment by using Phot. 143–144 as mirror pictures.

Hold one end of a ruler in your left hand (forming an axis with two fingers) and play with the other end – with your right hand – different rhythms on the table. The ruler was thus used as a one-armed lever.

Now, if you hold the ruler in the middle (with your left hand) thus having transformed it into a two-armed lever, and play rhythms with your right hand in such a way that the other end of the ruler strikes the table from below, you will feel that the motion is an entirely different one.

When two children are astride a seesaw, each will instinctively try to swing his partner up high, in order to attain a smooth motion. One who cares only about pressing down his own side will bump himself soundly on the ground.

In piano playing we can, therefore, achieve expediency in our movements only if we continually take care "to play from below", that is if we try to realize that we ourselves are striking the string from below.

This concept is based on reality, and our ears will have the sensation of a satisfactory sound only if we strike the string on this basis. The movement is apparently downwards. Our fingers do indeed move the keys downwards. But from the point of view of the working process, and also according to the ear, this movement is directed upwards, if we bear in mind that we strike the string with the hammer.

Thus the "key-playing" pianist either does not pay attention to the music, or has to constantly force himself to calculate: "I have to carry out changes to this or that extent in order to produce the same sound by striking downwards, as if I had done it upwards."

Thus, for a "key-playing" pianist it is easier to concentrate on the motion than on the tone. As a result the rhythm, too, may become easily distorted, because his primary aim was the rhythm of his movements instead of the rhythm of the sounding tones.

If we observe the hand of a pianist playing with a good rhythm, we will notice that, although the tones sound in an absolutely correct rhythm, the movement of the hand seems to be lazy and negligent. The reason for this is that what we see is only the beginning of the movement. The setting in motion of the two-armed lever, resulting in the swinging action of the hammer, takes much more time than one would think. The hand takes into consideration the inertia of the key, it adapts itself to the limits within which the key can move and does not seek to mark the rhythm for the eye only but to realize it on the strings. Thus the tone will sound only a considerable time after the beginning of the movement. If we concentrate strictly on the tone production, its rhythms will determine exactly when and how much time before the movement is to be executed.[9] In the majority of cases

[9] A careful observation of drum playing will show a similarity in that it is the drum-stick and not the hand that commands the rhythm.

the cause of the recurring grave faults in rhythm may be found in the "short" swing-stroke. This is mostly the case when an otherwise good performance is interrupted by some "short" movements.

The handling of the key as a two-armed lever requires a tension-free state of the body. The increase in speed must be built up within the approx. 8 mm course of the key in such a way that the culminating point is attained precisely at the escapement level. Such delicate work can be executed only with a relaxed body functioning as an elastic support.

Concerning the notion of the relaxed state of the body, we find quite a lot of misunderstandings. In its literal sense it means a slackening or loosening which is only a part of the truth. The muscle tonus excludes any absolute relaxation and what we need in fact is not relaxation but elasticity, the springiness of the fencer.

We can go even further afield for an appropriate comparison by stating that the piano should be grasped – with the participation of the whole body – as intensively as the wrestler prepares to seize hold of his opponent. (This comparison is not quite appropriate in connection with soft playing where we might perhaps better speak of an affectionate embrace which is not of the same force but certainly of the same intensity.)

The full grasping of the keys requires the same elastic foot-work as that of the boxer or wrestler. This gives special importance to how far back we seat ourselves on the chair.

If we sit too far back, the feet are not yet able to prop themselves against the ground, if we sit too forward, they again become unable to do so because they have to carry the weight of the body. An appropriate seat enables us to lean on our feet, without putting our whole weight upon them and thereby reducing their elasticity.

Stanislavsky (p. 76, part II of the quoted work) describes the sensation of motion as a stream of energy. Indeed when playing the piano, we must have the feeling of energy streaming into our body through our feet and then flowing on through the trunk and arms into the piano. If an excessive tension develops somewhere in the body, it will hinder this feeling of streaming and therefore a stiffly upright sitting position and a slack slumped one will be equal hindrances to good tone production. We must, consequently, not "play from the shoulders" by leaning against the piano with the trunk. The arms must not hang down but the trunk and the feet must represent elongations of the arm. In this way, the entire body will be uniformly elastic like a wire spring.

When using a machine in everyday life, we have to concentrate on the machine and not on our body. When riding a bicycle we have to get into motion by pedalling and directing it with the aid of the handle bars. If instead of that we concentrate only on our feet or hands we will immediately tip over. Of course, the piano does not tip over if someone is playing badly on it – let us confess that this is found sometimes regrettable by us – but if someone pays attention only to his own movements instead of directly manipulating the piano, it will not tip over, the pianist will not get hurt but the music will.

Sometimes in everyday life it becomes inevitable for us to think of our own body when working but then this occurs only if something is wrong with our health. Proof of this can be found in certain African dialects where "I have a head" or "I have a foot" means: " my head is aching" or "my foot is aching." Thus, if one movement is "ill," i.e. if it is an inappropriate one, we have to pay special attention to it. But this must be allowed to occur only exceptionally. If our attention is absorbed with our own movements during piano playing, they cannot really be expedient ones, they cannot really serve the tone production.

Many pianists work themselves to death when playing by doing several times as much work as needed. At the same time – or to put it more correctly – for this very reason, the sounding of the tones is miserable. It cannot be otherwise because the pianist is not occupied with the piano and does not strive to make the instrument "sing" the tones, but rather only gets into a strained state and makes useless efforts by concentrating on himself. How much more simple it would be to become aware of the real situation and to induce the piano to "sing."

When discussing the emotional content we mentioned (p. 78) that the pianist is the director and the actor in one person. But we may go even further by saying that the pianist performs a composition to a certain extent by the same "transmission" as the puppeteer.

The piano – although it is incapable of playing, i.e. moving, instead of us like the puppet instead of the puppeteer – is just the same singing and talking about our feelings instead of us. But those emotions can be expressed only by the piano! It is in vain if I am rejoicing, and people see me exulting, but the tone of the piano does not express it. And it is of no use if I am crushed by sorrow but the piano does not sing about it. Of course the effect of the emotion can be seen on me! As C. Ph. E. Bach wrote: *"Man sieht und hört es ihm an"* (quoted work p. 122). But this is only of secondary importance when taking into consideration that we have to make the piano express everything, the tone of the piano has to be joyful or sorrowful, exultant or depressed. Through our playing we have to fill the piano with life just as the puppeteer fills his puppets with life when endeavouring to transmit his own feelings to the puppet.

For some pupils only bold comparisons are of use, so make him imagine he wants to teach the piano the compositions as if he were doing it with a singer.

Or make him imagine the strange scene of being in a circus where the animal tamer would execute the jumps through the flaming hoops with the lions sitting around and patiently observing the show. Is it not the same when a pianist makes himself work and does not care a bit about what the piano is doing? The pianist has to "tame" the piano in order to make it "jump" at his slightest gesture, and instead of that it is he who is doing the "jumping". (Alas, this is very often no mere metaphor, because one sees some wild piano players literally jumping at the piano by leaning against the keyboard.) Think of how the circus rider makes his horse obediently execute the most complicated figures by unnoticeable movements of his feet and hands. Of course the piano cannot be taught to carry out any independent spectacles. In this respect its "taming" is more difficult than that of animals. But be consoled by the fact that the piano is more manageable and less whimsical than a lion or an opera singer.

ALTERATIONS OF THE MOVEMENTS IN THE INTEREST OF THE SOUND

When executing some work, be it by means of a simple tool or a complex machine, we alter our movements while observing the result of the work in order to carry it out more and more exactly. In piano playing the aim of the work is to produce tones corresponding to our musical concept. Thus only the sound can give us direction as to how to alter our movements.

If an artificial satellite deviates from its planned trajectory, computing machines correct the trajectory. This is how our brain corrects – by the aid of experiences gained by sounding the previous tones – the apportioning of the force required for shaping the next tones.

It should repeatedly be kept in mind that this modifying work is almost entirely an automatic one even when practising. The modification which is carried out consciously can only be a rough one – it is almost like a caricature. The conscious aim can only be that we want a softer, sweeter or darker tone colour, but the detailed realization, the bringing into life of these tones, functions only by a "team-work" of complicated reflexes.

In the preceding chapters it has been stated that in piano playing the sensation of tone colour is not produced by the objective tone colours but jointly by the relative tone volume, the apportioning of the noise-effects and the agogic shaping. All this is formed by the aid of the musical concept. However, the connection between the musical concept and the movements required for its realization cannot be expressed in absolute values. The musical concept can only serve as a guide when sounding the individual tones. Innumerable slight modifications may prove necessary for the correct apportioning of force, depending upon momentary circumstances.

Even with an unchanging musical concept different individual movements are required not only depending upon the quality and state of the piano but also upon the acoustic conditions of the concert hall (its dimensions, form, furniture, crowdedness and even its temperature). The musical concept is the pattern, the realization of which should always be accommodated to the circumstances of the moment.

Thus, when sounding a tone, we will compare it with the "pattern" and we will modify the force required for the subsequent tones in accordance with the deviation of the sounded tone from our musical concept. This criticizing, comparing, correcting procedure is of course not carried out between two tones. The movements needed for the realization of a tone start almost simultaneously with the tone concept. But in the subsequent few notes, even if in a quick tempo, the experience gained through the first tone will have an effect.

The appropriate tone colour may be obtained only by means of an exact apportioning of force. This is the intermediary factor of the whole shaping. This is why the absolute simplification of the movements is of such infinite importance, this is the reason why the *naturalness* of our movements is so indispensable. If the tone of the pianist is "outside the piano," if he "plays on the strings," it indicates that his movements are natural and expedient. It shows that he has found the balanced position enabling him to produce tones by the aid of the simplest movements and by the use of the exactly required force. Thus he has transferred maximum muscular energy into tone. To summarize: the necessary modifications are carried out easily.

In such cases the tone colour of the individual note is not different and yet the general impression is as if every tone had undergone a change.

If the movements are not natural, i. e. not reflex-like ones, there is no sound basis for a modification. One time more force is applied than necessary and another time less than required and in the end the tone seems to be bad.

Thus it is clear that anything impeding the activity of the unconditioned reflexes in connection with these movements will be of fatal influence on this ability of modification.

Phot. 145
RUDOLF KERER

ON THE NATURALNESS OF THE MOVEMENTS

What is natural movement? Movement which is associated with unconditioned reflexes. Therefore we should carefully investigate those unconditioned reflexes which influence our movements when playing the piano. It would be difficult to establish any order of importance of these reflexes and even more difficult to strive even for an approximative completeness. But some aid may be furnished by our recognizing and strengthening several of the unconditioned reflexes affecting our movements.

BREATHING

Every instrumental performance is a kind of communication. Our musical concepts are made audible enlarged on the instrument. However, the fact of communication is linked with the mechanism of speaking and singing by strong unconditioned reflexes. The better we are able to apply the reflexes (linked also with our speaking), the more natural our playing will be.

When speaking our thoughts, phrases are communicated by the aid of the air current passing from the chest through the larynx and oral cavity with special groups of sounds of different pitches. The unconditioned reflexes of communication are thus connected partly with the mechanical execution, i.e. the producing of air and the work of the larynx and oral cavity respectively and partly with the special groupings of sounds.

Instead of his larynx the pianist employs the piano for producing sound. Thus the group of unconditioned reflexes associated with the work of the larynx and lips are eliminated. Only the reflexes connected with breathing can be used in the piano playing. These remind us to some degree of speaking and they aid us in achieving a certain speech-like performance. Because of this fact even more stress is laid on the primary importance of correct breathing in piano playing since this is the only mechanical connection between speaking and piano playing.

Concerning the breathing reflexes connected with speaking the following points must be taken into consideration:

1. Since the air stream is a prerequisite of every sound production, our body strives to assume a position, when singing or speaking, which will assure as natural and comfortable breathing as possible.

2. The streaming of air continues throughout all of the tone production, without any interruption. Speaking or singing is made impossible by retaining the streaming of the air.

3. The frequency of breathing is connected with the emotional content of the thoughts. We will breath more frequently in proportion to any increase of agitation.

If we consider point *1.* we again have an additional argument for the correct body posture and against the trunk bent excessively forward which hinders free breathing.

In accordance with point 2. we have to take continuous care to assure entirely free breathing during piano playing. Even when teaching beginners free and even breathing is to be considered as a kind of polyphonic task.

When considering point 3. we may become easily induced to apportion our breathing in accordance with the musical contents.[1] This would be a grave fault because the frequency of breathing must not be guided merely by the musical content of the piece (even this would not be an easy task) but also by the *mechanical work* to be executed which depends upon the different instruments and also upon the acoustical circumstances. But the frequency of breathing can be influenced even by the degree in which the air is used up in the respective room or hall in which we are playing, not to speak of the nervous state of the pianist which may increase his air consumption.

The apportioning of the breathing is thus impracticable and besides there is no need for it. The only thing one has to care for is to assure a continuously free breathing. In this way our breathing may accommodate itself to the emotional concept and the requirements dictated by mechanical circumstances. It will become automatized in a relatively short time just as it happens in the case of many hundreds of activities to be executed in everyday life.

Retained, jerky breathing also produces direct mechanical harms. The constant lack of air diminishes the elasticity of the trunk and will hinder the functioning of the body as an elastic support. At the same time this jerky, retained breathing will also hinder the free work of the shoulder joints. This gives rise in many cases to jerky playing.[2]

At an advanced state of piano playing it is rather difficult to settle and correct the retained, jerky type of breathing. But one should not spare one's efforts to do this! Think of a long-distance runner covering the distance with retained breathing. The same absurdity would result from a pianist's playing with retained breathing, of doing work that absorbs an incredible amount of energy. But which is worse than any mechanical harm: The pianist playing with retained breathing will – so to speak – continually lose his belief in speaking to his audience and of communicating something to them.

PARTICIPATION OF THE WHOLE BODY IN THE PIANO PLAYING

It has been stated in the chapter on the swing-strokes that the functioning of the whole body as an elastic support is of decisive importance. In analyzing the individual playing forms we shall also find that inappropriateness or unreliability of the elastic support is among the causes of almost all faults. This is because the body does not fully participate in apportioning the resistance.

The decisive role of this factor in piano playing can only be partly explained by physical causes because the many unconditioned reflexes aiming at the whole body's participating in every important work are of as much significance.

In our everyday life the muscle tonus of our *whole body* will increase when executing some important movement. (Of course, one should not concentrate on increasing the muscle tonus because if this is done consciously it will cause excessive contraction and tension in the pianist's body.) The finest and hardly visible movements executed during a surgical operation of the eye or the ear require the preparedness and aid of the surgeon's whole body. Even when adjusting a fine screw or

---

[1] Kurt Johnen, who deserves credit for dealing first with the breathing of the pianist (*Wege zur Energetik des Klavierspiels*. Halle, Mitteldeutscher Verlag) goes even further. He links breathing with the metre and even with pendulum-like swinging of the body. In my opinion this is detrimental to the delicate shaping of rhythmical expression.

[2] This is why it must be repeatedly emphasized that the pianist has to learn correct deep-breathing in the same way as the singer or the sportsman. If the lower, voluminous parts of the lungs are filled up with air it will give the feeling of an excellent support for the spine while leaving the shoulders entirely free. If, on the contrary, we take air only into the apex of the lungs–as it is done in most cases–the shoulders will become stiff and cramped.

cutting a complicated paper design our whole body becomes prepared and participates in ensuring exactitude of the work by an increased readiness. The employment of the whole body is felt to be quite natural with tasks requiring a great amount of energy. This is at least of the same indispensability in movements necessitating accuracy and subtlety.

Thus, when employing his whole body in playing the pianist will acquire a great number of unconditioned reflexes which will aid him.

DIRECTION OF THE EYES WHEN PLAYING

One of the reflexes of our working processes, reinforced by the experience of millions of years, is our looking at the work object. If, instead of that, we look at the work tool or any other object, our movements will instantly become uncertain. (E.g. while cutting wood we do not look at the axe but at the wood to be cut.)

This innate reflex is so strong that even those who have been *blind from birth* will always look in the direction of their work.

In piano playing the string represents the work object and the key constitutes the tool. Therefore, one should not look at the keys, because to do so will force one to use them as one-armed levers and to play as if the keys produced the sound. It goes without saying that one does not actually look at the string either: we mean to say only that the head is to be turned in the appropriate direction. Thus, to look upwards or sidewards is not a perfect solution either, even if not as bad as to look at the keys. Let us not tire of reminding the pupils – and last but not least ourselves – that the direction of looking is a factor which may considerably improve or spoil playing.

The above – seemingly unimportant – factor in reality decisively influences piano playing. Remember the great performers you have heard. Everyone of them directed his eyes forward in his most inspired moments.

Pavlov in one of his lectures gives an account of certain experiments made with white mice. Unconditioned reflexes were established through sounding electric bells so that at their ringing the animals had to run to the feeding place.

"The first generation of mice needed 300 repetitions in learning to connect the ideas of feeding and of ringing, i.e. to run to the feeding place at the sound of the bell. The second generation needed

Phot. 146
MONIQUE DE LA BRUCHOLLERIE

only 100 repetitions in order to attain the same result, the third generation 30, and the fourth only 10 repetitions. The last generation I saw before leaving Petrograd learned this lesson after 5 repetitions. The sixth generation will be put to the test after my return to the city. It seems very probable that after a certain time the new generation will run to the feeding place at the sound of the bell without any preceding lesson." (New Researches on Conditional Reflexes, Science, Vol. 58, 1923, No. 1506, pp. 359–261.)

Mankind learned through the experience of millions of years to look in the direction of the work. It is impossible to shake off the effect of such a deeply innervated reflex. Or is it conceivable that man should learn so much more slowly than a white mouse and that the practice of millions of years should leave no trace? Or might the recurring idea prove true according to which "these rules do not apply to the arts" – in other words, that the artist is no human being? Or is it only the pianist who is no human being?

There might seem to be some justification to the counter-argument that continually looking ahead could cause uncertainties in the skips and in large shiftings of the hands. If we were to look ahead without interruption, this will indeed cause difficulties in certain cases – although much less so than might be expected. But then there is no question of this. If the skip makes it necessary, we may, of course, glance down at the keys. If we are really looking ahead, this will not require any changing of the head's direction. A good sight-reader, too, will sometimes look down at the keys. We may look down as much, when playing without notes, but under no circumstances more often. Thus, when playing without notes, the right position of the head will be determined by the principle that it must differ as little as possible from the position assumed in sight-reading.

EFFECT OF THE EMOTIONAL CONTENT ON THE BODY POSITION

The emotional content of a particular composition strongly influences the body position through the movements producing the sounds. This is why in the foregoing chapter on sitting we insisted on full freedom of movement.

Every emotion is connected with certain characterisitic forms of movement and thus each emotional state of mind has its corresponding movements. These have become unconditioned reflexes on the basis of the practice of thousands of generations. Joy, friendship, and other pleasurable feelings are thus connected with open movements, while anger, annoyance, sorrow, with closed ones. If the movements carried out when playing the piano are not in conformity with those dictated by the emotions, our movements will be artificial and forced. It follows that every predetermined postural attitude is harmful to our playing. The state and position of the body must be determined by the emotion and not inversely. Thus the position of the body depends essentially on the musical concept. Sitting with one's body leaning continually forward is irreconcilable with a joyful mood or the expression of a released, happy state of mind. On the other hand, a constant open position of the body would be just as faulty because it is impossible to reproduce resoluteness, anger, etc. in such a position.

The predetermined body position will cause serious harmful effects and these effects made by such a stereotyped body position will even be more serious with a talented pianist with colourful musical concept. With a talented musician the body position required by the musical content is linked with the atmosphere of the composition by a forceful unconditioned reflex. Thus it will get into conflict with a body position forced upon the body which has no connection whatever with the musical content.

This duality may easily force the pianist to renounce the more subtle expressive nuances.

But what will happen if over a long period we again and again strengthen the harmful innervation represented by an incongruence between the emotional content and the body position?

Sooner or later grave confusion will follow, and this will not only make the playing uncertain but will react detrimentally even upon the emotional content, by setting limits to the latter, restraining it, and finally causing it to degenerate.

Phot. 147
IMRE UNGÁR

THE CONNECTION OF THE ACOUSTIC SPATIAL REFLEX WITH THE MUSICAL CONCEPT AND THROUGH IT WITH THE BODY POSITION

The ability to adapt ourselves to a certain space or room when producing the tone is an unconditioned reflex. In the course of many thousands of years the volume of the produced tone was influenced – in addition to the emotional content – by the distance across which it was intended to give signal by the sound. In other words: the dynamic level of the tone production depends partly upon the emotional content which arouses it and partly upon the distance across which the tone is to be transmitted. It is evident that the same phrase would be pronounced in a different way if talking with someone in a small room as compared with the manner of performing this conversation on the stage.

Now the question is: does anything else change besides the dynamic level? Try the following experiment: Speak a phrase and then repeat the same phrase with the same tone volume but form a speaking tube with your hands and imagine you are speaking to a person 75–100 feet away. (It is very probable that although you want to speak with the same tone volume you will involuntarily use a greater one.) On close observation you will notice that in the second case you apply completely different agogics, you articulate your speech in a different, more intelligible way.

Our acoustical adaptation to a certain space is such a deeply rooted reflex that it is sufficient to imagine a space or auditorium of a certain dimension to adapt our voice to that space. This is why the actor is able to declaim even in a small room in the same way as on the stage. By imagining himself as being in the theatre he adapts his voice and rhythm of speaking to the acoustic conditions of the stage.

Like singing or speaking, instrumental performing is essentially also a kind of communication, the only difference being that the transmitting organ is not built into our body. Thus it is evident that the musician playing on an instrument is also greatly influenced by the need to accomodate to the particular dimensions and reverberation of the room because they require dynamic and agogic alterations, i.e. changes in the musical performance. This accommodation is very important also with violin and wind instruments, but in the case of the piano it is of the utmost interest.

The piano has undergone great changes in the course of time. The common characteristic feature of clavichord, harpsichord and piano (of the old type) is their small tone volume and at the same time a soft, sensitive tone. (Even C. Ph. E. Bach wrote that the piano was for playing figured bass in the orchestra because of its small tone volume.) The small tone was caused by the thinness of the strings. Later on stronger strings were used as the piano grew more and more to be the special instrument of the concert halls. The continual increase of the thickness and consequently the increased tension necessitated the application of the iron frame. While the tone colour of the first pianos was very similar to that of the string or wind instruments, the tone colour of our modern pianos reminds us almost of that of bells. Compared with the tone volume of a violin or a flute one could say that the piano of today is constructed for large halls. Even its pianissimo is intended to be heard across a long distance.

The piano is a big sound amplifier because of its mechanical structure, its mighty soundboard and its strong strings. It is clear that grave troubles in the reflexes may arise if someone aims to use such a large sound amplifier to play only for himself, i.e. to amplify the tone only for himself. This is exactly the same as talking into his own ears by means of a high-capacity sound amplifier. In consequence of such a contradiction to our acoustic space-reflex distortion may arise in piano playing. It is at this stage that the pianist starts "to play flabbily" on the piano, i.e. not only reduces the dynamic degree more than is required but also plays with stereotyped dynamic contours and distorts agogics almost into a caricature.

In order to get an idea of the extent of the distortion it will suffice to compare two data. An average room of an apartment has about 2800–3500 cubic feet of air while that of the concert hall of

Phot. 148
BÉLA BARTÓK

the High School of Music in Budapest is 350,000 cubic feet. On the other hand, the tone volume of a concert-grand is not very much stronger than that of an upright. But even if taking the twofold tone volume, it is still ridiculous compared to the hundredfold cubic content.

This is the main reason why the so-called "concert-hall routine" is indispensable for concert performers. The ability of immediate accommodation to the instrument and also at the same time to the acoustic conditions of the concert hall can only be acquired by a certain amount of practice.

Therefore it can easily be seen that, even when practising, we always have to imagine ourselves in an auditorium or a large open-air place, like the actor imagines himself on the stage when studying his part at home. *The imagining of a large space will automatically "set in" the appropriate greater intensity, the agogics and dynamics corresponding to a large space.*

Concert pianists often complain of being unable to play well in a room; they "feel in the mood" only in a concert hall. There is a certain antagonism between imagining ourselves in a concert hall while playing in a room and between the requirement always to modify our movements depending upon the sound. (See p. 86.) Indeed, a certain "concert-hall routine" is also absolutely indispensable from that point of view. But if we are already accustomed to accommodating, sounding the tones in a concert hall we will be able to imagine this "concert-hall tone" also in our room, although, of course, this will be never of the same value as playing in a real concert hall.

Imagining playing in a large place or hall is also of importance from the mechanical point of view. When the pianist imagines himself playing in a large hall and transmitting the sound across a large distance he modifies also his body posture. The body positions of certain emotional states do not always exclude the passivity of the arms or hands and the lack of elasticity of the trunk. (E.g. sadness, grief.) However, the fact that we not only have to experience these emotions but also to express and convey them through the piano to the audience, requires a certain activity of the body. We have to get the sensation that the energy producing the tone streams through our body, fingers and the keys into the strings and spreads from there into the concert hall.

A bent trunk or loosely hanging arms are harmful, detrimental not only because they diminish the functioning of the body as an elastic support but also because they are in contradiction to the body posture required by unconditioned reflexes; i.e. they are contradictory to the body position given by the emotion and the activity needed for transmitting the sound across a large distance.

Activity of the body is sometimes accompanied by a slight bending of the trunk. (This can only be seen when the respective mood too [agitation, passion, desperation, worry, etc.] requires an increased activity.) Some methods—misled by this hardly perceptible bending—require piano playing with continuous bending forward. This will evidently hinder the expressive playing because it is detrimental to sit in a *predetermined* active body position. The intensive tone concept may at any time produce the appropriate body position, but by no *predetermined* body position will it be possible to attain a far sounding tone, i.e. a shaping of the melodic contours corresponding to a large open space, from both the points of view of dynamics and agogics.

The transmitting of tone across a large distance, the "sonorous sounding" of the instrument (attention: even the pianissimo may sound sonorously!) must be made a principal requirement in piano playing—even when teaching beginners. Only that piano playing can be good and natural which accommodates itself to the sound amplifying character of the piano.

Some reflections must be made also on some other aspects of the acoustic spatial reflex. Sometimes one is embarrassed to find that a performance, which did not sound particularly good to us, gives a much better impression when re-listening to it on the radio. The reverse case is even more frequent. Performances having made a deep impression in the concert hall, will sound colourless and dull on the radio.

This contradiction is also to be found with theatrical performances. In a theatrical performance the actor has to take into consideration the real actual space (theatre) in his articulation and even when speaking to his partner standing near him he will articulate more distinctly, accommodating himself to the acoustic conditions of the theatre. All this is different when speaking before a microphone. The performance of the actor will be life-like—almost independently from the dimensions of the studio—if he adjusts the dynamics and articulation of his speaking exclusively to spaces described in the script. He may speak as if talking to himself—if the text is to express meditation—and may whisper as if he spoke in a small room.

However, an instrumental performance before a microphone must never be of the same room-like character as talking into the microphone. Every instrument is intended for a certain magnified projecting of the melodies living within us. We strive to communicate our musical concept in a form perceptible to many listeners. Thus it is fundamentally contradictory to the technique of every instrument if we play only for ourselves, if we do not make the instrument sound sonorously. This is definitely the case with playing the piano. Since the piano is, according to its whole structure, a big sound amplifier, it is clear that the concert-hall character of piano playing must be conserved also when playing into the microphone.

The pianist, however, finds an almost unsolvable task before him when playing into a microphone. He has to play as if he performed in a large concert hall because—as stated above—this is required by the special character of the instrument. The studio, where his performance is taken on records or tapes, is in most cases large enough and so it has a considerable reverberation. This reverberation, however, depends not only upon the dimensions of the room (hall) but also in even greater measure upon its structure. The microphone, on the other hand, is usually set up very near to the instrument and so it "hears" everything in a different way than the performer. *The performer plays as if "talking" to a large distance and the microphone is listening to it from quite close at hand.*

It has been stated above that the dynamics and agogics of an artistic performance are transformed and altered depending upon the dimensions of the place. But a still more important relation exists between the sounding, or more correctly the reverberation, of the room and the tempo. It has been proved by the experiments made by Márta Sz. Karsai (research worker of the Research Group for Acoustics of the Hungarian Academy of Sciences)[3] that the tempo of a composition has to be accommodated within certain limits to the reverberation of the concert hall in which the piece is played.

Hence it follows that a talented performer with a fine ear who accommodates his playing to the actual sounding will not recognize his own performance listening to it on the radio or on records, because neither his tempi nor his agogics, indeed not even the dynamic proportions of the melodies will be found correct by him.

Building up a special style of playing before the microphone is by no means the solution. This would make no sense and would lead to an even more grave distortion of the compositions which were imagined and destined by the composer to be played under the conditions of concert-hall acoustics. (Such microphone-styled playing will sooner or later spoil or even destroy the technique of the pianist.) The right way to be followed in broadcastings and recordings would be to pay much more careful attention to natural sounding of the tones. Care should be taken, on the one hand, to arouse the impression in the radio listener that he is seated in a concert hall rather than quite close to the piano, and, on the other hand, to enable the performer to hear – at least approximately – the same thing as the microphone.

Since agogic elements play a great role in the tone-colour sensations aroused by the piano playing, the appropriate place of the microphone is most important not only from the point of view of the acoustic space reflex but also from that of a beautiful tone colour. When recording a piano concert good results may be attained by one microphone if the acoustic conditions are favourable, but with solo piano performances much better results are obtained by applying several microphones. One of them, set up near to the instruments, will assure the sonorous sounding of the tone, while the others will "bring in" the reverberation of the concert hall in order to arouse the impression of reality in the listener.

ON PRESERVING THE NATURALNESS OF THE MOVEMENTS

Our innate ability aids us in preserving the naturalness of our movements in piano playing, too. However, in the event of incorrect practising, inexpedient movements will gain more and more ground and their gradual increase may spoil our whole technique.

Not only wrong movements applied while practising – i.e. wrong movements innervated in the course of piano playing – are harmful. Sitting or walking with a stiff body, incorrect breathing habits, rigid neck posture, etc. may also spoil piano playing as much as the innervation of wrong technical elements.

---

[3] The author of this book also participated in one of these experiments. A part of Brahms's "Variations on a Theme of Haydn" was played from records. A "jury", consisting of ten well-known musicians, had to vote on the question, which of the 21 recordings was the best. The voting of the committee was almost unanimous. Almost always the same recordings received 10 marks. There was even in instance when almost everybody wrote on the voting-slip: "This is conducted by Toscanini," and cases, on the other hand, where the performance was said to be scandalously amateurish.

At the end, it was declared to everyone's astonishment that in all the 21 occasions the same record was played and that only a slight, hardly perceptible change in tempo and reverberation had been made by the aid of a special device.

This thesis is also inversely valid. Good movements, innervated during piano playing, have a liberating effect on our other movements, too.

The close interconnection existing between our bodily movements shows that in piano playing correct movements can be acquired only by simultaneously developing our general faculty of motion. Naturalness and simplicity are to be attained in all our activities if we want our piano playing to be natural and simple.

It follows from the interconnection between the movements that the development of piano technique may also be furthered by systematic gymnastics. Well-selected gymnastic exercises will assure the proper innervation of the most important movements and the harmonious development of the muscles. By employing gymnastic exercises results will be attained in a shorter time and more surely than if we confine ourselves to practising exclusively on the piano.

The greatest advantage of gymnastic exercises lies in the aid they furnish the pianist in learning the respective movements exactly and in elaborating them without weakening the necessary contact between the musical concept and the movements required in piano playing. Teaching new kinds of movements directly at the piano without any preparatory work will often result in forming a number of wrong interconnections. By exactly innervating the necessary movements through gymnastic exercises before we begin to practise a new kind of movement, we will reduce the possibility of error and thus considerably shorten the time required for practising.

However, not only the specific movements preparatory to piano playing must be practised, but any other physical exercise, which assists the harmonious functioning of our muscles, renders our movements free, and gives them the required momentum, will prove useful. All our movements are under a common direction in the nervous system. In liberating one set of motions, the others, too, will be improved. Only such exercises must be avoided as they are based on the overburdening of particular muscle groups and thus innervate strained, convulsive motion.

This book, of course, only deals with arm and hand gymnastic exercises for pianists. However, every instrumental performer has to do systematic physical exercises assuring the harmonious functioning of the whole body. (See chapter on "Complementary Gymnastic Exercises.")

ON PRACTISING

REPETITION AS A MEANS OF STABILIZING NEW CONDITIONED REFLEXES

The central nervous system issues thousands of commands in the form of unconditioned reflexes. In the course of learning, these reflexes become continually completed by new conditioned reflexes.

If the concept of a tone and the corresponding movement producing the adequate sound on the piano is repeated often enough, new conditioned reflexes will develop.

The effectiveness of the repetition is best assured by proper apportioning. Many methods have been elaborated and acclaimed as the only correct ones.

However, repetition involves certain dangers, too.

According to Pavlov, the forming of conditioned reflexes is impeded by the weakening or temporary change of the stimulus.

Repetitions easily diminish the intensity of the musical concept. The emotion uniting the tones will weaken, since one of the most difficult things on earth is the exact repetition of an emotion.

The fading of the emotional content as a result of repetition involves the danger of the technical work becoming an aim in itself. If the emotional content loses its intensity, it can easily happen that we practise something entirely different from what is required by a good performance.

The only method of preserving the emotional content from damage is to try with each repetition to penetrate deeper and deeper into the essence of a composition. The repetitions are to be continued only as long as we feel this development of our emotions.[1] If we feel that a composition is of no interest to us any more, if we don't find new possibilities in its interpretation, any further practising will harm not only the performance of that particular composition but even our whole technique. In his Preface to the transcriptions of Paganini's Caprice Schumann wrote the following: "Even that which is most beautiful will, if it is enjoyed at the inappropriate place or to excess, give rise to indifference and disgust..."

In this connection the following objection can be made: The continual emphasis on the emotional content may lead to an "ecstatic" way of playing which again would lead to a separation from the musical content of the composition. This danger may indeed arise but only if we exaggerate everything under the pretext of ecstatic playing. This inevitably means a falsification of the composition we are performing.

Such ecstatic playing replaces the genuine, profound feeling of the themes of the composition by a *continuous* exaltation, by a *continuous* nervous tension.

The continual "pathos" makes impossible the expression of fine nuances and differences because it treats everything alike. Coarse jokes and fine witticism, weeping and laughing, fury and

---

[1] Stanislavsky: *The Work of the Actor*. I, p. 16. "I have found the great secret! You must not ride the same subject to death, and you must not repeat to excess the same worn-out conception."

Phot. 149
CLIFFORD CURZON

joy become equally expressed in a transfigured way which will be nothing but a more or less successful caricature of the composition.[2]

Most pianists believe that their playing will only be effective if they are able to create a special atmosphere of emotional tension. Unfortunately sometimes even the professors strive to increase the "degree of heat" of the playing in order to augment the "thrill" of the performance. This is a grave error! The ardour, the "degree of heat" must never be apportioned or added to a composition by the performer, it must stream from the piece. If, e.g., a scherzo of Beethoven suggests to us a young peasant dancing with his sweetheart, why does it need any strained, ardent performing? Or, if the music is intended to express a perfect calmness, or even an overcoming of the problems of life, why does it required any sensational, thrilling type of performance?

The continuous superlatives, the constant emphasizing of everything means nothing else than insipidity itself. If everything is found by the performer to be a culminating point in the composition, it will be just as tedious as if nothing had been stressed. In everyday life, too, it would be most comical if someone laid a special emphasis on each of his words. Experiences of everyday life should be related in a plain, ordinary way.

Thus music, if it wants to reflect life, cannot consist of mere culminating points because life, too, has its plain work-days. What makes musical compositions really interesting are the continuous changes and contrasts of wave crests and wave troughs, the variations of the emotional tension. By reproducing this a more interesting and thrilling performance will be achieved than by any "heat-degree".

A musical composition may be interpreted in many different ways – each one of them being equally correct – but for the performer, at the moment of playing, only one true way of performing may exist.

We are aided by a long series of unconditioned reflexes in expressing our emotions in a sincere and inspired way. But different reflexes are linked with telling an anecdote or delivering an animated speech, and still different ones to performing a ballad or a joyful dance. Even this apparently exact term: "joyful dance" contains an immense amount of variational possibilities. Just to mention two extreme cases: dance of fairies and rural dance. But, are even rural dances of uniform character? They are different not only according to their respective region but also depending on whether they are danced by old or young folk, boys or girls, or a loving couple. *Every emotional nuance is linked with a certain series of reflexes.* These reflexes – together with those required by the instrument in order to sound the tone – will produce the tones adequate to our musical concept.

Thus, if the pianist performs everything with a continuous emotional tension it will disable him to develop a correct technique and to find the infinite scale of tone-colouring possibilities. The artificially "overheated" way of playing will prove detrimental mainly for talented musicians. They will feel continually disturbed and worried by the feeling that their playing is not true, not natural.

---

[2] Stanislavsky: *The Work of the Actor.* I, p. 74. "Try to play love, jealousy or hate 'in general.' What does this mean? It means playing only an insignificant part of the passions or a few of their elements. Actors playing their role 'in general' give the audience only small fragments of feeling, passion, thought, logical action, human behaviour."

"It is almost ludicrous to observe how this playing 'in general' is accompanied by sincere excitement and strong emotions. It is impossible to convince such actors that their playing lacks passion and feeling and that they do no more than to reproduce slight traces of them."

(I, p. 43.) "Actors belonging to the more or less nervous type arouse emotions in themselves by artificially exciting their nerves. This is the source of the unhealthy extasy, the stage-hysteria which has as little psychical content as the physical emotions aroused in an artificial way. Neither this nor the other one is of artistic value because we do not see the expression of real feelings of the actor filling the role with life, but only shamming, 'putting on a show', affectation. However, this kind of acting, too, may attain its aim, can create some connection with life, may arouse some effect because the artistically uncultured spectator is unable to judge correctly the obtained impressions and will content himself with rough falsifications. The actors, belonging to the above described type will assert with real conviction that they are the true representatives of art and have not the faintest idea that the work is no art at all but bungling."

Troubles will also arise in the series of reflexes because those required by the musical concept wil differ from, or will be contradictory to, reflexes required by a *continuous* pathetical way of playing The greatest differences will be found in works of great composers which were written with a deep knowledge of the possibilities of the piano. These compositions are to be played in their only true way. This will enable the pianist to find also the best technical solutions.

It must be supposed that many performers are misled by the fact that piano playing always requires an intensive activity which of course goes together with a certain tension. (The muscle work is executed by means of contractions, i.e. a certain increase of tension.) The general level of muscle tonus[3] shows an increase with every action, and also changes with the emotional state. It is evident that these two factors – the expressing of emotions and intensive activity – will result in a considerable increase of tension.

The level of tension is augmented also by the fact that the performance is carried out in a large concert hall, it is intended to communicate emotions to many people present there. However, the increase of the level of tension is not contradictory to the differences of tension required by the nuances of expression. On the other hand, reversing this process and considering the high level of nervous tension as the starting point of artistic performance, not only will a caricature of the musical concept result (because everything is pathetical) but in addition the playing itself will become stiff and cramped.

Thus the real deepening of the emotional content is made impossible by the ecstatic way of playing. And it will also be impossible for the emotional content to deepen if we concentrate our attention, even if only temporarily, exclusively upon our motions under the pretext of "practising." The sticking to the emotional content is apparently made superfluous by the fact that if we concentrate primarily on the movements they will be learned by a relatively little number of repetitions. This way of practising – although giving good results in a short time – will prove harmful in the end because the connection between the musical concept and the movements will weaken and fade away. The repetitions have built up a connection between the individual movements instead of between the movement and the tone, which means that the movement has become an end in itself. Such playing becomes indifferent and pays attention mainly to the succession of the tones, since it is not guided by the emotional content but by some vague tone concept, which only ensures to the tones a certain order of succession.

It would be a great fault, however, to think that concentration on the problems of motion has now become entirely superfluous. On the one hand, the emotional content and the musical concept, and, on the other, the movements which transform them into sounds must always maintain their mutual equilibrium and have to develop in proportion to each other, or else the pianist will get the impression of being an actor without a voice.[4]

The formation of new conditioned reflexes is hindered also if a disparity arises between an unvarying tone concept and varying movements. Hence, it is of special importance that, in practising, *the same movements should always be connected with the corresponding tone concept*, and that changes in the movements should conform with changes in the tone concept.

---

[3] The muscles are, even when resting, in a state of a certain contraction. This is called the muscle tonus. (See p. 117.)

[4] Stanislavsky: *The Work of the Actor*. II, p. 91. "There are actors who are habitually out of voice. As a result, they are apt to croak, to spill forth their words and to distort everything they seek to interpret, while in the meantime their spirit is taking wing. Try to imagine that a dumb person would like to express in words his gentle, poetical feelings towards his beloved. But in place of articulated sounds, only a repellent, hoarse noise issues from his throat. He distorts the beauty he experiences within himself and prizes above all else. This distortion drives him to despair. The same thing happens with an actor, who, inspired by profound emotions, is endowed with a bad voice."

THE ATTENTION

Repetition is of use only until the attention begins to weaken. Practising carried out without full attention will cause more harm than good. Therefore the pianist should not sit down to practise when he is tired. A few minutes' rest will multiply the results of his work.

The most harmful and dangerous thing is to sit down at the piano in a bad mood. It makes no difference what the cause may have been: the tension in international politics or a slight impoliteness experienced in the bus; the pianist will already be unable to concentrate on the music or even on his movements. In addition, anger and annoyance induce a tension of the muscles, which will hinder the infinitely sensitive accommodation required in using the key as a two-armed lever. Even with a pianist of good motion mechanism it may in such cases happen that he beats his instrument. However, to *beat* the instrument means to spoil the whole adjustment of the mechanism, because he will play as if it were the key which produces the sound (see chapter on "Expediency").

The violinist has it somewhat easier. Even the worst violinist would not dream of beating his instrument because it is clear to him that he is able to produce a sound with his instrument only by pulling his bow on the strings. If he does not do this well, the instrument will – by means of terrible squeaking, howling and other infernal tone – signal that it has been treated unkindly.

The task of the pianist is rendered ticklish by the fact that the instrument produces musical sounds not only when touched in the proper way but "endures even the worst ill treatment". And since to beat the piano is a simpler solution than to make music on it, a special type of "pugnacious" pianist has developed who fights a veritable boxing match with his instrument.

Practising always requires full attention from the aspect of motion, too, and the whole body must be in readiness. Every thought and movement must be at the service of tone production: this task cannot be entrusted to the arms or the fingers only. *We have to feel responsible for each tone.* In practising, too, our movements will be right only if each tone is felt by us to be important and if we concentrate on each tone with all our power.

If the movements of the pianist are inexpedient, the tones he sounds will not reflect his concepts. The tones will not reproduce what the pianist wanted to express. This is why a great many people have recourse to the solution of not listening to their own playing at all. They concentrate only on the things going on in their imagination and so they lock themselves up "hermetically" in their musical conception.

This is the reason why some excellent musicians – who manifest a refined musical taste when criticizing the playing of others – fail to notice even most blatant mistakes in their own playing.

Grave conflicts may thus result if the pianist is unable to heed the actual sound produced by his own playing. Watchful attention is an indispensable requirement of good practising because it registers even the slightest deviation from the musical concept and thus enables the pianist to correct the slightest faulty nuances in his performance. So, just as incessant self-observation while playing in a concert and concentrating on what was not correct may be regarded as detrimental, the other extreme, i.e. lack of self-criticism while practising, is at least as wrong, if not worse. *In our practising we must inexorably and indefatigably perfect our execution.* To achieve this, a high degree of concentration is a prerequisite.

Thus correct practising calls for uninterrupted concentration. This is furthered:
a. by proper distribution of the time of practising,
b. by variety of the material.

Individuals differ with regard to the length of the time they are able to practise with full concentration and without getting exhausted, and even the same pianist will change according to his momentary physical and psychic condition. The time during which we are able to concentrate without getting exhausted and suffering no detrimental consequences is generally 25–40 minutes. Thereafter it is absolutely necessary to rest for a shorter or longer period.

Emil Sauer in *Meine Welt* (p. 80) quotes the following words of Nicolaus Rubinstein: "It is quality and not quantity which constitutes the essential part of practising. Four hours daily, divided into two equal parts (in the morning and in the evening) is abundantly sufficient. Practising beyond this time is harmful. By mechanical finger-work nothing can be attained other than the risk of killing even what little spirit is left in us. Mechanical practising is a stupid and senseless thing when it is not the brain which predominates."

Variety in the material to be practised may be secured partly by the method of not insisting on immediately learning the individual parts of the piece perfectly; instead, the separate voices or smaller coherent parts should be learned alternately. We are barely capable of paying attention to more than three or four successive repetitions, but, after having practised some different parts, we will be able to continue our work with renewed energy and interest. This does not mean, of course, that our work should be unsystematic. Even in variety there must be system.

For instance, when practising a Fugue for three voices of the "Wohltemperiertes Klavier", we have first to take each voice separately one after the other, striving to bring out their specific character as much as possible. The tones should not be played mechanically, even when playing them for the first time. Every badly sounded note is a poison which impedes good, spontaneous playing even in the future.

Next, the playing of the voices should be combined. The alto and bass, the bass and soprano, and the alto and soprano should be played together, alternately. In the meantime, we have to repeat again separately those voices which are not plastic enough. Only after having finished this, may we approach playing the three voices together. In the beginning, each group of themes or intermediate part of the fugue must be practised as a single unit.

Do not work too long a time on the same material. Variety must be assured also by practising more than one composition during the same period of time.

The principle of variety also requires one to work if possible on pieces of different style at the same time. The same musical or technical problem will be seen from an entirely different aspect and our attention will thus be directed more thoroughly to the solution of the problem.

SLOW PRACTISING OF FAST PLAYING

If no technical difficulty arises in the playing of a musical composition or in a part of it – and supposing that the intensity of the musical concept does not decrease during the repetitions – a comparatively small number of repetitions will be sufficient for learning it. However, if technical difficulties stand in the way of the solution, the number of repetitions must be increased considerably.

But increasing the number of repetitions does not necessarily lead to a favourable result. With a constant fast tempo one may not notice certain parts of wrong details. The danger of this is even more increased by the decrease of attention caused by the great number of repetitions. Therefore, in order to eliminate the fault, a way of enlarging the technical detail which has caused the fault must be found. To do this, a temporary slower tempo is needed.

In slow practising the enlargement and exaggeration of the respective details must be considered as a technical principle. The main advantage of the slower rate-setting is that we thus become enabled to bring to the surface and to enlarge the faulty kinetic factor (at the expense of other factors) in order to rectify it. There is a great difference between slow practising and playing in a slow tempo. In slow practising the technical solutions are *temporary* and *distort* the proportions of the single factors for technical purposes. In playing in a slow tempo the technical solutions are *final* and give a tone effect corresponding to our tone concept.

Thus, when playing a scale slowly, we stress the finger-strokes and strengthen the work of the fingers (at the expense of the other factors), or sometimes exaggerate the rotatory movements in skips, or give a more vigorous activity to the forearm in staccato playing, etc. The distortion of the proportions of the single components will, however, distort also the tone effect, and thus slow practising will – on account of our emphasizing the kinetic aims – harmfully affect the spontaneity of our playing. Practising with these aims is a "necessary evil" and it must be reduced to the smallest possible extent. This can be realized only through an analysis of the most efficacious and most precise ways of executing the movements, in order to automatize them within the shortest possible time and with the smallest possible amount of work.

Slow practising – a slower rate-setting – creates favourable conditions for automatization of the movements because all our attention can thus be concentrated on the execution of the movements. Since our aim is the automatization of the movements, colouring and dynamics may be applied only up to the extent to which they do not endanger the accuracy of the movements.

Slow practising of fast playing can be utilized for the following purposes:

1. Facilitation of memorizing;

2. Automatization of the movements corresponding to the different key-groups (innervation of the order of succession of the keys, learning of unusual fingerings);

3. Correction and perfection of the swing-strokes with regard to each note of the musical detail.

The perfection of the swing-strokes may serve two aims:

3a. Improvement of the control, fullest possible checking and consciousness of the movements.

3b. Development of velocity, i.e. perfection of the swing-strokes in order to make them appropriate to attain optimal velocity.

The only prerequisite of practising in accordance with paragraphs *1, 2,* and *3a* is, that the retardation of the tempo leaves us abundant possibilities to imagine each tone of the respective musical part in its relation to the other tones. Thus, in this case the tempo of the practising cannot be determined. Any slow tempo will answer our purposes as long as it preserves the musical units and is appropriate to the execution of the movement required in the fast tempo.

In excessively slow tempo, e.g., we are inclined to execute every stroke with the arm instead of the fingers. This kind of practising can be solely used for the purpose of memorization. The sequence of tones and the fingering, too, may be automatized by this method, but the outcome will be that our technique becomes spoiled because movements, other than those needed in the performing of a composition, will be automatized.

Faulty practising (one might say: "counter-practising") is the reason why many "dexterous" pianists discover after a certain time that – although practising as much as before – their fingers will not obey as they did once. Thus, it may happen that performers – who knew no technical difficulties whatever at the age of twenty – are, at the age of forty, unable to master technical problems solved with ease 20 years earlier. The cause is to be found in their having replaced the originally correct movement associations by faulty ones.

If the aim of slow practising is the improvement of the control (when the fingers "run away," or the playing becomes uneven) our experience proves to be expedient to apply a variety of slow tempi. When practising control we should endeavour to attain perfect domination over every small detail of the movements both in slow and in fast tempi.

Phot. 150
MONIQUE HAAS

DEVELOPMENT OF VELOCITY

The development of velocity requires exceedingly careful investigations because it is under the pretence of developing velocity that pianists do an immense amount of work in finger technique which dissipates so much energy and concentration. Under the assumption they are developing velocity pianists separate their movements from the musical concept and thus hinder their own technique which would enable them to be a real executor in the service of music.

This chase after velocity is entirely senseless. Our muscles and nerves are able to execute very fast movements without any special practising, even faster movements than needed for the virtuoso piano playing. The only problem is, how to make this velocity applicable. If care is taken to transform the greater part of the applied muscle energy into tones, the pianist will discover within himself the ability for displaying velocity not even suspected before. But it should be repeatedly stressed here that the most important prerequisite of velocity is the speed of the musical concept. Practising automatizes the work of the fingers and arms to the musical concept. This work can be performed more economically by slow practising and thus a gradual improvement of the automatization can be attained. However, in both the development of control and that of velocity the decisive part is always played by the musical concept.

Thus, the development of velocity requires – from the mechanical aspect – only the perfecting of the swing-strokes and rendering them suitable for attaining maximum velocity. An improvement of the single swing-stroke can only be attained if in slow practising exactly the same movements are executed as in fast playing, i.e., if the same movements are really improved which are later applied in playing.

How can we be certain that exactly the same movements will be executed both in slow practising and in fast playing? By taking care that the proportion of the factors which are characteristic for the movement is not changed in the retardation.

What are the characteristics of a swing-stroke? Primarily, it must be made clear, from which joint it is to be executed, what distance must be covered in what time and whether the stroke is of a continual or changing velocity. As the control (the braking) influences the velocity it is evident that – in order to find out the respective laws – a swing-stroke, entirely free from any control, must be analysed. Therefore, in our investigations of the kinetic laws the maximum velocity must be taken as a basis, in which the role of the control in the individual strokes is so slight that it can be left out of consideration. (At maximum velocity our attention is concentrated exclusively on the lightning-fast execution of the swing-strokes.)

In piano playing this velocity is needed rarely and only in exceptional cases. This kind of playing may easily become unmusical. In our analysis, however, this marginal case must be used as a basis in order that, by reducing the control, the proportions of the single factors may better come to light.

ANALYSIS OF VELOCITY PLAYING

The highest degree of velocity in piano playing is attained by playing with finger movements. (In what follows, we shall designate very fast finger-playing by the term "velocity playing".) Therefore, we have to analyse velocity playing, i.e. its limits, and within these limits determine the characteristic laws of the swing-stroke.

1. In velocity playing the active swing-strokes are executed by the first joint of the fingers. Use of the second and third joints would diminish the velocity. (See pp. 127–128.)

2. At maximum velocity each note is sounded by a free swing-stroke and, therefore, the ratio of distance (course) and time can be considered as a constant one. By free swing-stroke we mean an energetic, resolute downward stroke, prepared by raising the finger. The fingers are raised high but without straining them. The movement must not be braked either during the raising or the striking. In examining the swing-stroke in its details, we find that the speed varies. However, when taking the total time as basis, the proportion of distance and time may be considered as constant.

Phot. 151
ROBERT CASADESUS

3. At maximum velocity the number of swing-strokes executed during a second is **extremely** high. In this case the absorbing of the rebounds of the keys requires a considerable amount of muscle work on the part of the elastic support.

Now, taking into consideration all these characteristics of velocity playing, our task will be to execute the slowing down of the finger movements in a way which will not cause a considerable change in the character of the movement. Since in fast tempo the determining factor of the ratio between the distance and time is the free swing-stroke, each swing-stroke must be kept free in the retardations.

When slowing down the tempo, we increase the time allotted to each individual tone. In order not to change the ratio of distance and time, the distance, too, must be enlarged. From this it follows that in slow practising of velocity playing the limits of retardation are determined by the length of the arc which the fingers are able to describe.

If the tempo is slowed down independently from the limits of the movements which our fingers are able to execute the swing-strokes will not be free but will become more and more controlled proportionately to the retarding. However, since at maximum velocity the swing-strokes can be considered as free from control, we may state that the braking of them may distort the changes of speed characteristic of the free swing movements. An equal fault would be committed by hastening the individual swing-strokes when practising. This, too, would hinder the attaining of maximum velocity. Therefore, in slow practising of velocity playing we have to execute always entirely free swing-strokes, because only in this way may we obtain a maximum tone volume (compared with the energy employed).

The aim of the swing-stroke is tone production, and we must, therefore, endeavour to achieve the required tone volume by the most economical and expedient movement possible. This – seemingly obvious – statement has to be stressed repeatedly because many pianists concentrate, in slow playing, solely on raising the arm or fingers, instead of on tone production. "The fingers must rebound into the air, and in octave-playing the hand has to bounce like a rubber-ball," they say, and the result is an innervation which is exactly the contrary of the required tone.

When, in slow practising, we execute a free swing-stroke, the movement itself is not slowed down but only enlarged (i.e. the ratio of distance and time remains unchanged). The tempo of the touches, i.e. the time consumed by a single swing-stroke, would thus seem to be determined solely by the length of the fingers just as the speed of a pendulum is determined by its length.

If the time required by the swing-stroke were actually determined by the length of the fingers, the third and fifth fingers would be unable to execute free swing-strokes in an equal time-period. In reality, however, we know that the contrary holds true. Although the time consumed by the swing-stroke is influenced by the length of the fingers, this is not the main factor in determining the tempo. The speed at which the swing-strokes executed with full-length finger-motion are felt by us to be free is determined, in the first place, by the nervous and muscular systems. This tempo may be considered as constant for the same technical problem and with the same pianist.

In slowing down, the proportion of the resistance required for the swing-strokes will also change. We have already seen in analysing the weight-effect that the resistance has to be diminished in direct proportion to the number of strokes. Thus in slow playing less resistance (weight-complement) is needed than in fast playing. In slow practising the resistance has to be even more reduced than in slow playing because otherwise the fingers could not execute the swing-strokes freely and the overburdening would prevent any enlargement of the movements. Thus, in practising velocity playing slowly, we have to diminish the weight-effect to a considerably larger extent than in slow playing; indeed, our playing will be practically weightless. By reducing the resistance to a minimum the fingers have to perform greater work because they also have to absorb a great part of the rebound of the keys. The surplus energy required for this is furnished easily by the finger muscles because the enlarged movement increases the force of the strokes. The "weightless" arm is thus a prerequisite of the swing-stroke executed with large movements.

APPLICATION OF SLOW PRACTISING

Slow practising is almost indispensable in learning the individual technical forms (see chapter on "Fundamental Playing Forms"), but slow practising of compositions must be reduced to a minimum.

Only musical passages of special difficulty should be practised slowly. (Not even a Chopin étude should be played slowly from beginning to end.) This is the more important because the relaxation of attention results in the movements becoming distorted. Slow practising, requiring a longer time, may consequently cause serious harm.

The control and development of velocity can never be exactly separated in slow practising of velocity playing. Slow practising is, to a certain extent, equally useful both from the point of view of velocity and from that of control, because in good control practising the accuracy of the swing-strokes, too, will always improve, and at the same time a minimal control will always be applied when carrying out velocity-developing work. In order to attain maximum benefit from the details of practising, stress will sometimes be laid on the control and sometimes on the development of velocity. Their ratio will change according to our momentary technical possibilities and to the tone effect to be attained, respectively.

The method of practising must always be adapted to the momentary physical and nervous condition of the pianist. It must be taken into consideration that control practising is generally more exhausting than that of velocity developing. Thus, the same composition should not be practised by the pianist always in the same mechanical way.

In the course of practising one has to lay stress sometimes on the control and on other occasions on the development of velocity — as the circumstances require. The best guarantee of correct practising is for us to acquire the ability to recognize which of the two is the more useful at the time. In part we do this consciously, in part by instinctive adaptation to our momentary physical condition.

The means of practising change to an even greater extent when we take the different styles into consideration. Entirely different means are needed in practising a Bach scale than in learning a scale of Mozart's. Scales in composition by Beethoven or Chopin, again, must be practised in another way. It follows that there is no generally valid prescription regarding slow practising. In each case we have to consider separately and with the utmost care to what extent control or the development of velocity has to be stressed.

In some cases excellent results are attained by both forms of practising, taken separately.

If we find that our playing is uneven, the parts which "run away with us" have to be practised several times at an intently controlled very slow speed.

If, on the other hand, we do not attain the desired tempo and find that our hand is not agile enough, we have to practise with free swing-strokes, executed under minimal control, and with our attention directed entirely to the execution of the swing-strokes.

Scale, passages and glissando-like progressions in general which require a quick tempo in one direction only, should be practised mainly with free swing-strokes (but not *solely* thus). In progressions with frequent changes of direction, however, practising with entirely free swing-strokes is a "double-edged weapon", because we are unable to master our hand, and it will "run away". This means that exclusive velocity practising is serviceable merely in technical exercises, because every progression abounds in directional changes. In re-education, however, velocity practising may render excellent help, because it will free the pupil's hands from constrained movements as if by magic.

In order to determine the proportion of control and velocity practising, let us take as an example Chopin's Etude in F minor (Op. 25).

Example 19

It requires very many changes in direction (after two or three notes) and extremely delicate dynamic shaping, at the same time it calls for a quick tempo and lively velocity playing but without any mechanical "scintillating." The changes of direction and the subtle dynamic contour necessitate intently controlled practising, so that the swinging motion of the single finger cannot be entirely free. Control is provided by the careful forming of the lifting and striking movements; the finger-end is precisely directed during the course of the entire swing-stroke, and it depends on our will which stroke will be stronger or weaker. (We must never think of the actual finger-tips but always to imagine their elongations, i.e. as if the fingers reached the strings. This conception gives us a sure protection against the stiff, rigid raising of the fingers where the second joint carries out the greatest movement instead of the finger-tip.)

Despite the enlarged movement (involving increased noise), the fingers have to strive for the most beautiful (the most noiseless) tone possible. This is apparently contradictory to the requirement of enlarging the finger movements in slow practising because a less beautiful (noisy) tone will be obtained by the finger's striking from higher position. However, in slow practising the enlarging of finger movements is indispensable. The primary aim here is not a beautiful tone but rather the best possible tone within the movement executed in accordance with the slow tempo.

Because of the control we are unable to make full use of the freedom of action of the fingers and thus the tempo is somewhat faster than if our aim were merely the practising of velocity. In order to assist in the control the fingers are – in accordance with the fast tempo – flexed into a bent position. (The degree of bending varies individually depending on the length of the fingers.)

If our aim were solely the development of velocity we would have to practise with entirely released fingers, partly in order to make full use of their freedom of action and partly to increase the activity of the interossei (the muscles of velocity). However, the aim of velocity practising may also be attained by enlarging the movements proportionately to the slowing down of the tempo and by executing the strokes vigorously (without excessive braking). Of course, here, too, the rule applies that a pianist with cramped hands has to choose a method of practising which comes nearer to the free swing-stroke, i.e. he has to employ less control and play with more released fingers.

RHYTHMIC VARIANTS

Rhythmic variants also come within the compass of control practising. They are applied in cases where learning necessitates so much repetition that it inevitably causes the diminishing of attention. This is the case when connecting certain difficult "grips" (German: Griffe), in unaccustomed positions of the hand, and – which is the most frequent case – in unaccustomed fingerings.

It must be made clear that even the best executed rhythmic variant is but a necessary evil because, no matter how colourfully and musically this variant is played, it has nothing in common with the music upon which it is based. When analysing the piano tone we have seen that the dynamic contours and the rhythm are closely interconnected. A change of the rhythm disturbs this equilibrium. Thus, in compositions technically mastered by the pianist in every detail no variants must be employed because they are decidedly detrimental from the point of view of a really delicate dynamic shaping.

We always have to ponder carefully, which rhythmic variant is to be chosen for the purpose of specific technical details. For instance, in practising plain legato progressions, the application of repetitive rhythms will hardly prove expedient, because it may result in arm thrusts instead of the required finger-strokes. At the same time a sforzato prescribed within the legato progression will be facilitated if the tone played sforzato is practised also with repetitions. As in finger-technique, the variants to be applied in octave and chord progressions must always be chosen so as to correspond to the aim of the final technical solution. The aim of the rhythmic variants must always be to show new sides of the technical difficulties and to reduce the danger of automatism by the new variants.

As a completion to control practising of Chopin's Etude in F minor (Op. 25) the following variants may sometimes be of use:

Example 20

But the following variant should be avoided:

Example 21

On the other hand, the study of Etude in G flat major (Op. 25) is facilitated by the following variant:

Example 22

The rhythmic variants are useful in cases as indicated above, but care must always be taken to apply them only in cases of the utmost necessity, i.e. in the event their use is prompted by some special difficulty. In our opinion the bar-by-bar elaboration of the compositions to be performed, by the aid of rhythmic variants, is decidedly harmful. As a warning example let us quote the rhythmic variants as given in Cortot's edition of Chopin's Sonata in B flat minor (3rd movt.)

Example 23

These rhythmic variants, for instance, serve no other purpose than to hack to death the startling effect of the two chords, and in addition even spoiling the grip. But then, can those two simple chords be of any difficulty for a pianist capable of playing the first movements? Obviously not! It seems that this movement, too, had to be equipped with rhythmic variants for the sake of completeness.

Rhythmic variants are incorrectly applied mainly by pianists who do not establish a close connection between their technique and their musical concept. By applying the rhythmic variants a certain external accuracy can be attained in the action of the fingers and the arm but – this work having only an end in itself – such playing will always give the impression of coldness even if the musical concept of the pianist is correct. His fingers will not execute exactly what he wants because their movements were not automatized to the music but only to each other.

Phot. 152
WALTER GIESEKING

SYNTHESIZING MOVEMENTS IN SLOW PRACTISING

We have to clarify the role of synthesizing and adapting movements in slow practising. In fast playing, e.g., with fast scale, synthesizing is comparatively easy because it can be merged in the movements of inward and outward direction. When slowing down the tempo, however, the progressing movement shifting sidewards will be less able to carry out the synthesizing and so the latter will require a continually increasing attention and concentration. The uniformity of the progressing movement will be lost in proportion to the slowing down and therefore the progressing movement has to be executed more and more during the stroke of the thumb.

When slow practising fast playing there is apparently no need for synthesizing because as a consequence of the minimal resistance one has the sensation that the upper arm does not assist the finger or the forearm in executing the active swing-stroke.

However, the functioning of the upper arm in apportioning the resistance, and even the synthesizing carried out by the whole body, is always needed because while the fingers are executing their swing-strokes the upper arm and, as its continuation, the whole body functions as an elastic support. The more we withdraw the axis of rotation of the active swinging unit from the keyboard the less resistance is needed, but a minimal resistance is always indispensable.

Synthesizing movements are thus necessary in all kinds of practising, but in slow practising they represent the strongest link with the music, because the swing-strokes – enlarged as they are as a result of the retardation – cause distortion in both the colouring and the dynamic levels.

If, e.g., in slow practising of scales we do not apply any synthesizing and our arms hang down passively, we will sooner or later involuntarily overburden our fingers. This overburdening will hinder the free motion of the fingers in slow practising, and clean finger-work will be replaced by "shaking".

ADAPTING MOVEMENTS IN SLOW PRACTISING

What will happen to adapting movements if we reduce the tempo? Are we able to augment the adapting movements in practising fast pieces slowly, in the same way as we enlarge the stroke of the arm or the fingers? Are adapting movements needed at all in slow practising?

Let us examine these questions one after another.

In the broken tonic chord, e.g., there is both rotatory and vertical adapting. If we increase the rotation, we will be compelled to play without moving our fingers. At the same time, vertical adapting is also forced into the background. (The only value of such practising is to fix the chord-touch, but this is more easily attainable by simple chord exercises.)

Practising with motionless fingers is not only a waste of time but – like any other useless motion – decidedly detrimental. It will automatize entirely senseless, rigid and clumsy movements which should never occur in playing.

It is also erroneous to stress the vertical adapting movements, again at the expense of finger-motion. (The so-called "rolling" or "dispersion.")

Augmentation of the adapting movements cannot be carried out proportionately to the slowing down, on account of the fact that *the same musical part requires different adapting movements, depending on the tempo in which it is played.* A case in point is the arpeggio. The smooth, beautiful rendering of a slow passage requires many adapting movements, because the progression, on account of the thumb, is no easy task. In the case of a fast passage or the slow practising of it the role of adapting movements is negligible because they will gradually melt into the synthesizing movements as the velocity increases.

The adapting movements can thus not be enlarged in slow practising. We always have to execute the adapting movements required by the particular swing-stroke of the forearm or finger.

The proper solution must, therefore, be found with the aid of our musical concept and motion instinct. From the point of view of the adapting movements, our only conscious task is to ensure that the arm is free to carry out the appropriate movements. Our striving after delicate, colourful playing will be our most reliable guide in finding the adequate adapting movements.

When adapting movements do not assist us in executing a given swing-stroke (e.g., if we enlarge the adapting movements in practising) *we will actually destroy our faculty of adaptation.*

It is, on the other hand, a gross error in slow practising not to aid the swing-strokes by adapting movements. In this case, the fingers and the forearm will not execute the strokes from the most convenient position, and their motion will thus become strained and rigid.

We have to emphasize repeatedly that the adapting movements play an important role in slow practising, too. They have the aim of rendering the amplified finger and forearm swing-stroke more comfortable.

It is their role to shift the centre of gravity according to need, to equalize the differences in the force of the fingers and to change the position of the arms in accordance with the various key-groups. But in doing so, they should never distract our attention from the execution of the swing-stroke by the active unit, but rather must subordinate themselves to this work.

In slow tempo different adapting movements are needed than in fast tempo; and still other movements are called for in slow practising. All these adapting movements have the common characteristic of being useful only to the extent that they associate themselves naturally with the active unit and assist in the execution of its tasks.

Phot. 153
SVIATOSLAV RICHTER

Phot. 154
ALBERT FERBER

ON THE ROLE OF THE VARIOUS JOINTS

In the execution of the individual swing-strokes every joint of the body participates either as an elastic support or an active swinging unit.

In order to decide which joint is the more suitable to execute a certain function, one has to compare the possibilities inherent in the anatomical structure with the requirements of the piano playing. Let us examine one by one the joints which are able to execute the active swinging movements. Then let us investigate both from the point of view of the bones and of the muscles, just how far the individual joints are capable of executing quick or fine movements. Comparing all that with our experiences gained through piano playing we may obtain a firmer basis than carrying on our examinations by excluding one or the other viewpoint.

Before starting a detailed analysis let us familiarize ourselves with some general elements of the anatomy of the muscles.

The middle, fleshy part of the muscle is called muscle belly. One of its two ends (at its immobile starting point) is called "origin," the other end (where the work is executed) "insertion."

The muscles of our limbs are so-called antagonistic muscles, i.e. they are arranged so that the action of one set of muscles is opposed by the action of another set. Since a muscle executes its work by contraction, another muscle – whose action opposes the first – is needed to replace the bone (previously moved by it) into its original position.

Fig. 23

The muscles end in tendons. The tendon is a fibrous connective tissue of compact, parallel fibres. It is always considerably thinner than the muscle. If the muscle is considered as a motor, the tendon functions as a transmission belt, transmitting the muscle force. On parts where the tendon might sustain injuries during the motion, e.g. when moving over the many-edged carpal bones having an irregular form, the gliding of the tendons along the bones is facilitated by the serious tendon sheaths.[1] (Having recourse to a mechanical comparison it may be imagined as if protecting a wire rope by a tube filled with oil.)

Even without any special command coming from the nervous system, the muscles are in a state of a continual slight contraction. This is called muscle tone or tonus. This is why a slight cut of some tenths of millimetres made by a razor blade will widen to the tenfold: it is pulled apart by the antagonistic muscles. The more developed and trained the muscle, the higher is the level of the muscle tonus. However, this must not be confused with the jerky contraction of the muscles because this does not mean any greater muscle force but only a squandering of the force.

The medium position of the joints is also determined by the muscle tonus. Thus, e.g., the first finger-joint (metacarpo-phalangeal joint) is pulled by the antagonistic muscles in both directions. If

---

[1] The most frequent cause of the inflammation of the tendon sheaths is the work carried out under excessive strain. (The pianist "presses" or forcibly lowers his wrist during the work of his fingers, or presses his arms while the wrist carries out its active work.)

the tonus of the two muscle groups is normal, i.e. not abnormally increased or decreased, the fingers will be held in resting (medium) position by the tonus of the antagonistic muscles. However, with pianists the one-sided development or even a cramped contraction of the flexors is often found, and, as a consequence, the fingers also assume a continuous flexed position because in the piano playing the work of the flexors (executing the stroke) is considerably greater than that of the tensors (carrying out the lifting). Since in everyday life a greater demand is made on flexors, a compensatory development of the extensors should be cared for by gymnastics.

HIPS

Starting the swinging motion from the hip joint is applicable only exceptionally and in combination with the activity of other joints. Its aim is to produce peculiar (grotesque, crude) tone effects. These tone effects are needed comparatively rarely and therefore the movements of the torso serve mainly to bring the arms into appropriate position, particularly in relation to the higher and lower pitch ranges. (When playing with both hands on the upper octaves we are compelled to bend slightly to the right, etc.)

Thus the spinal column (rachis) is not employed with the aim of executing an active swing-stroke but its more appropriate function is that of an elastic support. One of the main guarantees of sensitive playing and fine dynamic contours is the elasticity of the spinal column. Hence it follows, that a grave fault is committed by a pianist when executing continuous bending with one of the lower vertebrae, instead of the active swing-strokes of the upper arm or in addition to these movements. This will be most detrimental to the expressiveness of the playing for the very simple reason that even pianists have but one trunk and if he moves his trunk instead of his arms, he deprives himself of the possibility to arouse the most different tone-colouring effects by the aid of his two arms. No less harm is caused in the shaping of the swing-strokes either because the spinal column is very appropriate to function as an elastic support (because the great number of vertebrae is able to absorb even the strongest rebounds) but it is entirely unfit to execute active swing-strokes on account of its structure and its relatively small muscle amount.

It is equally a great fault if the hips are used by pianists for a pendulum-like bending forward and backward during playing, because it disturbs the functioning of the vertebral column as an elastic support. This does not exclude, of course, the bending of the trunk forward or backward according to the emotional content (see p. 92).

THE SHOULDER JOINT

The bones of the shoulder-girdle are the collar bone (clavicle) and the shoulder-blade (scapula). They are freely embedded in the muscles and only the clavicle is articulated with the breast-bone (sternum).

The upper arm consists of one bone only: the humerus.

The joint at the upper end of the humerus is hemispherical, and cylindrical at the lower end (trochlea).

The hemispherical joint plays a large part in giving the greatest freedom of action to the shoulder joint.

The upper arm moves easily and freely in every direction, but its rotation is cumbersome. This can be applied only in connection with other movements, e.g. those of the shoulder-girdle; it is incapable of any independent, active functioning (e.g. tremolo).

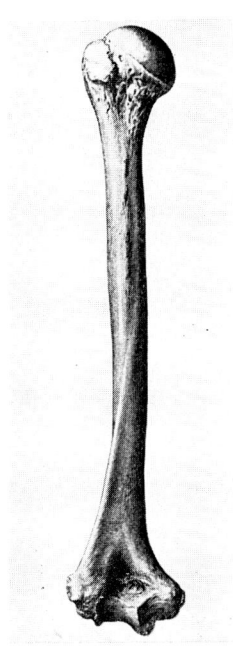

Fig. 24
THE HUMERUS

The additional, complementary movements of the clavicle and the scapula are indispensable in assuring the complete freedom of the upper arm. However, the fact that these bones are movable has been misunderstood by some teaching methods (especially those of the weight technique). These methods state that the movements of the upper arm will be executed in the most perfect way if they are linked with the movements of the collar bone and mainly with that of the shoulder-blade, or possibly the entire active movement is executed by the two bones of the shoulder-girdle and not by the humerus. This is a typical example of the theories born at writing-tables and contradicting in every detail the practice of everyday life. If we examine the movements of the shoulder joint, we may see that in the course of our everyday life many hundreds and thousands of movements are executed starting from the shoulder joint—i.e. without any active shifting of the shoulder blade and clavicle. One may even say that all the important movements of the arm are started from the shoulder joint. Similarly the surgeon, watchmaker or mechanic execute their work, requiring great precision and care, from the shoulder joint just as one of our finest movements, caressing, is executed from the shoulder. If, instead of a movement started from the shoulder joint, *the shoulder-girdle itself* moves, an awkward, cumbersome movement will result. This is why one has to avoid pulling up or even moving actively the shoulders. Thus, when speaking about "playing from the shoulders" in the following chapters we will always mean the active movements of the upper arm and not those of the shoulder-girdle.

The whole arm is set in motion by the muscles of the back, the shoulder and the chest. These muscles are capable of executing the most delicate movements, because owing to their huge size, they can easily move the arm, and their antagonistic functioning renders a perfect balancing of the arm possible. The considerable muscle mass has a great deal to do with the fact that the shoulder joint is so suitable for executing delicate movements. Even the whole arm, representing a considerable weight, is easily and with perfect accuracy moved by these mighty muscles. (In the language of the pianist: we play "from the shoulders," "from the chest.")

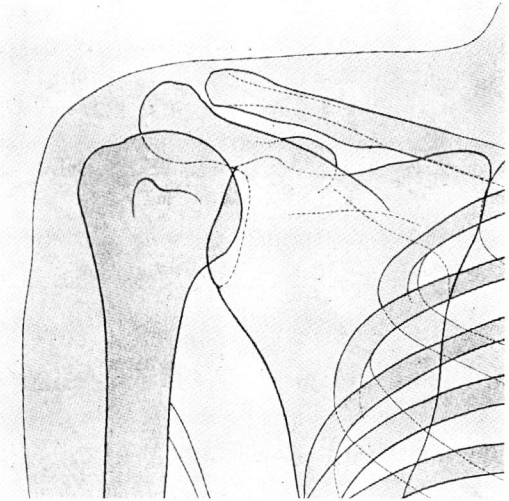

Fig. 25
CONTOURS OF THE SHOULDER
Dorsal view. Sketch based on an X-ray photograph

THE ROLE OF THE UPPER ARM IN SYNTHESIZING

As stated on page 32, the whole body of the pianist functions as an elastic support and thus participates in the synthesizing. Within this work, however, the most delicate regulation is carried out by the shoulder joint. The mighty muscles, moving the upper arms, enable us to perform very exact movements.

It must be stressed that neither the wrist nor the elbow joint is capable of delicately apportioning the resistance. While the shoulder joint is considerably higher than the keys the wrist and elbow are on the same level with them and so the hand or the forearm can work only as a lever. This means in other words that the slightest movement of the forearm in the elbow joint causes a considerable shifting at the fingers.

The so-called forearm playing is in most cases caused by incorrect, faulty sitting and body posture. It can be caused by the unfavourable proportion of the upper arm and the forearm (short upper arm and long forearm) or a very long arm compared with the trunk. The cause can be also poor teaching, e.g. if the pupil presses his upper arms to his trunk.

The shoulder joint is very often wrongly used in the synthesizing. If the upper arm "hangs down loosely" — as is frequently demanded by some teaching methods — it will be unable to hold up the rebound of the key and to transmit it to the spinal column. The rebound of the key will shock the arm and move it from its place. The functioning of the shoulder joint will be correct if we have the feeling that the trunk is an elongation of the arms. In that case the shoulder joint will smoothly transmit the rebounds; these can be absorbed without any hindrance in the trunk and feet. In its external form this movement often goes together with a slight lifting, elevating the arm. This does not mean, however, that anything can be attained by a mechanical lifting, with an "elevated position" of the arm. The arm must be "behind" the hand and the trunk "behind" the arm. This requires different positions in each case but the prerequisite of it is always the fullest elasticity.

ACTIVE SWING-STROKES OF THE UPPER ARM

Tones requiring special care in shading are always sounded by a movement starting from the shoulder joint because we are enabled only in this way to carry out perfect direct swing-strokes. Special importance to this way of tone producing is given by the fact that the swing-strokes of the upper arm are relatively free from noise-effects, they "carry well". The noise-effects can be best reduced through the upper arm swing-stroke because the weight and force of the arm produces a correspondingly round and full tone even with minimal motion.

The less noise the tone of the piano contains — compared with its volume — the fuller and more carrying it will be. Such a sonorous tone is thus obtained by avoiding — i.e. reducing to a minimum — both the upper and the lower noises.

The upper noises can be easily avoided by starting with the fingers at the level of the keys. Thus one of the preliminary conditions of a beautiful sonorous tone is already created by the direct swing-strokes.

It is a more difficult task to avoid the lower noises. We can do so only when force is applied merely for a very short time — namely until the point of escapement is reached. If force is applied beyond the escapement point and we push or press the key to the key-bed, the lower noises will increase, and we shall obtain "wooden," "rapping," "dry" tones.

To attain a staccato effect, it is always necessary to make use of certain noise-effects. These latter should, therefore, be applied even when the staccato is played by the upper arm.

Upper noises will be added to the tone by the upper arm's executing an indirect swing-stroke (the fingers descend through the air instead of starting the stroke on the key-surface). The "pinched" staccato produces lower noises. The different kinds of upper-arm staccato are achieved by varying the application and blending the two kinds of noise-effects, accompanied by modification of the tone duration.

The most characteristic feature of the swing-stroke of the upper arm is the utilization of the arm's mass to produce the greatest possible force through comparatively small movements. The whole arm participates in the swing-stroke so that the hand, too, cannot remain passive and the finger-ends must always be taut. (The word "finger-tip" is intentionally *not* used because under this notion generally a point immediately next to the nail is meant, while that part of the finger touches the key only in the case of strongly bent position.) Passive, loose finger-ends lead to an increase of the noise-effects and generally result in unreliability of tone production. *The finger-ends practically have to blend with the key because only thus will we feel that the keys are elongations of our arm (like the hammers of the cymbalom player) and that with their aid we are playing directly on the strings.*

Depending on the required tone volume we employ larger or smaller movements. The form of the movement will also change, in proportion to the participation of the wrist and the elbow.

The various kinds of upper-arm swing-stroke are complemented by the motions of the wrist and the elbow. The participation of these two factors changes not only according to the desired tone colour, but also in accordance with the physique of the pianist. As a general rule, however, we may state that the more massive the tone required (e.g. imitation of wind instrument), the more desirable the use of the arm as a whole. Sometimes we apply such small swing-strokes that the movement is hardly visible, but in order to produce a fortissimo effect a special solution, the so-called spindle-motion, will be required.

In the spindle-motion the arms are imaginarily elongated up to the axis of the key. Thus, one end of the motion is the shoulder joint, the other is the key's axis. The arm moves like a skipping rope.

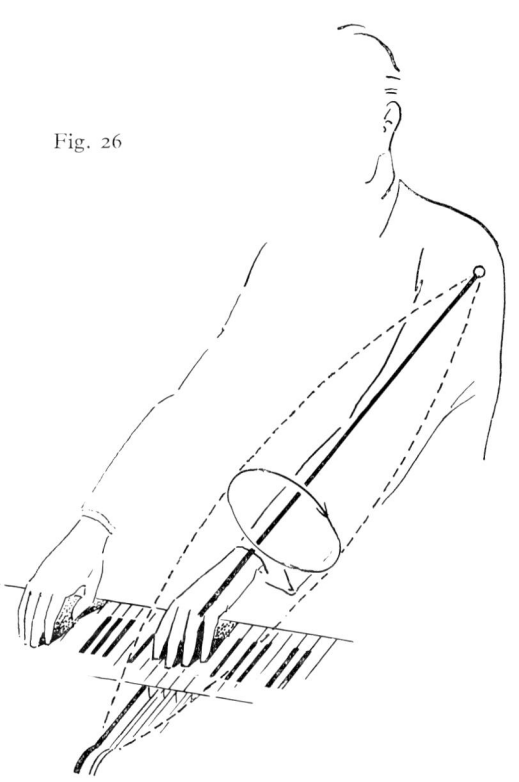

Fig. 26

It is very important to imagine the key as an elongation of the arm. If we picture the point of contact with the key as the end of the lever, only a fraction of the force employed will be transformed into tone. (As if – instead of tone production – our only aim were to turn and swing the arm.) By joining in our imagination the key with the arm we are able – within the spindle-motion – to employ our whole energy towards setting the key in motion. Only thus can we obtain a tone volume proportionate to the force applied.

If we attempt to achieve a fortissimo effect merely by vertical movements, we will obtain extremely strong lower noises. Such swing-strokes are well suited to dark tone colours and the impression of black moods. The excessive employment of this kind of stroke will, however, cause uncertainty in contour-shaping, because the constrained motion thus imposed upon the arm has a very disturbing effect. Although in certain cases dramatic expressiveness is heightened by such a touch – indeed, it may even happen that the required colour can be obtained in no other way – care must be taken to avoid adapting it as our constant playing form.

Excessive motion of the upper arm also occurs very frequently. This will happen almost always if the whole amount of force is not transmitted to the strings. This leads also to faulty innervations just as does the opposite extreme, namely in cases when the arms are not employed. If the movement is always larger than necessary, it becomes impossible exactly to associate the extent of the motion with the tone volume.

Synthesizing is also needed with the swing-strokes of the upper arm. We have to take special care to apply synthesizing movements here because after executing the individual swing-strokes our arm is inclined to become passive. (In such cases the main part in the synthesizing and in the apportioning of the resistance is played by the spinal column.) We must also see to it that our arm, far from becoming passive even after sounding relatively long, sustained notes, prepares itself for the next swing-stroke. (The hand of the conductor of an orchestra seems to be motionless when indicating the fermata, while in reality it expresses the intensity of the tone.)

THE ELBOW AND RADIO-ULNAR JOINT

The forearm consists of two bones: the radius and the ulna. The radius is connected with three carpal bones through a joint, but the ulna has no connection with the carpal bones.

On the upper end of the ulna we find a cavity designed to receive the cylindrical surface of the humerus. The elbow joint is of the hinge type, particularly suited to the display of agility. Although the hand and the forearm constitute a great mass it is, nevertheless, moved with a considerable velocity by the muscles of the upper arm. A repetition velocity of 8 strokes per second is attainable for every trained pianist.

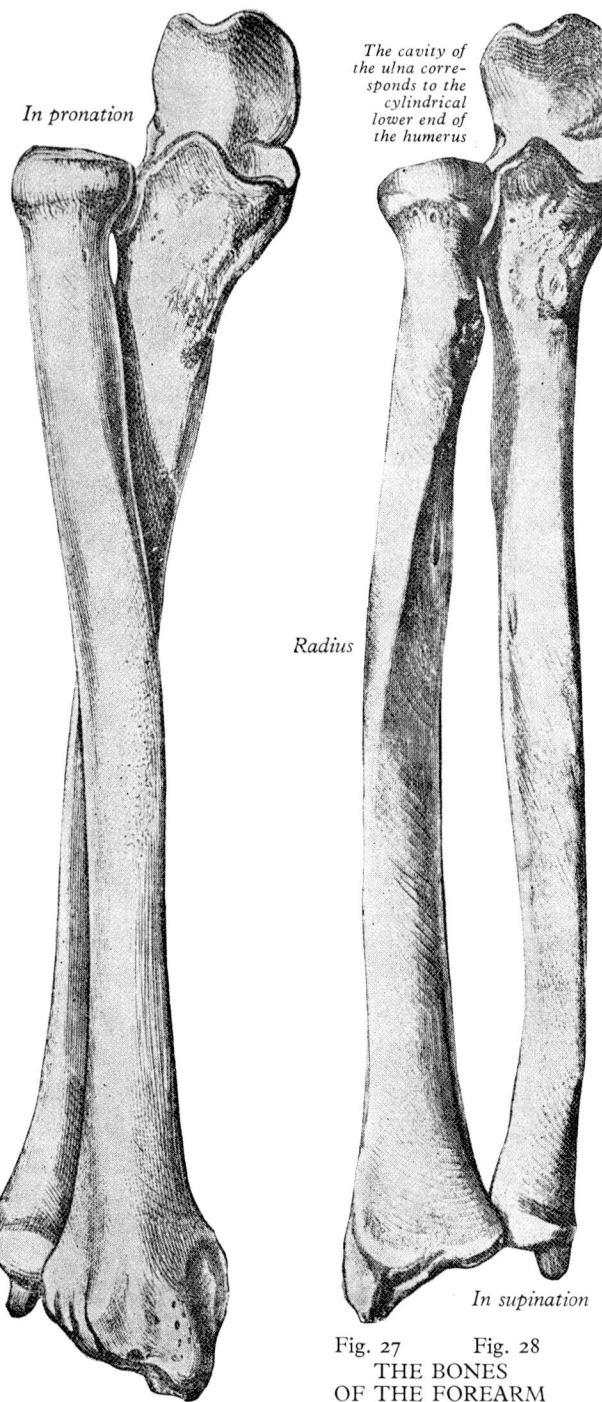

In pronation

The cavity of the ulna corresponds to the cylindrical lower end of the humerus

Radius

In supination

Fig. 27   Fig. 28
THE BONES
OF THE FOREARM

Within the group of muscles moving the forearm and located in the upper arm, two require mention: the biceps and triceps (the former is used in bending, the latter in stretching the forearm).[2] In piano playing the stroke is the work of the triceps, the action of raising is a function of the biceps.

When one is playing in rapid tempo, the biceps and triceps perform their work with the aid of the so-called *vibrato technique* (see p. 154).

In vibrato playing the large stretching movements are interrupted by short flexions. This has the advantage of enabling the muscles to change their shape while in action, thus reducing fatigue. Flexion also may be interrupted by brief stretching movements, but this is more difficult because in this case the larger movement does not pass in the direction of the stroke.

The radius is able to effect rotatory movements both around its own axis and around the ulna. As the hand is fixed to the radius, it rotates together with the latter.

The ulna participates only to a minimum extent in the rotation: the movement is executed almost entirely by the radius.

There are two rotation positions of the forearm and hand, namely, pronation (twisted so the palm faces downward) and supination (untwisted so the palm faces upward). In pronated position the two forearm bones cross each other diagonally while in supinated position they are parallel.

The tendon of the biceps when pronating the forearm is wound around the head of the radius. When the biceps contracts, the tendon uncoils, and in doing so it turns back the radius. (Just as we set a top spinning with the aid of a string.)

[2] If the muscles start with two or possibly three heads separately and melt into one muscle belly, we speak of two- or three-headed muscles, respectively.

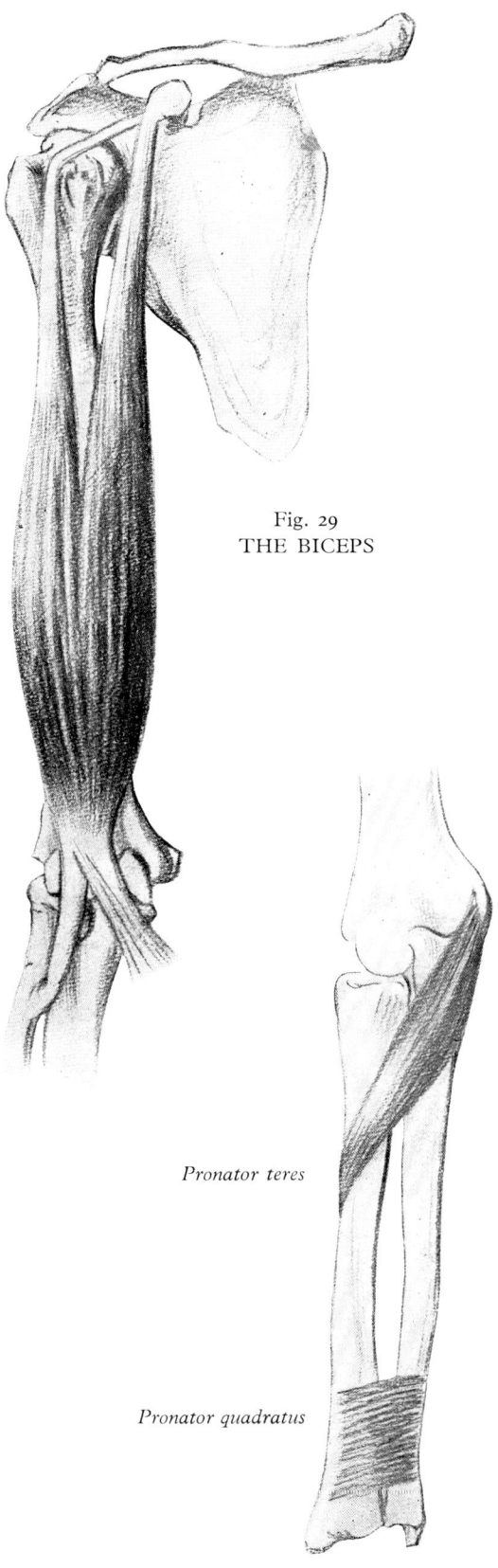

Fig. 29
THE BICEPS

Pronator teres

Pronator quadratus

Fig. 30
THE PRONATORS

When the arm is extended, the biceps is unable to effect any supination, and we are compelled to perform this action almost entirely with the aid of the supinator muscle situated in the upper part of the forearm. The "output" of the supinator is, of course, far from the mighty biceps, and therefore our arm is to be slightly flexed when playing a quick tremolo.

The muscles participating in pronation are the pronator teres and the pronator quadratus. Both of these muscles pull the radius and the ulna towards each other, but the pronator teres functions in addition as a flexor of the forearm. (Fig. 30 shows that one head of the two-headed pronator teres starts at the humerus and the other head at the ulna.) Since the pronator teres — like the biceps — functions also as a flexor, pronation may be effected more easily with bent arms.

In piano playing mostly a rather strong pronation is needed. This is uncomfortable particularly for beginners. Therefore, a child when beginning to learn piano playing tends to "lay down" his little finger: the pronation required for finger action is felt to be too strenuous.

We have to insist on attaining that degree of pronation which enables freedom of action on the part of the fingers. It would be a grave fault, however, to demand constant strong pronation instead of the amount absolutely necessary for executing the movements freely. In a relaxed position, i.e. resting position of the arm, the bones of the forearm are in a semi-pronate position. A deviation of this resting position is admissible only in so far as it is needed in order to execute the movements freely. Thus the degree of pronation will not be of the same constant degree during the piano playing. So, e.g., octave playing requires much less pronation than finger technique, and, when playing sixths, the little finger reaches the key somewhat from the side.

As one may see there is a considerable difference of force of muscles in favour of the biceps and the supinator (carrying out the supination).

Supination is — as a consequence of the participation of the biceps — much more energetic than pronation, stressing the fifth finger is thus easier even in the quick tremolo.

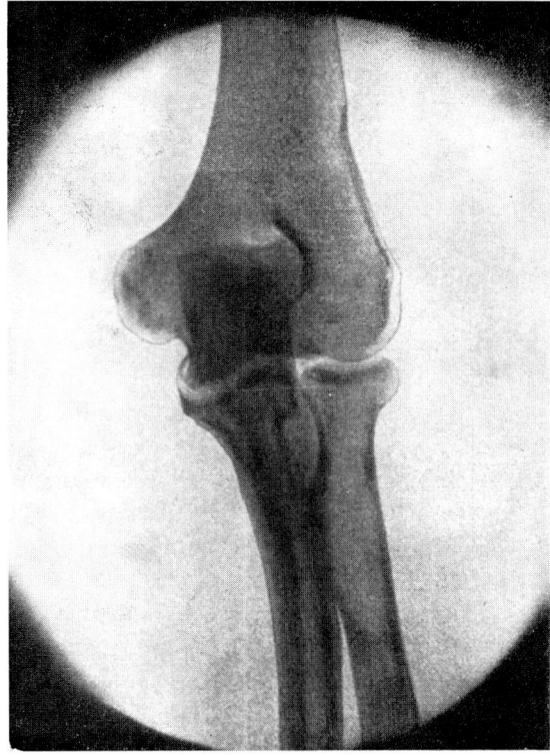

Fig. 31
Extended arm in supinated position

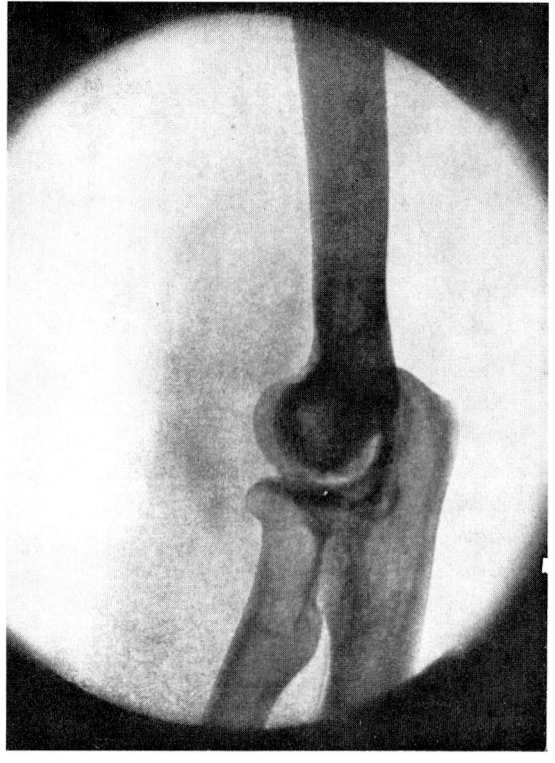

Fig. 32
Extended arm viewed laterally

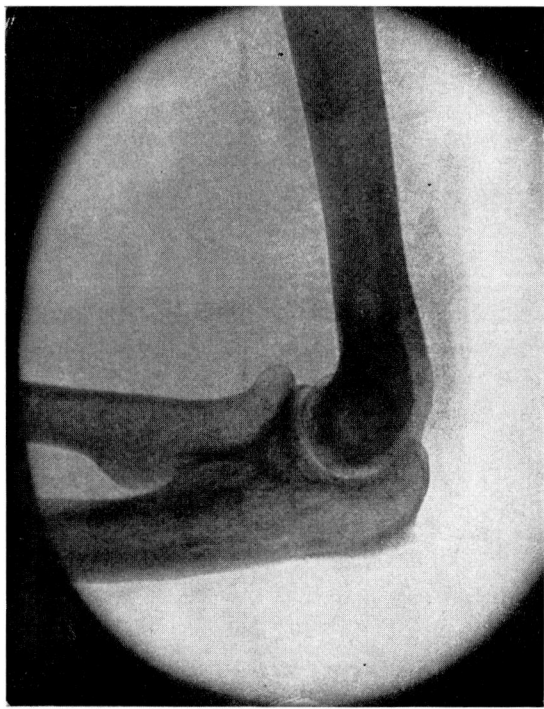

Fig. 33
Arm bent at a right angle, lateral view

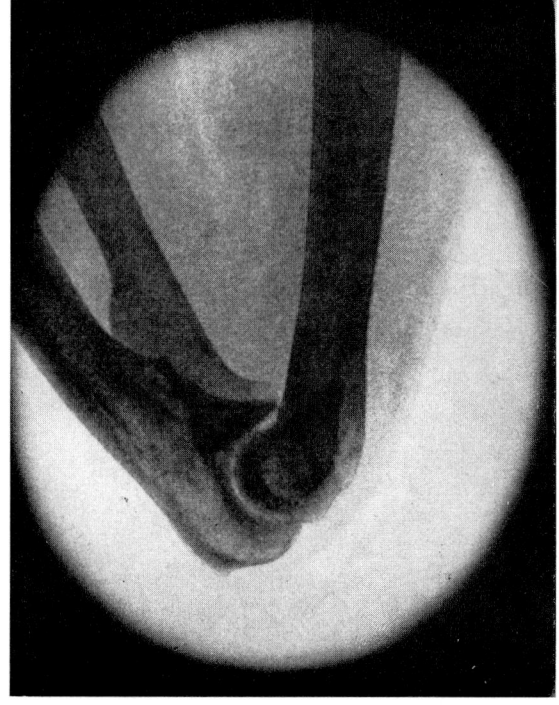

Fig. 34
Fully bent arm, lateral view

The elbow joint is a typical "quick", agile joint: the quickest movements can be executed starting from this joint. As mentioned above, a repetition velocity of 8 strokes per second is a speed easily attainable by any skilful pianist; a virtuoso is even able to execute ten strokes per second. So, it is no mere chance that high demands are made by composers on the octave technique. (See the well-known octave passages in Tchaikovsky's Piano concerto in B flat minor, Chopin's Polonaise in A flat major and Liszt's Transcription of "Erlkönig".)

However, the elbow joint is much less capable of playing an important role in the apportioning of resistance, of the weight-effect. The forearm, having the elbow as its rotation point, will function as a lever in the apportioning of the resistance and this makes any delicate differentiating impossible. Thus the elbow joint in its functioning as an elastic support has the role of transmitting, forwarding the elasticity, i.e. a link of the series of articulations absorbing the rebound.

THE WRIST

Three of the carpal bones are connected with the radius through joints. The carpus consists of 8 tiny bones of irregular shapes situated in 2 transverse rows. When bending the hand and moving the wrist, both rows are in motion. This enables the wrist to assume a beautiful rounded form when bending the hand. As the rows are mobile both in relation to the radius and in relation to each other, we are able to move our hands laterally in the direction of the ulna (ulnar flexion, abduction), as well as in the direction of the radius (radial flexion, adduction).

The metacarpal bones are joined to the second row of the carpal bones: one for each finger.

X-RAY PHOTOS OF THE LATERAL MOTION OF THE HAND

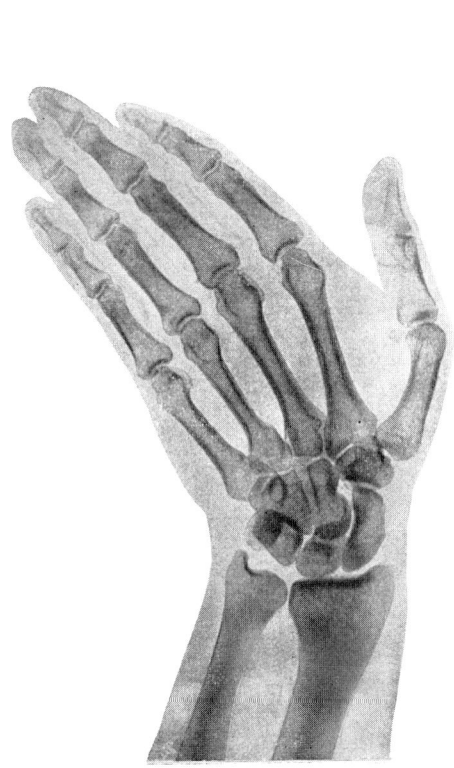
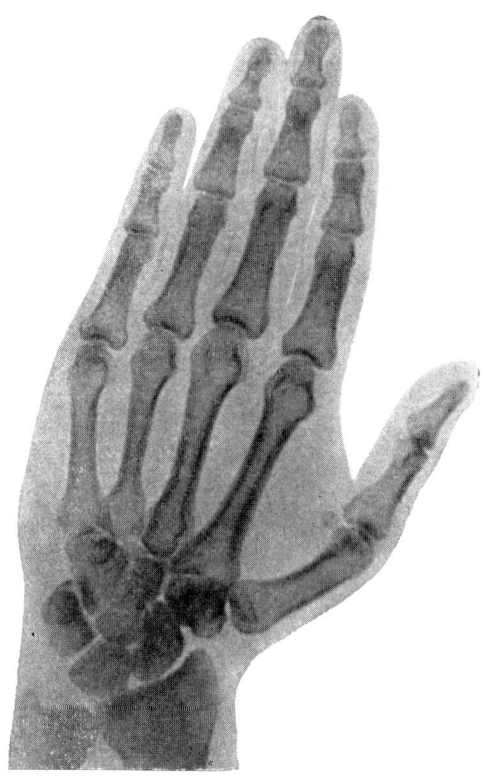

Fig. 35
Ulnar flexion

Fig. 36
Radial flexion

Thus, the wrist consists of three rows of joints:

1. those between the radius and the carpal bones,
2. those between the two rows of carpal bones and
3. those between the carpal and metacarpal bones.

The complicated structure of the wrist indicates that it is unfit for quick movements and its function is to give softening, balancing effect to the work of the other joints. Even the location and weakness of the muscles of the wrist seems to prove that the wrist is only to a most limited degree capable of working independently.

The lateral motions of the hand are made possible by the extensors and flexors of the carpus, but they are considerably less fit for flexing or bending the hand because their tendons are fixed on the carpus, i.e. in the immediate neighbourhood with the rotating point.

The flexing and extending of the hand are executed by the aid of the finger muscles and not by the muscles of the wrist. This is the reason why there can be no wrist technique equal to finger or forearm technique; the wrist will always execute complementary movements. (This was recognized even by Hugo Riemann: *Katechismus des Klavierspiels*. Leipzig, 1905.)

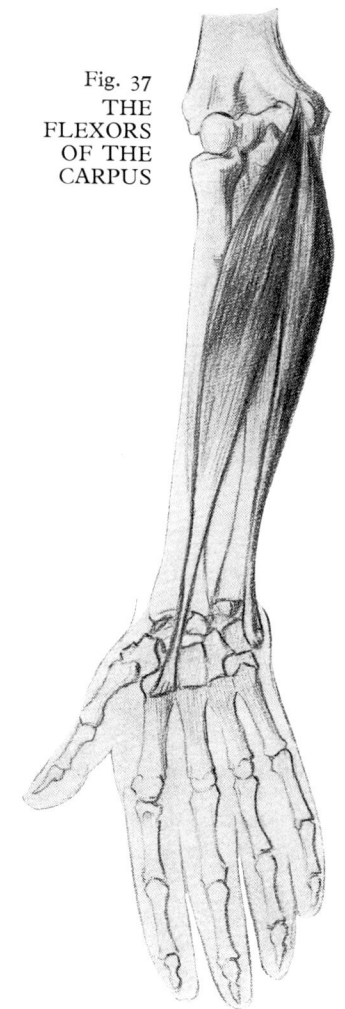

Fig. 37
THE FLEXORS OF THE CARPUS

THE BONES OF THE HAND

Fig. 38
Back of the hand

Radius

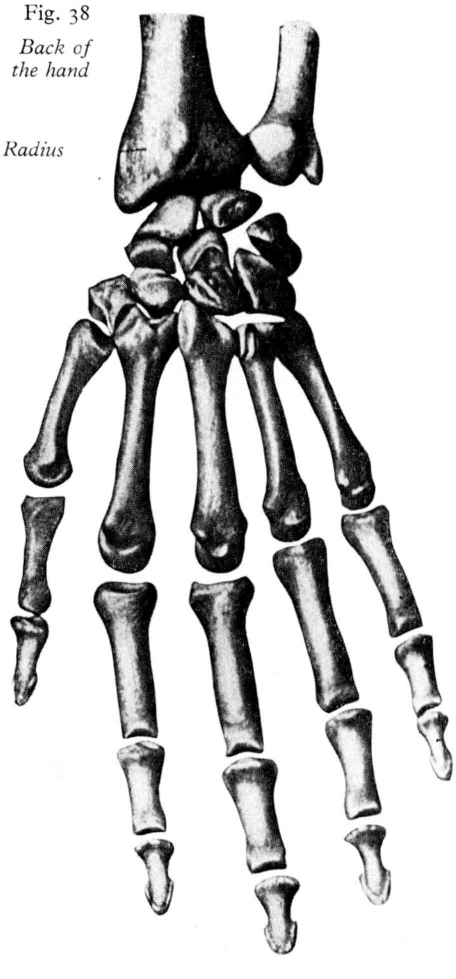

←— *ulna* —→

Bones of the carpus

Bones of the metacarpus

First phalanx (Knuckle phalanx)

Second phalanx (Middle phalanx)

Third phalanx (Nail phalanx)

Fig. 39
Palm

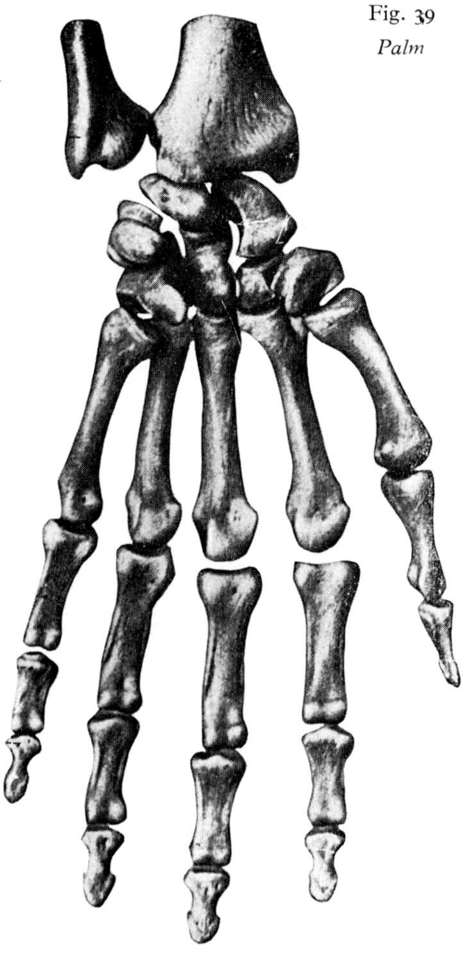

THE FINGER JOINTS

The metacarpal bones are connected with the phalangeal bones at the metacarpo-phalangeal joints.

The finger provided with the greatest freedom of action is the thumb, which owes its great mobility to its special saddle-shaped carpo-metacarpal joint (in contrast to the metacarpo-phalangeal joints of the 2nd, 3rd, 4th and 5th fingers) and its intricate muscles which form the mass (thenar eminence) at its base.

The thumb consists of two phalanges while the other fingers consist of three.

If one allows his arms to drop to his sides in a naturally relaxed, hanging position, the fingers will assume a slightly bent position. This is the medium position of the finger joints which is maintained by the normal tonus of the finger-extensor and finger-flexor muscles.

The following finger muscles are located on the upper part of the forearm: the deep finger flexor; the superficial finger flexor; the joint finger extensor; the muscles moving the thumb; and the muscles aiding the independent motion of the forefinger and little finger.

Of this intricate array of muscles, the superficial and deep finger flexors and the finger extensor are of principal concern to the pianist.

The belly of the superficial finger flexor divides into four tendons which then split and insert into the sides of the base of the second phalangeal bones of the four fingers. The belly of the deep finger flexor divides into four tendons which pass through a split in the corresponding superficial finger-flexor tendon and then insert into the base of the third phalangeal bones of the four fingers.

The belly of the finger extensor also splits into four tendons. Each of the latter has two insertions; the first is at the base of the second phalanx; the second one at the finger-end. Thus both the superficial and the deep finger flexors have their antagonistic muscles.

In piano playing the finger functions as a one-armed lever.

The fact that the second phalanx has a separate flexor, as well as a separate tensor branch, seemingly justifies the view that the finger-stroke should start from the second finger joint. Although the part thus set in motion is actually shorter, the above view is nonetheless erroneous from the mechanical point of view. If the second phalanx were to be moved by the superficial flexor, the force would act (since its point of insertion is at the base of the phalanx) at a point near the fulcrum of the lever. This would require more energy and thus would be more fatiguing than to move the finger-tips. (In addition, the finger-tips would be passive and weak.) It follows from this that we would be compelled to make use of the deep flexor if we were to start our stroke from the second joint.

When executing a stroke with the deep finger flexor starting from the first joint (metacarpo-phalangeal joint) of the 2nd, 3rd, 4th or 5th fingers, our muscles have the task to prevent simultaneously the hand from shifting. This is achieved by means of the extensors, and it is easily made, because the metacarpal bones are joined to each other and thus the hand is easily held by the common finger extensor, i.e. by its branches for the other fingers. In this "fixation" the extensors of the carpal bones have an important role also.

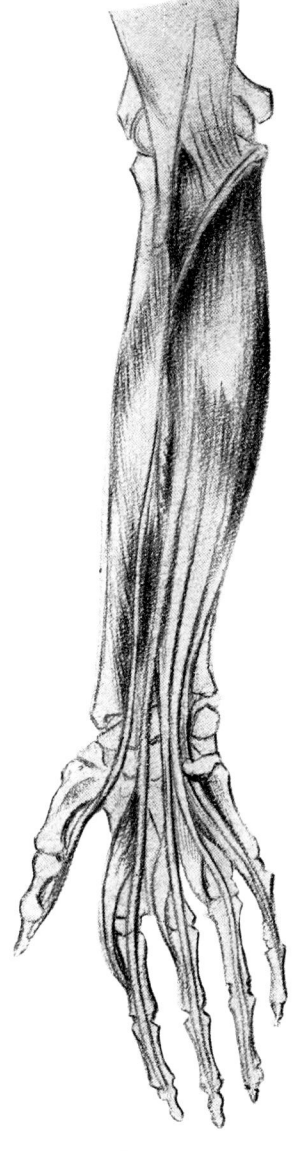

Fig. 40
THE DEEP
FINGER FLEXOR

But what would happen if we were to execute a flexion starting from the second (1st interphalangeal) joint? In this case it would not be sufficient that the other branches of the extensor balance (by their muscle tone) the pulling of the flexor. The functioning of the extensors of the carpal bones would also be insufficient because a pull of the extensor of the finger at its insertion into the base of the second phalanx must be applied in order to prevent the first phalanx of the second finger from shifting.

And what happens when elevating the finger? Again the extensor does the work but in this case it is executed at the insertion into the 3rd phalangeal bone. Thus the extensor is in continuous action both with strokes and elevations and so it fatigues in a very short time because it carries a twofold burden and this will hinder both velocity and the exactitude of the work.

According to some views the independent bending of the third phalanx is of extraordinary importance in finger technique. Some writers even assert that pianissimo playing is the work of the third phalanx.

The independent flexing of the third phalanx can be done only on the basis of faulty innervation. By means of the two insertions of the extensor muscle we are able to immobilize either the finger-tip or the first phalanx. In the latter case, we use the insertion at the base of the second phalangeal bone, whereby the finger-tip is completely relaxed. The second phalanx can be kept motionless only with the aid of the insertion of the extensor at the finger-tip. Thus we can succeed in independently bending the third finger joint only in the event that the extensor does not fully respond (in consequence of faulty innervation) and dominates only the second phalanx. Insisting on independent flexion of the third joint thus hampers proper innervation and gives rise to inaccuracy in the work of the extensor in its important role from the standpoint of velocity.

The work of the superficial and the deep finger flexor, being independent of each other, enable the finger to execute strokes with uniform energy, independently from the extent of the flexing. The setting of the joints into differently stretched and bent position is made by the superficial finger flexor while the stroke is executed by the deep flexor.

Even the shape of the first joint is more appropriate to execute active swing-strokes than that of the second and third joint. The reason for this is that the active swing-strokes of the fingers are executed very frequently – one might even say: in the majority of the cases – not in a perfectly vertical direction but mixed up with more or less lateral movements. From among the finger joints, however, only the first joint is capable of executing lateral movements. Taking into consideration also that both the flexors and the tensors may display their effect more easily on the first joint than on the other two, one may state that only the first joint is suitable for active swing-strokes while the second and third joints serve for determining the desired extent of the different bendings.

Within the group of muscles of the hand, the interossei are of greatest importance from the point of view of piano playing. These originate at the side of the metacarpal bones (together with the lumbricalis muscles completing their functioning): their tendons become united above the first phalanx with the tendons of their common extensor. So if, e.g., only the interosseous muscle of the second finger (located sidewards from the thumb)

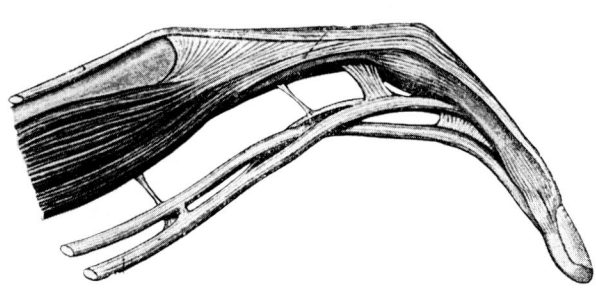

Fig. 41
TENDONS OF THE THIRD FINGER

The interosseous muscle, proceeding from the side of the metacarpal bone, and the tendons of the lumbricalis muscle (functionally complementing the interosseous muscle) are united over the first phalanx. (The upper, thicker bundle of muscles is the interosseous.) The illustration clearly shows how the tendon of the superficial finger flexor is divided into two parts and gives passage to the tendon of the deep finger flexor (adhering to the finger-end)

contracts, it will draw the second finger towards the thumb. If, however, the interossei, located on both sides of the second finger, are moved at the same time, they will first extend the third phalanx and after that, by means of further contraction of the muscle, bend the first phalanx.

This interesting threefold function of the interossei has important consequences in certain fields of piano technique. The functioning of the interossei is most easily executed from a slightly extended position of the fingers because then even the slightest contraction of the muscles acts as a flexing factor. Since they are situated near the fingers – the distance covered by the tendon being short between the motor and the attainable place of the work – they play a particularly important role in rapid finger technique, especially in velocity playing. Thus, their development is a prerequisite of finger velocity. For this reason the proportion between the length of the fingers and the length of the back of the hand is – to a certain extent – an indication of the ability to acquire velocity. The shorter the fingers in proportion to the back of the hand, the better they execute quick movements. We may note how the hands of professional pianists become transformed as a consequence of much exercise. The palm becomes broader and more thickset because of the strengthening of the interosseous muscles. Both brilliant tone effects and soft, dim passages are easily attainable with the aid of the interossei. This made the use of them so desirable for the romantic style of piano playing. Since the interosseous muscles function most easily in connection with a somewhat extended finger position, the romantic school preferred the use of certain tonalities requiring many black keys. Of course, this was not done on the basis of some anatomic concepts but only because they felt that the tone effects, imagined by them, were attainable in these tonalities. This is why Chopin, for instance, hardly composed anything in D major (bent position) but made ample use of D flat major and A flat major (stretched position).

It is certainly no mere chance that we find so many piano pieces of Mozart composed in D major. The clearly drawn contours required by Mozart were most easily attainable in the bent position forced on the player by the D major (by a maximum employment of the long flexors and extensors).

Mention must be made of the opponens pollicis muscle of the thumb which pulls it towards the little finger and of the opponens digiti minimi muscle of the fifth finger which pulls the little finger towards the thumb. Combining the action of these two opponent muscles plays an important role in giving stability to the hand.

Phot. 155
THE HANDS OF CLARA HASKILL

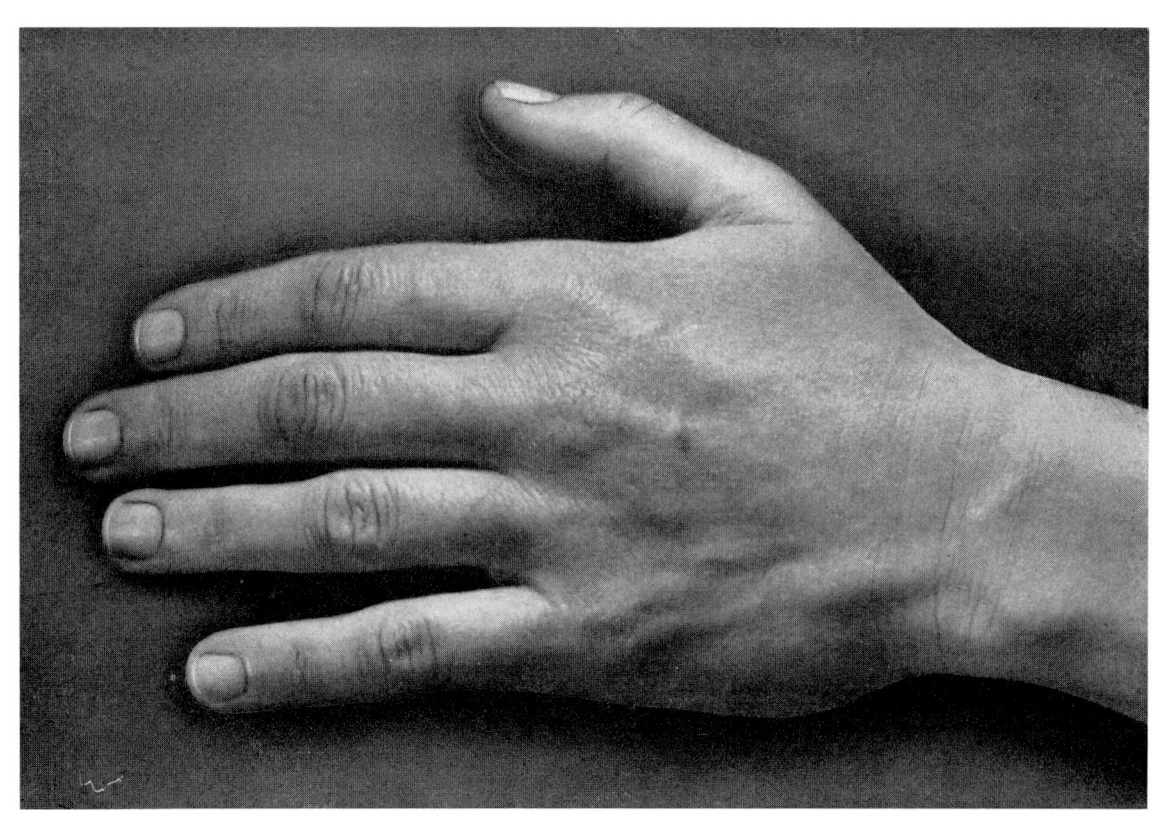

Phot. 156
THE HAND OF ANNIE FISCHER

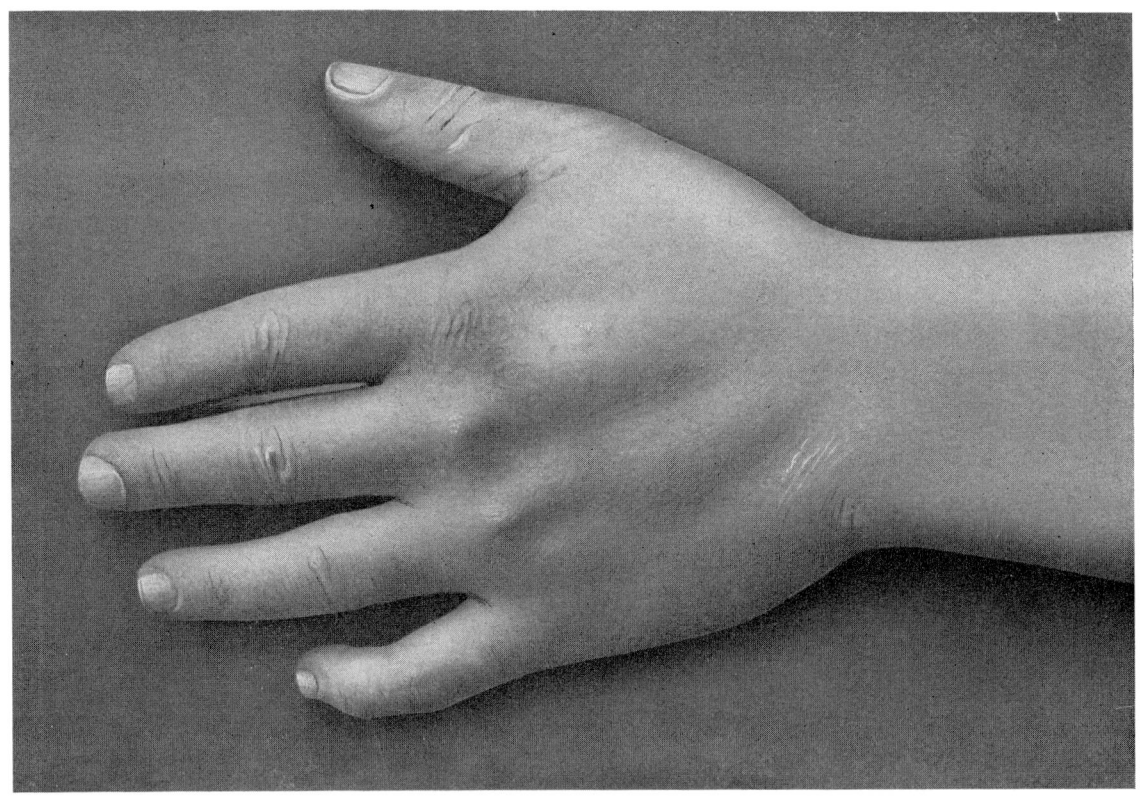

Phot. 157
THE HAND OF THERESA CARREÑO

STRUCTURE AND FORM OF THE HAND

HAND STRUCTURE

Because a hand structure favourable for piano playing gives a great advantage to the player, it is often considered an indispensable prerequisite of a pianistic talent. In fact, the greatest pianists, without exception, had good hand structures and so some general rules concerning the hand structure can be derived from examining the hands of the virtuosi. Where an unfavourable hand structure is a hindrance to the pianist on his way leading to a good piano technique, the study of the components of the different types of hand structure will lead to remedial measures which will compensate for the structural deficiencies. (The photographs throughout this book furnish abundant material for the study of the laws established by the writer.)

The characteristics of hand structure are the following:

1. The proportion of the length of the fingers (phalangeal bones) to the back of the hand (length of the metacarpal bones).
2. The proportion of the fingers to each other.
3. The proportion of the length of the individual phalangeal bones in each finger.
4. The proportion of the thickness of the fingers to their length.
5. The form of the finger joints.

1. The shorter the 2.–5. fingers compared to the back of the hand, the more applicable is the use of the extended fingers, the more favourable it is for the velocity of the fingers. The shorter the fingers, and at the same time the longer the back of the hand, the quicker and more reliable is the work of the fingers. In the case of long metacarpal bones both the interossei and lumbricales muscles (i.e. the muscles of velocity) are long.

If the fingers are long compared to the back of the hand, they are compelled to take up a strongly flexed position in order to strike the key nearer to the point where the thumb strikes. Or, if we insist on playing with fingers with an extended position, the long fingers will force the back of the hand to take up a steep position. In the first case strongly "controlled" movements will be possible which will be detrimental to the facility and ease of playing, while in the second case the finger work starts from a strongly flexed position and thus its effectiveness will be diminished.

The length of the thumb may, up to a certain extent, compensate for the unfavourable ratio between the other fingers and the back of the hand. If the thumb is long, less "pulling in" of the fingers is needed and so the back of the hand may assume a less steep position. The relative length of the thumb is one of the most important factors of good – or bad – hand structure.

2. The less the difference between the length of the fingers, the easier to equalize their striking power. The playing of trills may also be performed more easily if the fingers are of nearly equal length because one does not have to compensate the difference in length by a stronger flexing of one of the fingers.

3. The longer the first phalanx is compared to the second and the third one, the more favourable is the proportion of the phalanges. (If the first phalanx is short, one is more apt to strike from the second joint: this is a disadvantage from the mechanical point of view.) If the first phalanx is long, the finger will move easier as a unit which is — as will be seen later — an important prerequisite for the development of velocity.

4. The thickness of the fingers is also an important factor of a good hand structure. There is a wide-spread belief that thin long fingers are advantageous in piano playing since broad fingers, unable to get between the black keys, may hinder the play. But taking a look at the hand of the world-known pianists, possessing the most beautiful tone colour and also the greatest velocity, we will find that they all have, almost without exception, massive and sometimes even thickset fingers. (E.g. Anton Rubinstein or Theresa Carreño, Annie Fischer or Sviatoslav Richter.)

But it is entirely out of question to find an absolute measure for the thickness of the fingers producing a good tone colour. This is also rather a question of the proportions. If the ratio of the phalanges to each other and to the back of the hand is favourable, even thin fingers will produce the sensation of a massive tone. (See the hand of Chopin.)

5. The reliability of the work of the fingers may be influenced also by the form of the phalanges of the fingers. Weak or strongly backward-bent phalanges hinder the work of the fingers as units and thus the reliability of their movements.

On the basis of the above characteristics one might be inclined to think that only pupils whose hands conform to the ideal norms may learn piano playing. The only portion of truth in the above statement is that pupils with entirely inappropriate hand structure will have to do extraordinarily hard work to acquire a good technique.

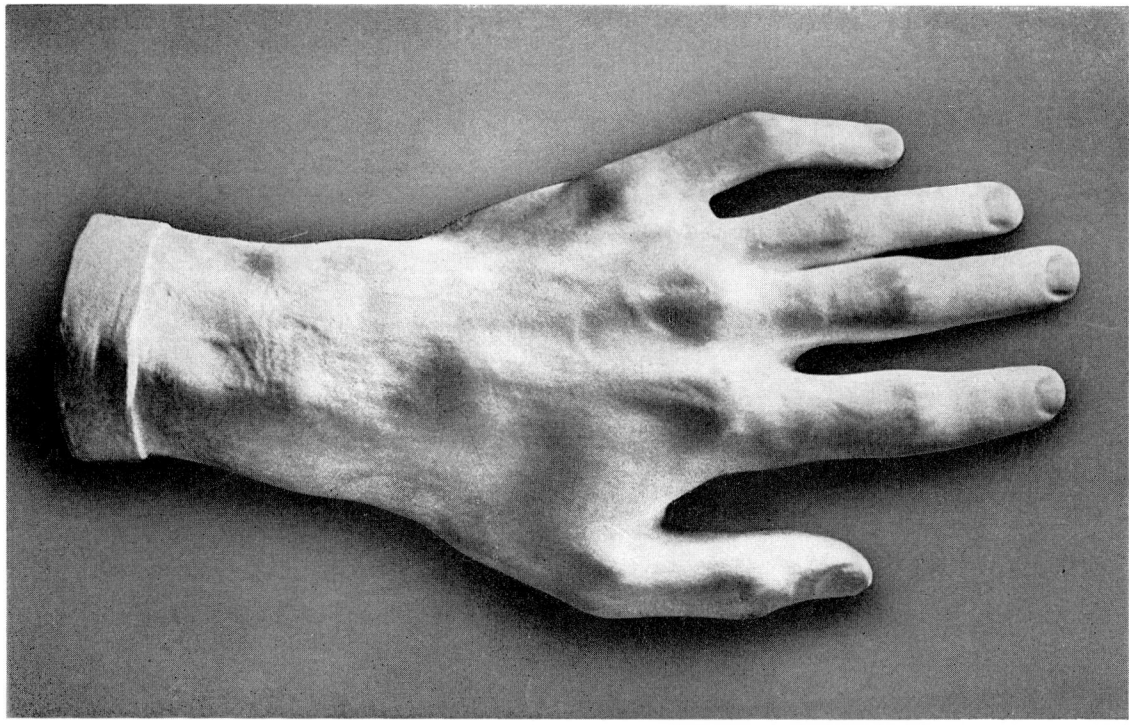

Phot. 158
PLASTER-CAST OF THE HAND OF CHOPIN

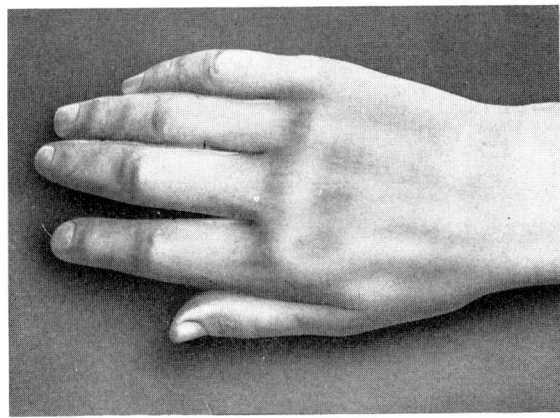
Phot. 159
THE HAND OF MENDELSSOHN (PLASTER-CAST)

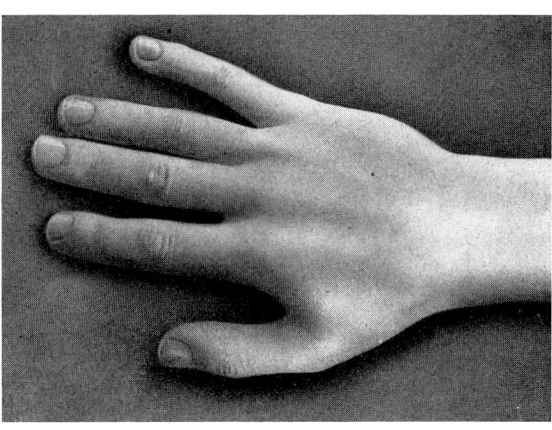
Phot. 160
THE HAND OF HANS VON BÜLOW

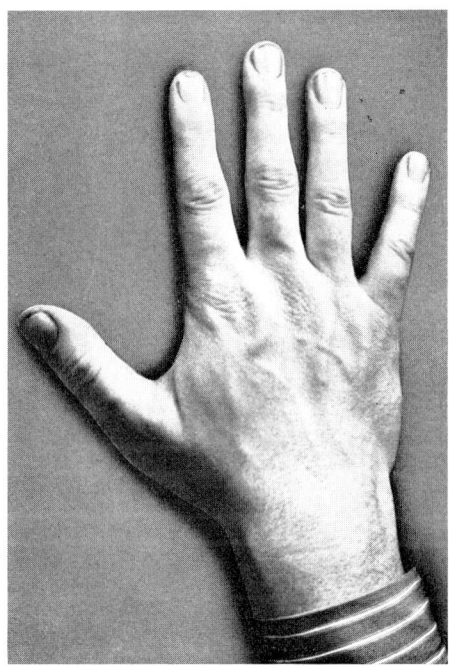
Phot. 161
THE HAND OF S. RICHTER

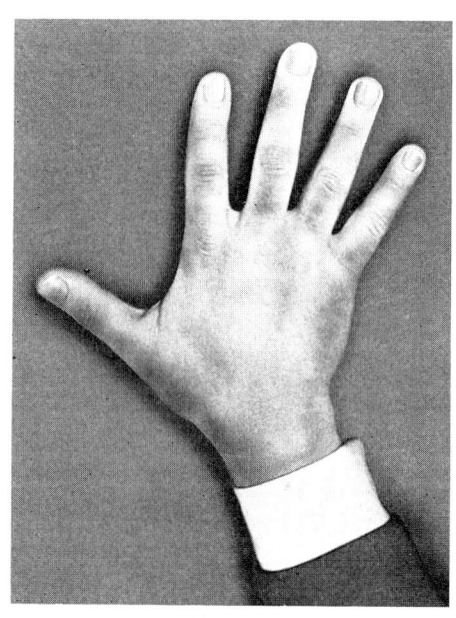
Phot. 162
THE HAND OF E. GILELS

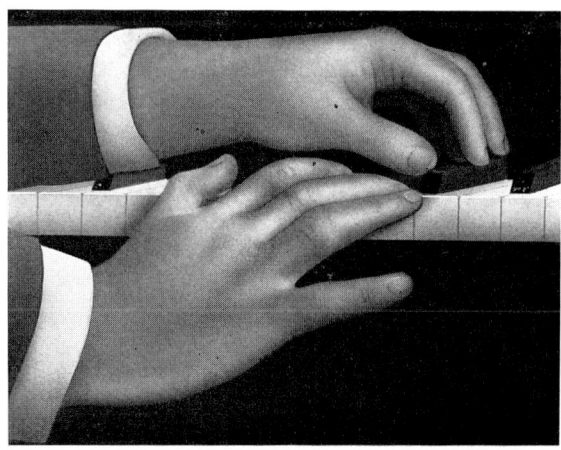
Phot. 163
THE HANDS OF E. D'ALBERT

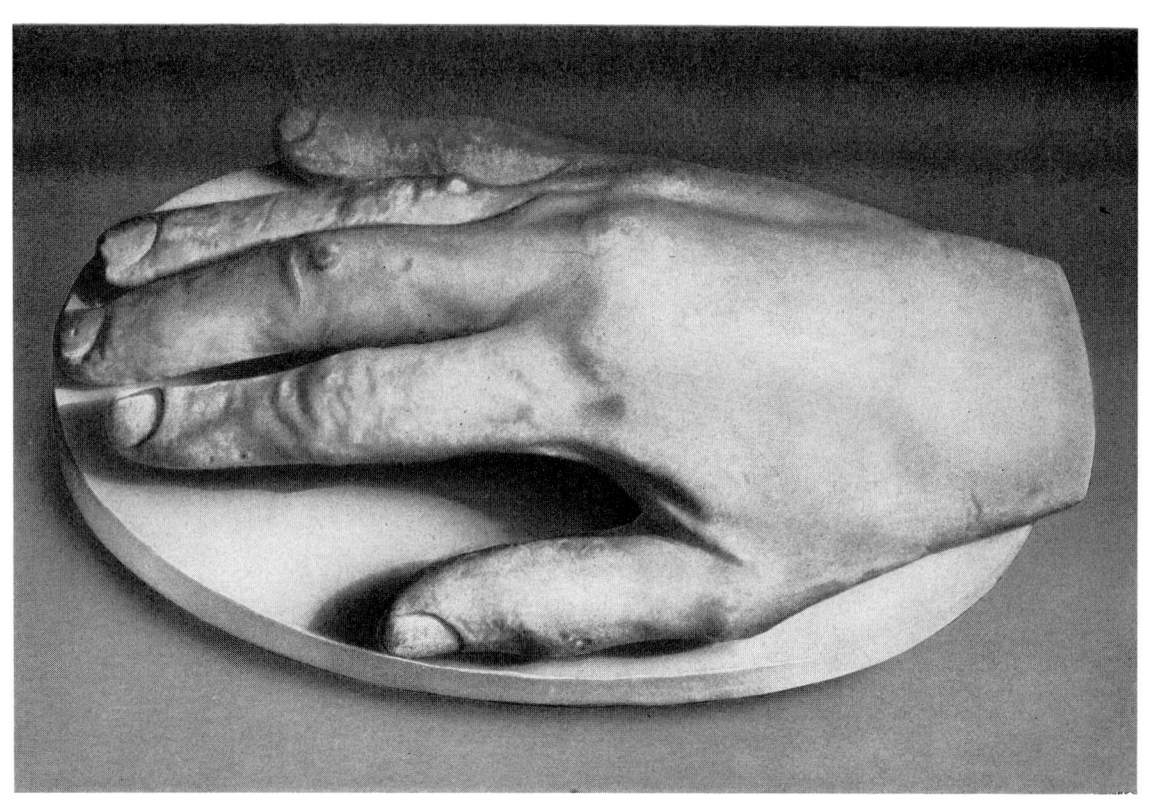

Phot. 164

PLASTER-CAST OF THE RIGHT HAND OF FRANZ LISZT

Phot. 165

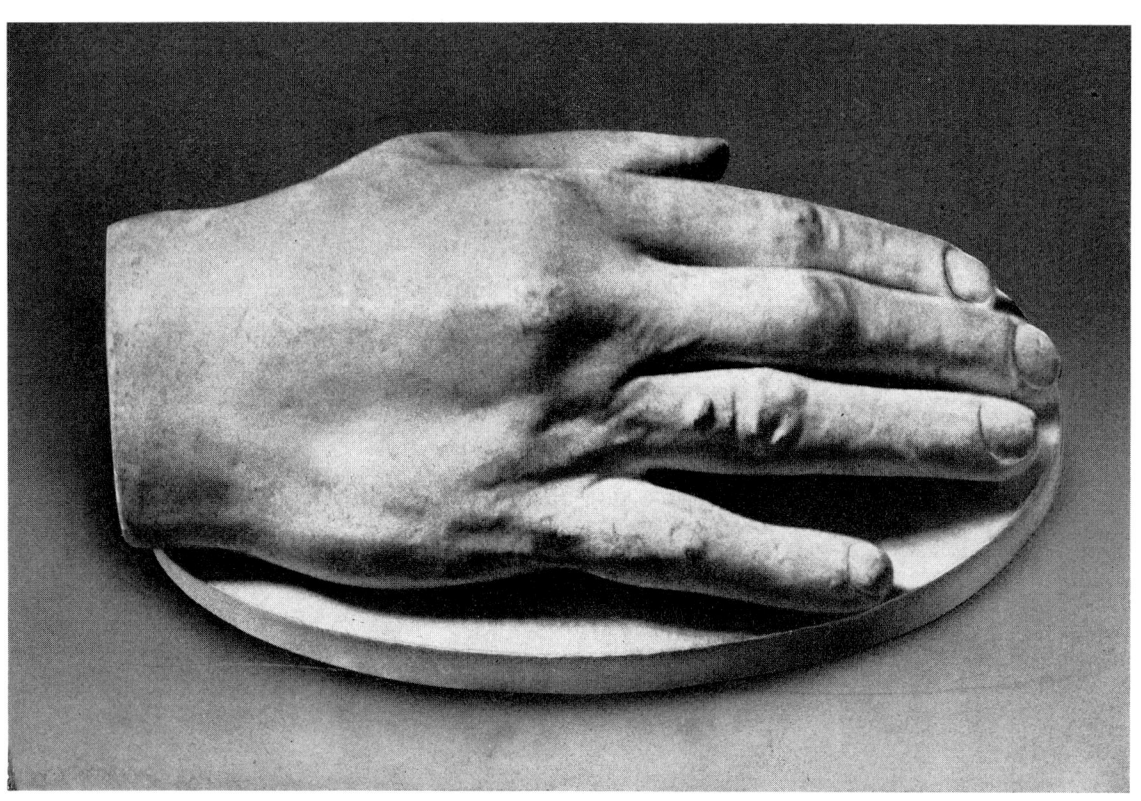

It is indispensable for the teacher to recognize the advantageous and disadvantageous qualities of the hand structure. Otherwise if the pupil solves some task with more difficulty because of some deficiency of his hand structure, the teacher might ascribe it to the lack of the pupil's musicality.

However, it would be a mistake to draw final conclusions solely on the basis of the hand structure. The quickness of the nervous system reactions, the spontaneity of the muscle work, and the ability of simultaneous application of the different movements are also to be taken into consideration. (Polyphony of the movements.) The appropriate proportion of the forearm and upper arm (short forearm compared to the upper arm) and, in general, the short arm or the extraordinarily developed muscles of the shoulder will aid in the overcoming of the difficulties.

But above all, the most important is the pupil's loving and understanding the expressive possibilities of the instrument.

The way to compensate for any deficiencies of the hand structure is to develop the respective muscle groups. The interossei and lumbricales can be compared to a motor. The larger the motor compared to the fingers, the easier the work will be executed. It follows from this that if we want to increase the velocity of the fingers we have to find some way of enlarging the motor. The back of the hand and thus the interossei and the lumbricales cannot be elongated but there is another solution: to increase the output of the motor. It is true that the muscles cannot be elongated but their thickness can be increased. This aim was served by the finger exercises of MacDowell (1861–1908) which strengthened the interossei by lateral movements of the fingers. Instead of keyboard finger exercises a simpler and more effective means is supplied for us by gymnastic exercises. (See: gymnastic exercises 32, 33, 41, 42, 46, 47.) But it is in vain to have a motor of a greater output if the fingers are unable to transfer the energy, supplied by the motor to the keys. The unfavourable proportion of the length of the phalanges, the excessively thin fingers and the fragile joints will endanger the sureness of the finger movements and the use of each finger as a unit.

There is a common remedy for all of them. In order to increase the stability of the fingers the flexor and extensor muscles and the muscles of the hand should be strengthened (see: gymnastic exercises 26, 27, 28, 48). In addition to this, gymnastic exercises are also needed to prepare the fingers to work as a unit, because fingers with an unfavourable structure acquire many faulty innervations in their activities of everyday life. (See: gymnastic exercises 34, 35, 36, 37, 38, 39.)

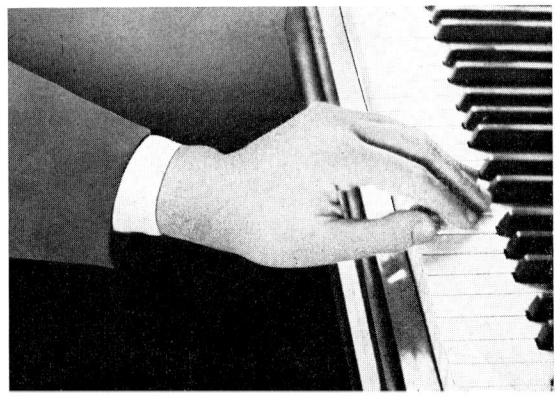

Phot. 166

A short thumb forces the back of the hand into a steep position. Velocity, power, and dynamic sureness of the finger-stroke will be impaired on account of the knuckles pressed upwards

Phot. 167

A player with short thumb can play the white keys only in bent position. This is possible only with strongly controlled movements

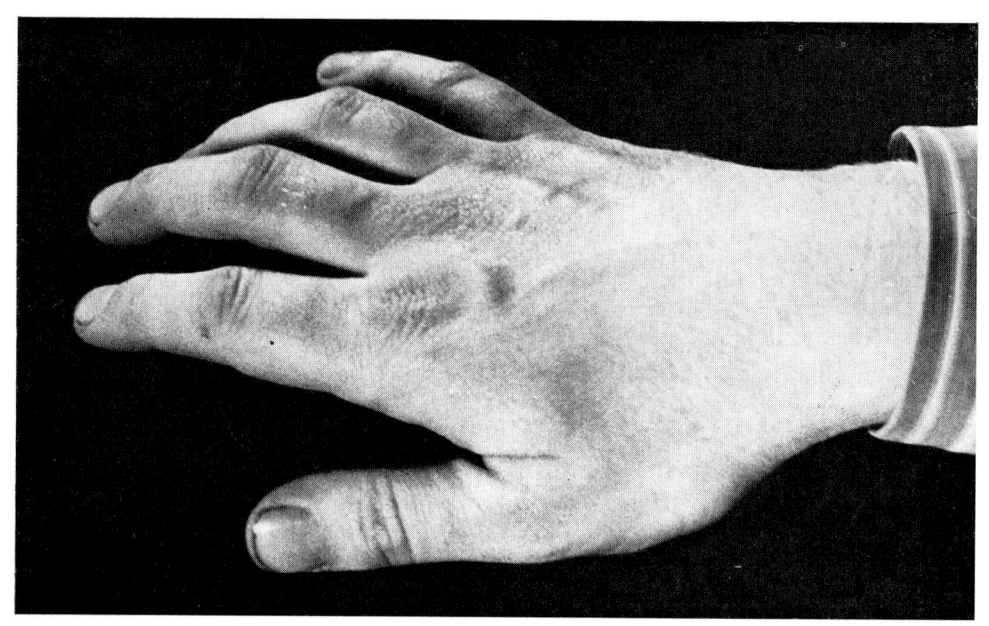

Phot. 168
THE HAND OF SVIATOSLAV RICHTER

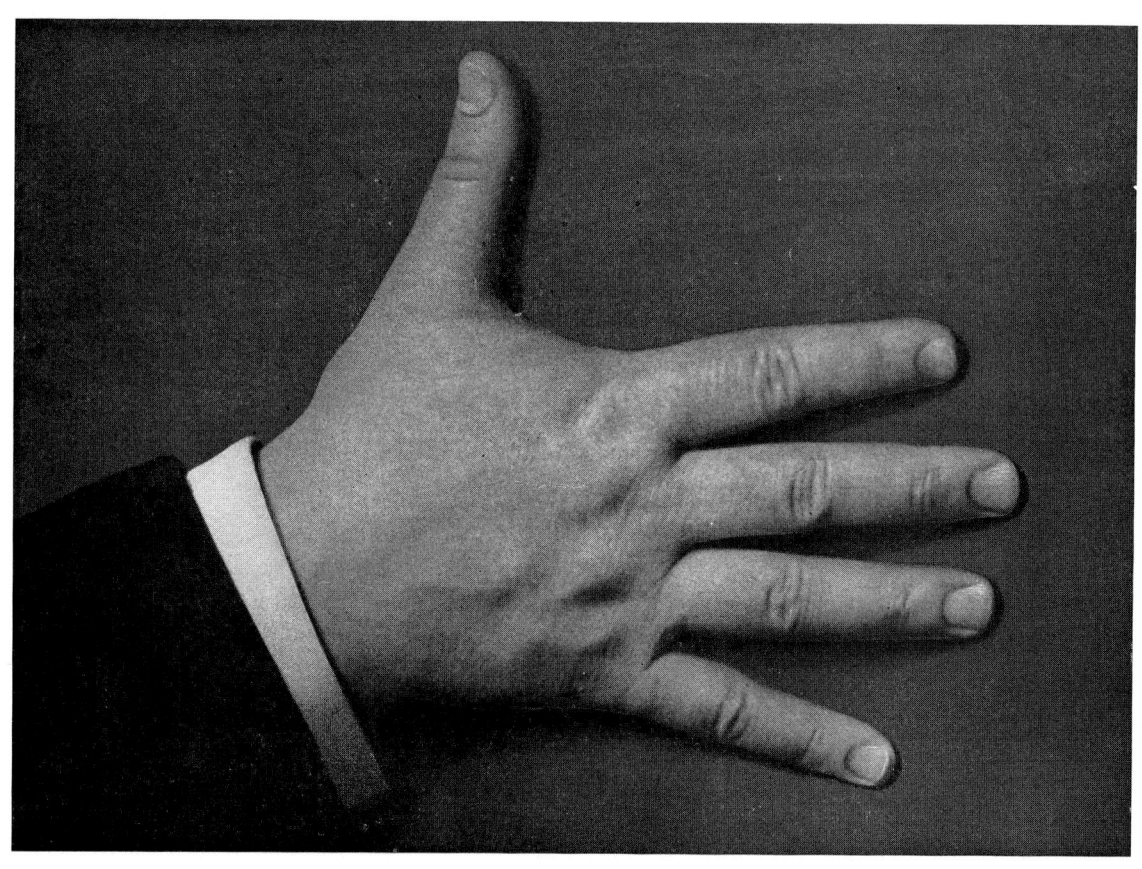

Phot. 169
THE HAND OF JAKOV ZAK

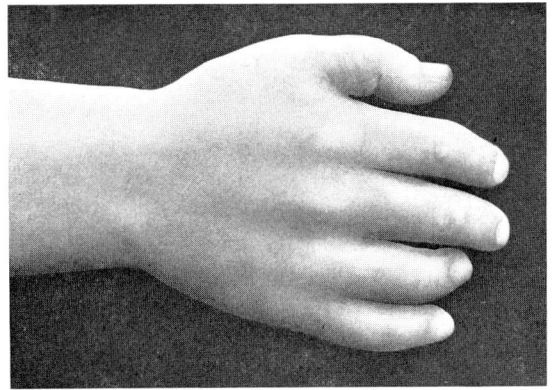 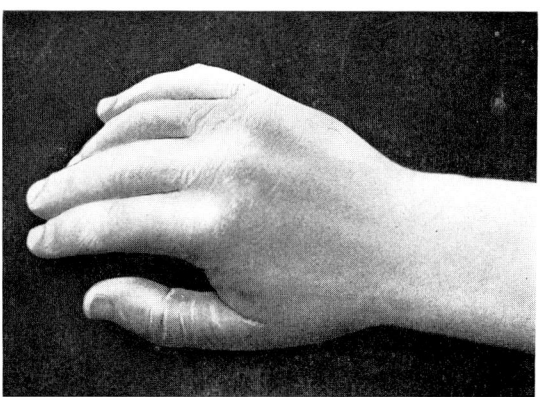

Phot. 170 Phot. 171
PLASTER-CAST OF ANTON RUBINSTEIN'S RIGHT HAND

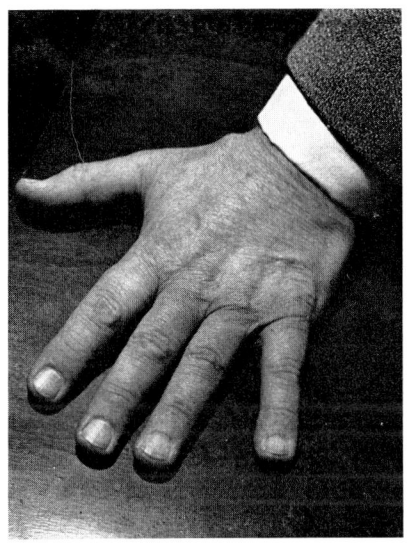 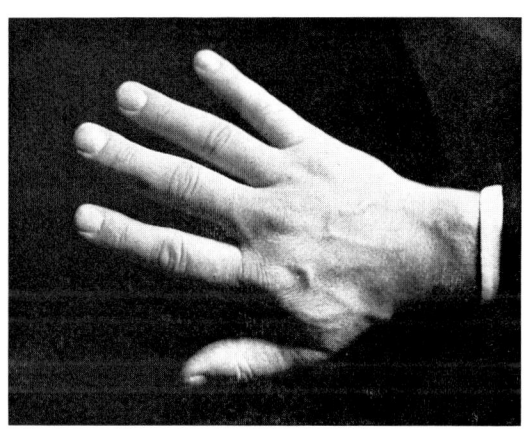

Phot. 172 Phot. 173
THE HAND OF CARLO ZECCHI THE HAND OF RUDOLF KERER

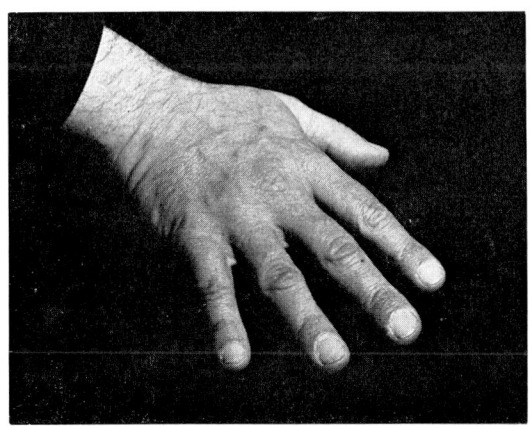 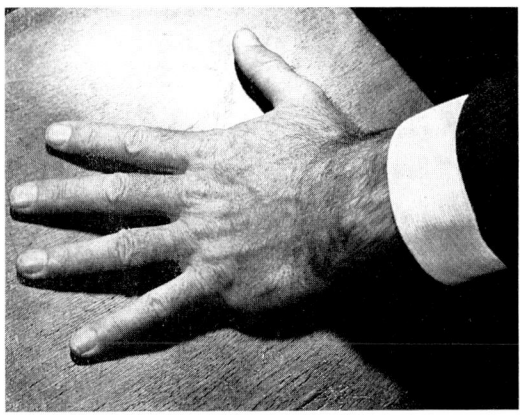

Phot. 174 Phot. 175
THE HAND OF LEV OBORIN THE HAND OF GYÖRGY SÁNDOR

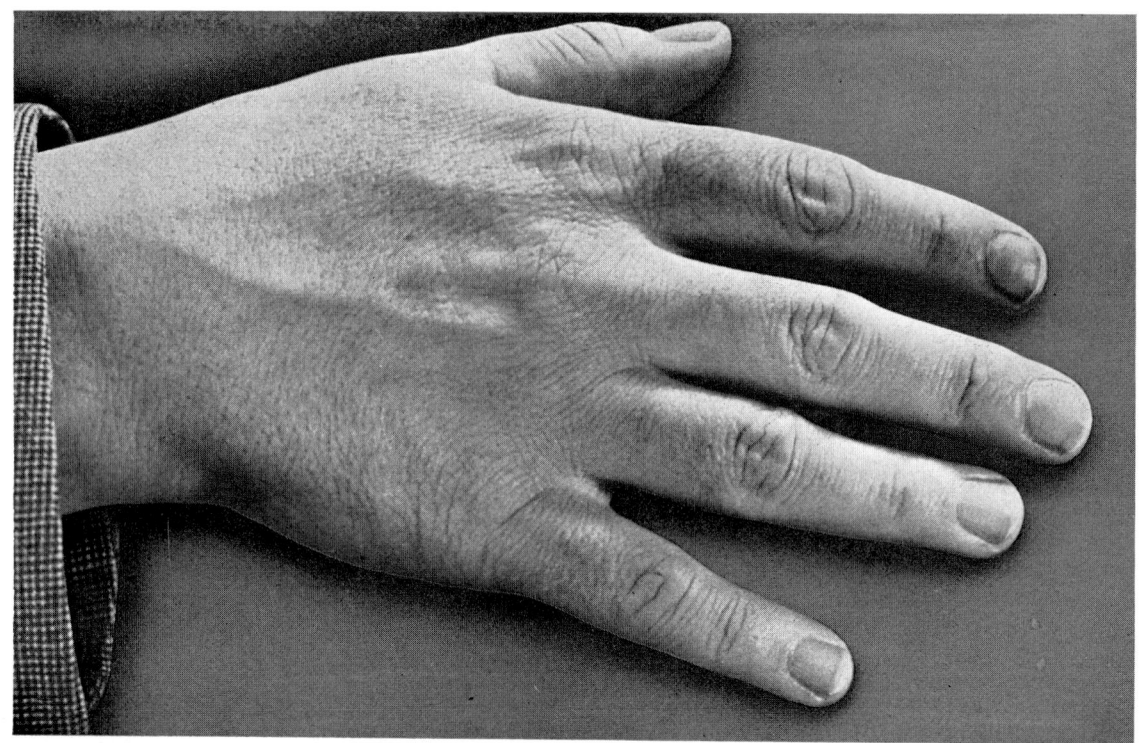

Phot. 176
THE HAND OF ISTVÁN ANTAL

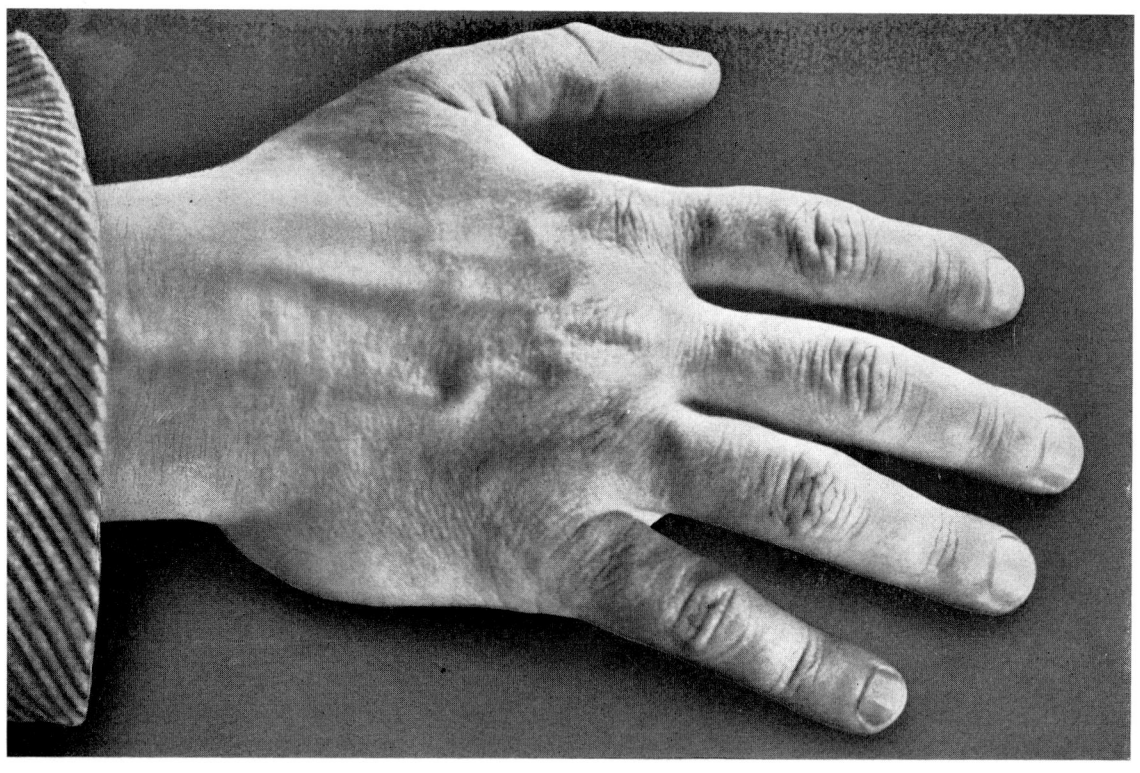

Phot. 177
THE HAND OF IMRE UNGÁR

FORM OF THE HAND

In the foregoing chapter mention was made of the medium position being determined by the muscle tone. The form of the fingers and mainly of the hand in their resting, i.e. medium positions, is determined by the tone of the muscles. Thus the form of the hand depends not only upon the structure of the hand but also upon the development of the respective muscle groups. If the flexors are stronger than the extensors, the hand will assume in the resting position a slightly bent posture, and if they are weaker, the posture will be a more stretched one because the extensors will draw the fingers outwards.

Since the form of the hand is determined by the proportion of the development of the muscles, it may prove wrong and even dangerous to teach a particular finger position in accordance with some previously determined pattern by setting the hands in a mechanical way. Alteration in the form of the hand may be attained only through changing the equilibrium of the muscles. This is a problem of education and practice.

In the case of a firm octave touch, e.g., the thumb will be bent in the first and second joint while it is strained outwards at the carpo-metacarpal joint. Attempts are frequently made to assume this octave position by means of practising a passive, adjusting, setting of the thumb. Actually, the thumb will sooner or later get used to the position acquired in this passive way but precisely on account of its passivity it will bring about the overburdening of the first joint which may easily result in disability. Due to frequently repeated passive adjusting it may happen that the thumb will bend (adduct) helplessly inwards when striking the key.

The rigid setting of the thumb in a constant form would be also wrong from another point of view. The position of the thumb has to vary also in accordance with the distance of the span. Thus the setting of the thumb required at a given moment is always determined jointly by the span and the balance of the muscles.

Thus if we want to alter the form of adjusting the thumb, the equilibrium of the muscles has to be altered. Through the active use of the thumb, the sensation of its constant activity will give work to the flexors and it will adduct the thumb more inwards. The frequent playing of octaves strengthens the opponent muscles and this will also aid in adducting the thumb. All of this must be completed by appropriate gymnastic exercises in order to make the muscles – to be strengthened – work in their full length. (See: gymnastic exercises 37, 38, 39, 48, 55.)

The form of the fingers and thus of the whole hand changes according to the equilibrium of the muscles. However, this relation cannot be reversed. The mechanical setting of the hand or the unnatural forcing of a hand-form may cause a change in the equilibrium of the muscles only by means of weakening or even temporary discontinuance of the work of certain muscle groups, which will result in diminishing the total output. Thus the "secret" of piano playing must not be sought in various hand-forms which have been presumed to be infallible such as the enforced raising of the knuckles to the same height, the rigidly erect little finger or the "apple" or "grape" position, etc.

As seen above, the position of the thumb varies according to the span, and the flexion or extension positions of the fingers will vary still more depending upon whether we play on black or white keys and in what succession these keys follow each other.

Piano playing cannot be considered to be inextricably linked to any constant hand position, constant hand-form and so even in the beginning of teaching piano playing one must not be bound to a *certain* hand-form. This means not only a waste of time but it may impede free natural playing.

The most active use of the fingers and playing with the finger-ends must be made the pupil's aim rather than the constant form and/or position of the hand. The active work of the fingers will always create the most expedient hand-forms. The teacher's explanations should help the pupil to find the natural movements and consequently the most suitable momentary hand position. The pupil will always find himself faced with new tasks in connection with every melodic passage. These tasks cannot be solved by a specific hard-and-fast formula. The position of the hand may differ even in the same key-position, depending on variations in the structure of the hand of different pianists.

Since in playing with extended fingers one can more easily attain the sensation of a perfect "amalgamation" of his fingers with the keys, the playing with extended fingers is always more expedient than playing with flexed fingers. One has to play always with "entirely" extended fingers as far as the given possibilities permit it. However, the possibility of playing with extended fingers changes with every musical composition, with every bar and with every pianist. So e.g., if many white keys follow one another, the thumb will not even get to the keys on account of the fully extended fingers. In such cases the pianist is compelled to flex his fingers. If his fingers are long, he has to flex them more strongly than those with short ones. On the other hand, a pianist with long thumbs is able to play with extended fingers in cases when that would be entirely impossible for any other pianist.

When playing scales in chromatic thirds the pianist with long fingers and short thumb will be forced – when striking with the first and third fingers – to flex the third finger strongly. However, this strong flexing is in this special case not harmful because it is necessary. If, on the other hand, the flexion goes beyond the absolutely necessary extent, it will make the fingers passive and will cause a whole series of faulty innervations.

Thus, playing with extended fingers "as far as the given possibilities permit it" may sometimes mean playing with very strongly flexed fingers. But this will not greatly hinder good playing, the "amalgamation with the keys", provided that the bent position of the fingers is *motivated* by something. Only detrimental is a hand position fixed independently from the musical conception, i.e. if flexed fingers are used when the tone colour requires playing with extended fingers. The most frequent fault is the excessive flexing of the third (and the longest) finger. Work should not be spared in correcting this fault because its elimination will result not only in a sudden improvement of the velocity but also in a freedom of expression and an increase in the tone volume.

Phot. 178
JAN EKIER

The position of the fingers during playing is influenced by the following factors:

1. The apportioning of the noise-effects (The different flexions of the fingers will emphasize the corresponding noise-effects.)
2. Tonality (Order of succession of the keys.)
3. Dynamic grade (Flexed fingers when playing louder.)
4. Tempo of the play (Flexed fingers when playing slower.)

These factors will very often operate contrarily to each other. In a slow scale, e.g., more flexed fingers are needed than with the same scale played in a fast tempo. If, on the other hand, we want to play the same slow scale with softer tone colour, a certain extending of the fingers will prove indispensable.

Two general rules can now be stated:

The flexed position is more favourable to the sharp contours because comparatively great muscle activity is required for the execution of small movements. (When striking with flexed fingers the first phalanx must be in a parallel position with the escapement level.)

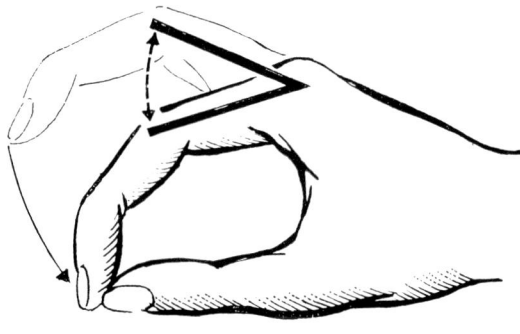

Fig. 42

In playing with extended fingers – when the fingers may be regarded as elongations of the keys – it is easier to attain soft tone effects.

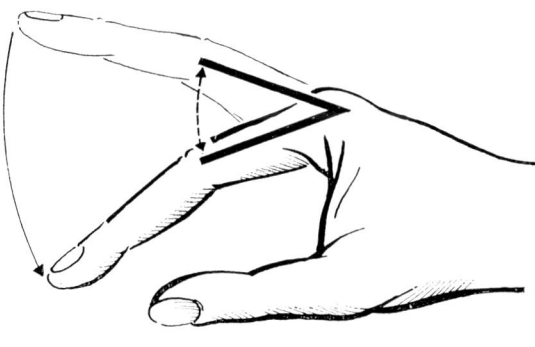

Fig. 43

At the same time the extended position is also of advantage from the point of view of both velocity and tone volume because in this position small movements of the muscles bring about large movements of the finger-ends and the activity of the muscles will become less tiring.

THE FUNDAMENTAL PLAYING FORMS AND THEIR VARIANTS

Piano technique is based on the fundamental playing forms, i.e. scales, octaves, chords, trills, etc. These forms represent general types valid for the playing of every pianist.

It may, for instance, be stated that the main constituents of scale playing are the finger-strokes and the synthesizing movements of the arm. We are able to define the circumstances under which the fingers and the arm will execute their work best. The playing form established in this way is valid in scale playing without exception.

Since the fundamental playing form contains only general features, it cannot become a medium of individual musical expression.

Musical expression requires a transforming of the playing form – depending on the style of the composition and the individual content. This transformed playing form – called playing variant in the course of what follows – has no general validity. The movements applied in the individual variant differ from pianist to pianist, because the musical concepts of each artist – giving rise to and defining these movements – are also different.

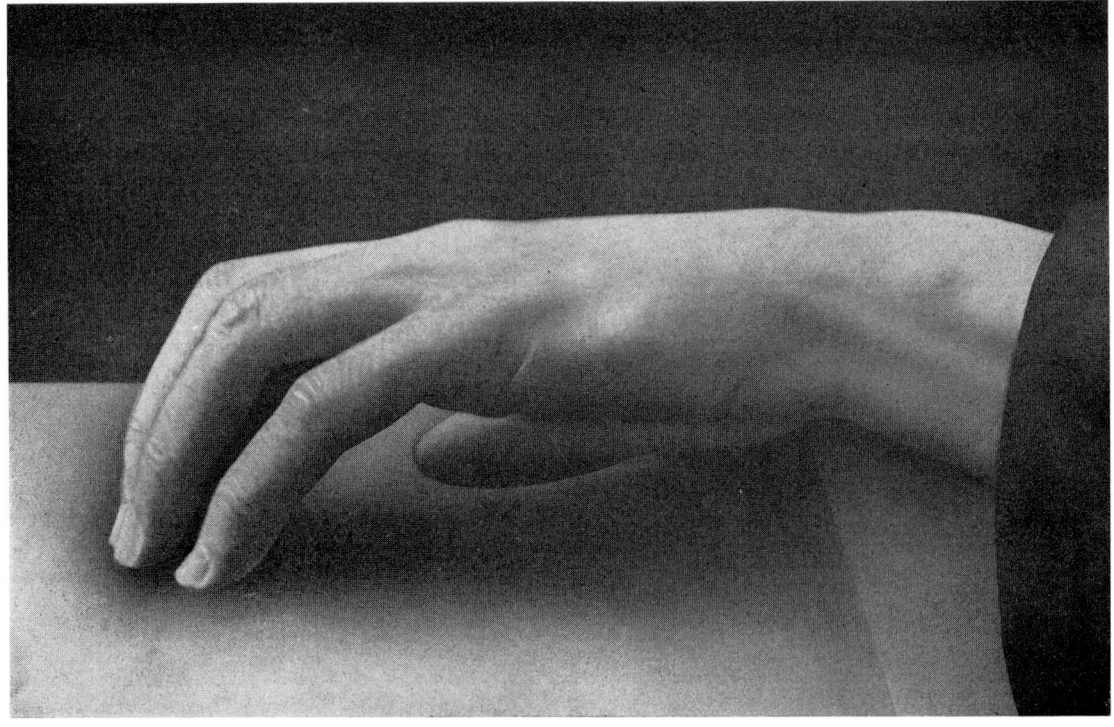

Phot. 179

THE HAND OF EMIL SAUER

Thus in some variants of scale playing, divergences may occur in the proportion of the finger work and the synthesizing movement of the arm. The variant will differ, depending on the amount of adapting movements employed by the pianist, on the extent to which the finger work needs to be supplemented by rotation or by active swinging movements, and on how much noise-effect is applied.

Here, too, certain types of movements will develop, because the performer will more often apply those movements which give reality to his concept, and he will fix these by means of repetition. However, as the variants are closely connected with the music, the proportion of the components of movements, too, will vary in accordance with the musical concept. The playing of the same motif will require different nuances – and thus different variants of movements – when playing the exposition of a sonata or the recapitulation, and they will be still different if the same motif occurs in the development.

Thus any attempt to define a large number of variants (e.g. 24 kinds of octave-touch) would impede the musical concept. To force the movements into patterns would also paralyze the imagination.

Some methods recommend that downward progressing sequences of seconds be executed by wrist motion, i.e. by sounding one tone through lowering, the other through raising the wrist. This is regarded as the only solution, but leaves out of consideration the fact that different dynamic and rhythmic structures require different solutions, e.g. greater or lesser wrist or arm activity or more vigorous work of the fingers.

The most important playing forms must be practised systematically in cyclical form (i.e. they should be repeated in equal phase as, e.g., in the scales).

While practising the variants requires special artistic work, the cyclical practising of the playing forms serve to improve the physical condition. (A similar role is played by sports in the work of a dancer.) Therefore, when practising octave scales the use of passive wrist is the right one because this is most frequently needed in musical pieces and not the active or even "pinched" wrist.

To practise the variants independently from the music – in the form of finger exercises or even études – is inexpedient. The only proper way of practising the variants is to play pieces of different styles and to work out technically each slightest detail with the utmost care. By playing pieces of various styles, we shall develop our capacity to create variants and our playing will thereby gain in colour and expressive force. (From the point of view of technique, too, it is harmful for somebody to specialize as a "Chopin player" or "Liszt player", etc.)

Phot. 180
JAKOV ZAK

THE TECHNIQUE OF OCTAVES AND CHORDS

THE USE OF THE HAND AS A UNIT

The forms of the technique of chords and octaves comprise also the playing forms in which the active finger stroke plays no role and the hand works always as a unit. Chopin, e.g., is so consistent in this respect that he includes the scales in thirds (played with the same fingers) with the octave technique (because the hand works as a unit), and the octaves played *legato* and with changing fingers to the double-grips.[1]

The use of the hand as a unit is also facilitated by the anatomical construction of our hands, since fingers 2–5 have three common muscle bellies (the finger extensor, the superficial and the deep finger flexors). Therefore it is relatively easy to make these fingers execute the task as a unit,

Phot. 181
HANDS OF VLADIMIR HOROWITZ

(e.g., the firmness, the "harnessing" of the hand), because this may be carried out on a uniform command. However, if we desire only the firmness of the first and fifth fingers, a more complex set of commands is needed: one command that tautens the first and fifth fingers and in this way "harnesses" their joints, and another command which inhibits the execution of that part of the previous command which concerns the second, third and fourth fingers (because the command was issued towards all of the five fingers). The two opposing commands will obviously be detrimental to each other, i.e., if fingers 2, 3 and 4 are held in a relaxed state, fingers 1 and 5 cannot be firmly fixed enough. (Although the first finger has no common muscle belly it has a common nerve supply with the other fingers.)

Using the hand as a unit requires in every case a certain "held", fixed, rigid position of the fingers. This is achieved by the simultaneous contraction of the extensors and flexors and the interossei and the lumbricales. (The muscles hold the fingers like a pole tethered with ropes.)

One of the most effective ways of making the hand firm is for the little finger and the thumb to tauten each other mutually, i.e. in this way both fingers are strongly drawn towards each other by the opponent muscles. The smaller the span required, the more powerfully the opponent muscles must act. (The optimal effectiveness will be attained, here too, in the medium position.)

---

[1] Commentaries to the études composed for the *Méthode des méthodes* of Fétis and Moscheles.

Acquisition of the ability to tauten the fingers in octave playing will be facilitated by practising smaller intervals, i.e. repeated sixths and scales in sixths. The preparation is bound to take a long time, especially when the pianist's hand is unable to span an octave without effort. (Effortless spanning of the octave is attained only by pianists who are able to play tenths when their hand is extended to the maximum.)

If a firm grip has already become automatized in a smaller tone interval e.g., on sixths (or with pianists with very small hands: on fifths), we may gradually extend it. A large hand is not an absolute and indispensable prerequisite for good octave technique but pianists with small hands need more thorough and longer preparation.

The force needed to keep the fingers taut changes according to the force of the rebound of the keys. Thus, piano requires less muscle effort for this purpose than forte, and in slow tempo less effort is needed than in fast tempo. The least amount of muscular effort to keep the fingers fixed is required in the direct swing-strokes, because here the rebound is absorbed wholly by the shoulders (and will not in the least affect the finger-ends).

Phot. 182
ARTUR RUBINSTEIN

Excessively intensive clenching may be detrimental to the accuracy of the swing-stroke because it weakens our sensation of the key as an elongation of the fingers.

The tautening of the hand must not be an aim in itself. One must not concentrate on the fingers' tautening each other but rather their grasping the keys jointly. This is facilitated by imagining the tautening of the fingers in an elongated form (imagine having fingers of 50 cm!).

Care must be taken also to pronate the hands only to the least, i.e. absolutely required, extent. The maximum velocity and sureness of the forearm is attained in the medium position. Therefore the little finger has to strike – as far as possible – always with its side in chord and octave playing.

The excessive tightening of the fingers may result in cramping or rigidity; thus the fixing of the hand must never be more than absolutely necessary.

The fixing of the hand can be attained in two ways. The using of the common extensors and flexors to this end has the disadvantage that – since their tendons lie across the wrist – the latter, too, will become fixed. Thus the more strained the muscles the more difficult the motion of the wrist will be. If we want to use the wrist even when tautening the hand, the fixing of the fingers should be carried out mainly with the interossei and lumbricales. However, since in order to make these muscles fix the hand a considerable contraction of the muscles is needed, the fingers must be brought into a stretched position. By stretching the third phalanx the interossei and lumbricales will obtain enough strength and so only a minimal use of the long extensor and flexor will be necessary in order to fix the fingers.

It can be stated therefore, that in the playing of octaves the slightly stretched position of the fingers is the most expedient because the required firmness of the hand (without straining the wrist) can be attained only in this way.[2]

Thus, in octave playing each of the fingers has an equally important role despite the fact that, as a rule, only the two extreme fingers touch the keys. And what is more: since the third finger is the longest one, our attention must be concentrated on that one. By concentrating on the third finger one can most easily attain the moving of the whole hand as a unit.

In chord playing all five fingers must be kept equally taut, both as regards the fingers held aloft and those which — in their role of elongations of the arm — strike the keys.

THE DYNAMIC SHAPING OF THE CHORDS

The firmness of the hand is a prerequisite of the dynamic shaping of the chords, too. If the fingers keep the chord grip we will be able to attain a large volume by a comparatively small amount of energy, and at the same time we may reproduce even the most delicate dynamic nuances. If, on the contrary, the fingers "hang loosely", the technique of octaves and chords will not be reliable dynamically either, because it will be uncertain how much of the force of the arm will be transmitted to the keys. Our efforts to make up the loss of force at the fingers cause jerky and clumsy playing.

Only the clinched position enables us to regulate precisely the relative volume of the individual chord tones.

Within a single chord a different volume of the individual tones is obtained partly by a corresponding shifting of the centre of gravity (with the aid of rotation) and partly by adjusting the fingers to different stroke heights. The finger held somewhat lower than the others will swing the key with a larger force. (The danger involved in holding the fingers at different levels and thereby disturbing the simultaneous sounding of the chords, is only apparent. The time-delay is almost imperceptibly small.)

Phot. 183

---

[2] When playing octaves some players will slightly bend their second and possibly even their third fingers in order to increase the firmness of the whole hand. Let us check the correctness of this solution by gymnastics.

Move your wrist, first actively, then passively, with extended fingers and, after that, try the same movements with the second finger bent. You will distinctly feel that the motion becomes stiffer and more strained as a consequence of the bending.

Why is it then that some excellent performers, nevertheless, bend their second finger in playing octaves?

Pianists who do not make their whole hand taut will notice that octaves sound better when they are playing on black keys. (Bent position.) With some fingers bent, they feel their hand is firmer and so the sensation of firmness becomes automatically linked with the bent position. This, however, forms an exception to the rule and the majority of pianists find that the correct functional solution is to play the octaves with slightly stretched fingers.

When using many black keys, the fingers have to be slightly bent, or else the hand will not have enough room – at least until Prof. Dr. Otto Goldhammer's (Leipzig) invention (a keyboard with longer keys) will have gained ground. The short pianoforte keys have resulted historically from the use of instruments with more than one keyboard. Long keys oblige the hand to cover too great a distance when changing from one keyboard to another, as is the case to this day with the organ. However, insistence on the use of short keys in the case of the piano causes unnecessary self-torture.

Dr. Goldhammer applies white keys with a forepart of 60 to 70 mm and black keys of 100 to 110 mm. Moreover, he gives up the oblique widening of the black keys so that the narrow part of the white keys attains a width of 18 mm. (This narrow part is uniformly wide and does not change as in the case of the old keyboards.) The abandonment of the obliquely shaped keys enables the fingers to operate comfortably even between the black keys. (See p. 169.)

Phot. 184

The dynamic shaping of chords is an important means of expression. With its aid the sounding of the chords not only becomes more beautiful but will also be clearer and more intelligible from the musical point of view. In the six-four chord the tonic, e.g., should in most cases be struck somewhat more strongly than the bass (the dominant) tone. In dominant seventh chords the seventh, and in minor chords the third, must be played more softly. In order to underline the musical continuity, we accentuate every characteristic leading tone progression and every alteration. The tone volume is modified also by a more vigorous sounding of the tone which forms a part of the melody, a particularly difficult task when the tone carrying the melody appears in the middle of the chord. A similar modification is required in the case of the higher chord tones, which are naturally weaker than the lower ones; the difference must be compensated by a more powerful touch.

Such complex work cannot be carried out consciously in all its phases. The movement to be realized must become automatically linked with our musical conception. The simpler the movement, the easier it is to associate it with the musical idea. This is why it is of such importance that our hand and finger should reliably transmit the movement of the arm.

If the fingers do not "give" and if we are able to direct the action of all joints by a simple act of our will, the corresponding movements will very soon become automatic. It suffices to imagine the tones and the functions of a chord: our hands will instantly assume the corresponding shape and our fingers will take up that position which enables them to apportion the tone volume correctly.

If, on the other hand, the work of the fingers is inaccurate and inexpedient, it will be very difficult to associate the appropriate movements with the musical concept. In each case, we will have to search again and again for the position in which – according to the momentary situation of the fingers – we can strike the chord. If, instead, we maintain the chord position, the arm action will easily and rapidly become automatized as regards the required positions and distances.[3]

The constant clenching of the hand in chord position and, within it, the constant change in the position of the fingers, require maximum finger activity. Although the fingers, in octave and chord technique, function as elongations of the arm – and their independent motion consists only in adjusting themselves to the respective key-positions – we, nevertheless, always have to strike with the finger-ends; we must always "feel" the finger-ends.

THE ROLE OF THE FOREARM IN THE OCTAVE TECHNIQUE

When dealing with the role of the individual joints it has been stated that the strokes of the arm are the fastest when executed from the elbows and are the most exact and delicately shaped when executed from the shoulders. In the octave and chord technique active swing-strokes can be executed both from the shoulder and from the elbow but the independent active role of the forearm will come into prominence only with the increase of the tempo. As to the wrist, we have seen that it is not very suitable for fast movements because the execution of them is hindered by the complex joint structure and small muscle amount of the wrist. (See p. 126.) Therefore the wrist motion is almost never used for the execution of independent active swing-strokes, it is applied only for com-

---

[3] The unchanged chord position is very useful also in sight-reading. One of the greatest difficulties of sight-reading will be overcome if we are not compelled to adjust the fingers one by one to the touch of a chord consisting of three or four tones; instead, the sight of the notes will at once induce the fingers to assume the correct position.

plementing (actively or passively) the active swing-strokes of the upper arm or forearm. (It has to be repeatedly emphasized that the synthesizing work of the upper arm is always indispensable. The pianist must always have the feeling that the stroke was started from the shoulders.)

The different playing variants of octaves and chords develop from the differently proportioned movements of the shoulder, elbow and wrist. Different styles and musical conceptions and even different tempi call for different playing variants.

In order to execute the variants, differently proportioned work of the shoulder, elbow and wrist is needed – depending on the physical structure and the muscles of the pianist. It is absolutely impossible to state generally valid norms of the octave technique for the individual variants. Thus it is wrong to split up the octave technique according to the individual variants, so e.g. to divide the octave into 20 or 24 dynamic or tone-colour variants. It would be equally wrong to make a distinction in the octaves on the basis of functioning by separating them into octaves carried out by the upper arm, forearm or wrist.

It is much more important to find the laws according to which the participation of the individual joints increases or decreases in the octave technique. Let us examine the possibilities of the increased participation of the joints in the octave technique from the point of view of the tempo, dynamics and tone colouring.

In the individual swing-strokes the delicate regulation of the tone volume is almost impossible when playing from the forearm. In such cases the possibilities for the dynamic shaping are ensured only by the functioning of the elastic support, the weight completion. Hence it follows that, whenever possible, upper-arm swing-strokes must be applied and the octaves must be played from the entire arm. This is of special importance in slow tempi where in the control of the individual swing-stroke or in the apportioning of the noise-effects even the slightest faults will become conspicuous.

However, the sounding of the octaves by swing-strokes of the upper arm will prove impossible even in medium tempo. Thus with the increasing of the tempo the forearm will come gradually into the foreground.

When analysing the technique of octaves from the point of view of the requirements of velocity we may state that the most economical movement, i.e. the fastest tempo (the marginal case of velocity) can be best attained if the forearm and the hand (up to the finger-tips) function as a unit and so the quick movements of the elbow joint can be transmitted through the finger-ends to the keys without any loss. Thus in order to attain maximum tempo in playing octaves we can not employ wrist movements, not only for the reason that the motion of the wrist is clumsy and requires more time than the arm movement, but also because by using the wrist we would execute a complex motion involving in itself a certain retardation.

In the fastest tempo the forearm carries out very small swing-strokes because its mass is a considerable one and the required kinetic energy can be attained by a relatively small velocity, i.e. by small movements. (See p. 27.) However, when slowing down the tempo we are forced to enlarge the swing-strokes of the arm in order to conserve the continuity of the motion.

As a consequence it follows that when slowing down the tempo the strokes should be carried out from proportionately increasing heights. Thus by raising the arm to greater heights the pianist would carry out superfluous work and, moreover, the strokes, started from a higher position in order to produce the sound, would involve more noise-effect. If, in order to avoid this, the swinging motion were stopped by the pianist between the individual strokes, a jerky and dynamically uncontrollable playing would result.

COMPLEMENTARY WRIST MOTION

The requirement to conserve the continuous motion of the forearm and simultaneously avoid excessive motion (and thus the superfluous noises) of the arm seems to be an insoluble antagonism.

The ideal sounding would be obtained, in octaves, too, if our arm functioned as an elongation of the key, by executing direct swing-strokes. This is, for the most part, impossible because the forearm (which we had to employ already with relatively minimal tempo in order to execute the active swing-strokes) functions as a one-armed lever with the elbow as its axis. The solution is to be found in applying the wrist. The active or passive use of the wrist, carried out simultaneously with the forearm movements, enables us to keep the fingers – even in slow tempo when the arm is elevated to a considerable height – quite close to the keys.

How can it be achieved that the fingers do not withdraw too much from the keyboard (in order not to obtain more noise), but the movements of the arm be just the same continuous? Since the development of modern octave technique – and in order to attain the above aim – the work of the arm and the hand has been coordinated in the following way: the hand passively takes over the movement of the arm, i.e. it always lags behind the motion of the arm. This movement is similar to that of the flail used in the threshing in olden times.

By the aid of the movements of the hand we may – even in the technique of octaves – have almost the sensation of executing direct swing-strokes and thus, when playing chords and octaves, *we feel as if we were shaking the piano*. (Attention! This is not identical with the shaking of our own hand: the maximal motion is to be imagined to take place in the hammer and not in our hands.)

When employing the wrist motion special care must be taken that the hand should not lose the proper chord-shape and the finger-ends should strike with the same active sensation as if they were moving. This is so much more difficult to execute because the hand receives the arm's energy passively and this may lead to a passivity of the fingers. In such cases the force received from the arm is to be transmitted to the keys and this requires an activity – or putting it more correctly – an increased elasticity of the fingers.

If 10 to 15 persons have to move a large weight but two of them have direct access to the object, these two persons have to take over the force of the remainder in order to be able to carry out the work. This is realizable, however, only if they themselves take an active part of the work, otherwise they may get hurt by the forces acting upon them from two directions. In the same way, octave playing with passive fingers result in the overburdening – and possible disabling – of the joints (especially the first joint of the thumb).

The work of the upper arm, forearm and wrist may be intermingled in various proportions. Fresh, sharp tone colours are obtained by adding a certain amount of wrist activity to our playing. In this case the upper noises are increased by the large hand motions. To obtain a hard tone, accompanied by considerable noise, we use arm strokes (without wrist motion) even in slow tempo.

If the hand hardly leaves the keyboard – while the arm simultaneously executes vigorous strokes – we obtain an almost declamatory, rhetorical effect which is one of the characteristic tone colours of Liszt's octaves.

When playing portato or legato in slow tempo, the hand does not leave the keyboard, but – as in starting a new bow-stroke in violin playing – it will glide after the arm.

In octaves, played legato, too, the wrist work is also of great importance because here a diminution of the noises is required. However, it must not be left out of consideration that without a certain amount of noise the octaves will lose their characteristic effect. Without a noise-effect sounding in a certain proportion, only voices progressing simultaneously in octave distances but no real octave effect will be obtained. This is why the coupled octaves of a Moór piano or a harpsichord will, if we play without noise, produce only different colour effects but they will never arouse any octave effect. (The separation of the octave playing into double-grip technique and octave technique made by Chopin is obviuosly based on the difference of the tone colours. See p. 145.)

Phot. 185–190

Fast octave with complementary wrist action

(István Antal, 32 pictures per second)

The moment of the set-off

The arm is already rising. The hand still lies on the keyboard

The hand at the highest point

The picture is entirely indistinct because of the extreme speed

The set-off moment. The arm rises anew

Phot. 191–196

Chord-progression with complementary wrist motion

(Beginning of Liszt's E flat major Concerto. Annie Fischer, 48 pictures per second. Every second frame omitted)

The set-off moment of the G-C-G chord

Example 24

The arm begins to rise, the hand lags behind

The arm rises considerably, but the fingers still hold down the keys

The hand, too, begins to rise

Phot. 197—202

The arm at the highest point. The hand is already on a level with the arm

The arm is sinking. The hand is still moving upwards

The picture is somewhat blurred because of the speed. The fingers already touch the keys

Set-off moment of the C-G-C chord

The arm rises, the hand still holds the chord

VIBRATO

The maximum velocity of the active work of the elbow, i.e. of the strokes of the forearm, can be attained by moving the forearm as a unit. The greater velocity we want to attain the smaller the movements of the forearm should be, and with a maximum tempo the fingers should not leave hold of the key. Therefore, to attain maximum velocity in the forearm strokes, we apply a special technique, the so-called vibrato. (Also known as repetition technique.)

In the vibrato, the swinging movements do not arise from equal lifting (bending) and striking (stretching) motions, but a single stretching motion is interrupted by several short flexions. In the vibrato our finger-tips thus do remain at the same place while executing the consecutive strokes but advance continuously and smoothly inwards from the edge of the key and then come back outwards somewhat more rapidly. In this way our hand is in continual motion on the keys. (When drawing our hands outwards, a steady bending movement is interrupted by short stretching movements, an action which is more difficult to execute.)

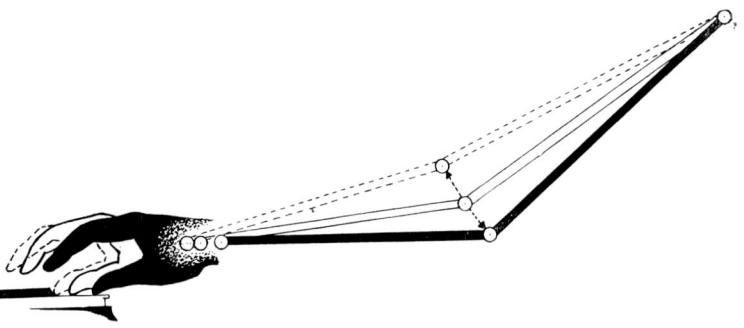

Fig. 44

In this type of vibrato playing, the tone volume is generally even and the tone colour obtained is satisfactory but the tense movement of the forearm, forced to cling to the level of the keys, is rather tiring and so this kind of vibrato is not suited for playing longer progressions. It is also disadvantageous for the fingers to change their positions on the keyboard continually, as it involves the danger — on account of their awkward position — of sounding false notes between the black keys.

But how can the problem be solved of increasing the motion of the arm and at the same time keeping the fingers gripped on the keys? How can both of these antagonistic requirements be met? There is but one solution. While keeping the finger's grip on the keys one has to let the wrist rise and sink, i.e., allow the possibility of a free forearm motion. (At the same time, the upper arm carries out forward-backward movements.)

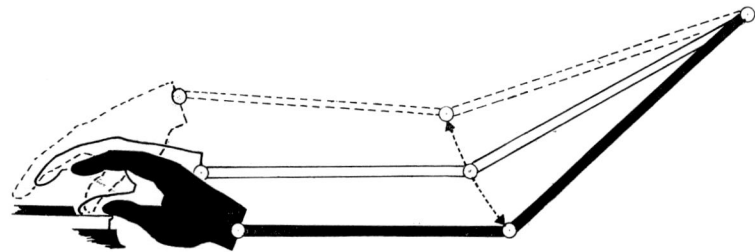

Fig. 45

The rising and sinking of the wrist with the vibrato must never be apportioned; it is dictated solely by the requirement of executing the movements as comfortably as possible. With vibrato, too, we have to imagine the motion of the hammers. If, instead, we concentrate on the wrist, "short" swing-strokes will result.

Example 25

Schubert-Liszt: Erlkönig.

Example 26

Schumann: Op. 7. Toccata

The vibrato played with an unmoved wrist will be "massive", vigorous and more suitable for dynamic shaping, but more tiring for the pianist.

By resorting to wrist motion, we obtain a less even vibrato (although it is partly compensated for by active hand work), and the dynamics, too, will be much less reliable. On the other hand, it is suitable for the playing even the longest octave passages.

The vibrato can be successful only if the hand and the fingers are perfectly firm and able to transmit without any loss the relatively small amount of force developed by the forearm. The fingers have to cling to the keys, so to speak, and in this manner to transfer even the smallest movements of the forearm. If the hand is unable to transfer the force unimpaired, we are compelled to add a considerable amount of force to the single strokes, which means the application of separate lifting and striking motions even in the fastest tempo. Besides being very exhausting, this will noticeably slow down the tempo. The greatest advantage of the vibrato, however, lies precisely in the fact that we are able to attain a fast tempo by a minimal display of force and, at the same time, a large tone volume by adding the weight complement of the upper arm.

The technique of octaves belongs – from the point of view of the motion functions – to the simplest playing forms. The reason for the relative rareness of good octave playing is to be found in the fact that even the least inexpediency of the movements will be detrimental to the velocity and force of the octaves. Because of the simplicity of this playing form an exceptionally important role is played here by the physical constitution of the pianist. There is no other field of piano technique where the well-developed muscles and the good proportion of the parts of the body (short forearm compared to the upper arm) would secure such an advantageous position to the pianist. But even if it is not attainable for everybody to play the octave passages of Liszt's Sixth Rhapsody with 140 M/M, everybody, without exception, is capable of acquiring a technique of octave playing enabling him to perform classical and romantic pieces well. The very simplicity of the playing form ensures a relative facility of learning the playing of octaves. In octave playing the same tempo may be attained as in clapping one's hands – once we have learned to clench the hand in the proper manner. If the maximum tempo of the octave lags behind that of a mere clapping with the hands, it is evident that the force developed by the arm does not reach the keyboard, and the player is, therefore, compelled to apply more force to the single stroke, resulting in reduction of the tempo. In the event of correct movements the tempo of the octaves may pass even beyond that of clapping because the elasticity of the keys diminishes the work needed for the lifting.

THE FINGERING OF OCTAVES

The fingering of the octaves is determined in the first place by the desired musical effect. We must not make a rule even of playing octaves with black keys with the fourth finger. According to Chopin, e.g., octaves played with fingers 4 and 5 alternatively belong to the technique of double-grips, and in his opinion in octave technique (thirds, sixths, octaves) the same finger should always be used. At the same time other composers – Liszt, for instance – preferred to play the chromatic octaves with alternating fingers. Thus our guide must be only the desired musical effect. When playing chromatic octaves fortissimo, the fifth finger must be put on both the black and white keys, because the larger arm movements required for this will be helpful for the fortissimo playing. In piano, however, we play chromatic scales with the fifth finger only if we want to give a stress to the staccato character of the scales. Leggiero and portato, too, can be more easily attained by means of using fingers 4 and 5 alternately.

In the octave ostinato of the middle section of Chopin's Polonaise in A flat – requiring a pianissimo effect – we may use the fourth finger, while in the crescendo the fifth finger should be applied in order to obtain a vigorous sound.

Example 27

In the octave variations of the Paganini Etude in A minor of Liszt's, Sauer even employs the third finger.

This legato fingering permits a very close touch and a soft playing of the staccato octaves. We thereby obtain the most beautiful leggiero effect. If we were to play two octaves lower, this fingering would no longer be suitable because there it does not produce a staccato effect. The lower staccato tones require more noise-effect – i.e. strokes from a greater height and with a more distinct separation.

Example 28

THE PREPARATION OF CHORD PRACTISING

As a basis for the technique of chords and octaves the firm tautening of the fingers should be practised first. However, it is not expedient to practise them separately in the chords and octaves because the innervation of the octave span, acquired in the practising of the chords, gives an almost unfailing sureness for the playing of octaves. The practising of the chords must be prepared by means of gymnastic exercises. Nowhere in the field of the technique of piano playing do gymnastic exercises bring such immediate results as in octave and chord technique. The coordinated tautening (clenching) of the fingers (the firm chord-grip, chord-touch), the transmission of the force without any loss (reliable dynamics)--i.e., all that which is the prerequisite of an economic playing of octaves—can be better attained by gymnastic exercises than by practising them on the piano.

In order to prepare the use of the forearm and hand as a unit exercises 9 and 10 should be repeated frequently. The practising of the passive role of the wrist is facilitated by exercises 21 and 22, and its semi-activity by exercise 15. The coordinated clenching, tautening of the fingers and the energetic action of the opponent muscles is to be prepared by exercises 51 and 52.

THE PRACTISING OF CHORDS

It has been stated before that the different variants of the chord and octave technique are obtained from the differently proportioned work of the elbow and wrist. As this proportioning can be most different, depending upon and in accordance with the tone concept, the variants of the chords and octaves are best practised in the compositions. It is only the firm chord-grip of the hand which must be practised separately, i.e., independently of the music, and this practising may be connected with the preparation of velocity.

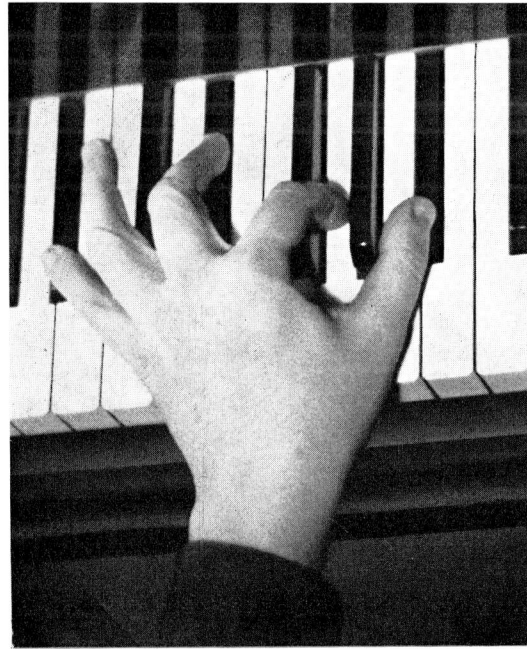

Phot. 203

E flat major. Six-four chord, forte-touch. The strong bending of the second finger forces the third finger to bend inward, too. When diminishing the dynamic degree the fingers assume a more extended, stretched position

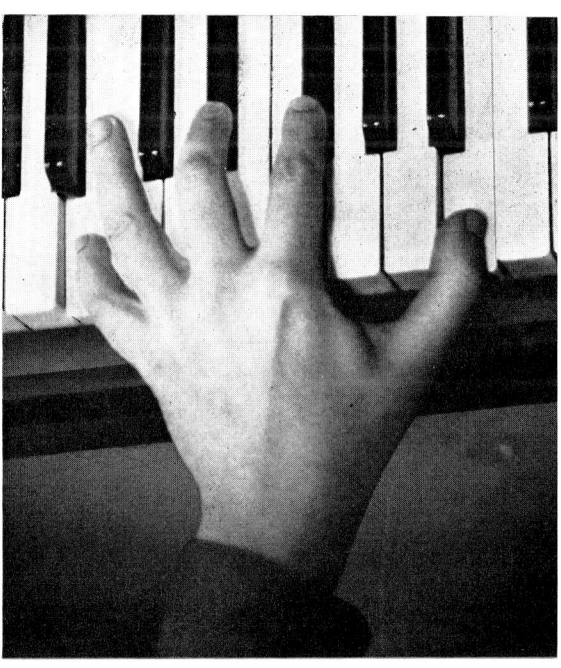

Phot. 204

B major common chord, forte-touch. The second and third fingers on the upper keys, despite the forte-touch, are in a relatively extended position because the short fingers are playing on the white keys. In the fortissimo, a further bending is necessary

Thus, one has to execute forearm exercises in which the hand and the forearm form a unit. It is apparently in contradiction with the foregoing to practise the forearm chord-strokes in a slow tempo, because it has been stated that – whenever the tempo permits it – the upper arm must be used for the sounding of chords. Indeed, in pieces we must never play slow chords with the forearm. However, in the last case our aim is the slow practising of fast chords. By slowing down the tempo the movement can be observed better and corrected. As in the technique of octaves and chords the work of the forearm has an exceedingly important role, the most important one from among the three components (hand, forearm, upper arm), i.e. the activity of the forearm is to be stressed and improved. Although in the final musical performing the use of the forearm is impracticable, one still has to lay an emphasis on it when practising, because if the forearm and the coordinated tautened hand do not work correctly every stroke will become gradually worse: worse tone colour, decrease of the endurance and decrease of the tempo will result. (If you are still not convinced may I remind you that fixing a flat tyre is not an absolutely necessary part of car driving but still one would not undertake a drive with a flat tyre.)

Since the main aim of our practising is the improvement of the using of the hand as a firm unit, special care must be taken of tautening the entire hand and of paying attention to the non-playing fingers. As a matter of fact, these fingers need even more attention than the playing ones because they have to hold the chord position as if playing together with the other fingers.

Do not practise the firm grip on full chords. They are most expediently practised by dividing them into groups of two notes. In the C major tonal chord, for example, the C-E third should first be struck four times consecutively, followed by the E-G and finally the G-C, each of them four times.

Example 29

The swinging movement is carried out solely by the forearm in a calm and slow tempo like the forearm circling in gymnastics. (See p. 254.) The upper arm does not furnish any real weight-effect – any detailed dynamic shaping – but still has a synthesizing function in order to enable the forearm to execute swing-strokes from the most advantageous position. (See chapter on "Slow Practising of Fast Playing.") The tempo of the single strokes must not be accelerated or retarded when changing the position (e.g., from the tonal chord to a sixth chord). This is at the same time a preparation for chord skips.

We have to concentrate on clenching the finger-ends even while touching the keys, because only this will enable us to execute the touch with the least expenditure of energy. We must have the feeling of being able to maintain the hands indefinitely in the chord position without getting exhausted.

The fingers have to function as elongations of the forearm and so they should not execute any striking movements simultaneously with the movements of the forearm. A fault, very frequently found with pianists, is that the fingers make a kind of scratching movement when touching the keys. This does not strengthen the stroke: its effect is the opposite and weakens the force of the stroke. (The same as if, when striking on a nail with a hammer, the hammer-head carried out strokes independently from the shaft of the hammer.) The desired firmness of the fingers is best attained by an imaginary prolongation of the fingers which hold an object tenderly.

If the grip is really firm, the hand will not modify its form when touching the keys; the fingers will not "give". To attain this end it is also necessary – when executing this exercise – that the arm should lower itself to a point *determined by our own motion command* and not as far as the key-bed permits.

Every difficult grip (German: *Griff*) may be practised in a similar way, i.e. first by dividing it into groups of two tones and afterwards repeating the entire chord several times.

It is very important that the full energy transmission should not be hindered by any "giving" of the wrist or the knuckles. It is *equally incorrect* if

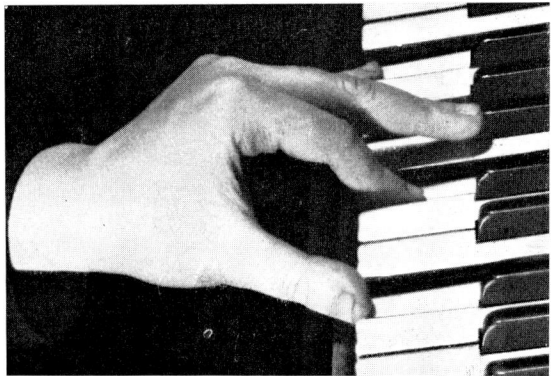

Phot. 205

the knuckles are pressed upwards (what is called "finger support")

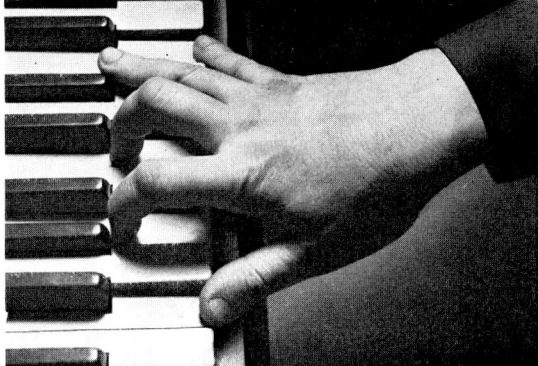

Phot. 206

or the knuckles "give"

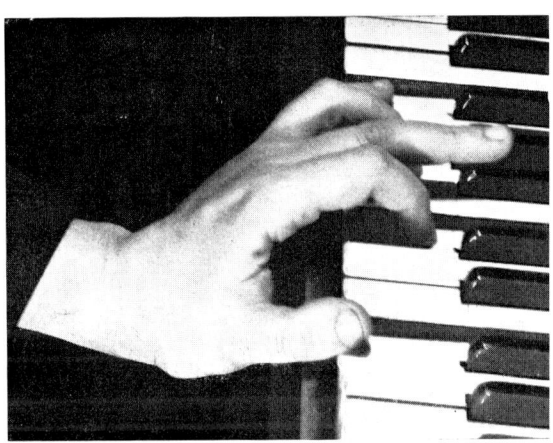

Phot. 207

Phot. 208

or the performer plays with low or high wrist position.

A forced position of the knuckles and the wrist permits only a fraction of the arm's force to reach the keyboard because the fingers will not be active enough. The chords must always be practised as if the finger-ends were moved directly from the elbow joint. (We should shorten the arm in our imagination.)

If the single chords do not present any difficulties, except the task of connecting them, it may be advisable to play the chords individually without repetition. The hand should remain on the keyboard after executing the stroke so that the chord continues to sound (as if we wanted to keep the key on the escapement level). But no pressure should be exerted on the key nor must there be any further weight-effect on the part of the upper arm or even, worst of all, any leaning against the key. In slow practising, we have to play chords which are built into finger-technique parts in the same way.

When practising single difficult chords and skips, we have to apply the pure forearm swing-stroke with minimal synthesizing movement. But when playing musically coherent parts, the full synthesizing movement of the upper arm is also indispensable. This is the more important because the essential chords should always be sounded by means of an upper-arm swing-stroke.

Skips of chords presenting no positional difficulties may be practised immediately with full chords. Repeat each of them twice, without any difference of duration between the chords played in the same position and those played with skips.

Example 30

The chord position of the fingers has to remain entirely firm even during the skip; this also applies to the non-playing fingers. By this means, we attain, within the shortest time, a perfect sureness in chord-skips because we have to pay attention only to the skip (since the hand maintains its previous shape). In the chord-change the fingers automatically assume – while in the air – the required new position, and thus the swing-stroke may be executed with a perfectly firm hand. (During the skip the entire hand should not be relaxed. Only the fingers which have to change their position should move.)

THE PRACTISING OF OCTAVES

In the playing of octaves special difficulties arise through our endeavouring to conserve the tautened firm grip of the hand during the complementary work of the wrist. Therefore it is advisable to begin the practising of the octave technique by repeated sixths. The span of the sixths is small enough to enable even pianists with small hands to preserve the sensation of clenching (tautening) the hand. The training will be more secure if we begin with repeated sixths than immediately with scales in sixths, because the playing of a scale makes the task of keeping the hand taut more difficult.

When practising sixths, the most useful method is to repeat each eight times in succession.

Example 31

The task of the wrist is to take over the swinging motion of the arm and to enlarge the arm stroke. We should have the feeling that the hand bounds of itself (without, however, bouncing like a rubber ball).

We should concentrate exclusively on the strokes and acquire the sensation of sounding the tones by means of a light motion and clear strokes of the hand.

After practising the sixths eight times in succession through a scale pattern, ordinary sixth scales should follow.

This scale in sixths must be practised only in C major. This requires a comparatively increased hand action because of the absence of those larger movements of the arm which would be called for by the alternating use of white and black keys. We must not endeavour to replace the increased motion of the hand by enlarged vertical motion of the arm, i.e. by strokes from a greater height, because this would smother the role of the hand and thus merely lead to faulty velocity exercises, instead of preparing for passive wrist action.

Phot. 209–213

Chord-exercise

(F major, 32 photos per sec.)

The figures between the pictures refer to the number of frames left out

The moment of the set-off

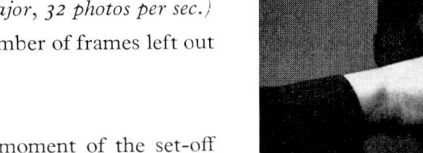

3

The arm is rising. It may be clearly seen that the position of the fingers and the wrist does not change either in the process of lifting or when executing the touch

9

The hand at the highest point

22

The sudden increase in speed is evident from the indistinctness of the picture

The hand at the moment of touching the keys. The blurring of the picture proves that the movement has not yet been slowed down noticeably by the braking action of the key resistance. This resistance increases up to the moment of the set-off, as may be seen from the clarity of the first picture

Phot. 214–219

Sixth-repetitions

(32 photos per sec.)

The hand immediately before the set-off moment

The arm rises for the new stroke

The wrist gets into a strongly bent position because of the passive lagging of the hand

The arm begins a new movement downwards, the hand is still directed upwards

Phot. 220—225

The hand at the highest point

The speed of the stroke increases, as proved also by the indistinctness of the picture

The hand at the moment of touching the keys. The second, third and fourth fingers are not braked directly by the resistance of the keys. In consequence of this, their speed decreases only insignificantly, as shown by the indistinctness of the picture

The set-off moment. The second, third and fourth fingers are already touching the keys. (The performer must not be conscious of the changed handform, or else his grip will be too weak)

It is an invariable rule that the scales in octaves should be practised with a passive wrist.

With increasing tempo less and less time is left for the hand's action, because hardly has the movement begun when we are already compelled to carry out the next stroke. The fingers have to tauten each other and the force of the grip must be increased proportionately to the intensity of the stroke. The opponent muscles must be brought into functioning by slightly pulling the fifth finger and the thumb together.

The non-playing fingers – especially the third (and longest) finger – have to lead the hand. This directing function of the non-playing fingers ensures the activity of the entire hand and, thus, the full transmission of the force.

Scales in octaves are to be practised with each hand separately at first. They should be played with both hands together only when we are capable of playing them one-handedly in uninterrupted parallel chains in all keys.

Example 32

In the case of broken chords, the chromatic direction is more suitable.

Example 33

Practising of the vibrato should begin with repetitions executed with a single movement. In order to facilitate assuming a clenched position, we should use sixths. Three or four tones should be played with a stretching motion, i.e. inwards along the key.

Example 34

In the next exercise a short bending motion is joined to a long stretching movement. Its rhythm is the following:

Example 35

When striking the first sixth, we must gain enough momentum to sound the subsequent seven tones in one movement. If the clenching (tautening) has already become automatized in the course of the previous chord exercises and we are able, even at high speed, to concentrate on the active sensation of the fingers, we will learn to play even the quickest repetitions without difficulty. This rhythm should first be practised by means of repetitions and afterwards in scales.

Example 36

It is unnecessary to practise this scale slowly, because slow chord practising will have set up the required innervation already. Here our task is confined to becoming accustomed to the speed and the success of the exercise depends only on our courage and self-confidence.

If we do not succeed in attaining the proper tempo, it may be considered as a sign that our hands are still passive while playing. To overcome this, there is no choice but to execute the chord exercises with more concentrated attention, to learn how to clench the hand better with the aid of gymnastics, and to increase the activity of the fingers.

After having mastered the vibrato of the arm in scales, we may proceed to a combination of repetitions with the octave vibrato.

Example 37

Now let us see the chord repetitions. These should be practised at first with movements advancing continuously and smoothly inwards from the edge of the key and then coming back outwards, as described for vibrato, afterwards with the aid of passive wrist motions, while maintaining the same point of contact with the keys. The forearm strikes with sharp little movements; the swing-strokes are so small that the fingers hardly leave the key.

Example 38

For constant exercising of the wrist vibrato, one should select some characteristic vibrato octave passages, such as the beginning of "Erlkönig."

BROKEN CHORDS

The playing of broken chords is based also on uniform chord touch, but the active swinging motion is executed by the fingers and not by the arm. The difference between this and ordinary finger work is that the fingers here assume the corresponding chord position and are thus compelled to strike in a rather stretched state. The outer fingers consequently need more help than usual. This aid is furnished by the different adapting movements, by shifting the centre of gravity, by rotatory and vertical movements, all of which assist in counter-balancing the differences of force caused by the various finger positions.

Phot. 226–230

Fast chord-playing

(Schumann: Aufschwung, Sviatoslav Richter, 24 photos per sec.)

Example 39

226

227

228

229

230

226 After the set-off of chord f^1-b^1 flat-d^2 flat

227 Sounding chord e^1-b^1 flat-c^2

228 The right hand after sounding c^2. The blurredness of the picture and the closedness of the fingers show that the hand has just performed the change of fingers and only now is going to assume the next position

229 Before sounding c^3. Note the activity and uniformity of the octave grip

230 The sounding of c^3

In the slow practising of broken chords, the sureness of the chord touch and the enlarged movements of the fingers should be practised separately.

Rotation and vertical adaption cannot be increased without deforming the movement, and it may, therefore, be advisable to avoid them in slow practising. (See p. 114.) Instead, the entire attention should be focused on the finger work. If, in addition, the chords, in unbroken form, are practised separately, even the most difficult broken chords can be played easily.

Any systematic training in the playing of broken chords (such as is employed in scale practising) is a waste of time. All the more important, on the other hand, is the careful elaboration and systematic practising of parts of compositions containing broken chords. This will enable us to automatize – in accordance with the musical concept – the proportionate blending of the components in the different variants. This is the only sound way of practising the complex, multiple movements required by the playing of broken chords. By recognizing and learning the various playing variants of broken chords we attain perfect security in performing them, and our playing will become more and more colourful and expressive. On the other hand, if we choose only one type and always practise only these "broken chords *par excellence*," our playing will become monotonous and expressionless.

ARPEGGIO

The arpeggio is a particular category of broken chords. The tones are held down, after having been sounded, and thus at the moment of striking the last tone the whole chord sounds together. In the music of the XVIIIth century the arpeggio sign did not mean only the simple breaking of the chord but also a "waving to and fro" of the tones of the chord, sometimes also through several octaves.

C. Ph. E. Bach: Fantasia in A major

Example 40

Couperin uses the arpeggio

upwards from below, and   downwards from above.

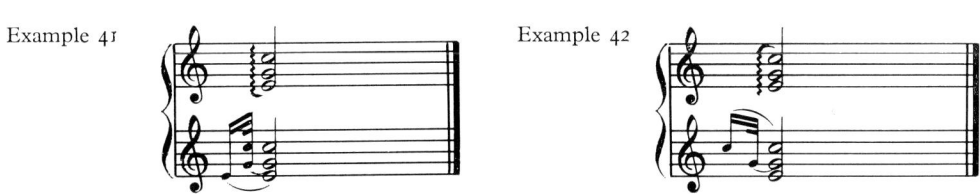

Example 41   Example 42

The greatest fault to be committed in the execution of the arpeggio is to sound the notes by a rotation movement. Equally faulty is the solution of sounding the tones by active finger work. The correct solution is to endeavour to sound each one almost by a direct swing-stroke, united by a slow, wide spindle movement executed by the entire arm. The lower half of this spindle movement is larger than the upper one and the whole movement is larger than usual. The centre of gravity must be shifted – so to speak – from tone to tone and the hand must be perfectly tautened even though the grip is so large that we are unable to span the chord with one stroke. Thus, the arpeggio is always the work of the upper arm and within this framework the rotation and finger work carry out only a minimal complementing activity.

In cases where the execution of the arpeggio requires a wider span than that of the hand, the execution of the spindle motion becomes complicated because it has to comprise smaller or larger skips. In such cases the tone to be struck by the aid of the skip is "grasped" with a small recurving arc. (See films on pp. 180–181.)

The theme of Liszt's Paganini (A minor) Etude is very rarely heard clearly.

Example 43

The cause of our missing the right key is almost always due to the fact that the fifth finger of the right hand tries to attain the highest note by a rotational movement of the forearm and so it bumps against the key instead of grasping it. But how could one bump against something "appropriately?" In such cases the finger only "tolerates" being shifted, and this obviously will be detrimental to its sureness. If, on the other hand, we give the finger an active task to accomplish – the sounding of a tone or the grasping of a key – it will be able to execute this task with an absolute sureness and facility because the expedient movement of the "grasping" is an inherited unconditioned reflex practised also continually in our everyday life.

Phot. 231
CLAUDETTE SOREL
playing Chopin's Op. 25 A flat major Etude

The natural movement, the "grasping" of the key has an even greater importance in such wide arpeggios:

Example 44   Chopin: Op. 10, No. 11

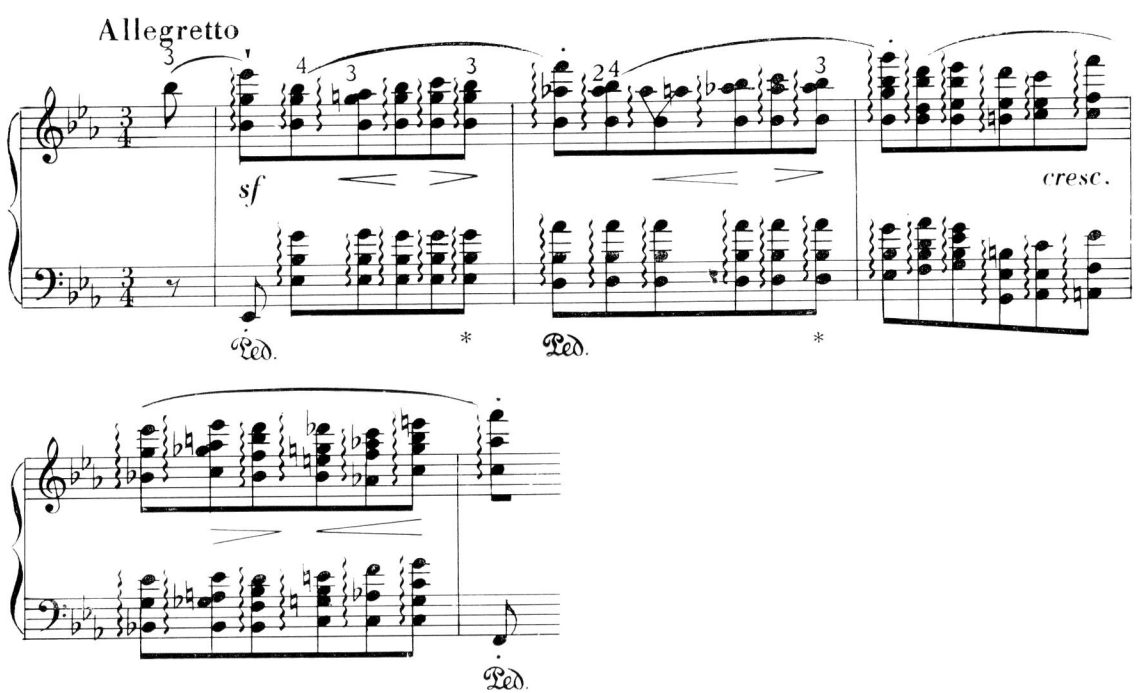

The correct striking of the tones is perhaps somewhat less difficult than in the Liszt Etude because the hand may remain constantly in a wide grasping position instead of having recourse to finger technique. On the other hand, the soft sounding of the tones, the intensive life of the voices and the shaping of the dynamic contours with its many nuances, will present a most difficult and delicate task. For the correct execution of these arpeggios each key has to be grasped separately and each one of them must be separately felt within the wide sweeping spindle movement of the arm.

Phot. 232
GOLDHAMMER KEYBOARD

169

THE TREMOLO

The most important factor in tremolo technique is the rotation of the forearm.

The axis of the rotatory movement is at right angles to the axis of the key and we are, therefore, unable to evoke the same perfect sensing of the key and concentration on the escapement level, as when executing vertical movements. The tones produced by rotatory movements have a mechanical sound, and there is no possibility of dynamically shading the individual strokes. For this reason the tremolo motion should be employed only in fast tempo. As long as the tempo permits, a vertical movement is preferable and the tremolo motion should be added only to the degree which may be required by the noise-effects. (See under "Adapting Movements.")

On account of the mechanical sound of the lateral strokes, any stress we may wish to lay on a tremolo tone must be achieved with the aid of the upper arm. The rotatory movement continues unchanged but the tones to be stressed call for an added stroke on the part of the upper arm.

Although a dynamic shaping of the individual strokes is not possible, it is perfectly feasible in fast tempo to shape the dynamic contours of the tremolo as a whole through the weight-effect of the upper arm. Crescendo and decrescendo are thus achieved by altering the weight-effect and not by increasing the force of the single strokes. In slow tempo, the synthesizing movement no longer suffices to permit dynamic shaping; hence we have to increase the number of adapting movements and active upper-arm swing-strokes in order to attain a dynamic tone shading. In the slow tremolo, the rotatory movements become overshadowed by the vertical adapting movements.

As the composition of the movements in a tremolo is extremely complicated, the proportions in which their components should be combined from case to case can be determined only by the tone concept. An enlarging of the rotatory motion in the tremolo, for example, results in a sudden increase of the upper noises.

THE PLAIN FOREARM TREMOLO

Rotation, from the point of view of the action of the joints, is more complicated than any other swinging movement. In order to obtain the proper tone effect—notwithstanding the difficulties —we have to work out carefully the most expedient form of rotation.

The rotation is carried out by the forearm. The first prerequisite is thus full transmission by the hand of even the slightest movement of the forearm. *A firm chord position is imperative also in the tremolo, just as in octave and chord technique.*

The strengthening of the upper or lower tones on the tremolo is also brought about by displacing the centre of gravity. It is easier to stress the fifth finger than the thumb because supination is carried out by one of our strongest muscles, the biceps.

The plain forearm tremolo requires a flexed elbow position. The upper arm does not move, nor does the direction of the axis of rotation change. In the plain forearm tremolo the degree to which the elbow is bent will consequently be determined by the position in which the biceps is best capable of utilizing its force. Since the biceps slackens when we extend the elbow, we are compelled to bend our arm slightly in order to execute a plain forearm tremolo.

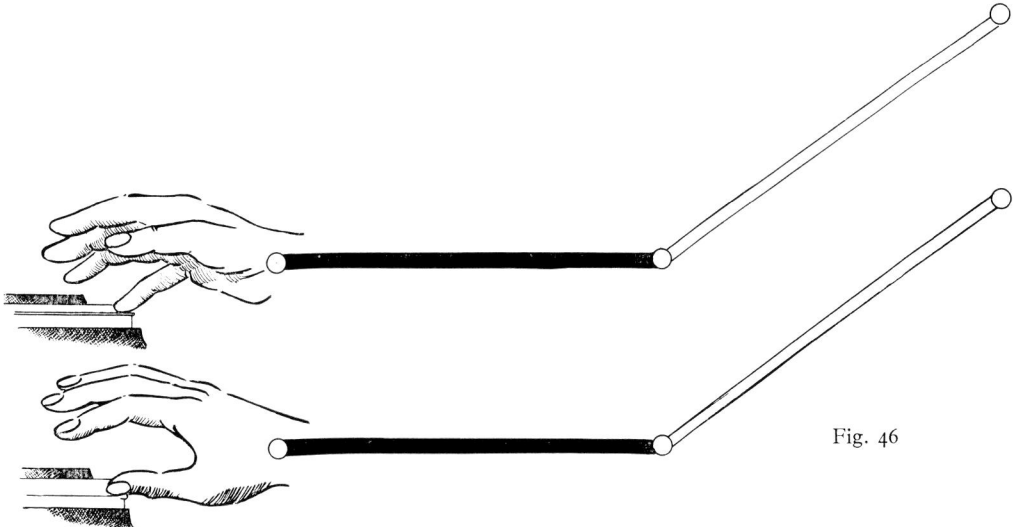

Fig. 46

The muscles executing the rotation – other than the biceps – are rather weak. Because the rotatory strokes do not permit any heavy overburdening, the limits within which the weight-effect may be increased are narrow. Therefore, if we want to produce a larger tone volume, the force of the stroke must be intensified by increasing the mass participating in the rotation.

THE SHAKEN TREMOLO

An increase in tone volume through a corresponding increase in the mass participating in the rotatory movement can be achieved by allowing a passive shaking of the upper arm during the regular rotation movement of the forearm. In this way, the axis of rotation becomes displaced from the middle line of the forearm towards the little finger. (We must not forget that the upper arm is passive in the shaken tremolo only from the point of view of the execution of the rotation, since it takes an active part in the shaping of the dynamic contours.)

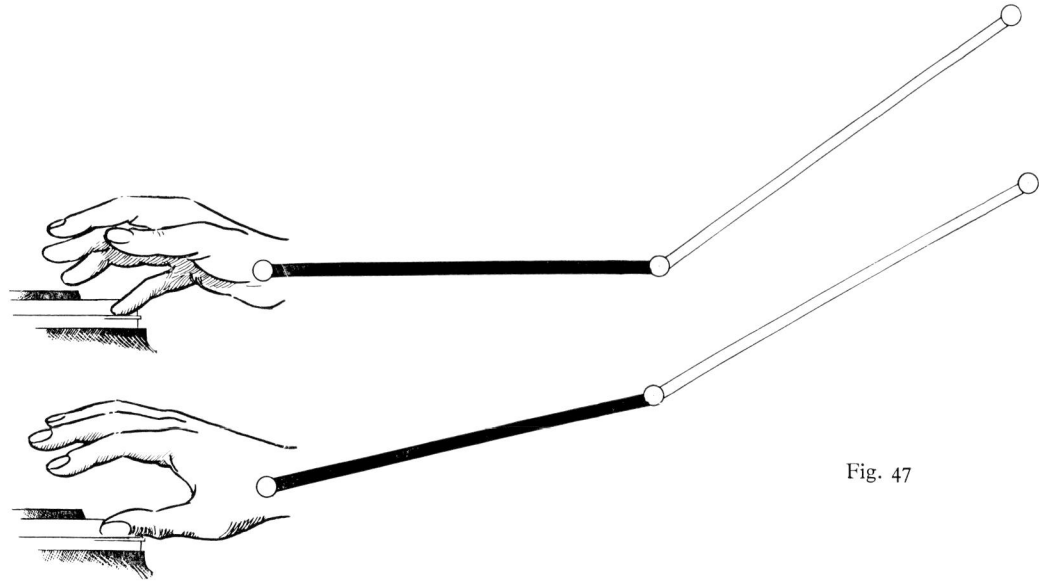

Fig. 47

The strokes of the thumb will thus become heavier, because the weight of the hand – as well as that of the arm – falls on the thumb. In the shaken tremolo the thumb strokes are consequently more easily stressed than the strokes of the little finger.

The shaken tremolo requires a somewhat more relaxed arm than the plain tremolo. The angle of flexing cannot be determined exactly because it depends on the kind of tremolo applied and it differs from individual to individual. In comparing the two forms, we may, nevertheless, establish the rule that the shaken tremolo requires a less flexed elbow than the plain tremolo.

PROGRAMME OF TREMOLO TEACHING

Since there is hardly any connection between the slow tremolo and the rotatory tremolo of the fast tempo, it is wrong to teach the rotation to beginners by means of special études or pieces. The tremolo is more easily learned by leaving the complicated slow tremolo until later and beginning with the plain tremolo in which rotation is to be employed without the introduction of other movements.

Learning the slow tremolo requires no special studies. If our adapting movements are correct, we will also be able to perform the slow tremolos in a colourful, variegated manner.

Example 45   Schumann: Piano quintet, Op. 44

Example 46   Beethoven: Sonata in C minor, Op. 111

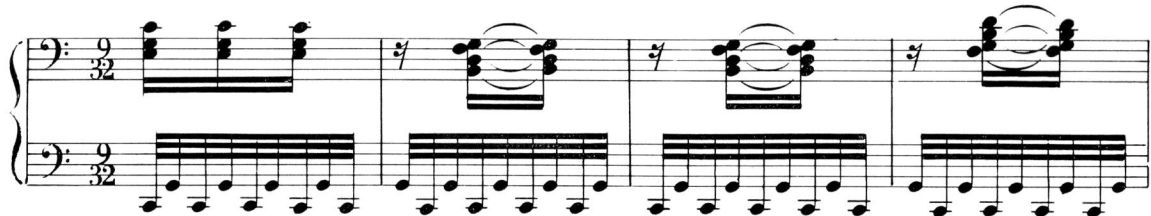

Acquisition of the tremolo necessitates a certain knowledge of octave and chord technique. If – on account of uncertainty as to the proper chord position – we are forced to carry out excessive rotatory motions, we will hinder the development of correct innervation. By means of a firm chord position, however, we may acquire a fast and reliable tremolo technique with little effort.

The tremolo should be prepared for by gymnastic exercises in the same way as the chord technique.

The innervation of the most economical rotatory movement can be more easily attained through gymnastics than at the piano. The increase of the rotatory motion, too, is realizable only through gymnastics. In no other way can we make full use of the rotatory possibilities of the forearm which are so indispensable for the development of speed. (See p. 255.)

TREMOLO PRACTISING

Both the plain and the shaken tremolo can be applied only in fast tempo without the noises and automatism of the lateral strokes becoming disturbing. If the tempo of the tremolo is only a little slower than the maximum tempo, each tone of it should be played as if we wanted to sound only that single tone by a direct swing-stroke. In order to find the appropriate position let us try to play a tremolo using both hands. Each hand should strive to "get hold" of the keys as if grasping each key separately. We should also try sometimes to play broken octave scales by this method: by playing the lower tone with the left and the upper tone with the right hand.

But even when playing in maximum tempo no appropriate tone colour will be obtained if we play the tremolo by consciously executing exclusively neutral strokes. The lateral strokes must be amalgamated with the feeling of the direct swing-strokes and the catching, grasping of the keys. The arm and the whole body have to work in accordance with the direct swing-strokes. One has to feel that the apportioning of the resistance is so delicate that it would be able to execute changes with each tone separately.

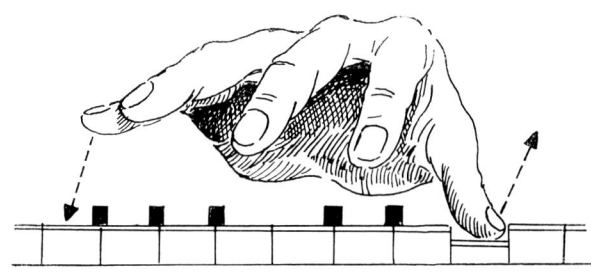

Fig. 48

In tremolo practising we have to start from tremolos played in a medium velocity; this is the most frequently encountered type in the pieces.

In the beginning it is advisable to practise only the plain octave tremolo (for smaller hands the sixth tremolo). When practising chord tremolos, let us first take those in which the thumb strikes alone and the chord is sounded together with the stroke of the little finger. This, too, may be played by means of a plain tremolo.

Example 47

If the common (tonic) chord is sounded simultaneously with the stroke of the thumb, we apply a "shaken" tremolo.

Example 48

The tremolo does not necessitate any constant practising. Once we have mastered it technically, it suffices to engage in occasional tremolo gymnastics and, from time to time, to repeat some tremolo part of a fairly difficult piece.

The slow practising of the tremolo should be continued only for a very short time, because its sole aim is to make us conscious of the muscular functions. If, however, we practise it only in fast tempo, many accidental movements may be innervated, and thus it will become impossible to blend consciously the rotation with the weight-effect, the "shaking" of the upper arm and the accentuation provided by the active swinging of the upper arm.

The adaptation of plain forearm tremolo to the piano and its proper innervation is easily attainable by slow practising. At the same time a retarded execution of the shaken tremolo (combined with various supplementary movements) is inexpedient because we cannot increase the separate components proportionately. Such tremolos are, therefore, to be practised solely in the original tempo in which they appear in the respective musical compositions.

Slow practising of rotation is carried out in octave (or sixth) position. The work is done entirely by the forearm; the upper arm has a synthesizing function but does not provide any weight-effect. However, it should not be passive, but hold itself in readiness for its synthesizing task. The finger-ends must be kept very taut in order to prevent them from changing their mutual position either during the rotation or after the stroke.

The axis of the plain rotatory motion lies approximately between the second and third fingers (on the basis of a straight line drawn from the elbow). In slow practising the rotation should be carried out around the axis. (See Fig. 48.) In the chord tremolo, the axis becomes displaced and, therefore, this tremolo must not be practised in a retarded tempo. The degree of displacement of the axis also changes with the tempo, and wrong innervations may consequently be acquired by slow practising.

Force should be applied only at the beginning, and it should cease before the end of the movement, whether of pronation or of supination. (As if spinning a wheel around an axle.)

Under no circumstances should the arm repose on the keyboard at the moment when the little finger or thumb strikes the key.

The hand, after executing the stroke, must be immediately prepared for the next rotatory movement. In the case of simple rotation without weight-effect, the keys will not sink down to the bottom of the key-bed. If we depress the key entirely, we incur the risk — by leaning against the key — of carrying out a larger rotation than needed.

As the act of leaning goes together with a lifting motion of the upper arm, slow practising, in this case, becomes valueless because such motion is inexecutable in fast playing. The slow practising of the tremolo is of use only if the force acts by intermittent jerks without *pressing* the key to the key-bed.

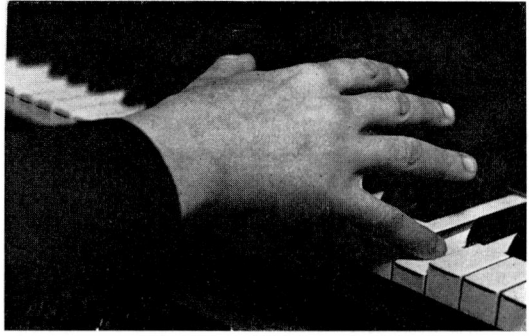
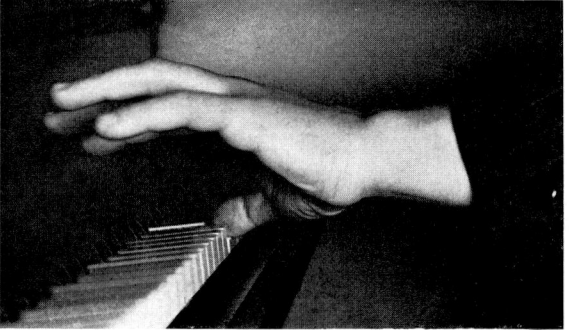

Phot. 233   Phot. 234

BROKEN OCTAVES

The playing of broken octaves is also based on tremolo technique. However, the progression here presents a special problem.

There are two possible solutions:

1. After both tones of the previous broken octave have been struck, the arm "skips" into the next position.

2. The progression takes place with the aid of rotatory movements, in which case the positional change of the arm will occur – depending on the direction of the scale – either with the first or the second tone of the broken octave.

In playing the broken octaves of the C major scale with the right hand upwards,

Example 49

we are able to advance to the new position after having played both tones of a single octave. The thumb always strikes by means of a pronating movement, the hand maintains a firm octave position and the arm advances further at the moment of pronation.

Fig. 49

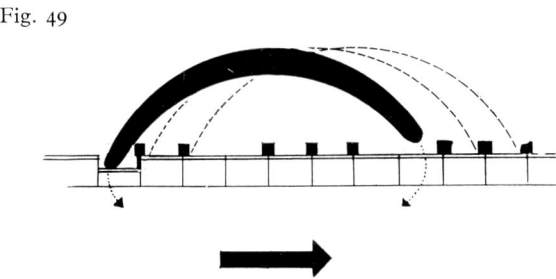

The playing of the same scale downwards sets a far more complicated task.

Example 50

After each broken octave we can, if we maintain the octave position, advance only by playing the next octave with a jolt resulting in conspicuous accentuation. The reason for this is that the arm has to move inwards, i.e. in the supinating direction, while the thumb strikes in the pronating direction.

A solution of this kind may be applied only when we wish to divide the broken octave scale into groups of two tones.

Example 51

Fluent playing would thus seem to require that the arm progresses together with the stroke of the little finger. This would – if the hand remained in octave position – only result in broken sevenths instead of broken octaves. Precise broken octaves can, however, be obtained by stretching the hand to the span of a ninth.

Fig. 50

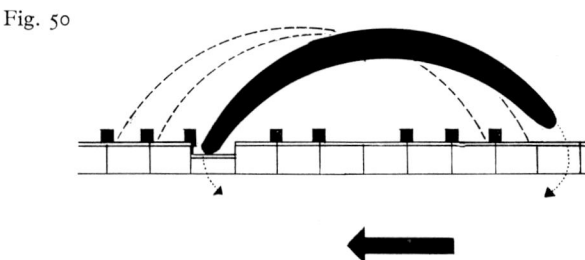

If the octaves are broken from above, both hands have to assume a ninth-span, when progressing upwards.

Example 52

Slow practising of the broken octave scale should be carried out in a manner similar to that of a tremolo. The principal difficulty arises from the necessity of a ninth-span when progressing downwards. What is needed is a plain forearm rotation without any weight-effect in order that the progression may more easily fuse with the rotatory motion.

Slow practising of both the tremolo and the broken octaves must be alternated with playing them at the fastest tempo. The alternation of slow practising and fast playing – by compensating and complementing each other – will facilitate apprehension of the correct functions.

SKIPS

The technique of skipping may also be considered as a branch of chord playing because its technical preconditions are firmness of the hand and immobile fingers. This applies not only to the chord skips but also to single-tone skips since the slightest movement of the extreme fingers influences the action of the arm. The arm is forced to execute smaller or larger movements according to the momentary span of the hand. If the movement of the arm does not remain the same when repeating the same skip, automatization will be rendered more difficult. Moreover, the quick execution of chord and octave skips with mobile fingers is virtually impossible, because the fingers have to find the grip and the touch again and again.

The skips are the most misunderstood elements of piano technique.

What is the skip? The successive sounding of two tones which are located at a greater distance from each other than the span of the hand.

One has to distinguish between the real skip (when the two tones of the skip belong together) from the case when one tone of the skip is the end of a musical phrase and the other is the beginning of another phrase. In such cases it is decidedly harmful to practise that skip separately. The first tone of the new phrase must be imagined intensively and then the whole melody must be practised by endeavouring to attain maximal expressive force and a beautiful tone.

When executing skips, it is a precondition of "catching," "holding" or "grasping" the key that the movement itself be really a grasping one. Just as we catch, or take hold of an object by the aid of our fingers, so the movement of the skip must also be led by the fingers. The uncertainty of the skip is caused mostly by the fact that the fingers are put on their respective place on the keys by the arm instead of the fingers' leading the arm, which would be the natural solution. (When the baby reaches for a rattle he grasps it with his fingers and does not lead his fingers with his arm.) Thus the skipping bass of the main subject of Liszt's "Feux follets" will be successfully carried out only if during the first and second fingers' playing the fifth finger remains stretched and ready to skip. If the fifth finger is not extended, the position of the hand will be contradictory to the requirements of the skip, because it is contradictory to our unconditioned reflexes. With such a faulty, relaxed hand the fingers tolerate, so to speak, being carried to the respective keys to be moved. (In addition, with such a faulty hand position the arm, too, has to execute a larger movement than with a firm grip.)

Example 53

A special difficulty is encountered by the circumstance that with every skip the horizontal movement of the arm, too, is needed and this lateral movement causes difficulties in the execution of the vertical movement required by the swing-stroke. It follows from this that the most frequently found fault with skips is that we concentrate only on the horizontal movement and not the vertical one which is directly producing the sound. Thus the horizontal movement becomes an aim in itself. The appropriate "amalgamation" of the horizontal and vertical movement can thus be achieved only if we concentrate with full intensity on the tone to be sounded, and, on the other hand, both the horizontal and the vertical movements are is expedient, i.e. only such and as large movements are executed as are required in order to produce the tone. Therefore, when executing the skip, we must not concentrate on the movement but on the tone to be sounded. In trying to establish an order of succession according to the importance of the components, one has to concentrate in the first place on the tone, secondly on the key (by the aid of which we obtain the required tone), thirdly on the direct swing-stroke preceding the tone production (vertical movement) and only in the fourth place on the horizontal movement to the key.

If we hammer a nail we do not follow with attention the whole motion up to its completion, but when starting the motion, i.e. still during the upward motion of the hammer, we imagine the hammer-head hitting the nail. In a similar way, one has to imagine with every skip, and at the very beginning of the movement, the tone to be sounded (as intensively as possible) and thus the most difficult skips will be carried out impeccably.

An analysis of the movements executed in a skip is of use only in order to eliminate any possible wrong movements. The movements needed for skip should be taught only to pupils who — either in consequence of their bad physical structure or wrong teaching — have innervated harmful movements.

When investigating the movements required in order to execute a skip, only the expediency of the horizontal movement, the simplest execution of the horizontal movement is to be determined.

1. The horizontal movement must be as natural as possible.

2. It must be executed along the shortest trajectory.

3. The music itself (its volume and colour) determines to what extent which parts of our body participate in the horizontal movements.

1. Our aim is: not to focus any attention separately on the skip but rather to concentrate with all our might on the tone production and leave the hands to find the most natural movements. If we do not forcibly innervate artificial motion elements, our hand will span the distance with the same unperceived spontaneity as it carries out innumerable complicated movements in the course of our everyday life. Nobody worries about the problem of how his hands will carry food to his mouth. If he still starts to think about it his movements will become clumsy and ridiculous. Here the consciousness of the movement will cause inhibitions. The same will happen if we concentrate on the movement during the skip instead of on the tone, and if we somehow try to establish the detailed execution of the motion. Leave it to the hands to find the most natural movement.

2. The horizontal movements should be carried out along the shortest route, the only restriction being that in the determination of the horizontal movement the tone concept must be the decisive factor. The movement carried out along the shortest route is not always identical with that one which brings into being the tone concept in the best possible way. The shortest trajectory would mean here that the hand passes closely over the keys and, touching the key, sounds the tone with a direct swing-stroke. This will work well only if one has sufficient time to sound both tones of the skip with direct swing-stroke. However, a stroke executed from a certain height is frequently needed to increase the tone volume, or, by adding a certain amount of noise-effect, to create the imagined tone colour.

3. From the aspect of tone colour it is of decisive importance to determine the proportion in which the upper arm, forearm or even the trunk is participating in the horizontal movement. Therefore, with skips, too, the execution must not be bound by pre-determined movement patterns. So, for example, the increased use of the forearm will produce sharper tones, but that of the trunk will produce massive, distortioned, cumbersome tone colours.

We have to avoid every unnecessary, superfluous movement. The horizontal movement is directed by the fingers, the whole arm simultaneously forming one single unit with them. The role of the elbow and shoulder joints, when participating in the motion, blend in different proportions according to the respective kind of skip. However, here too, the rule will apply that the forearm is not employed consciously, it is – so to speak – only permitted to participate in the movement and its functioning must be reduced to the necessary extent. With very large skips the trunk may even have to assist. However, if the trunk motion is applied *unnecessarily*, i.e. not in the interest of tone-colour production, it will not only bring about a cumbersome tone colour but will also render the skips uncertain.

The skips are divided into two groups:

1. Both tones of the skip are reached by even motion and result from indirect swing-strokes.

2. The first tone, struck by a direct swing-stroke, is used as if it were a springboard for reaching the second tone.

EVEN-MOTION SKIPS

An even motion is required first of all in repeated skips played in fast tempo, because they leave no time to prepare skips.

Example 54

Liszt: La Campanella

Single-tone skipping resembles an enlarged rotation. The height of the arc of rotation is determined by the convenience of the arm's motion. The hand should remain near the keyboard in order to abbreviate the arc of the movement as much as possible.

Note the rotatory movement of the forearm in the successive pictures of the next two pages. It may be clearly observed that thumb and little finger reach beyond the key to be struck. This proves that the hand, after having executed the skip, does not knock against the keys but brakes by the aid of a reverse-directed little arc, i.e. it is possible to move the key with a relatively controlled movement which is almost a direct swing-stroke. (Of course, the player must not think of the braking but must only imagine the most beautiful tone possible.)

The more extended the hand position the smaller the movement required. The limit of extensibility is determined by the firmness of the hand: the hand must not be stretched to a point which would affect the tautness of the fingers.

The slow practising of the skips is needed only to correct faulty functions.

The slow practising of single-tone skips is based on rotatory movements.

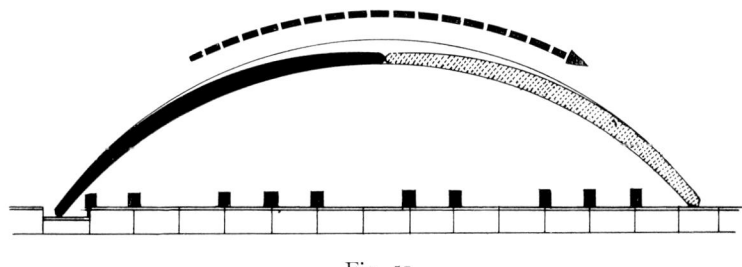

Fig. 51

Phot. 235–240

Skips executed by even motion

(La Campanella, Tamás Vásáry, 48 photos per sec.)

Phot. 241–246

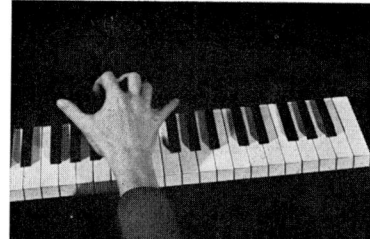

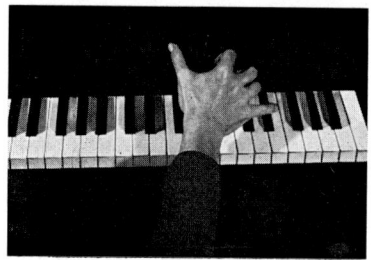

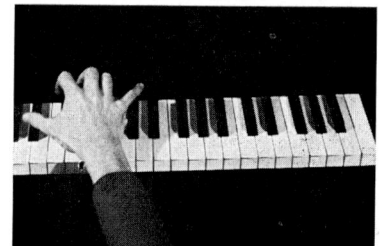
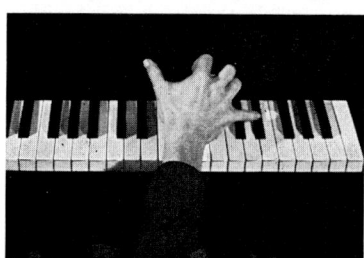
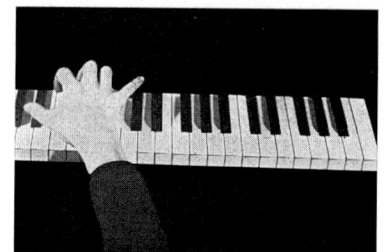
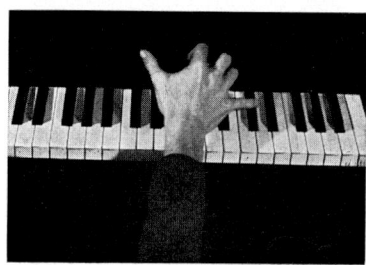
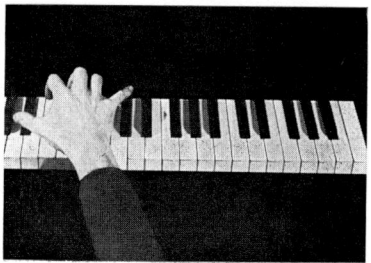

Phot. 247—252

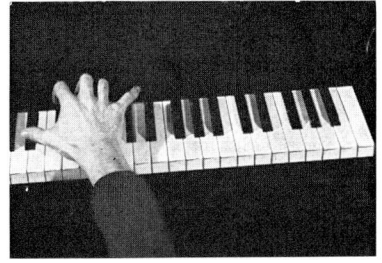

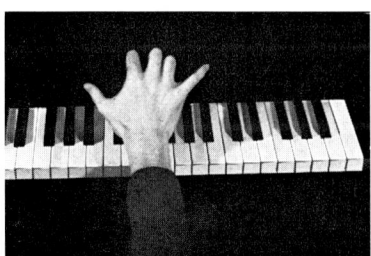

Phot. 253—258

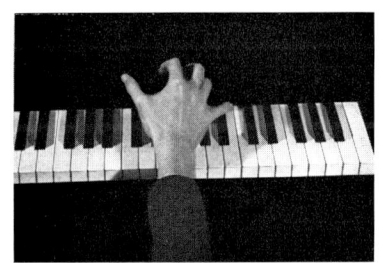

The pianist should not press the touched key down to the bottom of the key-bed but, on the contrary, should prepare instantly for the next skip. By slowing down we merely separate the strokes, while the skip itself is carried out with lightning speed. (Slow skips are always uncertain.) In the execution of the skip, the following factors are involved: a swinging movement (extension or flexion of the elbow) and rotation of the forearm; a slight rotation of the upper arm and a horizontal swing-stroke of the upper arm—this last being the essential executory factor of the skip. Such complex motion, if enlarged, would become distorted, therefore the rotational arc should not be enlarged even in slow practising.

If we want to stress or emphasize particular tones within skips executed by even motion, it is necessary to impart separate active movements to the upper arm, thereby altering the arc of the rotation. The stressing is attained, as a rule, by a higher stroke which results in a steeper curve. This should not be practised in slow playing, because the increased force will distort the movement and the overburdened arm will be unable to conserve the dexterity and ease required in skipping.

THE PREPARED SKIP

If the second tone is attained by employing the first tone as a springboard, there are three ways of executing the skip:

a. The first tone prepares the second one, which carries the accent.

Example 55 Chopin: Etude, Op. 25. No. 5

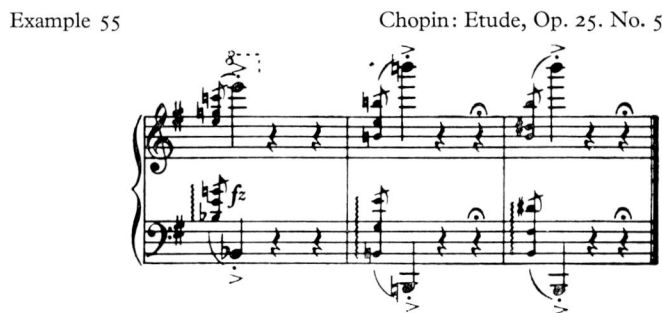

b. The second tone is lightly joined to the stressed first one.

Example 56 Beethoven: Op. 2. No. 2

c. After executing the skip with lightning speed, we do not immediately sound the second tone but wait for a short time above the key in question, in order to prepare for the next direct swing-stroke.

Example 57 Beethoven: Op. 31. No. 2

Example 58   Brahms: Sonata, Op. 2

Each of types *a* and *b* are always played with a single synthesizing motion. Type *c* occurs most frequently because here both tones of the skip can be produced by direct swing-strokes.

In all three types the arm glides flatly over the keyboard. The hand should remain exactly in octave position, thus facilitating orientation and increasing sureness.

In the prepared skip the musical contour shaping is easier than in the even-motion skip. When increasing the tempo of the repeated skips, however, we are gradually compelled to employ the latter. The musical concept of the player has to determine at which moment the transition from one type of skip to the other should take place. (The evenly executed skip is accompanied by more noise-effects.)

Whatever the type, a skip will be really good only if we do not concentrate on the skip itself, but on the tone to be sounded. Here again the correct solution will be suggested by the intensity of the musical concept.

CHORD SKIPS

In octave and chord skips the rotational movement of the forearm is not applicable because of the simultaneous sounding of the tones of the octaves and chords. The arc required for the skip in this case arises from the vertical motion of the forearm and the horizontal motion of the upper arm. In octave skips the arc is considerably higher than in the skips of single fingers.

Chord skips presenting no difficulties in the grip must be practised with the full chord. (If the grip is difficult, practise in the way given on p. 158.)

When executing skips with identical chords the grip of the chord must remain so firm that even the non-playing fingers do not move. Thus the skip will become sure in a very short time because our hand conserves the former grip and our whole attention is concentrated on the sounding of the next chord. The sureness will not diminish even with a chord change because the fingers almost automatically assume, still being in the air, the necessary new position and the swing-stroke can be executed by a perfectly firm hand. (The entire hand does not relax during the skip; only the finger having the task of changing its place should be moved.)

By slow practising of octave chord skips, it is possible not only to separate the individual strokes but also to enlarge the arc. This is, in general, more expedient than the separation of the strokes because by enlarging the arc the continuity of the motion can be conserved also during slow practising.

Phot. 259—264

The octave skip

(Beginning of the E flat major Concerto of Liszt, Annie Fischer, 48 photos per sec.)

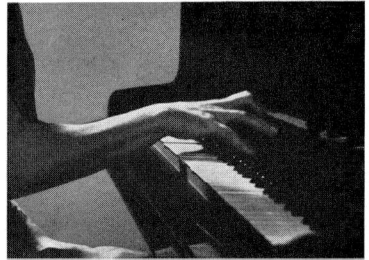

The semicircular movement of the arm begins after the sounding of the B flat octave

Example 59

The forearm—in following the circular movement—gradually rises higher and higher. The successive pictures show that the main task of the upper arm is to carry out a lateral movement. The circular movement is performed by the forearm

The forearm at the highest point of the circular movement

Phot. 265—270

During the downward phase of the skip the speed is increased. This is why the following three pictures are indistinct (until the hands are slowed by the braking effect of the keys)

The set-off moment in the A flat octave

The arm begins to rise along the receding arc

REDUCING THE ARM MOVEMENT WITH THE AID OF FINGERING

Proper fingering in many cases assists in reducing the arm movement required by the skip.

Example 60

Liszt: Paganini Study in A minor

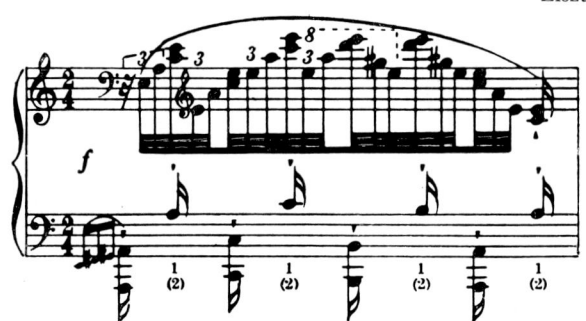

The fingering indicated in parentheses (employing the second finger) is the more widely accepted one. It has the drawback of the hand's losing its octave position and of the arm movement's becoming larger than in striking with the first finger. This makes the bass octaves uncertain. At the start of practising the use of the thumb seems more difficult, but if the octave position is firm enough automatization will soon take place.

The dreaded skips of Liszt's "Mephisto Waltz" are also more sure with the following fingering:

Example 61

The following passage from Kodály's "Dances of Marosszék" also causes the pianist much trouble.

Example 62

Universal-Edition, Wien.

The difference between the two fingerings is even more obvious here. In fast tempo, these skips can only be played with the aid of the first finger (thus diminishing the distance), if we want to avoid striking a false note.

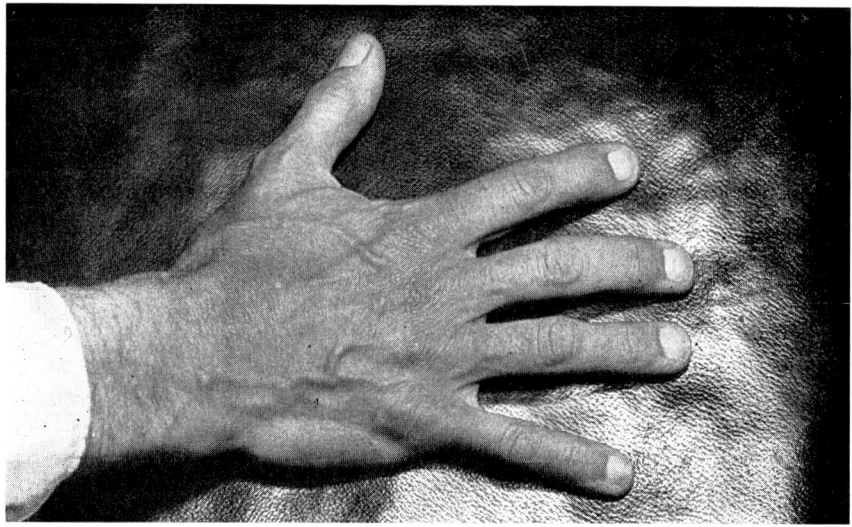

Phot. 271
THE HAND OF ROBERT CASADESUS

GLISSANDO

The tones of the glissando are not produced by separate swing-strokes but by gliding the hands over the keyboard in *one* movement.

The fingers must not be held stiffly. Let them spring elastically from key to key. This becomes realizable only by keeping the finger-ends taut and avoiding any relaxation of the third phalanx during the execution of the glissando.

The simplest way of playing the glissando is with closed fingers and the back of the hand turned towards the keyboard.

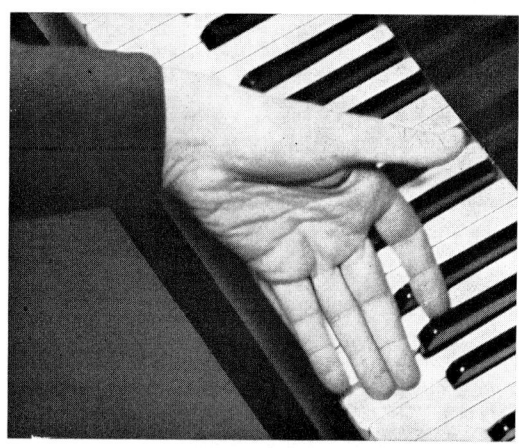
Phot. 272

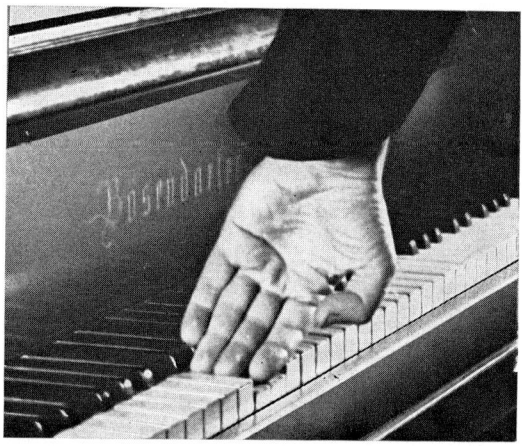
Phot. 273

LEFT-HAND GLISSANDO ON THE WHITE KEYS
It depends on the proportions of the fingers whether the glissando is to be carried out with fingers 3–4 or 2–3

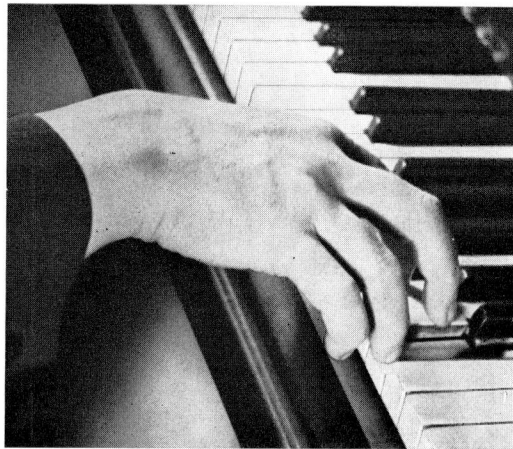

Phot. 274
GLISSANDO OF THIRDS

Played by fingers 2–4, or possibly, 1–4. The hand has to be turned in both cases in the direction of the playing, if we want to produce a smooth glissando and to avoid the finger's getting stuck

The sixth and octave glissandos should be prepared through separate practising by the participating fingers.

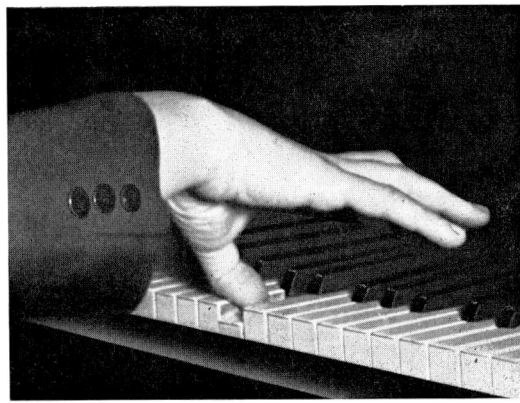

Phot. 275
GLISSANDO OF THE THUMB, INWARDS
The position of the hand as a whole assists the thumb. This position, however, must not be excessively rigid, because otherwise we get a jerky, uneven glissando

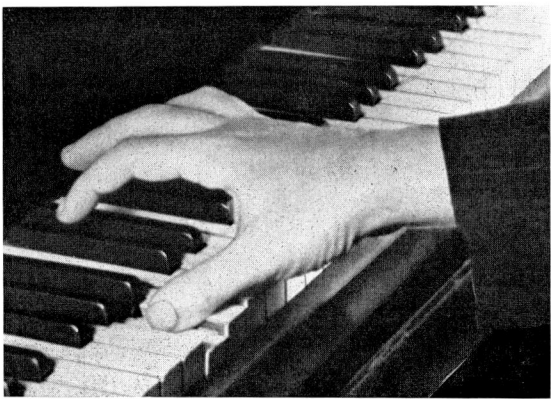

Phot. 276
GLISSANDO OF THE THUMB, OUTWARDS
The key must be touched with the side of the finger

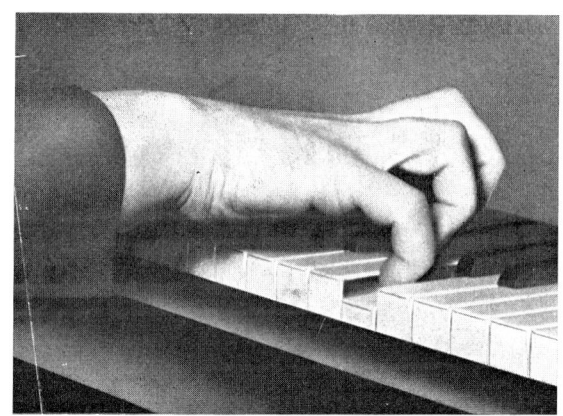

Phot. 277
GLISSANDO OF THE LITTLE FINGER, OUTWARDS
The strong bending of the third and fourth fingers increases the elasticity of the little finger

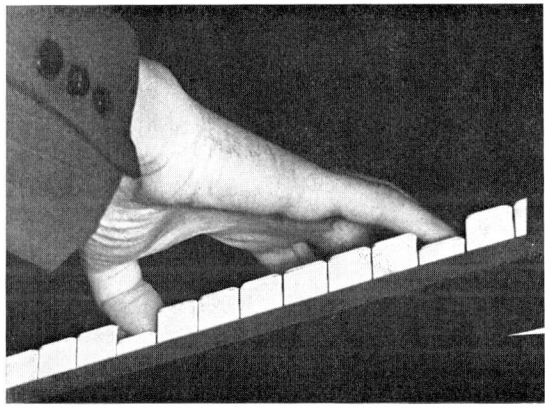

Phot. 278
OCTAVE-GLISSANDO, INWARDS
Players with large hands can perform it with bent thumb, while those with small hands have to execute it with straight thumb

FINGER TECHNIQUE

The most important subdivision of piano playing is finger technique. The work of the fingers is not only of great importance in the active swing-stroke of the fingers but also in transmitting the force of the arms to the keys. The incorrect action of a *single* finger may undermine the entire technique, while the development of finger technique has a favourable influence on the other playing forms, too.

As has been analysed in the chapter on "Swing-Stroke", the perfect "feeling", the full "grasp" of the keys can only be achieved by means of a direct swing-stroke. Since a perfect direct swing-stroke can only be executed by the whole arm, the perfect solution for the pianist would be to have ten arms at least, in order to have sufficient time to hold the keys even in the fastest tempi.

But could we not imagine each finger in the role of an arm? Yes, we could, let us suppose the finger to be an elongation of the arm.

If we want to acquire the feeling of the fingers being the elongations of the arm, the first prerequisite is the most delicate changing of the resistance (weight-complement, weight-effect). In other words: we must "stand behind" each tone. The most important requirement of good finger technique is thus the reliable, delicate functioning of the elastic support.

One of the reasons — sometimes the only reason — of a weak finger technique is a passive arm. The passivity of the arm becomes innervated mostly in the age of puberty. The arm of the pupil suddenly becomes larger and the development of the muscles is not in proportion with the development of the bones. Therefore the arm of the adolescent becomes passive — almost from one day to another. The fingers thus become overburdened which diminishes not only their velocity but also their expressive ability.

If the apportioning of the resistance is not sufficiently delicate, it will diminish both the force and the velocity of the fingers.

The weakness of the fingers is sometimes caused by holding the knuckles stiff (a by-product of the so-called rolling play). The back of the hand becomes in such cases a neutral territory between the fingers and the arm. This kind of technique is acquired by some pianists by means of long years of hard — and let us add: painful — work. They are even proud of how independently of their arms their fingers move; of how motionless their hand remains during the work of their fingers. This is sheer nonsense! The joints can have but two roles: either they belong to the active swinging unit or to the elastic support. Neutral "interposed" territories hinder both of these functions.

Therefore, a special task is thus to avoid allowing the metacarpal bones build up a neutral territory. They have to adapt themselves to the finger work even better than the arm does. They have to change their position constantly in order to assist the swing-strokes executed by the fingers as much as possible.

SHOULD WE RAISE THE FINGERS?

Many discussions are carried on over the problem whether it is correct to play with raised fingers or with fingers continuously held on the keys.

Apparently good results could be assured by each finger "starting on the key". This was a cardinal point of many theories and they have very many followers even today. But what does "starting on the key" mean? On closer analysis it turns out to be based on wrong observations. The fact that the pianist's finger touches the key does not guarantee at all that he will execute a direct swing-stroke. The preliminary condition of the direct swing-stroke is that the movement of the finger is carried out in the direction of the motion of the key. The "starting on the key" does not assure this. On the contrary: the fingers – on account of their constantly being held down – will become cramped and may be able to follow the direction of the key motion only to a lesser extent.

Thus, there is no other solution: the raising of the fingers is, up to a certain extent, always indispensable in finger technique. This is also required if we want to apply noise-effects, but from the physiological aspect it is absolutely indispensable.

Continuous tone sounding can be carried out only by continuous motion. If, however, the fingers are in constant contact with the keyboard it will be almost unavoidable that the single movements become separated by a certain jerky forced stopping. On the other hand, in order to "fill up" the whole time with the motion it is absolutely necessary that the finger leaves the keyboard.

A movement of a certain extent is also indispensable in enabling the fingers to apply sufficient force within the legato. Sometimes we even have to raise our fingers so high that it would arouse disturbing noise-effects. In such cases the tone corresponding to our tone conception can be attained by braking the finger at the moment of reaching the key. From the large movement it gained the necessary momentum and thus in the last moment it may sacrifice a certain part of this momentum in order to be able to cling to the key. Thus, the raising of the finger is carried out on such occasions in order to enable the muscles to execute larger movements. To avoid excessive noise the full velocity is not utilized, but we nevertheless obtain an appropriate tone volume because the output of the muscles is thus greater than it would have been if we had executed small movements. In slow tempo we are able to notice the braking even with the naked eye. (See in the slow-motion pictures on pp. 200–201.)

POSITIVE CONCENTRATION

One of the most effective factors in the proper training of the fingers is positive concentration. We have to concentrate on the fingers performing the strokes and not on what the other fingers do in the meantime. (It is definitely harmful, for instance, not to concentrate on the strokes of the second and third fingers, but on the position assumed in the meantime by the little finger.)

It happens that the fingers which are inactive at a given moment will *accompany* the active ones for some anatomical reason or because of wrong innervation. There is no harm in this if it has an anatomical cause. On the other hand, it requires considerable energy to keep the non-participating fingers immobile deliberately because this calls for a high degree of tension on their part. Faulty innervation will also be created by the concentration required to preserve the immobility of the inactive fingers, because it sets up a close interconnection between unnecessary and necessary movements. Hence we have to concentrate entirely on the active work, as a result of which the motion caused by faulty innervation will gradually lessen and finally disappear.

Concentrating on the inactive fingers arises, as a rule, from the conception that this will assist the independence of the fingers.

What do we mean – strictly speaking – by the independence of the fingers?

A finger is independent if its work is not hindered by the other fingers. The fingers which are kept unmoved, on the other hand, hinder the action of the finger engaged in striking and thus restrict its independence.

Thus it is erroneous to choose as a basis for training the fingers exercises in which the keys are held down. (During the action of particular fingers, the keys are held down or lightly touched by the other fingers, which remain motionless.) This kind of practising – if it is done without any forcing and straining – supplements the mechanical work required in training for polyphonic playing, but such a complicated task should be imposed on the fingers only after years of playing with free natural finger motion. Polyphonic finger exercises are useful solely at the highest level of study (for instance, when studying the "Wohltemperiertes Klavier"). It is entirely wrong, however, to use such exercises as an element – let alone as a basis – in teaching beginners. (It depends entirely on the individual whether or not this finger is needed at all.)

ANATOMIC PECULIARITIES OF THE FINGERS

In order to give a detailed analysis of finger technique, we first have to analyse the anatomic characteristics of the individual fingers.

The first finger is clumsy and slow because its base joint – enabling the thumb to stretch and move diagonally – is less suited to velocity than that of the other fingers. (The base joint of the thumb is not the articulation of the metacarpal bone and the first phalanx, but of the metacarpal and carpal bones.) One of the most important elements of finger technique – the "passing under" of the thumb (i.e. flexing it under the palm) is also a retarding factor because it requires a diagonal motion which is a result of forces acting in different directions. In practising, special care must therefore be taken of the development of the thumb's agility.

The thumb is an outer finger and much shorter than the neighbouring second finger. This inclines us in scales to apply a forearm stroke or rotation (instead of a thumb stroke), thus endangering not only the velocity but also the evenness of playing. (The dynamically exigent corner-tones of the melody are often played by either the thumb or the fifth finger. A beautiful tone is in this case, as a rule, only attainable by the active swinging motion of the upper arm.)

According to general belief the second finger is strong, skilful and reliable. On a higher level of performance its agility, however, leaves much to be desired, because the second finger is overburdened to the utmost and stiffened by the movements required in everyday life such as holding, grasping or pressing movements, and this detrimentally affects its work in piano playing.

The comparatively outer position of the second finger enables it to act as an elongation of the arm in striking the key. Therefore, we frequently tend to use rotation or shaking, instead of striking with the second finger. This renders our performance uneven in the same way as in the case of the thumb.

The third finger is the longest one, and – precisely on account of its length – is inclined to become passive. If we do not concentrate on keeping it taut, the third phalanx will "give" or bend inwards after the stroke. Placing the third finger into the chord position is more difficult than in the case of the others. This possibly is another reason for its passivity.

The fourth finger is connected with the third and fifth fingers by junctures, i.e. tiny bridges between the tendons. If the third and fifth fingers remain unmoved, the junctures will greatly impede the motion of the fourth finger. Hence the view that the fourth finger is weak and slow. Nothing could be further from the truth! The striking force of this finger is proportionate to its length and its agility even surpasses that of the other fingers. However, this striking force and agility will develop only if we give it the opportunity and use it to the same degree as the other fingers. The fourth finger is hardly used in everyday life, and thus we have to take special care to develop it in piano playing. It is a senseless and even harmful view that employing the fourth finger must be avoided as far as possible in velocity playing. We repeat: the fourth finger is at a disadvantage only if the neighbouring fingers are kept unmoved. This, however, occurs mostly in polyphonic playing in which case the fourth finger cannot be replaced anyway.

The fifth finger is one of our most muscular fingers. This is proved, among other things, by its role in octave technique. Its strokes, however, are weak on account of its shortness and small mass. In velocity technique and trilling we thus have to add to its striking force by carefully chosen adapting movements and by adequately shifting the centre of gravity. As it is an outer finger, we have to make sure that – as with the thumb – it participates actively and is not replaced by forearm strokes.

In the course of different musical epochs the technical role of the different fingers has undergone considerable changes.

Bach and Couperin used the thumb only in cases where this was necessitated by polyphony or some great stretching movement. The use of the thumb has gained ground only in the second half of the eighteenth century, acquiring in a short time an almost exclusive autocracy. The fourth and fifth fingers were pushed entirely into the background by the use of the first three fingers despite of the fact that these fingers are just as agile and important "singing" fingers as the other two. They are sometimes even more useful. Chopin fought for the "equal rights" of the fourth and fifth fingers not only in his brilliant Chromatic Etude but also in the theoretical field, by declaring that the fifth finger can by no means be considered a weak one and that it is superfluous to strive toward making the fourth finger independent from the third one. However, the use of the fourth and fifth fingers did not attain their deserved place even at the beginning of this century so that even Busoni stressed that "I try more and more to avoid the passing under of the thumb." (See p. 232.)

Thus, each one of the fingers is capable of displaying force and velocity. One only has to find the conditions under which the fingers are best able to carry out their work.

CORRECT APPORTIONMENT OF THE WORK OF THE JOINTS

The most expedient and most economical finger work is attained in the following way: The swing-stroke should be executed by the first joint, while the second and the third joints adjust themselves to the keyboard by bending or extending the fingers. (See p. 128.)

This apportionment of the work of the joints is required by our anatomical structure and it is hard to understand why everybody does not play in this way. Indeed, this is exactly how outstanding pianists do play, at least in the most difficult passages, where they can succeed only by applying the most natural movements.

In teaching, however, we very frequently find a wrong distribution of the work of the joints. While the process of lifting is performed by the first joint, it is accompanied each time by bending the second and third joints. Correspondingly, each stroke involves a stretching of the second and third joints. By this technique pianists strive to attain an even velocity and scintillating performance. The motion is, in fact, so complicated that the only way to carry it out is by extreme evenness eliminating any possibility of agogic and dynamic subtlety.

Despite such methods, a pianist with suitable hand structure and of outstanding musical ability will arrive at a natural way of playing under the pressure of technical difficulties. But woe to him who has a less fortunate hand structure and does not find the right movements instinctively. His whole energy will be absorbed by sounding the tones in an even tempo and a correspondingly even tone strength. As a result, he will become unable to give agogics and dynamics the necessary attention.

A technique of this kind requires an immense amount of practising. Finger exercises and scales have to be practised for hours, if only for the sake of warming-up, because the unnatural movements have to become automatized over and over again, which is impossible without constant mechanical

Phot. 279–283

Beginning of Chopin's Fantaisie Impromptu

(Annie Fischer, 120 photos per sec.)

The figures between the pictures indicate the number of omitted frames

Setting off the D sharp with the third finger

3

The fourth finger immediately before the set-off moment

2

The fourth finger sets off the F sharp

6

The most interesting moment. On account of the change of position, not a single finger touches the keyboard

10

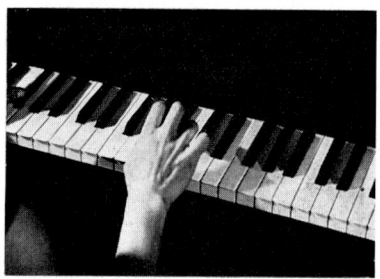

The thumb touches the A

1

Phot. 284—288

Immediately before the set-off

2

The moment of the set-off

3

The second finger before the touch

5

The second finger at the set-off of the C sharp

4

The third finger immediately before the set-off of the D sharp

13* 195

repetition. If this technique is applied, the adaptation of the separate strokes to the dynamic line becomes an insolvable problem because the movements get linked with each other instead of with the musical concept. The fingers thus attain a fluent motion but are unable to reproduce musical nuances. They do not provide either maximum speed or tone volume, nor are they capable of regulating correctly the noise-effects.

PREREQUISITES OF GOOD TONE IN FINGER TECHNIQUE

Good piano tone is considered by many people as merely a matter of natural endowment of the pianist. Tone quality is indeed decisively influenced by anatomical structure. The weight-effect comes much more easily to pianists with short, massive arms. A short thick finger transmits the force of the muscles more fully than does a long, thin finger and thus greater resonance will be achieved. Teaching, however, serves to compensate defective endowments. The fingers can be taught to transmit the impulse given by the first joint through the aid of the finger-ends and to pass on to the keys the weight-effect given by the arm.

Velocity, rhythmic and dynamic shaping, and conscious application of the noise-effects require the use of the finger as a whole as if the tip were moved immediately from the first joint. If the finger strikes as a whole single unit, the force and course of the swing-stroke will be accurately determined by the motion of the first joint.

The work of the second and third joints also contributes to economical finger motion by enabling the required finger position (flexion or extension) to be assumed with a minimum of change. Consequently within the swinging motion no inexpedient movement, no passive hitting with the fingers, no unnecessary bending or extending must be tolerated. (This is not contradictory to the statement that it is unnecessary to waste our energy on trying to eliminate accompanying movements of the fingers.)

We have to develop the "finger-end feeling", that is, the ability of consciously touching the keys with active finger-ends. However, it is impossible *to prescribe in advance* which part of the finger should touch the key.

One has to endeavour if possible to always strike with the soft part of the finger-pulp; it has to "cling" to the key. (With some key positions there is such a small possibility of this that the "if possible stretched finger" means in reality a strongly bent finger.) The larger the surface of the finger-pulp touching the key, i.e. the more stretched the finger, the more favourable will be the position for executing the direct swing-stroke. If, however, the finger touched the key in a fully stretched position this would diminish the "catching" and "holding" possibility. It is again the medium position which gives the most favourable precondition for the activity of the fingers.

The position of the fingers varies according to the succession of black and white keys. For this reason, flexions and extensions of different degrees are needed even *within a single phrase*. In strongly flexed position the finger-tips (but never the nails), and in extended position the fleshy parts of the finger should touch the key.

The finger-ends should approach the key by the shortest route, without any superfluous movements or detours. Any unnecessary movements in lifting the fingers should not be carried out either, but rather they should be allowed to resume the striking position by the shortest possible route.

The finger shall not glide along the key after having finished the stroke and any subsequent bending or extending movements of the second and third joints should not be permitted.

In slow practising both the tone volume and the noise-effect increase because the strokes are executed from a greater distance. For this reason, we are only partially able to realize our musical concept. However, an accurate elaboration of the finger action is indispensable also in slowing-down. Practising with passively dropped fingers will do more harm than good and will spoil our finger technique, while active finger work will enable us to attain results in an astonishingly short time.

APPLICATION OF NOISE-EFFECTS

Upper noises are frequently used in finger technique. The stronger the noise-effect we want to obtain, the higher the single finger stroke must be. When playing without noise-effect the fingers must be placed immediately on the surface of the keys. Thus it is very important to regulate the height of the stroke in accordance with the required musical effect.

The carrying capacity of the tone is augmented the more we reduce the noise-effect. A noise-free tone is felt by us to be more resounding and full, while excessively loud noises (compared to the tone volume) deprive the tone of its full resonance. It is essential that the proportion of the noise-effects to the strength of the tone be determined by us and that noise-effects be used or omitted intentionally and consciously and not left to chance.

The tone also loses in resonance if the second and third joints "give" when striking, and if the finger-ends are unable to transmit the force received without any loss. In such cases, the loudness of the noise is in proportion to the height of the stroke, but the tone amount is too small compared with the noise and the tone is not "concise" enough. The finger is unable to accomplish its task because it cannot transmit its impulse to the key, just as we are unable to strike with the required force when using a hammer with a broken handle.

We must have the feeling as if the fleshy part of the finger were concentrated on a such a tiny part as a pinhead, i.e. while almost grasping the key with our finger we feel the touching part is just a tiny point. If we can carry through both these tendencies, the finger will not "give", and no superfluous noise-effects will arise independently from our motion command.

The absolute amount of the noise-effect may, therefore, change even in the case of strokes of unchanged height. When carrying out active strokes with the finger-ends, the surface of the contact diminishes and the noise will diminish, too. (When striking with passive, "giving" second and third joints, a large surface will touch the key on account of the flattening of the fingers.) It is of still greater importance that, when carrying out the swing-stroke in a concentrated manner, the finger-ends are able to transmit the received force without any loss.

THE JOINT WORK OF THE FINGERS AND FOREARM

In teaching finger technique we are in general aware of the danger that the pupil will "shake" his hands, i.e. he will complement the functioning of the finger with an active forearm motion. The shaking must be really considered as a grave fault because, on account of its mechanical character, it makes every dynamic shaping impossible, sooner or later it forces the fingers into passivity and thus entails the rapid decrease of the ability to play in a quick tempo.

However, when fighting against "shaking" music teachers go into the other extreme by preaching an "entirely pure finger technique" which excludes almost entirely the work of the arm. We can judge how fatal this is for the dynamic shaping. It is also quite certain that the fingers – thus deprived of the assistance offered by the arm – will grow clumsy instead of becoming agile. But there is still another grave fault led to by the "pure finger technique." It hinders the pupil from developing the ability to connect the imagined tone colour with the work of the active swinging units almost automatically.

When dealing with the legato it has been stated that the legato appears in a continually changing content in each different style. So, e.g., many legato scales of Mozart, which would be wrongly played with portato or staccato, correspond to tone effects attained by violinists playing with separate bows. Such a tone effect is sometimes attained by us by changing the resistance almost from tone to tone, or sometimes, mainly in forte passages, the active work of the forearm will give aid to the fingers. In forte playing it often occurs that the work of the forearm will be more intensive than that of the fingers. But this is not identical with shaking either and so one should not mix them up. The shaking is mechanical and so it does not offer any assistance to the fingers, it may work only instead of them. It hinders the development of finger technique because it compels the forearm to execute active work when there is absolutely no need of it. On the other hand, if we want to attain a greater key velocity by applying a greater mass, and with this aim in mind we avail ourselves of the active work of the forearm, this will already be a help given to the fingers. (The force, i.e. the height of the stroke could of course be increased too, but this would completely change the tone colour in consequence of the proportionately increasing noise-effect.)

Thus it is obvious that both shaking and the continuous "pure" finger technique are equally nonsensical. Technical solutions can be determined only by the musical concept and there is no predetermined pattern which could serve as a basis for constituting generally valid and constant rules.

But how can we be assured that the pupil employs only the extent of arm motion required to complement the finger work? The only possibility for this is precisely the appropriate foundation of the finger technique. The fingers must always be active and one could almost say that the fingers have to dictate to the forearm to what extent they require active help. This activity – as has been mentioned in the chapter on "The Technique of the Octaves" – applies even in the case when the fingers execute no separate movements and figure only as elongations of the arm.

EXERCISES FOR THE DEVELOPMENT OF FINGER TECHNIQUE

Pupils with good movements and favourable hand structure learn the finger's active work (executed from the first joint) by simple imitation because it is a natural movement. Thus, when teaching beginners, special finger exercises are needed only in the exceptional cases of pupils with bad movements. On a more developed technical level, however, such great demands are put upon the fingers both in the field of velocity and in that of the display of force that special aid must be given to most pupils. So the necessity for special touch exercises arises to develop and aid the exact and loss-free work of the fingers.

Our aim is a more vigorous and clearer execution of the separate swing-stroke and so we have to find a way of assuring that only the fingers execute the strokes during the exercise. This can be checked if we let our arm "float" weightlessly and not even supply a minimal resistance. With relaxed, passive arms the exercise can be of no use. As the arm does not give any aid, it will frequently happen in the beginning that the key will not remain depressed but will push back the finger. The more accurately we execute the swing-stroke, the deeper the key will sink. At a certain depth, the weight of the finger will of itself suffice to hold down the key. When carrying out free swing-strokes, the task of holding down the keys cannot be entrusted to the finger muscles because this will make the finger stiff and passive, thereby endangering the freedom of the next swing-stroke.

(In reality not only the weight of the fingers but also the resistance of the finger muscles hinders the rise of the key. Our fingers are fixed by the antagonistic muscles even when we have the feeling of our fingers' being perfectly relaxed.)

We want to practise having the fingers execute their active swing-strokes from the first joint with maximal sureness. To promote this, we have to make exercises where no separate movements of the second and third joints (e.g., accommodation to the black keys) are needed.

The free movement of the fingers can be assured by preparing them in advance by appropriate gymnastics. If we want our finger to move really as a whole the second and third joints must not execute superfluous work because one has to feel where these joints are. The preparatory gymnastic exercises always begin with bending the second and third joints. (Nos. 34, 35.) Circling with the fingers (No. 33) follows afterwards with a view of restoring the equilibrium of the muscles, and to conclude gymnastic exercise No. 36 preparing the use of the fingers as a unit.

The position of the fingers, assumed in the resting position, will determine which one of the gymnastic exercises should be repeated more frequently. If the problem is that the third and second joints bend backwards, more bending exercises should be done. With cramped, bent-in fingers more circling exercise is to be used.

Put your right hand on the C-G fifth. The thumb should rest lightly on the C without depressing it. The other fingers touch the keys in a relaxed position, i.e. not in a strained extension but in the medium position. The separate swing-strokes must not follow each other very closely. Give yourself time enough to be able to execute the next swing-stroke again with full concentration. Strike with the same finger four or five times and then proceed to the next. It is most expedient to begin with the fourth finger because the swing-strokes are executed in the best way by this "specialist", applied in most cases only in playing of instruments.

Our aim is to achieve a really free swing-stroke: The finger, making full use of its freedom of action, should rise as high as it is able to do so without strain. The lifting must not represent any separate phase but merely be the preparation for the stroke. The proper conception of this movement will be facilitated by imagining we are sounding a large heavy gong. Imitate the swinging movement of the arm with the fingers so that the movement starts from the first finger joint instead from the shoulder.

The freedom and the vigour of the swinging movements of the individual fingers are dependent on their not being hindered by the other fingers. Therefore, the resting fingers must always be permitted to accompany the finger executing the swing-stroke. This accompanying movement is largest when the action is performed by the fourth finger and considerably smaller when carried out by the second or fifth fingers. After executing the swing-stroke the accompanying fingers have to fall back on the keyboard; they must not remain in the air. But it is equally faulty for them to lean heavily against the keyboard.

During the whole process of the swinging movement, i.e., both when lifting and striking, we always have to *rivet our attention on the finger-ends*. When playing with released fingers, we strike with the fleshy part of the finger-ends and try to narrow the stroke practically to a pinhead. (As if striking the key with a thorn protruding from the pad of the finger.)

The arm floats freely and aids the fingers by its constant adjusting movements. Although the active work of the fingers starts from the first joint, we must have the feeling of moving the keys directly from the chest.

Phot. 289
ALEXANDER BRAILOWSKI

Phot. 290–294

Touch exercise with the fourth finger

(32 photos per sec.)

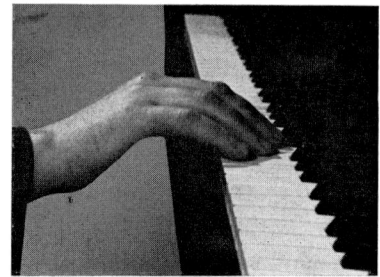

The fingers are in repose; they touch the keys lightly

12

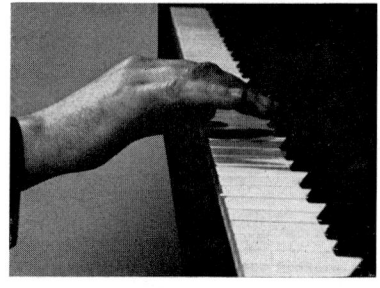

The little finger makes room by rising ahead of the fourth finger

3

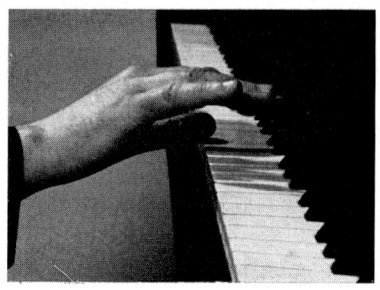

2

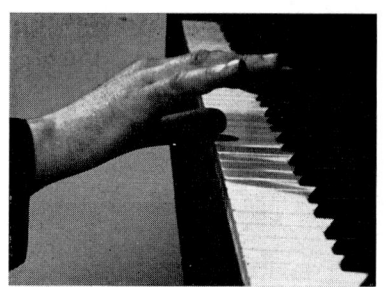

The fourth finger is already in a higher position than all the other fingers

1

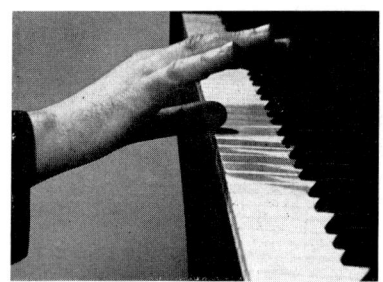

It may be clearly observed that the thumb — although it supports the hand — does not depress the key

5

Phot. 295—300

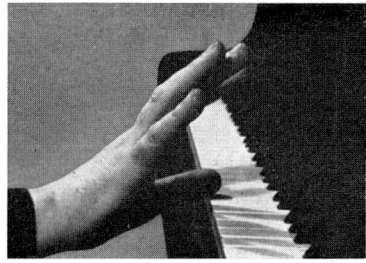

The fourth finger at the highest point

The fourth finger begins to move downwsrds

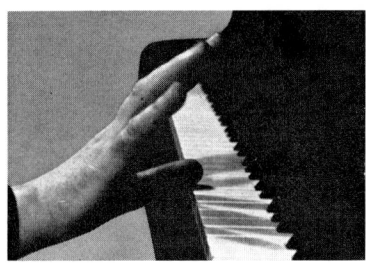

The increasing speed of the fourth finger is to be observed from the indistinction of the outlines

The picture becomes entirely blurred on account of the extraordinary speed

The fourth finger already touches the key, the other fingers are still moving

The moment of the set-off. The third finger already touches the key, but the second one — having risen last — is still under way

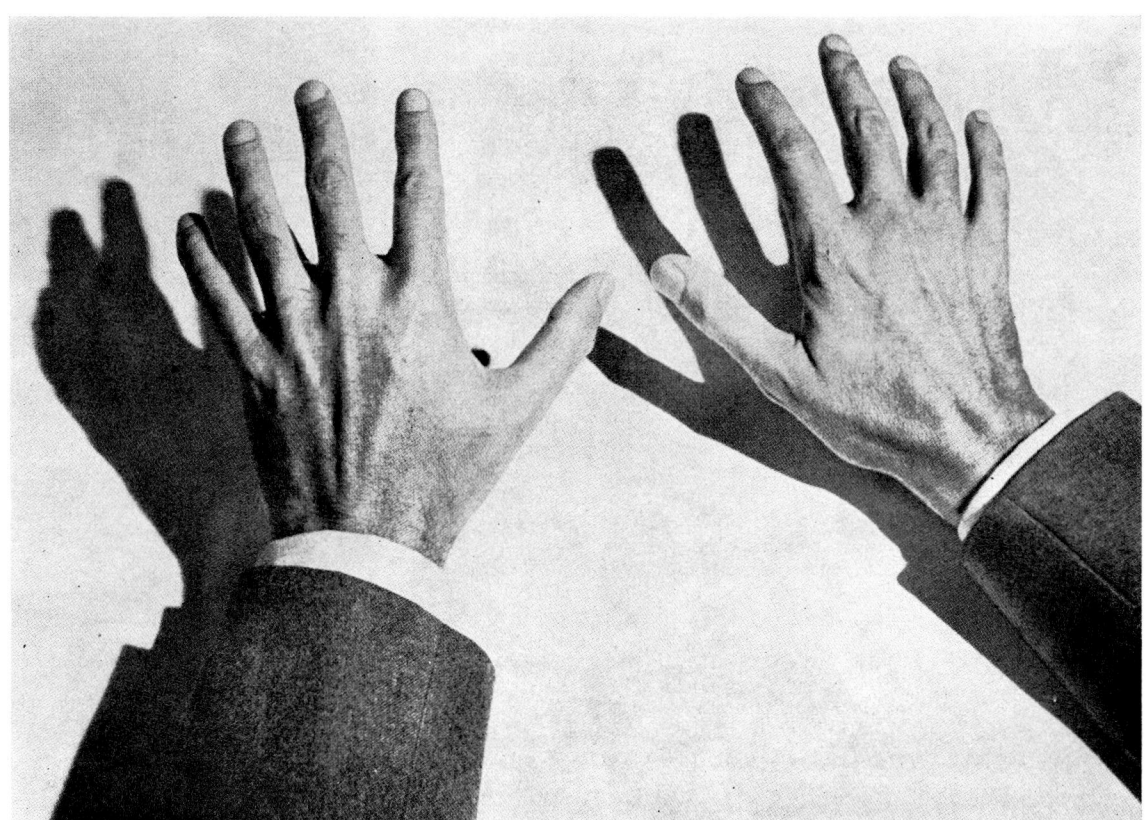

Phot. 301
THE HANDS OF ARIAS

This exercise cannot be carried out by the thumb because its freedom of action is hampered by the immobile arm and the deep position of the wrist. However, the thumb has an important function in that it supports the arm by lightly touching the keyboard. This makes possible the free suspension of the arm which would otherwise be impeded by the exhaustion of the muscles.

The free swing-stroke of the thumb can only be practised when the arm is also free to move. The wrist is then able to assume a higher position and will not hinder the motion of the thumb.

In this case the individual swing-strokes are not separated from each other. While one of the fingers strikes, the other gets ready for action and all fingers are in a state of constant preparedness. For this purpose, the fingers, after executing the stroke, wait in the air for the next stroke. Smooth playing is assured by the adjusting movements of the arm.

The most suitable exercise for practising the free swing-stroke of the trunk is some five-finger formula, such as the following Hanon finger exercise.

Example 63

The swinging movements must be linked with each other without any interruption. If each swing-stroke is free and as comfortable as possible, and the individual fingers make full use of their freedom of action, the tempo will be precisely determined as a result of this linking of movements. This tempo will be a comparatively slow one, but within it there must be no braking of the finger movements. The entire exercise has to consist exclusively of a series of free swing-strokes.

The thumb should carry out the same free and large movements as the other fingers. Adapting movements of the arm are indispensable for this purpose. They enable each finger to assume the most convenient striking position, but the arm must not take part in the swing-stroke nor should it oppose any resistance. (The application of weight-effect would render the fingers unable to utilize their full freedom of action, thus depriving their swinging movement of freedom and comfort.)

Because we do not apply any weight-effect, the tone cannot really be beautiful and well-sounding in this exercise. The single swing-stroke must nevertheless be carefully executed in order to attain the most beautiful sound possible. The tone volume, too, will increase proportionately to the gradually increasing clearness and accuracy of the swing-stroke. At the same time, the tone quality will also improve because the tone volume increases without any increase in the noise-effects or, rather, simultaneously with their diminution. Without weight-effect the tone remains thin, no matter how precise the swing-stroke, but this exercise, nevertheless, will assist in making the swing-stroke surer. (In actually performing a composition there is bound to be a weight-effect in any case!)

The above exercises are adapted exclusively to teaching the finger the correct swing-stroke. They must be practised by the two hands separately. To practise them constantly is superfluous and we should employ them only temporarily in order to master complete finger action. Pianists with suitable hands and a proper sense of motion will instinctively and without such special exercises find the most expedient way of using their fingers — as may be seen in the case of several excellent performers. But that which a few people can achieve by instinct can be attained by everybody as a result of consciously directed teaching.

Phot. 302–307

Progressive touch exercise

(32 photos per sec.)

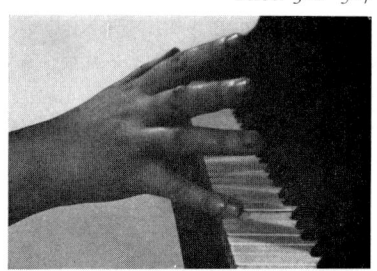

The fourth finger rises for the stroke

While the fourth finger executes the stroke, the others assume a still higher position in order to set free the fourth finger

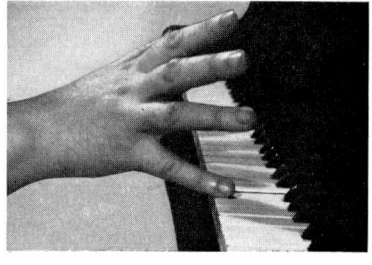

The fourth finger at the highest point

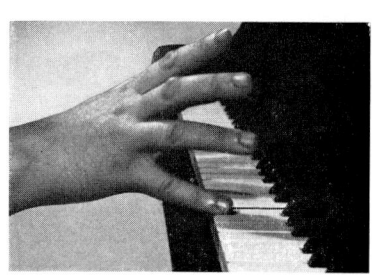

The indistinctness of the picture shows the increasing speed

The fourth finger already touches the key

Phot 308–312

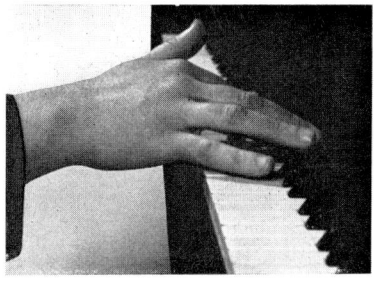

The thumb is ready for the stroke; the second finger still holds the key

30

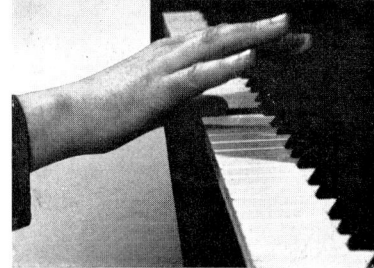

The first finger at the moment of the set-off. The second already risen

13

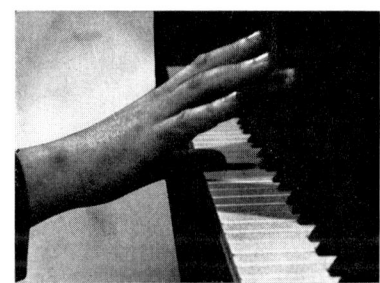

18

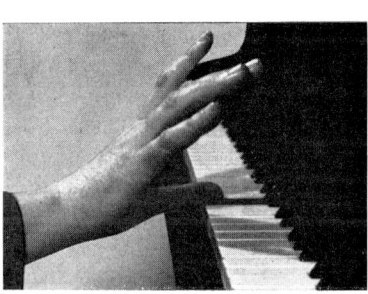

The second finger at the highest point

7

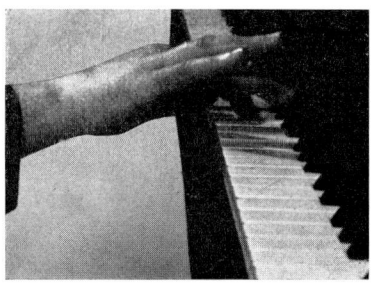

The second finger at the set-off moment

THE PLAYING OF SCALES

The playing of scales is one of the most difficult phases of piano technique. The pianist encounters quite a lot of special difficulties. In a good scale the strokes of the fingers have to follow each other as smoothly as if we had separate fingers for each key. We have to "swindle," i.e. make our hands progress in such a way that even the most attentive listener does not notice that the hand executed a shifting. The pianist has to overcome the laziness of the thumb which impedes the velocity of playing and he must not let the oblique stroke of the thumb cause differences in the sounding of tones. On account of the progressing movement of the arm the adapting movement of the arm and hand produce additional difficulties and a still more difficult task is to find the correct solution for the synthesizing in the course of which we have to equalize not only the different forces of the fingers but also have to take care always to obtain a tone volume corresponding to the melody despite the fact that the higher tones of the piano gradually weaken.

Since difficulties are the greatest in the fast playing of scales, the functions required in scale playing at maximum velocity should first be analyzed.

ARM MOVEMENT IN SCALE PLAYING

The task of the arm in the playing of scales — besides apportioning the resistance, i.e. synthesizing — is to ensure the smooth movement of the hand in changing position. What is the simplest solution?

From the aspect of fingering the diatonic scale consists of repetitions of three- and four-tone groups. On this basis the solution which appears simplest would be to divide the octaves into two arm movements and to make the position changes dependent on the fingering groups.

However, no such divided position changing is noticeable in the playing of outstanding pianists. When playing rapid scales they will glide their arms in a single movement along the keyboard, a movement that is as quiet as in playing a glissando. (If, e.g., one hand plays a scale while the other executes a glissando, both arms of the performer will move precisely in the same way: the movement of the hand playing the scale is just as even as that of the other hand executing the glissando.)

It is obvious that with the slowing of the tempo the arm motion can be gradually less and less uniform and the changing of position can become more and more separated. This does not, however, impede the uniform shaping of the scale because in slow tempo there is abundant time for the fingers to equalize the difference of force aroused by the uneven arm motion.

The synthesizing is facilitated by the fact that the resistance will change proportionally to the horizontal movement of the arm. Thus, e.g., when playing upwards, both the progression of the melody and the relative weakening of the piano tone require increase of the resistance in order to make us hear an equalized tone volume. On the other hand, when playing downwards the resistance decreases *simultaneously* with the horizontal movement of the arm. Since the changes of the resistance (weight-effect) are closely linked with the horizontal movements of the arm, we get the feeling that the horizontal movement is the medium of the synthesizing process. Do not forget however — as this would cause serious difficulties especially in slow tempi — that the synthesizing must take place in the direction of the strings and not horizontally.

The adapting movements of the arm have also an important role in the shaping of the dynamic contours of the scale. The work of the arm is completed by the horizontal movement of the hand and the raising and sinking of the wrist. The role of the adapting movements becomes increased in slow scales where they are quite indispensable not only in the dynamic shaping but also in their enabling us to attain a smooth noise-free playing. The prerequisite of good sounding of a slow scale is thus the relatively great number of adapting movements. With the increasing of the tempo, however, gradually smaller adapting movements are required and in the fastest tempi they become almost imperceptible.

Thus, practising the adapting movements consciously in scales played in a medium tempo or in the slow practising of fast scales will lead to faulty innervations. The automatization of the raising of the wrist is not only superfluous but also decidedly hinders the smooth flow of the scale. Pay full attention to the mighty sweeping movements of the arm (comprising even four or six octaves of a scale into one single unit) and leave the adapting to our muscle-feeling. (A prerequisite of this is, of course, that the rigidity and stiffness of our upper arm or forearm does not hinder the adapting activity.)

THE CHANGES OF POSITION OF THE HAND IN SCALE PLAYING

From the fact that the hand, too, takes part in the adapting process it follows that the position of the hand changes according to the height of the pitch register and the tonalities, i.e. the succession of the tones. However, these position changes can be neglected when considering that the pianist has to accommodate the position of the hand to the direction of the scale. Just as the arm connects the rapid scales through a single arm movement, it is evident that the hand must not divide the scale into several parts. It follows that the hand does not change its position either, as long as the scale advances in the same direction. (This statement applies only in a general sense, because the position of the hand undergoes slight changes depending on the height of the pitch register.)

The hand may assume three positions compared to the forearm: it elongates the arm either in a straight line or at an angle, bending towards the thumb or the little finger (radial or ulnar flexion).

The position of the hand is to be chosen with a view toward facilitating the finger work. Since in scales the most difficult task is the changing of the position, the fingers playing a role at that moment are the first to be taken into consideration. When playing the scales outwards the role of the thumb and of the second finger, when playing them inwards the roles of the thumb and the third and the fourth finger respectively should be analysed.

The thumb has considerably greater possibilities for a horizontal movement than the other fingers. For this reason the thumb does not need any particular help, the only thing to be assured is that it be not hindered in its horizontal movements by pressing the hands down.

Phot. 313
THE HANDS OF WILHELM BACKHAUS
The radial flexion of the right hand is clearly noticeable

Example 64

Schubert: Impromptu in F minor

Phot. 314
THE HAND OF ANNIE FISCHER
Rapid scale inwards (Schubert: Impromptu in F minor)

The most natural feeling of the hand can be attained if it is a straight continuation of the forearm over the keyboard (as suggested by Chopin). With an inward scale this is really an excellent solution because after the stroke of the thumb the third and fourth fingers respectively may assume their place over the proper key.

But what happens if the scale is played outwards by keeping the same hand position? The thumb will also find its place most easily in this position, but the second finger attains the proper key only at the price of a considerable jerk. How could we assure the same comfortable solution as has been done formerly for the third and fourth fingers?

Phot. 315
THE HANDS OF ALEXIS WEISSENBERG
The left hand in strong ulnar flexion

The reason why it was comfortable to play an inward scale with hands as straight elongations of the arms was that the hand turned in the direction of playing. Turn the hand also when playing outwards in the direction of the movement, if necessary even by a strong ulnar flexion, in order to enable the second finger to assume its place smoothly. The radial flexion, too, will—first of all in the extreme octaves—aid us in putting smoothly the third and fourth fingers on the appropriate key.

Thus, in a fast scale the hand will always bend in the direction of playing in order to assist the fingers in passing over or under. This gradually becomes more and more difficult with reduced tempo because as we slow down, the adapting movements of the arm come into prominence and the execution of these would be endangered by the maintenance of an unchanged hand position.

DIRECTION OF THE THUMB STROKE

The preliminary condition of the even, smooth progressing of the arm is that the fingers strike the keys obliquely to a certain degree and from the side. This has special importance with strokes of the thumb because the thumb executes more horizontal than vertical movements, and so it can better accomplish its task by striking obliquely and sidewards. If the thumb were to strike vertically, the hand would have to progress jerkily in order to shift the thumb into the new position. If the arm were to be jerked again and again into new positions after each group of three or four tones, the result would be a scale studded with accents and unevennesses. If the thumb strikes with oblique horizontal movement, on the other hand, it is capable of taking the lion's share of the movement itself and of distributing only the rest among the other fingers.

It is very important to decide in what direction the thumb has to strike. The direction must be chosen so that the rebound of the key does not brake but aids the progression of the arm.

If the thumb reaches the key by an oblique horizontal stroke *executed in the direction of the arm movement*, it will counteract the arm's progression. The resistance (counter-stroke) of the key acts in a direction opposite to the arm movement and the thumb will virtually get stuck in the key. Thus, the only possibility of smooth performance is to execute the thumb stroke in a direction contrary to that of the playing. (The thumb's action is similar to that of a hook used to swing a boat forward.) In this manner the resistance of the key does not hinder the arm's progress but, on the contrary, facilitates it.

PREPARATION OF THE THUMB STROKE

Thumb strokes carried out in a direction opposite to that of the playing require a certain preparation when playing a scale outwards. The thumb must be passed under the palm before the beginning of the stroke. Scales played inwards do not necessitate any preparation, but all the more attention should be paid to the free swinging motion of the thumb. We have a tendency to stiffen the thumb under the impression that it is already above the key to be struck and that it will suffice to strike downwards. In reality, however, the arm will already have moved further before the thumb stroke is carried out, and the thumb is forced to strike laterally at a wide bias in order to reach the key. This oblique swing-stroke will succeed only on condition that the movement has a free course also in the radial direction. Therefore, when practising slowly, the thumb must stretch to an apparently unnecessary degree, passing beyond the key to be struck. However, it is precisely with the aid of this stretching that the thumb will be able to execute the oblique swing-stroke correctly.

As the thumb is extremely clumsy and slow, its stroke must be prepared very carefully. In slow practising the thumb should begin to pass under the palm immediately striking, so that it will already have reached its place when the second finger strikes. This is very important because, in the fastest tempi, the thumb will reach its place only if it begins the preparatory movement simultaneously with the stroke of the second finger.

In slow tempo we are inclined to delay the preparation until the stroke of the third or fourth fingers. In fast tempo this will be unsatisfactory on account of the slowness of the thumb.

SLOW PRACTISING OF FAST SCALES

Scale playing is a complex motion. Slow practising of fast scales can, therefore, be correctly practised only by decomposing the movement into its components. The most important factor in playing scales is finger action, and, therefore, the swinging movements of the fingers in slow practising should be executed in a way exactly corresponding to the way they are executed in fast tempo. The amplitude of the swing-strokes should be enlarged concurrently with the slowing of the tempo.

When playing scales outwards we are compelled to decompose the action of the thumb and to divide it into the preparation and the stroke instead of executing a single unbroken swing-stroke. If we were to insist on a free and comfortable swinging movement on the part of the thumb even in playing scales in an outward direction, the preparation would not be innervated, thereby impeding the even flow of the scale.

When playing scales inwards, the thumb will, like the other fingers, execute comfortable, free swing-strokes. The preparation consists in a considerable stretching movement of the thumb enabling it to get at the key from the side.

In slow practising of fast scales an even motion of the arm will not prove serviceable because this sort of curbed, slow movement would stiffen the arm. The arm movement has to take place simultaneously with the thumb stroke. In slow practising each octave will thus be divided into two arm movements. This will not affect the synthesizing of the fast scale into one movement, provided we never lose the sensation of the upper arm's readiness for the synthesizing motion.

When changing position, the thumb and the arm will simultaneously carry out their contrary movements. The arm must not wait until after the thumb stroke when assuming a new position, because this would easily result in leaning on the thumb, and if that were to happen, the thumb would be compelled to depress the key. This would, on the one hand, cause an interruption of the synthesizing movement and, on the other, a faulty innervation, in consequence of the necessarily passive movement of the thumb. The innervation of this passivity would render the thumb (already inert by nature) even more incapable of agile motion. The perfect simultaneity of the opposite movements not only assures a uniform synthesizing movement but also the activity of the thumb.

Phot. 316–321

The action of the thumb in fast playing of the B major scale. Lateral view

(120 photos per sec.; every second frame omitted)

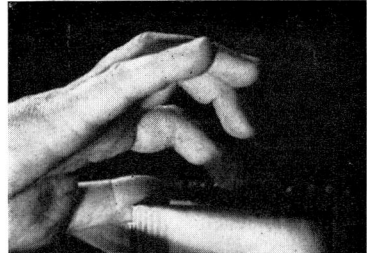

The thumb begins its movement simultaneously with the stroke of the second finger

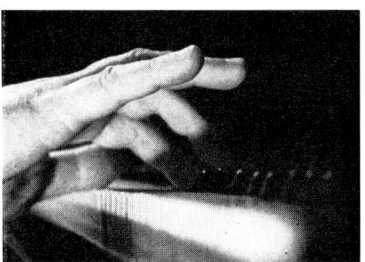

The second finger still touches the key. The third finger immediately before the set-off moment

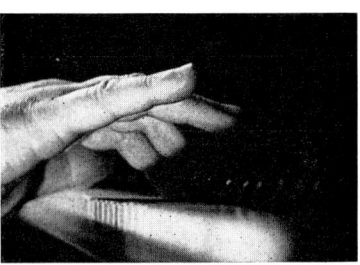

The third finger at the set-off of the D sharp; the second finger still touches the key. The thumb is already under the palm

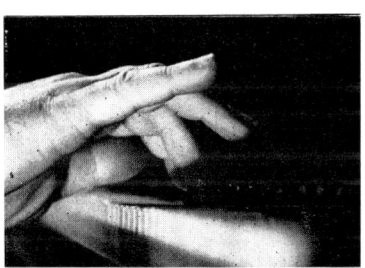

The third finger is still lying on the key. The thumb is preparing for the set-off. As may be seen, the thumb, in this picture, comes closest to the observer, i.e. it passes beyond the key in order to execute the stroke diagonally and in a direction contrary to that of the playing

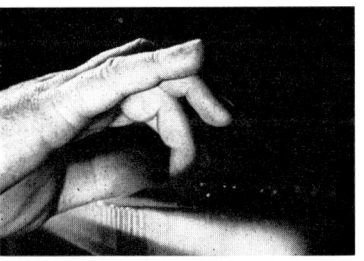

The third finger has just now released the D sharp. The thumb is 2/120 sec. before the set-off moment

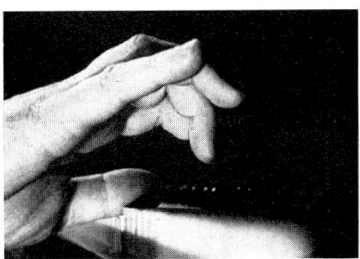

The thumb at the set-off of the E. Note how the hand in the pictures grows gradually larger. This proves that the movement of the arm is even

Phot. 322–326

Slow practising of fast scale

(The left hand plays a B major scale onwards. 32 photos per sec.)

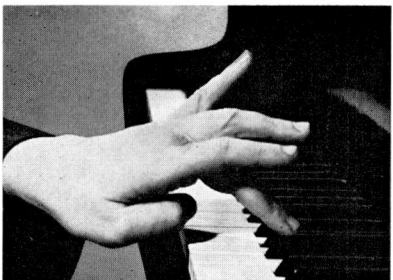

The third finger sets off the G sharp. The thumb prepares for the stroke

13

The fourth finger lightly touches the F sharp, the thumb rises in order to execute an oblique inward stroke

The fourth finger at the set-off of the F sharp

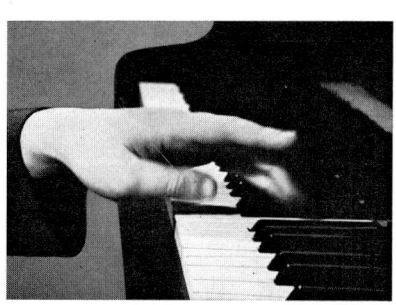

The picture becomes indistinct because the thumb executes the stroke by moving away from the palm with great speed, while the hand simultaneously changes its position

1

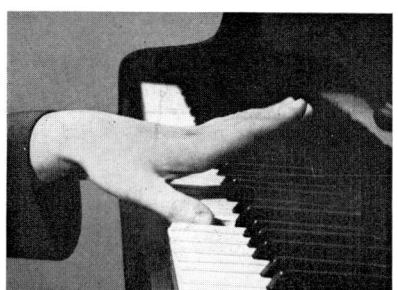

The thumb at the set-off of the E. As the movement of the hand is not controlled but free, it passes beyond the required position

12

Phot. 327–332

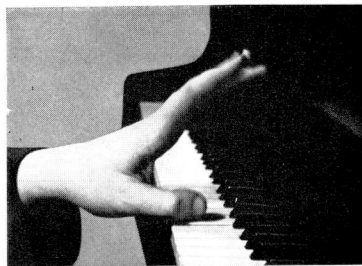

The second finger strikes with great speed as may be noticed from the indistinctness of the pictures. The thumb releases the E and begins its preparatory movement

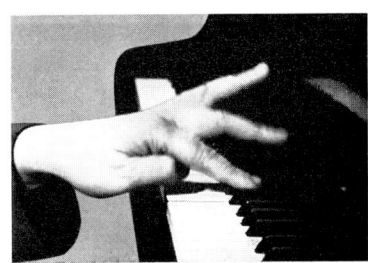

The second finger lightly touches the D sharp, while the thumb during the stroke assumes its position under the palm. It is very characteristic of the great speed of the movement that all this takes place in 1/32 sec.: on the preceding picture the beginning of the preparatory movement is still to be seen

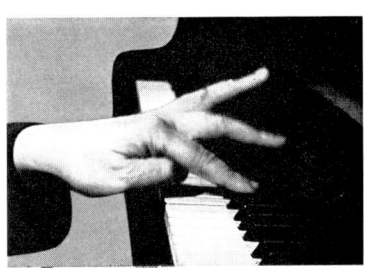

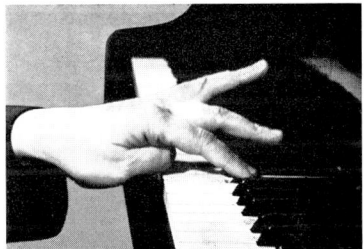

The second finger at the set-off of the D sharp

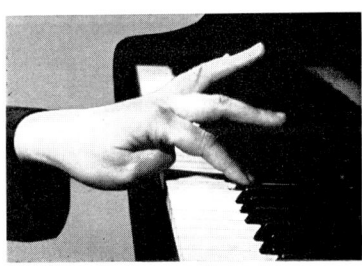

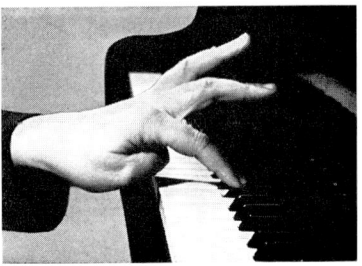

213

In slow practising of fast scales, the arm should give only a minimum – but absolutely indispensable – weight-effect. This weight-effect counteracts the rebound of the key, which thus is absorbed not only by the knuckle but also by the resistance of the arm and shoulder. (In slow practising the arm has no dynamic task whatever.) The resistance of the arm enables us to sound the tone energetically which is imperative in scale playing.

If in slow practising of scales we do not apply any synthesizing and our arms hang down passively, we will sooner or later involuntarily overburden our fingers. This overburdening will hinder the free motion of the fingers in slow practising, and clean finger work will be replaced by "shaking".

The scale must, therefore, be synthesized, both in slow practising and in slow or fast playing by a single sweeping arm movement. (In slow tempo this movement will not be a uniformly, smoothly progressing one and this will make the synthesizing process difficult.) In the case of scales or passages moving in the opposite direction we have to imagine ourselves opening our arms and as if the piano also opened simultaneously. Thus when our hand remains in reality in its place, we have the feeling as if it moved horizontally.

Scales must – even in the higher grades of schooling – be practised mainly by each hand separately, playing slowly and fast in succession. This is the best way to get the "feel" of synthesizing by means of a single movement and, at the same time, of clear finger strokes within this uniform arm movement. In the beginning, both fast and slow scales must be practised only in one direction and several times one after another, either merely inwards or merely outwards. The two directions must not be joined until we are able to play them perfectly and with great speed in one direction. (This applies only to the learning of fast scales and not to the scale playing of beginners. Slow practising of fast scales should not be started until the middle grade, i.e. when taking up the Sonatas of Haydn and Mozart.)

Special practising is needed for the intensively controlled scales of medium velocity (notably in mezzoforte and piano). Their virtuoso execution requires a superior knowledge of fast scale playing. In the course of practising we also have to increase gradually the speed of the scales of medium tempo, until the borderline between the manner of playing medium and fast scales disappears. A prerequisite of this is the most accurate shading of every tone in fast tempo, which requires a parallel and systematic practising of both kinds of scales.

The beginner's slow scale cannot be developed into a fast scale merely by gradually increasing the tempo. Certain faults would thereby inevitably become innervated because the slow scale requires many adapting movements, which are rather complicated to reduce gradually in the course of practising. If, however, we start practising fast scales even before those of medium tempo, it will lead us to the most essential technical solutions and ensure that between the manner of playing medium scales and the fast ones no other difference will exist than the quantity of the adapting movements applied.

SCALES IN THIRDS

The problems of scales in thirds are fundamentally the same as those of plain scales. The only difference is that in playing scales in thirds it is even more difficult to be certain that the changing of the position of the hand is carried out without jerks and that it does not cause any trouble in the dynamic shaping.

The work of the arm is the same as with plain scales but since changes of position occur here more often, the apportionment of the resistance puts the work of the whole body – and mainly that of the arm – to an even greater test. With a relaxed, passive arm a scale in thirds cannot be played with satisfactory tone volume even in medium tempo.

But the change of position is even made more difficult by the circumstance that in scales in thirds two fingers always strike at the same time. No noteworthy complications arise if the problem is only how to equalize the differences caused by the length and mass of the fingers. But it is of considerably greater difficulty if we have to co-ordinate two different functions, as e.g. the stroke of the third finger carried out simultaneously with the oblique thumb stroke. So it is no mere chance that this difficult problem is approached in the most different ways in the practice of teaching.

According to one of these views the main aim is to connect the upper voice and for the sake of this one has to sacrifice making the lower voice legato. But there are also opinions contrary to the above; according to these, only the lower voice should be connected. The common basis of both of the above theories is that the hand should be turned into the new position by leaning on the thumb which assures a perfect legato for the right hand in the lower voice and for the left hand in the upper voice. However, with both of these solutions it is unavoidable that, while one of the voices sounds really perfect legato, conspicuous pauses will occur between the tones of the other voice.

A better solution will be for the fingers, in changing position, to reach the keys simultaneously in their role as elongations of the arm. The fingers do not move when changing position and even the thumb stroke will not be prepared. Although in this case the voices do not become separated, the effect obtained is not satisfactory because the finger strokes become mixed up with arm strokes, resulting in unevenness and clumsy playing.

But what is the cause of the difficulties? Obviously the fact that it is very hard to co-ordinate the work of the third finger striking vertically and that of the thumb striking obliquely and sidewards. What was the solution with plain scales? The thumb had always to strike in a direction opposite to that of the scale. In scales in thirds this solution must also be followed, otherwise the rebound (backward stroke) of the key would display a braking effect. One has to find the way to make the third finger strike oppositely to the direction of the scale.

The difficulties are even more increased by the third finger's being the partner of the fifth one in the preceding tone. Thus, while we have the possibility of comfortably preparing the thumb to execute the stroke carried out in direction contrary to the scale, the preparation of the third finger is quite impossible because it is difficult even to bring the third finger over the proper key in time. There is apparently no other solution than suddenly to drag the arm there and to let the finger strike as an elongation of the arm but this will unavoidably spoil the sounding.

Thus, the third finger has to solve two apparently contradictory tasks. After having sounded the preceding tone it has to travel the distance of a fourth to the second key with lightning speed. And in addition it has to take care that the stroke is carried out in a direction opposite to the progression, i.e. parallel to the stroke of the thumb.

However, the two opposite movements can be co-ordinated as is always done in reality with the fast-playing scales in thirds. The third finger endeavours to attain the next key with a *semi-arc lateral stroke*. As the end of this movement is carried out in the direction opposite to that of the scale, the rebound of the key will also help the progression of the arm. This semi-arc horizontal stroke enables us to execute a smooth change of position in inwards-played scales also.

In fast scales the semi-arc stroke of the fingers is a minimal one but nevertheless it is indispensable for attaining an equalized sound and virtuoso tempi because the full activity of the fingers can only be assured by semi-arc horizontal strokes. (With changing the positions we are always in danger of the fingers' merely *tolerating* the shifting.)

Fast scales in thirds can only be played by employing side strokes of the fingers, even if their execution has been practised in some other way. If the fingers merely carried out vertical strokes — and did not participate in the lateral movements (change of position) their activity would be decreased. The active "feeling" of the fingers is absolutely necessary even with the strokes of the upper arm. (The helmsman steers the prow, even though the rudder is in the stern.) In a similar way, the arm's progression in slow playing is led by vigorous horizontal movements of the fingers.

Example 65

Let the right hand play an upward (outward) C major scale in thirds. The two initial tones are sounded with the aid of an upper-arm swing-stroke by the first and third fingers. There follows the vigorous striking of the *d* and *f* on the part of the second and fourth fingers but even before the tones *d* and *f* are sounded, i.e. before the key is reached by the second finger, the thumb should already assume its position under the fourth finger.

When it is the third and fifth finger's turn to strike, special attention must be paid to the activity of the fifth finger in order to avoid rotating the arm instead of executing the above stroke.

Phot. 333   Phot. 334

Phot. 335

The next step is performed again by the first and third fingers, while the arm "jumps" into the new position. The thumb and the third finger spread apart vigorously in order to reach the *f-a* third.

The thumb will easily perform the outward motion because, on account of its having been prepared by being brought under the fourth finger, it now has space enough to execute vigorous horizontal movements.

Care should be taken of the semi-arc shaped movement of the third finger. In the commencement of the movement it opens — like a pair of scissors — in the opposite direction to the thumb, but the semi-arc executed at the finishing of the movement helps the hand in its shifting.

In the inward (downward) scale in thirds, after the stroke of the *c-e* keys by the first and third fingers, the *b-d* will be sounded by means of an energetic semi-arc stroke on the part of the second and fourth fingers. When, simultaneously with the stroke of the second and fourth fingers, the first and third fingers are lifted, the thumb is to be spread out widely in order to get appropriate place for the enlarging of the oblique movement needed for the fast tempo.

The thumb, in preparing the oblique movement, passes beyond the key to be struck. However, even at reduced velocity, this lateral motion is by no means as large as that employed in the plain scale, because the simultaneous movement of the third finger strengthens the vertical component.

After sounding *a-c* now follows the semi-circular stroke of fingers 2 and 4 with the simultaneous change of the arm's position. At each successive change of position, fingers 2 and 4, or 3 and 5 continue to touch the keys by means of semi-arc horizontal strokes.

Example 66

When sounding the third *e-g* with fingers 3–5 the thumb is spread out again widely preparing the oblique movement. This spread position is still maintained throughout the stroke of the fingers 2–4 (sounding *d-f*) as can be seen in photo 336.

If we play scales in thirds with "sliding" fingering, the sliding finger always has to execute a strong horizontal movement in the direction of the scale. For example, in the A major scale in

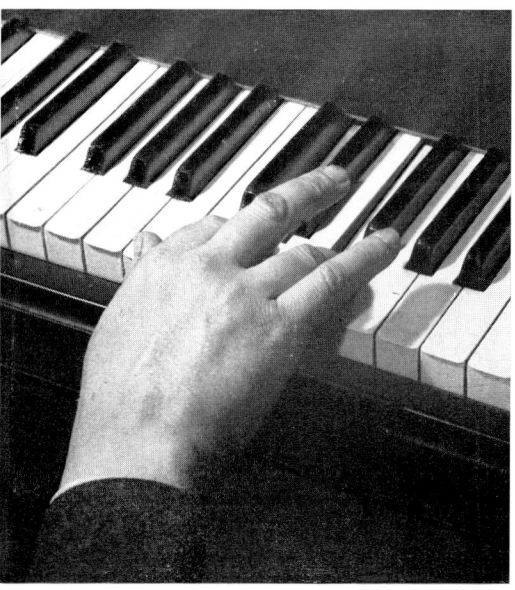

Phot. 336

thirds, played downwards by the right hand, the thumb after striking the *e* will sound the *d* with an energetic horizontal motion.

In fast tempo, the horizontal strokes melt into the glissando movement of the arm, but they require special care in slow practising. Without conscious lateral movement (of course ending by an arc-shaped movement) it may easily occur that the gliding finger will remain motionless and the arm will strike in its place as well as in the place of the parallel finger. Such confusion of arm and finger

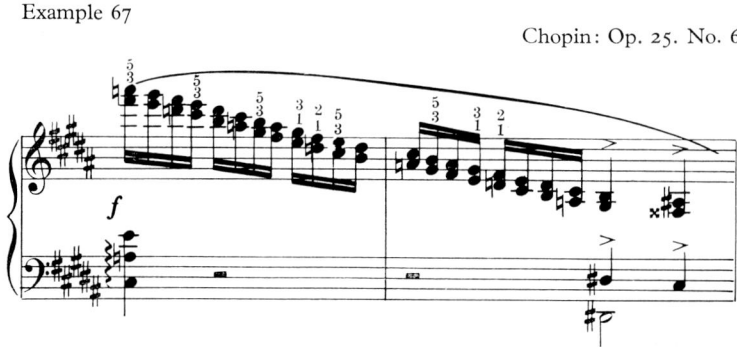

Example 67

Chopin: Op. 25. No. 6

strokes makes us unable to develop a smooth scale. (This does not contradict the requirement that any desired stressing should be accomplished by arm strokes. If, on the other hand, smooth, even playing is required, a uniform functioning of the fingers is imperative, of course.)

Practising of scales in thirds will be successful only if the plain scale has already been perfectly mastered in all tempi and if each pair of fingers has overcome the difficulties of the trills in thirds.

The gymnastics for thirds, given on page 259, will afford a valuable aid to the learning of the trills in thirds. This exercise will automatize the parallel motion of the 2–4 and 3–5 finger pairs, so that much time and effort at the piano will be saved.

They should be supplemented by employing the thumb in thirds executed in the air. In this case the finger-tips should be moved directly and perfect co-ordination of the action of the finger pairs should be striven for. The motion of the fingers should deviate somewhat from the medium position towards the stretching direction but in no case towards the bending direction. This best corresponds to the finger action required in piano playing.

PASSAGES

From the point of view of technique the playing of passages is essentially the same as that of scales, the difference being only that the difficulties found in the playing of scales are to be found in an increased form in passages. In passages we play broken chords through several octaves and thus their playing requires prior mastery of both chord and scale technique. The fingers operate exactly as in the playing of scales, but the hands remain in chord position.

As we encounter the same difficulties, we have to apply the same solutions as in the scales, viz.:

1. The arm has to "unite" the passage progressing in the same direction by one movement.
2. The hand must always be turned in the direction of the passage's progression.
3. The thumb always strikes contrarily to the direction of the passage.
4. The thumb stroke must be prepared in the best possible way.

The execution of the wide synthesizing movements of the arm is of special difficulty in passages played in slow tempo. If in a slow passage the synthesizing movement is not supported by adapting movements, the first, third and fourth fingers, respectively, will not reach the corresponding keys when changing position. Consequently, the arm will strike instead of the fingers and the arm will easily "melt" this stroke into the skip required to the execution of the changing of position. As the finger strokes become intermingled with the arm strokes we are compelled, for the sake of even sounding, to reduce the finger motion to a minimum, and consequently to produce the tones by rotation. The sound thus obtained will be hard and uneven despite every effort to the contrary.

The smooth performance of a slow passage, therefore, requires many adapting movements because the more we diminish them, the harder the tone becomes. The technique of a smooth passage should be our main aim in learning to play passages, since all playing variants can easily be deduced from it.

The slow practising of rapid passages poses a different task. Since the fast playing of passages (the same as in the scales) the adapting movements must decrease proportionately to the increase of the tempo, in the slow practising we also have to decrease the adapting movements. Adapting must be applied only to the extent required by the free execution of the swing-strokes of the fingers, because in the slow passages the adapting movements which are otherwise very important will narrow down to the movements of the finger with the result that the slow practising of fast passages will be absolutely useless. The finger movements are not to be decreased in the slow practising, but on the contrary, increased (just as in the case of scales). Therefore one has to take special care to execute each finger stroke resolutely and vigorously. The synthesizing process must, of course, also fully prevail in slow practising of passages.

When playing an outward passage, the action of the thumb has to be prepared already during the stroke of the second finger as we learned above in practising the scales. The stroke itself, however, has to take place simultaneously with the arm's assuming a new position. The execution is rendered difficult by the fact that the thumb does not reach the corresponding key because the arm is

Phot. 337–342

Fast playing of B major passage

(Annie Fischer, 120 photos per sec.)

The third finger immediately before the set-off of the F sharp

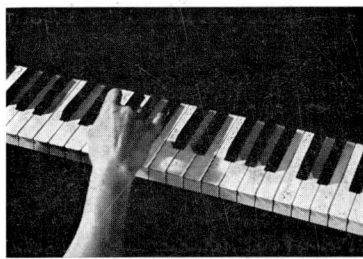

Note that the fingers keep the distances corresponding to the chord-position

The thumb already touches the B

Phot. 343–348

Immediately before the set-off moment

After the set-off the key sinks still somewhat lower

The second finger touches the D sharp, the thumb releases the B

The second finger before the set-off of D sharp

Phot. 349–353

Thumb stroke in B major passage played in outward direction

(120 photos per sec.)

The second finger rises, the third already touches the F sharp. The thumb gets ready to pass under

1

The thumb reaches the second finger simultaneously with the set-off of F sharp

3

The third finger is compelled to release the F sharp key because of the change of position, while the thumb takes its place. Note the even progression of the arm: On the series of frames it may easily be seen that the arm assumes the new position gradually and not by jerks

3

The thumb almost touches the B. It will be observed that the fingers conserve the chord-position even during the change of position

1

The thumb lightly touches the B

1

Phot. 354—358

The thumb at the beginning of the set-off

2

The set-off moment

2

The second finger prepares for the stroke

5

The second finger immediately before the stroke

10

The second finger at the set-off of D sharp. In comparing this frame with the first of the series, it will be noticed that the arm advances steadily even during the setting off of the D sharp

obliged to execute twice as large a skip as in scale playing. In order to attain a better innervation of the skip, neither arm nor hand should change their position while the thumb is getting ready: the fingers have to remain parallel to the keys up to the end.

The arm should not be allowed to lean against the keys after having executed the skip because this would be detrimental to the synthesizing movements. The hovering of the arm and the effortless synthesizing movement will be facilitated by the thumb's striking simultaneously with the skipping of the arm.

The changing of position causes difficulties also in the passages played inwards (downwards). After the thumb stroke the hand is unable to attain the required position by one skip and it has to execute the progression in two parts, i.e. partly during the stroke of the thumb and partly during that of the third finger. The finger, whose action is simultaneous with the skip of the arm into a new position, always has to perform a semi-arc horizontal stroke.

The pupil should begin practising passages only after he has acquired a perfect sureness in the playing of scales. Automatization of the chord technique should have been achieved previously in order not to disturb the vigorous finger strokes. Even so, it is very difficult at the beginning of slow practising of passages to maintain the chord position during the action of the fingers. For this reason, the practising of passages must be thoroughly prepared.

TRILLS

Trills are very frequently considered as mere musical decorative elements. This view may lead to grave faults because, although they can be elements of ornamentation, their main aim is to express intensified emotions. With the aid of trills, the dynamic shaping of the melodic line will become more colourful and rich. Therefore our main aim must be the rich and at the same time expressive tone of the trill instead of its velocity or even mechanical uniformity.

Perhaps no one of the playing forms depends to such a great extent upon the exact apportioning of the resistance, as does the trill. The slightest overburdening makes it slow and clumsy. It can be stated almost as a rule: if the pianist's trill is not good, it is caused by overburdening of the fingers. The fingers may attain the agility required for the trill only if we employ the muscle force of the fingers always to the extent absolutely needed, i.e. we provide for their always attaining the escapement level with the maximum of the given force. (See page 28.) This requires an extraordinary delicacy in the apportioning of the resistance, i.e. no pressing whatever must be tolerated.

The pupil must be able to execute uniform, evenly played trills but this does not mean that he has to execute merely mechanical, uniformly arranged trills (e.g. uniformly played semiquavers or demisemiquavers), or that he will attain a good trill technique by practising mechanical trills for long years. This concept is wrong from the physiological standpoint because a perfect uniformity can only be attained by applying an intensive control which is detrimental to velocity. But it is even more erroneous from the musical standpoint because to speak about "uniformly arranged emotions" would – to put it mildly – arouse astonishment in any human being. The trill may imitate for instance birds' singing and thus it is clear that it must be just as free and natural.

In real life in Nature there is only the free trill, so the trill as a means of expressing emotions can also only be free. However, this is not inconsistent with the fact that a trill may under certain circumstances be mechanical and uniformly arranged. For the work of our muscles the periodically arranged work, the regular repetition of the movements, is a preliminary condition and so the trill also becomes arranged into regular groups. However, this arranging must not be forced by sharp accents or even be "conscious" grouping of the tones in advance. The arrangement of the groups will be made by the muscles themselves in the most economical way. All this applies of course only to the free trill and not to those prescribed as uniformly arranged by the composer. If the composer needs uniformly arranged trills for the motivic structure of this work, the accents of the arranging will also play a role in the musical structure. But in these cases the composer usually prescribes the trill motion in a detailed way. In general it can be presumed that the sign of the trill means free trills even in those cases where the composer's explanation of the musical ornamentation prescribes uniformly arranged trills. Couperin, for instance, writes the following: "Although in the table of ornamentation the trills are prescribed with uniform notes, they must be, nevertheless, played slower in the beginning than when finishing them, but this increasing must be made imperceptibly···"[1]

[1] Couperin: *L'Art de toucher le Clavecin*. "Quoi que les tremblemens soient marqués égaux, dans la table des agrémens de mon premier livre, ils doivent cependant commencer plus lentement qu'ils ne finissent: mais, cette gradation doit être imperceptible."

The "regularly arranged" trill cannot be considered as a basis. This is proved also by Quantz and Leopold Mozart,[2] both of them mentioning that the velocity of the trill is dependent upon the dimensions and the reverberations of the hall in which the pianist plays.

[2] J. J. Quantz: *Versuch einer Anweisung die Flöte traversiere zu spielen*. Chapter IX, Par. 2.: "Nicht alle Triller dürfen in einerley Geschwindigkeit geschlagen werden: sondern man muss sich hierinne so wohl nach dem Orte wo man spielet, als nach der Sache selbst, die man auszuführen hat, richten. Spielt man an einem grossen Orte, wo es sehr schallet: so wird ein etwas langsamer Triller bessere Wirkung thun, als ein geschwinder. Denn durch den Widerschall geräth die allzugeschwinde Bewegung der Töne in eine Verwirrung und folglich wird der geschwinde Triller undeutlich. Spielet man hingegen in einem kleinen oder tapezierten Zimmer, wo die Zuhörer nahe dabei stehen; so wird ein geschwinder Triller besser sein als ein langsamer. Man muss ferner zu unterscheiden wissen, was für Stücke man spielt; damit man nicht, wie viele thun, eine Sache mit der anderen vermenge. In traurigen Stücken muss der Triller langsamer; in lustigen aber geschwinder geschlagen werden."

(Do not play all trills with the same velocity; you have to accommodate yourself both to the room in which we play and to the piece we are playing. If we play in a large room with great reverberation, a somewhat slower trill will make more effect than a faster one. On account of the resounding, the too quick movement of the tones will be blurred, in consequence of which the quick trill will be unclear. If, on the other hand, we are playing in a small or wall-papered room where the listeners stand nearby, a quick trill will be better than a slow one. One has also to distinguish between the pieces to be played in order not to mix up one with the other, as it is often done. In sorrowful pieces the trills must be played slower, in gay ones quicker.)

Leopold Mozart: *Gründliche Violinschule*. Chapter X, Par. 5.: "Der Triller lässt sich der Geschwindigkeit nach in vier Gattungen theilen: nämlich in den langsamen, mittelmässigen, geschwinden und anwachsenden. Der langsame wird in traurigen und langsamen Stücken gebraucht; der mittelmässige in Stücken, die zwar ein lustiges, doch anbey ein gemässigtes und artiges Tempo haben; der geschwinde in Stücken, die recht lebhaft, voller Geist und Bewegung sind; und endlich braucht man den anwachsenden Triller meistentheils bey den Cadenzen. Diesen letzteren pflegt man auch mit piano und forte auszuschmücken: denn er wird am schönsten auf die hier beygefügte Art vorgetragen."

Example 68

Par. 8.: "Der Triller muss überhaupt nicht geschwind geschlagen werden, sonst wird er unverständlich, meckernd oder ein sogenannter Geisstriller. Ferner darf man auf den feinern und hochgestimmten Sayten einen geschwindern Triller schlagen, als auf den dicken und tief gestimmten Sayten; weil die letztern sich langsam, die ersten aber sich sehr geschwind bewegen. Und endlich muss man auch, wenn man ein Solo spielet, den Ort beobachten, wo man seine Stücke aufzuführen gedenket. An einem kleinen Orte, welches etwa noch dazu austapeziert ist, oder wo die Zuhörer gar zu nahe sind, wird ein geschwinder Triller von besserer Wirkung seyn. Spielet man hingegen in einem grossen Saal, wo es sehr klinget, oder sind etwa die Zuhörer ziemlich entfernet; so wird man besser einen langsamen Triller machen."

(Par. 5. The trills are to be distinguished according to their velocity in four kinds: slow, medium, quick and increasing trills. The slow one is applied in sorrowful and slow pieces; the medium one in pieces with gay but still moderate and decent tempo: the quick trill is to be played in pieces full of wit and motion, and, to conclude, the increasing trill is mostly applied with cadences. The latter is also embellished with piano and forte, because it is performed in the most beautiful manner described here.

Par. 8. The trill generally must not be played too quickly because in that case it becomes unintelligible, bleating or the so-called goat-trill. On the thinner and higher-tuned strings we may play faster trills than on the thicker and lower-tuned strings, because the latter vibrate slower and the former ones very quickly. Finally, when playing solos, we have to take into consideration the room in which we intend to perform the piece. In a small room, which is, in addition, wall-papered, or in such a one where the listeners are very near, the quick trill will be more effective. If, on the other hand, we play in a large room, resounding very much, or when the audience is rather far away it is better to play slow trills.)

In the work of Fétis and Moscheles: *Méthode des méthodes*, published in 1840, as in the previous quotations only the free trill is described:

Example 69

226

The velocity of the trill must also be accommodated to the pitch. Short high tones require considerably faster trills than the tones of lower octaves, and with bass notes no fast trill can be played. This is why considerably less ornamentation is found in the bass than in the higher voices in the music of the eighteenth century. (See Par. 8 in the quotation of Leopold Mozart.)

Trills are divided – according to their technical execution – into the following three groups:
1. Plain finger trills.
2. Trills with alternating fingers.
3. Tremolo trills.

PLAIN FINGER TRILLS

Plain finger trills are always played with neighbouring fingers. This kind of trill is used when an extremely sensitive and agile trill rather than large tone volume is needed, i.e. when the agogic and dynamic delicacy of the tones of the trill is of more importance than their brilliancy.

Which pair of fingers will be found by the individual to be most suitable for trills, depends entirely on the proportionate length of the fingers. As a rule, it can be stated that the smaller the difference between the length of two fingers, the more easily and beautifully our trills will sound. If, e.g., the difference in length between the third and fourth fingers is smaller than that between the second and third fingers, the trill may be executed more easily with the third and fourth fingers. In the case of a long fifth finger, even the redoubtable trill with the fourth and fifth fingers is comparatively easy. But despite whatever differences there may be between the proportions of the length of fingers, one can learn and has to learn to play trills with any of the finger pairs.

TRILLS WITH ALTERNATING FINGERS

Alternating fingers are employed most of all in trills of long duration. The changing of the fingers increases our stamina and permits a larger tone volume, but at the same time reduces the delicacy of the trill. In trills with alternating fingers, the first finger always participates; either the first and second fingers alternate in conjunction with the third or the third and second alternate in conjunction with the first.

TREMOLO TRILLS

As indicated by its title the tremolo trill is a result of a rotatory movement (like the tremolo). On account of its large tone-effect combined with great speed and efficacy, this is the most frequently employed kind of trill. In order to facilitate the rotatory movement we always perform it with noncontiguous fingers, i.e. with the 1–3, 2–4 or the 3–5 finger pairs. The special position of the thumb enables us to play the tremolo trills with the 1–2 finger pair as well, but this is less convenient than the trill with the 1–3 finger pairs.

THE PRACTISING OF TRILLS

In learning to play trills the following exercises (believed to be composed by Mozart) are generally employed.

Example 72

The above exercise will be of more use if the trill is played almost entirely freely.
The evenness and uniformity of the trill can be more easily attained by the following exercise:

Example 73

These exercises, however, do not ensure ease and agility in trilling, and it is therefore of great importance to practise in addition free finger trills without any rhythmical arranging. The simplest method of doing this is the following: The trill should be started by an upper-arm stroke so that the fingers already find themselves trilling as they touch the keys. This cooperation with the upper arm gives the fingers a sense of sureness enabling them to execute the desired short trill with astonishing agility. (Gymnastic exercises No. 56 and 57 will serve as preparation.)

All three kinds of trills must be practised by each hand separately as frequently as possible.

Unfortunately, it is very frequent that pianists prefer the use of some kind of trills for technical reasons. This is definitely wrong. Only the requirements of the musical expression can determine which kind of trill is more favourable. Therefore it must be rejected if the pianist employs alternating fingers with a Praller or mordent just because in his opinion it is easier to play them correctly in that way. Employing alternating fingers creates entirely different dynamic effects which can be motivated only by the musical concept. Busoni, e.g., employed in his later years Prallers and mordents with alternating fingers more rarely than when he was young. But that was done not because of technical motivations but as a consequence of changes in his musical concepts. (See on page 232.)

The question of when to employ which kind of trill must be determined first of all by the pianist's musical taste, but the choice will also be influenced by his physical constitution. Some pianists will apply tremolo trills rarely, others will avoid plain finger trills, while still others will find the trills with alternating fingers inconvenient.

The choice of the trill to be employed must depend entirely on the individual characteristics of the pupil – while also taking his anatomic peculiarities and musical endowments into consideration. The type of trill to be employed by the pupil should not be prescribed but rather he should be allowed to choose in accordance with his own musical concept. Mastery by all fingers of the art of trilling and of all three kinds of trills is, however, a prerequisite.

THE TECHNIQUE OF REPETITION

When playing repetitions of a single tone, we employ either
1. the same finger (the strokes being executed from the arm), or
2. alternating fingers.

Neither of these two solutions can be regarded as having exclusive general validity, because each is appropriate for expressing a different musical concept. The two kinds of repetitions provide equivalent solutions in many cases and the musical concept or the physical endowments of the pianist will decide which solution should be chosen.

Example 74   Beethoven: Sonata in F minor, Op. 57

Repetition with one finger has the advantage that, at least in the majority of the cases, it can be executed by a direct swing-stroke. This is why it is most suitable for a delicate shaping of agogics and dynamics. As it is very difficult in soft playing to follow the dynamic line exactly, we in this case frequently apply the same finger. The delicate shaping of soft tones is facilitated by the fact that with one-finger repetitions we play almost without noise-effects. The vibrato-like solution with the same finger enables us to effect repetitions of long duration. Great dynamic changes (accents, sudden crescendo or diminuendo, subito forte or piano) are more easily realized by one and the same finger.

Repetitions with the same finger can also be used in very fast tempo if played only for a short time because in this case they sound excellent. The importance of playing with the same finger increases still more when repetitions with both hands are to be played.

Example 75

Liszt: Funérailles*

In playing repetitions with alternating fingers the upper noises come into prominence and the single tones become clearly separated from each other. Alternating of the fingers enables the pianist to execute very fast repetitions even for a long time. But a certain mechanical character of playing will unavoidably result. However, it is precisely this mechanical character which renders repetitions with alternating fingers exceedingly apt for producing a brilliant effect. Therefore, in very fast tempo alternating fingers must be applied almost without exception.

Example 76

Liszt: La Campanella*

Example 77

Liszt: Gnomenreigen

* The examples marked by an asterisk give original fingerings as used by the composer.

In alternating repetitions of longer duration the 4–3–2–1 or 3–2–1 fingering must be applied according to the rhythmical articulation.

Example 78   Bartók: Bear's Dance

In very fast tempi, the 4–3–2 fingering is also very serviceable if the repetition occurs in a periodically interrupted form or if called for by the rhythmical articulation.

Example 79

In certain cases, the fifth finger may be drawn into the repetition for the sake of the rhythmical division, but only if the fifth finger of the pianist is not much shorter than the fourth and does not force the pianist to draw in the other fingers excessively.

The use of alternating fingers will facilitate rhythmical articulation. This is the reason why we often – sometimes even too often – apply alternating fingers in playing the up-beat *(Auftakt)*.

Because of the rhythmical articulation, repetition with alternating fingers will sometimes prove preferable even in slow tempo.

Example 80

Beethoven: Sonata in D major, Op. 28*

Example 81   Beethoven: Sonata for Violin in A major, Op. 47

In most cases it is only the individual's musical conception which can decide whether repetition by means of the same finger or by alternating fingers is to be employed. This conception may, of course, change with the time. Busoni, for instance, wrote the following on the change of his conceptions in the course of twenty years: "···for the present I do not employ (or only very rarely) alternating fingers in repetitions. (The same with Prallers and mordents···)"[1]

The fingering of the last movement of the Kreutzer Sonata, for instance, may reflect considerable differences between the various musical concepts of particular pianists. Those who wish to emphasize the buoyancy of the theme will play the repetitions with alternating fingers. Those who want to stress the sublime humanism and the heroic character of the theme, will play the repetitions with the same finger. One of the culminating moments in Bartók's unforgettable rendering of the Kreutzer Sonata was the exposition of the second subject in the last movement. With the aid of single-finger repetition he successfully blended the exultation, love and heroism, expressed in the theme, into a wonderful entity.

---

[1] J. S. Bach. *Zweistimmige Inventionen.* (Busoni-Ausgabe, 1914). Vorwort zur zweiten Ausgabe.

···"Den Studierenden würde ich davor warnen, meiner 'Interpretation' allzu buchstäblich nachzugehen. Der Augenblick und das Individuum haben hier ihre eigenen Rechte. Meine Auffassung mag als ein guter Wegweiser dienen, nach dem sich Einer nicht zu richten braucht, der einen anderen guten Weg kennt."

"···Ich mache gegenwärtig vom Fingerwechsel auf repetierten Noten wenig oder gar keinen Gebrauch (ebenso bei Pralltrillern und Mordenten) und vermeide mehr und mehr das Untersetzen des Daumens.

Endlich halte ich mich bei geringen Details und Nebenmomenten nicht länger auf und der Ausdruck eines Gesichtes ist mir wichtiger, als der Schnitt seiner Züge."

(I should warn the reader against following my "interpretation" too literally. Here the given moment and the individual have their own rights. My concept may serve as a good guide not absolutely to be followed by somebody who knows a better way.

···At present I apply little or absolutely no alternating fingers with repetitions (and also with Pralltriller and Mordents), and neglect more and more the passing under of the thumb.

Finally, I do not concern myself very much with slight details and elements of secondary importance, and the expression of a face is of more importance to me than the cut of its features.)

ON THE PLAYING OF ETUDES

In addition to the scales and other cyclical forms a special way of practising the fundamental playing forms must be added: the playing of études. Etudes are musical compositions having as their aim the overcoming of a certain technical difficulty. This is attained by repeating the respective difficult technical formula as often as possible and in as many forms as possible. The structure of an étude is simple and its dramatic content is slight in order to enable the pianist to concentrate on the possibilities of technical solution.

The "material" of the étude is normally one single playing form which returns in as many variants as possible. Thus, a tremendous number of études can be found for practising a special formula of finger technique, broken chords, octaves, thirds, sixths, repetitions, tremolo trills, skips, arpeggios, etc. Good études will show us all possibilities of a given playing form by a great number of variants.

However, contradiction is to be found in the concept that inspiration for composing a piece should be given to us by endeavouring to overcome a certain technical difficulty. Delicacy of the dynamic and agogic shaping (serving as a basis of producing the tone colour) plays a decisive part in the technique and thus the latter always depends upon the musical concepts. Perhaps this contradictory character accounts for the fact that only great composers wrote études which are useful in every respect and which give an all-round development to technique. Only great composers have been able to compose études in which the technical aim gave inspiration to the musical concept which may be perfectly expressed by the given technical formula.

But what happens if the musical concept and the technical formula do not melt into an organic unit, i.e. when the étude is devoid of any valuable musical content? The playing of these études is harmful because if the technical formula does not express anything at all, the pianist's work can only be a mechanical, useless one, a mere muscle training of the fingers.

Unfortunately, the greater part of études consist of such pieces having poor musical content. "But the great advantage of études is precisely the fact that playing them has purely technical aims without any particular wish to express whatsoever, and they are played in order to develop a uniform equalized playing", might be argued.

In the course of the foregoing (see page 31) we have shown that an equalized playing cannot be achieved by indifferent, mechanical, uniform movements. It has also been proved (see page 107) that velocity and development of agility of the fingers and arm is independent from the playing of études. (A different problem is whether the playing of études provides a good occasion for pianists to practise the above abilities.) Thus the mechanical playing of études by renouncing from the beginning every musical expression cannot develop technique but indeed may prove harmful.

Upon closer analysis we find that when doing this mechanical playing of études the pianist neglects one of the most important elements of piano technique: the development and increasing of the delicacy of the resistance. *The most important basic problem of piano playing is the continual development of this ability.* The problem is exactly how to apportion the resistance (weight-complement) in the required extent. If it is less than exactly required, it will spoil the tone colour because it falsifies the dynamics, if it is more than necessary, it will even hinder the display of velocity. Thus practising may be useful only if it provides opportunity to develop the delicacy of the resistance in all the playing forms. Etudes may, consequently, be considered as useful, indifferent or harmful according to their giving or not giving opportunity for the pianist to develop – within the virtuoso work of the fingers and arm – the delicacy of the resistance.

An essential feature of an étude is the repetition of a technical formula as many times as possible. This too involves great dangers. A composer of genius must be one who is capable of repeating one single technical formula without doing this at the expense of the expression or of the musical form. At the same time, the composer must be a pianist of outstanding abilities in order to know the limit of solving the continuous repetition of one single formula through appropriate technical means.

As can be seen, both the musical and the technical prerequisites of a *good* étude are most severe. No wonder that the greater part of the études are unsolvable from the point of view of higher technical demands. They cannot be played perfectly because the continuous uniform motion is so tiresome that the pianist is compelled to apply some sort of *special étude technique* to be able to play the étude to the end. What is the secret of this "technique of étude playing?" The pianist has to give up entirely the dynamic shading, even that required by the poor musical content of the étude, and has to concentrate on sounding the tones with a relatively uniform volume and velocity.

When encountering technical difficulties in one of the masterpieces of piano literature we shall always find that the composer – having a "sense for the instrument" gives some solution to the problem. See, for instance, the upper voice of Weber's Perpetuum mobile:

Example 82

The continuous changing of the figurations gives abundant possibility for resting and refreshing the muscles and so the pianist is not hindered in the detailed dynamic shaping.

When comparing this with the following Etude of Czerny we see that the broken third are

Example 83

repeated 42 times. What does this mean? In order to give a *good* performance of this étude a more developed technique would be needed than for the Perpetuum mobile. (Supposing that we did not want to use the étude to destroy our technique and to diminish the delicacy of dynamic shaping.)

A well-known difficult part is the following episode of the Rondo in Beethoven's Waldstein Sonata:

Example 84

And indeed, the full energy of a pianist is required to perform this part in which the whirling flow of the triplets is seldom heard in a satisfactory performance even in concert halls. But how short this interlude is compared to the études of Czerny which are allegedly intended to prepare an easy solution for similar tasks.

Logics seems to be turned upside down here! Are pupils prepared to solve difficult technical problems by giving them *unsolvable* ones? Or – which is even worse – what kind of preparation is to make the pianist (under the pretext of études) practise entirely different elements from those to be solved in the musical piece? The broken octaves of a Beethoven sonata can always be solved but we could hardly say that about the Etude in E flat major of Clementi. (It is not accidental that Mozart called to his sister's attention that she should take care not to lose the lightness and suppleness of her hands while playing Clementi's works.) And "Gradus ad Parnassum" is still far from being as one-sided as the greater part of études having as their only aim the condensing of as many technical difficulties as possible.

What is the solution? Are we entirely to reject playing études? Would this not cause an irretrievable deficiency in piano teaching? It is indeed very difficult to give a clear-cut answer to these questions. Categorical rejection of playing études would be of course a grave mistake. The études of Cramer or Clementi, and even to a lesser degree those of Czerny, contain valuable musical material, let alone the wonderful compositions of Chopin or Liszt which are admirable pieces of music also condensing technical problems under the title of étude. There is but one thing to be stressed: *let us break away from the prejudice that piano technique can be acquired only by playing études.*

As strange as it may seem: a good technique may be learned in the first place by the playing of pieces, and this technique can be further developed by the aid of études, *good* études. Etudes may give us in certain cases the feeling of absolute sureness and – precisely on account of their simple musical structure – may enable the pianist to enjoy the smooth running of his fingers, the brilliant sounding of the tones, the virtuoso playing. But we must never forget that every étude requiring merely mechanical uniform work of our fingers instead of an expressive performing and dynamic shading is senseless and harmful.

Most of the works of Couperin and the other French harpsichordists fulfil also the task of the ideal études. The development of the technique of ornaments gives a better guarantee for the agility of the fingers than any number of tiresome études.

FINGERING

Proper fingering is an important constituent of clear musical shaping. At the same time it creates the preliminary conditions for the most convenient solution of the problems at hand. If we omit considerations of comfort, the fingering chosen by us may prove to be inexecutable when playing at the required speed. Still graver faults may ensue from our paying attention only to the convenience of the fingering because the result is likely to be in contradiction with the musical concept.

The rules of fingering have arisen from practical experience. However, as some of these rules contradict each other in part, the musical effect should determine which of them is to be preferred in the particular case. For this reason the teacher should enable the pupil to acquire the faculty of always choosing the fingering best adapted to the musical solution and to the physical make-up of the individual.

A logical fingering becomes rapidly associated with the respective key positions, so that comparatively few repetitions are required to establish it. In the course of practising more and more fingerings will gradually become automatized to the point where they may finally be applied without much thought even in sight-reading. (The so-called "instructive" fingerings cause more harm than benefit. Particularly detrimental is the principle: "The more difficult, the more useful", because it hinders the automatization of the correct fingerings.)

The most important rules of fingering may be summarized as follows:

THE SPECIAL ROLE OF THE THUMB AND THE LITTLE FINGER

In the case of alternating white and black keys, the first and fifth fingers should be placed on the white keys on account of their shortness. Using the thumb on black keys forces the other fingers to bend considerably if they do not also come on black keys as for instance in Chopin's Etude in G flat major Op. 10. The passing over and under of the fingers is also made difficult by the short fingers coming back on black keys. Thus, smooth scale playing requires that the thumb be placed on the white keys.

Example 85   Liszt: Spanish Rhapsody

For the sake of the musical expression, however, both the thumb and the little finger may be placed on the black keys. So, e.g., in a scale of Liszt's Spanish Rhapsody (Example 85) both the thumb and the little finger are placed on the black keys in order to carry out less passing under, in order to attain a glissando effect of the scale. In general, blurred tone effects are produced in this way more easily, because the short finger – by being placed on a black key – also forces the other fingers to execute smaller movements. Since the role of the fingers diminishes by this solution, the vertical adapting movement of the arm and its rotation, too, will have to offer more aid to the sounding of the tone.

Example 86
Beethoven: Sonata in A major, Op. 2, No. 2

In Bach's Invention in D minor, both the little finger and the thumb are placed on black keys for the sake of the synthesizing.

Example 87

The use of the little finger on black keys is found much more frequently than that of the thumb because the little finger does not force the other fingers to assume such a rigidly bent position.

Example 88 Liszt: Paganini Study in E flat major

Example 89
Beethoven: Sonata in E flat major, Op. 30, No. 3. Scherzo

PASSING THE FINGERS OVER AND UNDER

It will be easier to pass the thumb under if the preceding finger is on a black key. Similarly, passing over is easier if the next finger strikes a black key after the thumb has played a white key. The lateral movement of the thumb needs considerable space, so that both over- and underpassing are hampered when the finger – under which the thumb should be passed – is on a white key. This is the reason why, e.g., the left-hand D major or G major scales are executed more easily and smoothly if the fourth finger falls on the F sharp.

ROLE OF THE FINGERING IN THE SYNTHESIZING MOVEMENT

Proper fingering may be of considerable assistance in carrying out the synthesizing movement and in shaping the dynamic line. Well-chosen fingering will render the tonality and the harmonic structure more palpable.

Let us analyse the fingerings of the D major and G major scales – mentioned above in connection with passing under of the thumb – also from this aspect.

If we play these scales with the left hand from the key-note, then the dynamically appropriate fingering will be as follows: the fourth finger will be placed on the E in D major scale and on the A in the G major scale. Thus it will always be the fifth or the first finger which plays the key-note – upon which the dynamic line is based – and the entire scale may be performed with a single momentum. If we were to place the fourth finger on the F sharp, in each one of the two scales two over- and underpassings would have to be executed, both in the initial and in the final octaves. This could give rise to a blurring of the dynamic line striving towards the tonic. The G major scale in the concluding part of Liszt's Paganini Etude should therefore be played with the fourth finger placed on the A, while in the Etude in E flat major (see Ex. 91) the fourth finger touches the F sharp because here the left hand accompanies the right hand at a distance of a sixth, i.e., it starts with a third.

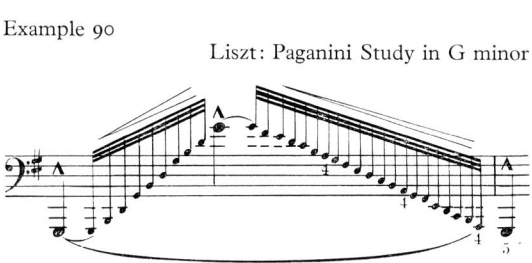

Example 90 — Liszt: Paganini Study in G minor

Example 91 — Liszt: Paganini Study in E flat major

In scale playing both fingerings are needed. Systematic training is required only for the more difficult scale – that with the fourth finger on the white keys – the more so because the scales starting from the key-note occur more frequently. Thus both fingerings should be mastered – i.e. practised by us – in order that we may always choose the more appropriate one.

Broken chords also sound better when we apply a fingering which assists the synthesizing movement.

Example 92   Beethoven: Sonata in F sharp major, Op. 78★

For the sake of the synthesizing movements we frequently apply "sliding" fingers, i.e. two successive notes played by the same finger.

Its most frequent form is that of sliding from a black key to a white one.

★ The examples marked by an asterisk give original fingerings as used by the composer.

In this example from Beethoven fingering the smooth sliding of the fourth finger is considerably difficult, but the smooth carrying out of the resolution can be achieved only in this way.

Example 93 — Beethoven: Sonata in D major, Op. 28*

Example 94 — Bach: Invention in D minor

CROSSING

When placing the hands in a new position, it is often better to use the method of crossing rather than that of passing over or under.

Crossing is applied most frequently in connection with the third finger. In outward progression the third finger will cross over the fourth one, while in inward progression it will cross over the second finger.

In *Obras de musica* by Antonio de Cabezon (1510–1566) we read the following:

"Ascending passages with the right hand are played with the third and fourth fingers; descending passages with the second and third fingers, the thumb being counted as first. The left hand, ascending, begins with the fourth finger, goes on to the thumb, then starts with the fourth, and so on. Descending, the process is reversed."

As can be seen, Cabezon employs only the right hand in crossing perhaps because it is more agile. It follows that the action of the thumb of the left hand does not represent a passing over and under in today's sense. This can also be proved by the fact that one of J. S. Bach's predecessors, Nicolaus Ammerbach, gives in his work *Orgel oder Instrumental Tabulatur* (Leipzig 1571) the same fingering for F major played with the left hand, and the fourth finger touches the C after the first finger is placed on B flat. This, indeed, cannot be considered as a passing over, in today's sense.

The passing under of the thumb came into use in Bach's days. But Bach himself hardly made use of it. (See Example 98.) As we can see from Example 97 Couperin used no passing under even in scales in thirds. The thumb was used only at the beginning and end of scales, in the case of rather wide spans. C. Ph. E. Bach had already used the modern fingering in the playing of scales but he still frequently applied crossing.

Neglect of the thumb may have different reasons. The sensitive tone of the clavichord did not permit any ample use of the thumb, and in scales a beautiful tone colour was more difficult to obtain when passing the thumb under. In the upper manuals of the cembalo and the organ the use of the thumb is inconvenient because it forces the arm of the player into a high position. Moreover, the keys of the

Phot. 359

ancient instruments were so short that there was hardly any room left for the thumb even on the lower manual. (See p. 147.)

In order to study the crossing, compare the following scale fingerings:

Girolamu Diruta: *Il Transilvano* (1625)   Example 95

Henry Purcell: *Lessons for Harpsichord and Spinet* (posth. 1696)   Example 96

François Couperin: *L'art de toucher le Clavecin* (1717)   Example 97

In the following piece Bach supplied his own fingering which provides abundant instances of crossing.

Example 98   Applicatio (Clavier-Büchlein für W. Fr. Bach)

A good example of the application of crossing is the fingering of Chopin's Study in A minor, Op. 10.

ROLE OF FINGERING IN SHIFTING THE CENTRE OF GRAVITY

Appropriate fingering facilitates the shifting of the hand's centre of gravity during playing.

A good example of this is the old rule of fingering which indicates when the third or fourth fingers should be used in common chords. This rule is based entirely on the proper proportioning of the weight of the hand. To ensure the correct shifting of the centre of gravity, the hands must be kept in as natural a position as possible. The fingering must, therefore, be such that the fingers are neither spread apart nor drawn together excessively, i.e. the hand must not be strained or bent.

In the common (tonic) chord of the right hand the only suitable fingering is the following:

Example 99

because to apply the fourth finger for as wide a span as a fourth would be nonsensical.

The same applies to the sixth chord where the fourth excludes the use of the third finger.

Example 100

In the six-four chord it is still more difficult to decide whether the fourth or the third finger should be used. In the case of unbroken chords the solution depends on the width of the position which the two outer fingers, i.e. 4–5 or 3–5, have to assume. If the distance to be spanned does not exceed a white-key third

Example 101

the fourth finger should be used. If the span is larger, it is preferable to use the third finger.

Example 102

In the case of the tonic chord played by the left hand the same rule applies.

ADAPTING MOVEMENTS WITH THE AID OF FINGERING

Different tone colours require application of different "quantities" of adapting movements. The fingerings must be brought into accord with these. If noise-free tones are desired, the fingering has to render free arm action possible. In Liszt's above-mentioned Etude in E flat major we attain a smooth, noise-free tone by applying the fifth finger. The fourth or third fingers are to be used on the E flat only if we want to stress "brilliance" of the tones instead of their suppleness. (Few adapting movements.)

In the following passage from Schubert's Impromptu in A flat major, the fingering given by the composer practically forces the arm into adapting movements.

The use of the third finger shows that Schubert wanted to attain a noise-free, smooth effect.

Example 105   Schubert: Impromptu in A flat major*

On the other hand, Liszt apparently envisaged a more virtuoso effect, because in the issue edited personally by him, he indicates the second finger in similar passages where Schubert did not prescribe any fingering.

Example 106

CONSIDERATION OF PECULIARITIES OF THE INDIVIDUAL FINGERS

In determining the fingering, we have to take into account the anatomic structure of each individual finger. On account of their varying length, mass and situation, each finger is suited to the solution of different problems. However, it must also be called to attention again that there do not exist such things as good or bad, weak or strong fingers. Each one of the fingers is suitable for the playing if applied appropriately. (See p. 192.) The thumb is suited for sounding independent tones only when playing forte or fortissimo but here it may produce a special massive sounding. The little finger is employed only for the finishing of diatonic scales, but, as it was proved by Chopin's Etude in A minor, it is excellently utilizable in chromatic scales. For this reason, the same theme will sound entirely different if we change the fingering, because each finger requires different adapting and – if called for – complementary movements.

REPETITION OF THE SAME FINGERING IN CHANGING OCTAVE POSITIONS

The repetition of a movement in the same position and under the same circumstances facilitates the automatization. Therefore one of the oldest rules of fingering is that in scales the same fingering must be played in successive octaves. This applies of course not only to scales but also to all other playing forms and to themes which must be played with the same fingering when reappearing in different pitch registers, even when it proves to be inconvenient to some extent, e.g. in very low or very high pitch registers.

FINGERING IN SEQUENCES

From the rule that the same themes must be played with the same fingering when they reappear in different pitch registers it follows that the same principle must be followed in fingering in sequences. Thus, in playing of sequences each member of the sequence should be played if possible with the same fingering in order to make the repetitions more conscious. An exception must be made if keeping the same fingering causes inconvenience of movements. (E.g., if the thumb or the little finger had to be placed on the black key.)

In the lower voice of Bach's Two-Part Invention in C major it is advantageous to place the thumb on the black key because this tone is followed by a part of a scale started by the thumb.

Example 107

The same motif in the upper voice – in the last member of the sequence – requires a change in the fingering, because if the thumb is put on the black key, the other fingers will be forced to assume a cramped position.

Example 108

PHRASING

An appropriate fingering must facilitate phrasing. In a fast tempo or when the other hand simultaneously plays a difficult part, it will be difficult to avoid faults, unless we take the phrasing into account. In arranging the fingering it is also of great importance to consider the style as far as possible. In the style of Bach, e.g., the proper solution of phrasing will be found much easier by making use of crossing.

Changing of position is of eminent help in emphasizing the phrasing. Correct phrasing of Bach's above-mentioned Invention will be considerably facilitated by the following fingering:

Example 109

Appropriate fingering also aids in accentuating. When repeating the accents, the stressed tones should always be played by the same finger. The stressed tones should be struck — whenever possible — by the thumb.

Example 110   Liszt: Paganini Study in A minor

TREMOLO FINGERING

In fast finger playing, a brilliant tone effect may be produced by the addition of tremolo movements. The plain chromatic scale serves as a good case in point.

Example 111

For the sake of the tremolo we use here the second finger only in playing the two consecutive white keys but otherwise we employ the first and third fingers. (To achieve tremolo effects, the fingering should in general call for the use of non-contiguous fingers, as we have seen in the tremolo trills.)

If a supple rather than a brilliant scale is desired, we should in the inward playing of the left hand put the fourth finger on the F sharp and in the case of the right hand on the B flat. Thereby less of a tremolo movement will be needed and a softer tone effect will result.

Example 112   Example 113

Example 114
Beethoven: Sonata in D major, Op. 28*

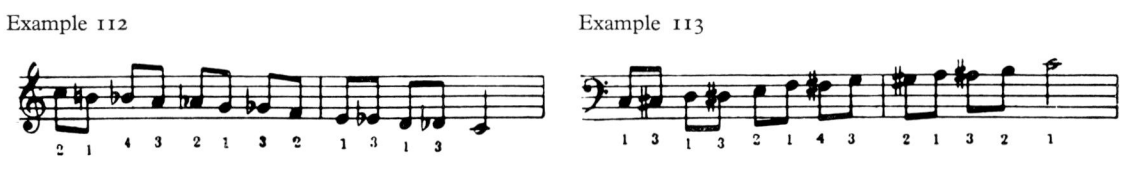

Example 115   Beethoven: Sonata in G major, Op. 31, No. 1*

DIRECTION FINGERING

In Example 112 we employed the fourth finger only in the inward-directed chromatic scale so as to achieve a soft tone effect but did not apply it in the outward direction. The fingers with higher numerals turn the hand inwards; therefore, when executing outward-directed passages, we have to employ fingers with lower numerals. Appropriate fingering helps to turn the hand in the playing direction. Hence we can use the term: "direction fingering".

C. Ph. E. Bach writes in his "Versuch über die wahre Art das Klavier zu spielen" (in the chapter on fingering) that in certain broken chords played downwards the use of the third finger is more convenient than that of the fourth.[1]

Example 116

This was the first formulation of the principle of direction fingering.

Application of direction fingering is a very important factor in playing passages. The passage of the C major six-four chord, for instance, when played outwards with the right hand is more brilliant and reliable if the E is struck with the third finger, but when played inwards it will sound well only if we employ the fourth finger.

Example 117

Beethoven: Sonata in D major, Op. 28*

Example 118

---

[1] "Der gute Vortrag, sowohl als das vorhergegangene, erfordern bisweilen eine kleine Änderung der Finger bey diesen Brechungen. Besonders findet man zuweilen bey gewissen von oben herunter gebrochenen Accorden den dritten Finger bequemer als den vierten, ohngeachtet dieser letztere natürlicher bey denselben Accorden, wann sie auf einmahl angeschlagen werden, eingesetzt wird."

In the penultimate bar of Liszt's Paganini Etude in A minor the F is played by the fifth finger.

Example 119

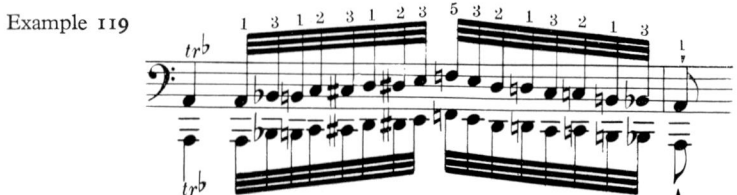

The 3–5 fingering produces a tremolo effect, but of even greater importance is the fact that if we use the fifth finger, the hand will be turned inwards. Application of the second or third finger on the F key would render virtuoso playing practically impossible.

A contradiction may seem to exist between scale fingerings with crossings, as mentioned before (see p. 239), and the principle of direction fingering, because the former prescribes the use of the third and fourth fingers outwards and of the second and third fingers inwards. In reality, however, this is also a direction fingering, because the third finger (being the longest one) strikes over the fourth or second finger. This use of the third or fourth finger automatically turns the hand outwards while the second and third fingers turn it inwards.

A very good example for the application of direction fingering is the playing of chromatic minor thirds. According to the principle of direction fingering, the fingers with lower numerals must be employed in the outward direction and those with higher numerals in the inward direction.

In playing an outward-moving chromatic scale in minor thirds the fifth finger is used in the upper voice (right hand) and in the lower voice (left hand) only on the two white keys. The other tones are played with fingers 3 and 4. In the other voice fingers 1 and 2 should be used. Apparently we also have two possibilities here. Either the second finger will slide from black to white keys or the thumb will slide from one white key to the next. The drawback of the sliding of the second finger is that the contact with the keyboard diminishes on account of the bent finger and this will weaken the dynamic expression. Obviously this is the reason why Chopin decided to apply the sliding of the thumb (as is to be seen in the fingering of the Etude in Thirds).

Example 120 Chopin: Op. 25, No. 6*

However, when playing inwards, the fifth finger should be employed as frequently as possible, because this furthers the turning of the hand into the direction of the playing.

Here Chopin's fingerings are not such a reliable guide as in the outward scale, because in the Etude in Thirds we find two different solutions.

In the following part he employs the fifth finger wherever possible:

Example 121

In the concluding scale of the étude, however, he applies the fourth finger even in cases where – according to the principle of direction fingering – the use of the fifth finger would provide a more favourable solution. He thereby contradicts not only the fingering of the part quoted above, but also among others the fingering of the Etude in A minor, Op. 10, where in the downward movement he uses the fifth finger throughout.

The fingering given in parentheses facilitates smooth playing of the final scale of the Etude in Thirds.

Example 122

The Etude in A minor offers ample opportunities for applying direction fingering.

The practising of this étude will be facilitated by playing the chromatic scale at first with the following fingering:

The use of direction fingering enables us to overcome many technical difficulties which trouble us when applying the usual scheme. However, the principle of direction fingering should be applied not only in solving technical difficulties. Its use will generally facilitate the work of the arm and render our playing more natural, thereby furthering quick automatization.

COMPLEMENTARY GYMNASTIC EXERCISES

The gymnastic exercises[1] given below are intended, first of all, to facilitate correct innervation of the movements required in piano playing. They serve, in addition, to complement systematic keyboard training and – in the event that no piano is available (journey, summer holidays, etc.) – to replace actual practising.

Such complementary training is necessary because the movements required at the piano do not make thorough use of the full mobility of the muscles. Gymnastics help to develop the muscles more quickly because, in addition to the smaller and strongly controlled movements required by the instrument, they also involve full and free movements.

It cannot be determined exactly how often the exercises should be repeated. The following rules may, nevertheless, be regarded as generally valid:

1. Never work to the point of fatigue.

2. Only exercises carried out with full concentration can be of use.

3. Even when exercising with a single finger joint, the whole body should be kept ready for action in a relaxed posture.

---

[1] Traces of the use of gymnastic exercises reach as far back as Couperin *(L'art de toucher le Clavecin)*.

"Les personnes, qui commencent tard, ou qui ont été mal-montrées feront attention, que comme les nerfs peuvent être endurcis, ou peuvent avoir pris de mauvais plis, elles doivent se dénoüer, ou se faire dénoüer Les doigts par quel'qu'un avant que de se méttre au clavecin ; c'est adire se tirer, ou se faire tirer Les doigts de tous les sens ; cela met d'ailleurs les Esprits en mouvement ; et l'on se trouve plus de liberté."

(People who begin late or who have been badly taught must — in view of the possible hardening of their sinews or because of bad habits acquired by the latter — take care to make their fingers flexible or to have them made so before sitting down to the harpsichord ; that is to say, they should pull their fingers in all directions, or get someone else to do it for them. This, moreover, will enliven their minds, and give them a feeling of greater freedom.)

Hand gymnastics as an aid to musical studies were first advised by E. W. Jackson (Great Britain) who delivered a lecture on this subject also in Budapest in 1864. His book on the subject is entitled *Finger- and Wrist-gymnastics*.

In 1897 a book was published in Budapest by Anna Lukács-Schuk, under the title: *Reform of Piano Teaching*. This work was subtitled: "A new method of teaching the piano, by the applying of which even pupils with less ability will attain an artistic technique within a comparatively short time." The author relates that her grandfather, Joseph Fischer M. D. invented hand gymnastics for her in order to free her from playing études six hours a day. By the aid of these exercises her technique improved so much that she "was heaped with praises" by her teacher, Franz Liszt.

Liszt was very much interested in the finger exercise practised by Anna Lukács-Schuk, so that he followed Dr. Joseph Fischer's advice and made his less-developed pupils execute hand gymnastics during the school-year 1886—1887.

"In this way we will give striking proof of the supremacy of this new method, because I am convinced that less-developed pupils, taught by the new method, will soon surpass even the best pupils having been taught according to the old one," said Liszt.

"For now," he continued, "we will keep the whole thing in secret and we will present it to the public only on the basis of facts and sure results because this is the only way to convince the stubbornness of the people of the old school, opposed to every innovation."

1. Describe a circle vertically with both shoulders. The arms hang inactively while the shoulders move.

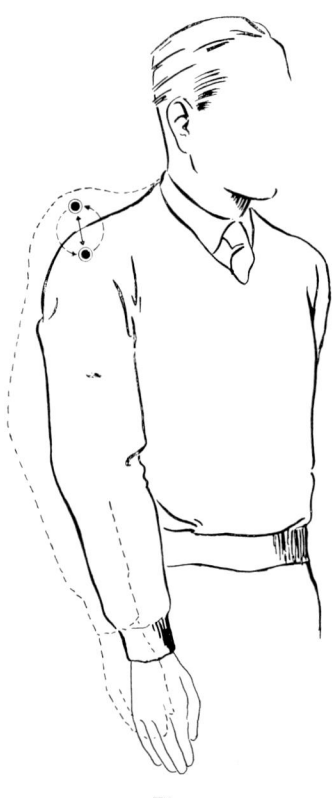

Fig. 52

2. Synthesizing circle. As the arms are raised, the backs of the hands at first face one another, but when arriving approximately at the level of the face, the fingers begin to rise so that, by the time

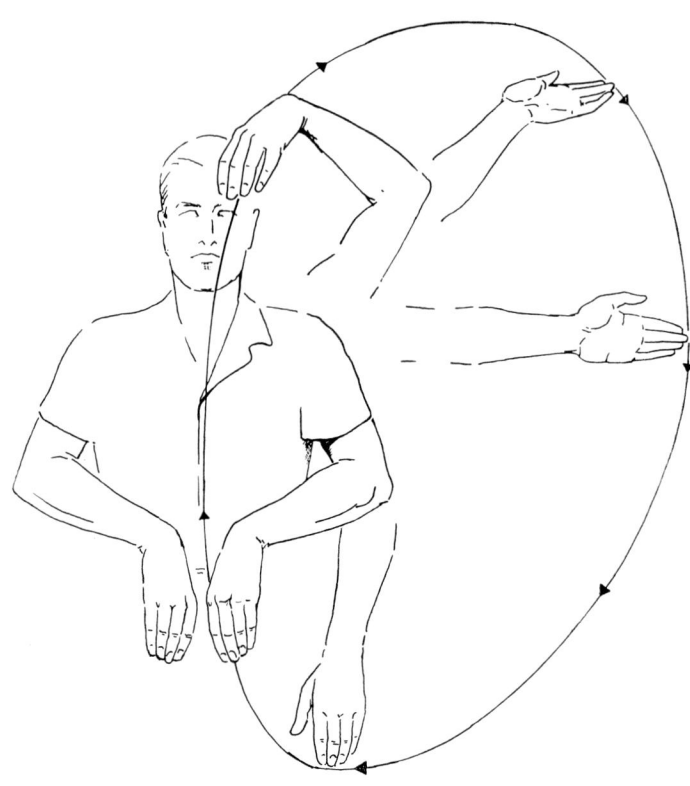

Fig. 53

Unfortunately Anna Lukács-Schuk did not describe in her book the exercises but enclosed the appraising statements of several well-known doctors of that time.

E. Piccirilli, in his book published in 1914 (Rome) under the title *Gimnastica e massaggio della mano* (Gymnastics and Massage of the Hand) and containing 14 exercises, especially flexions and circlings, mentions Liszt as having also applied hand gymnastics.

He quotes a passage from a letter addressed to him to the effect that Tonassi, the outstanding violinist and conductor of the Scala, had shown a child some gymnastic exercises designed to overcome certain difficulties in piano playing. Tonassi, on this occasion, had added: "I have seen Liszt engaged in these exercises before sitting down to the piano, in the days when we used to play together."

Another part of the same letter reads as follows: "Among the real masters of music who were my friends in Venice, there was an excellent pianist who was also the organist of S. Simon Grange. Being blind from birth, he had been a pupil of the Institute for the Blind in Padua. He was also a well-known composer."

"One day the question was discussed of how to overcome the constant stiffness of the fingers of students learning in a certain private institute. The blind man (his name was Luigi Modulo) said: 'I am going there and you shall see how I overcome it.'"

"He employed the same movements as Tonassi. Asked where these exercises came from, and whether he had invented them himself, he said: — 'No, they were shown by Liszt to a friend of the director of our Institute in Padua.' The institute visited by Modulo later produced the best students."

Among the few works recently issued, the book by R. Prentice (*Hand Gymnastics*. Novello Publishers, London) should be mentioned. This work gives several excellent strengthening exercises and emphasizes the importance of concentration during the execution of gymnastic exercises. The above-mentioned works of Jackson and Prentice have been used in part as sources for the composition of the exercises published in this book.

the arms are stretched, the fingers are already pointing upwards. The arms rise directly in front of the trunk and descend laterally with a wide-stretched, gentle movement. In descending, the palms revolve forwards, and by the time they have reached the lowest point, they face inwards. At the beginning of the new circle, the hands are again back to back.

When the hands are tired, they must be refreshed by executing synthesizing circles. Thus we avoid over-exertion. Pianists, especially those whose hands become easily cramped, have to interrupt practising as many times as possible by making some synthesizing circles.

As we have seen in the chapter dealing with the joints, the role of the shoulders is of a decisive importance. Weakness of the muscles moving the upper arm may hinder all our technical work. An impeccable action of these muscles is indispensable for every pianist, but the development of the shoulder muscles is particularly necessary in the case of piano players with long arms.

3(a). Swing the arms forwards, then laterally so that the finger-tips describe the upper half of a circle. Endeavour to swing your arms very high. This exercise should be carried out daily as many times as possible, gradually increasing the number of repetitions (5–15).

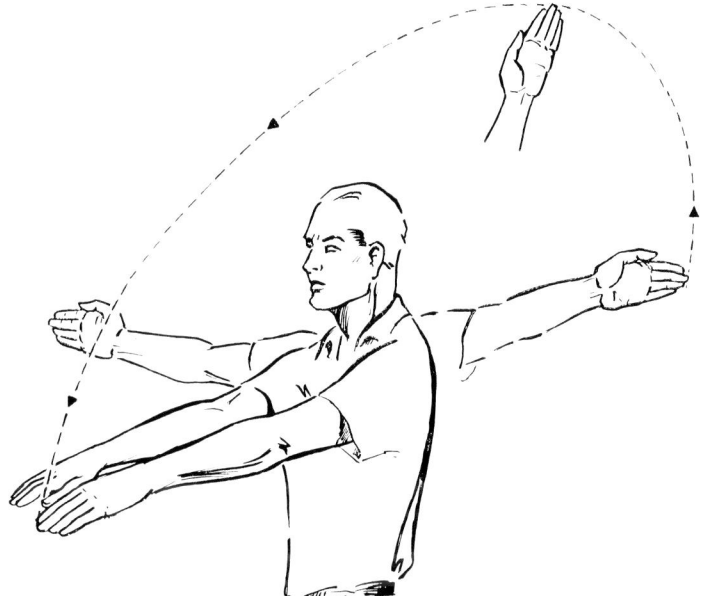

Fig. 54

3(b). The same exercise with lower semicircles. (This exercise may be inserted among other exercises for relaxation.)

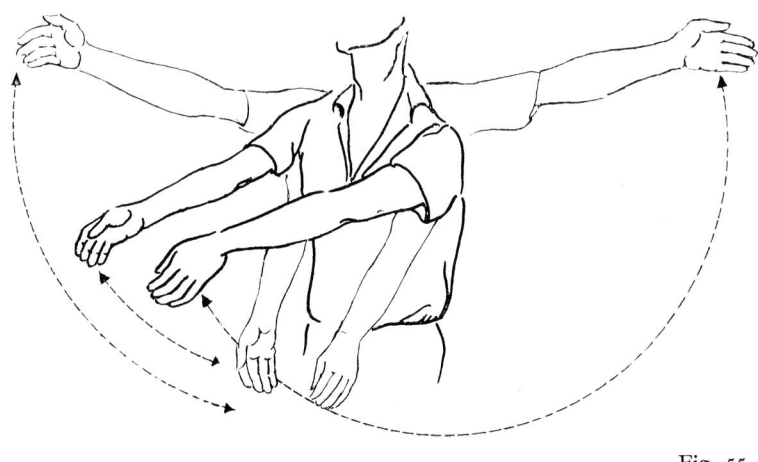

Fig. 55

4. Describe alternatingly smaller and larger lateral circles with easily extended upper arms (e.g., four small and four large circles). Each arm should form a single unit from the finger-ends to the shoulder. The circling motion should always be vigorous. We must have the feeling that the arm is being led by the finger-ends. This is possible only in a relaxed position. Avoid any tension.

Fig. 56

5. Describe swingful small circles with your arms extended forwards. The circles must be commenced first upwards and then downwards. We have to imagine ourselves having arms of 30–45 feet and moving them directly from the shoulder joint. The elbows must not execute any separate movements but they must not be stretched rigidly. The palms are turned somewhat up as if balancing something on the end of our imaginary arm.

6. Describe a serpentine line with your arms comfortably extended forwards. You have to imagine yourself pointing to an object far away (for example a car approaching us on a serpentine road, winding up a mountain side), i.e. you lengthen your arms in your imagination to that point. The tempo must always be slow. Exercise each hand separately.

Pointing at an object is an instinctive, inherited movement which shows us how the whole arm may be felt as an entity without any tenseness.

The finger-end feeling in piano playing corresponds to the feeling experienced in pointing. The only difference is that in the first case we lengthen our arm (in our imagination) not to a distant point but to the string.

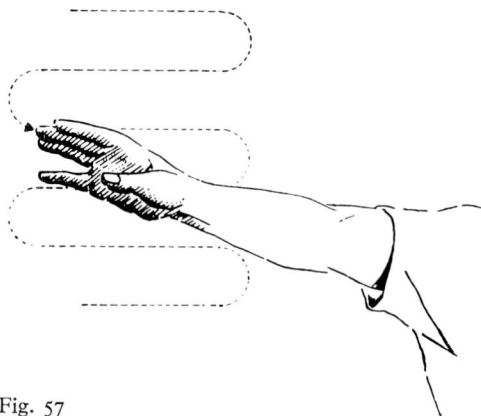

Fig. 57

7. Swing the right arm upwards while the left arm, bent at the elbow, touches the right shoulder with the hand. Then alternatively swing the left arm upwards and touch the left shoulder with the right hand.

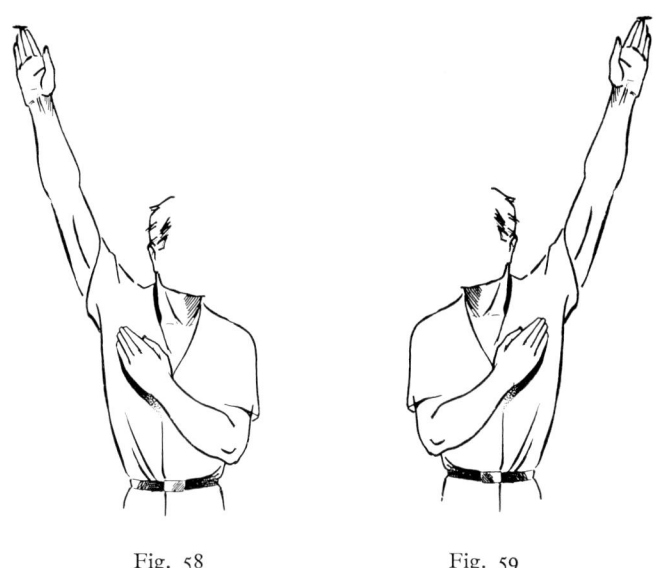

Fig. 58 Fig. 59

The exercise must be executed at a slow tempo but the arm should arrive at the highest position with a single energetic swing.

8. Lateral arm position. Palms directed upwards, fingers extended. Bend the forearm, keeping the upper arm motionless and relaxing the wrist completely. Stretch the arm again with extended fingers, but this time the palms are directed backwards. Return to the bent position. In the next stretching movement the palm faces forwards, in the succeeding one downwards; after every stretching we return to the bent position. In stretching, the fingers are vigorously spread apart, while in bending the wrist and the fingers should become loose. The exercise should be practised with both arms simultaneously.

Fig. 60

9. Preparation of chord practising. Lift and lower the forearm from the elbow. The hand remains all the time in firm chord position; one should feel as if the finger-tips were being moved directly from the elbow. All five fingers are firmly fixed, the little finger and the thumb being always turned towards each other. If the finger-tips (i.e. their imaginary elongations) are kept taut, the chord position can be maintained for a lengthy time without exhaustion.

Calm, even motion without any swinging. Practise each hand separately.

10. Forearm circling. The upper arm hangs limply from the shoulder and does not take an active part in the movement. (It gives way passively.) In order to execute this a perfectly relaxed state of the shoulder joint is required. The exercise should be practised with both arms simultaneously with swingful vertical circles, executed in opposite direction.

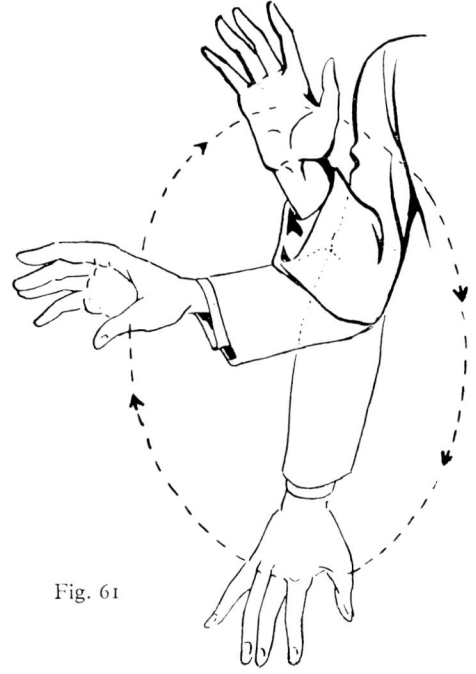

Fig. 61

11. With the upper arm in horizontal-lateral position, and with the forearm kept as near as possible to the level of the upper arm, describe horizontal circles around the elbow, the latter serving as a centre. Simultaneously with the forearm, the wrist also executes circular movements which widen the circle of the forearm. Each hand should be practised separately.

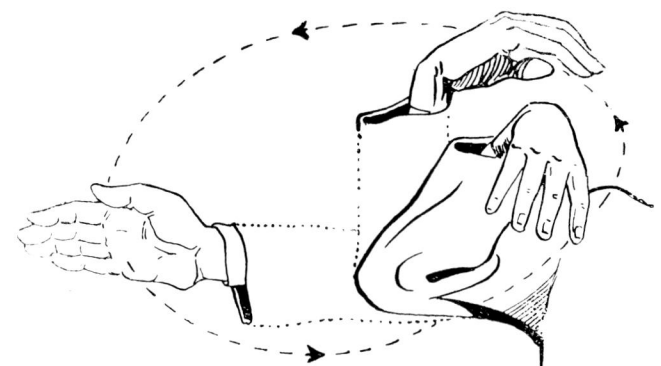

Fig. 62

12. Rotation of the forearm around an imaginary axis running from the end of the third finger to the elbow. The hand assumes a firm but not cramped chord position, the fingers remaining without motion of their own, as if holding with their imaginary elongations a big ring. The movement should be soft slow, and covers about an eighth of a circle. It is important that the rotation should always be executed exactly around the imaginary axis. Practise always with each hand separately.

13. The same exercise as under No. 12, but with a rotation swift as lighting and a bigger movement. ($1/3$ of a circle.) The force operates only at the start and the hand revolves only as long as the impetus of the initial swinging motion is effective and the rotation continues without strain. In this way, any shifting of the wrist will be avoided. Remain one or two seconds in the extreme positions so that you can concentrate fully on the next rotation.

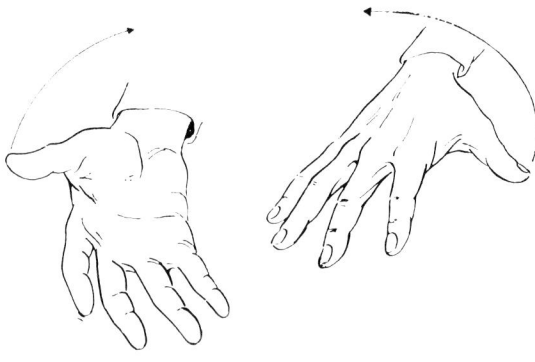

Fig. 63

14(a). Swinging movement of both wrists with softly extended fingers drawing the upper half of a circle in opposite directions. The motion is directed by the finger-ends ("long" fingers) but the hand forms a single entity, the fingers do not execute any separate movements. First describe upper, then lower half-circles, in opposite directions.

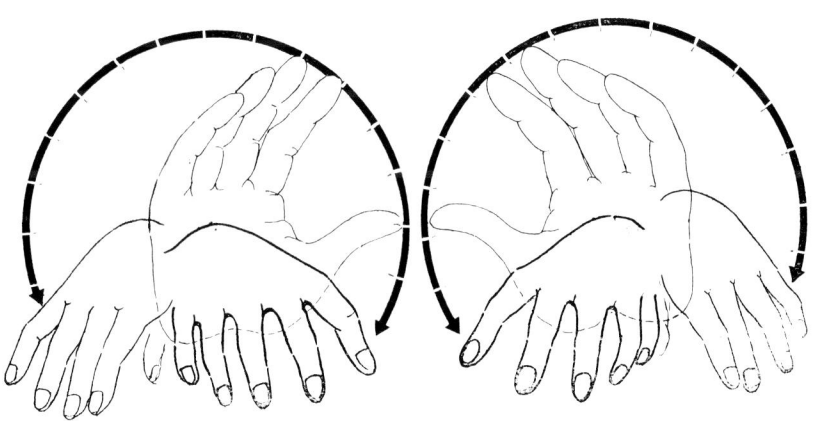

Figs. 64–65

14(b). Having achieved an impeccable execution in opposite directions, practise these exercises in the same direction.

15. Circling motion from the wrist. The movement is initiated by the lower arm, as if swinging a weight attached to a cord in a circle. Be sure to give the movement the character of a swinging motion and to describe the circles with imaginary elongated finger-tips. Practise this exercise with both hands simultaneously in opposite directions, the left hand first circling clockwise, the right hand counter-clockwise (which we shall call a downward circle),

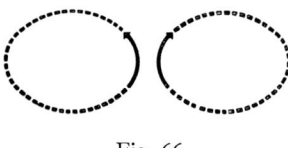

Fig. 66

and then vice versa (upward circle).

Fig. 67

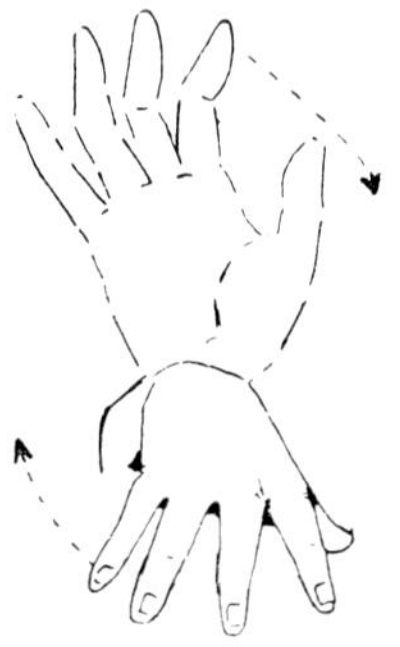

Fig. 68

The momentum is given by the motion of the forearm. Thus it is not only inexpedient but even harmful if the circling is executed with immobile forearms. But care must be taken that the movement of the forearm is minimal. This is, generally, almost imperceptible but in our "feeling the movement" it makes a great difference because with unmoved forearm the motion is felt stiff and rigid. The circles will be swingful only with the activity of the forearm.

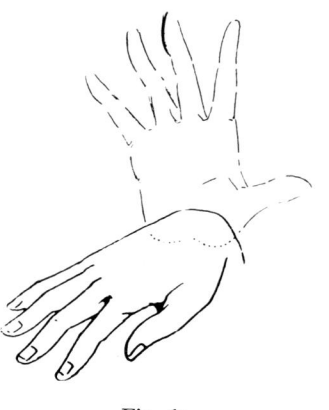

Fig. 69

16. Bend your wrist relaxedly. The fingers also should be in a slack position. Suddenly spread your fingers wide and at the same time swing your hand upwards into a stretched position, then release it again. The spreading movement is initiated by active finger work, while in the relaxing phase the hand should drop passively.

17. The contrary of exercise No. 16. From an extended, yet relaxed hand position swing your hand with spread fingers into bent position, then calmly lift it again into the starting position.

Fig. 70

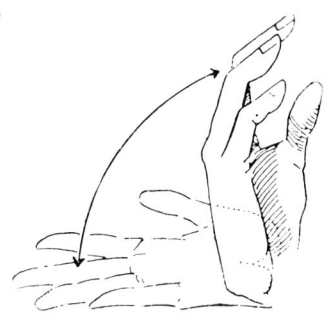

18. The forearm is turned upwards, the hand gently bent towards the upper arm. Now, swing the hand with spread fingers into a stretched position.

19. The contrary of exercise No. 18. Swing the hand with spread fingers into a bent position.

Fig. 71

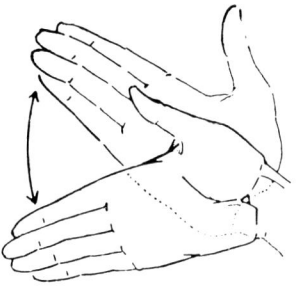

20. Move the hand from the wrist upwards and downwards, with the palm facing inwards. (Lateral movement.)

Fig. 72

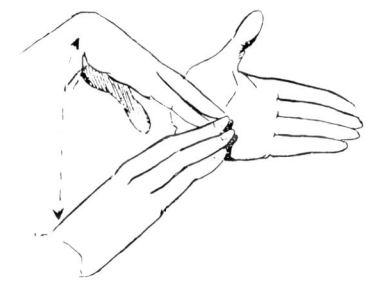

21. Hold the extended left hand with the palm turned inwards. Touch the left palm lightly with the middle finger of the right hand, facing downwards, then alternately lift and lower the right forearm from the elbow without shifting the point of contact with the left palm. (The upper arm does not take part in the movement.) The right hand must form an entity as if the finger joints were incapable of any movement. The wrist is the only joint which executes a passive movement. (It is important to concentrate on the motion of the forearm and not on that of the wrist in order that it should move passively.)

Fig. 73

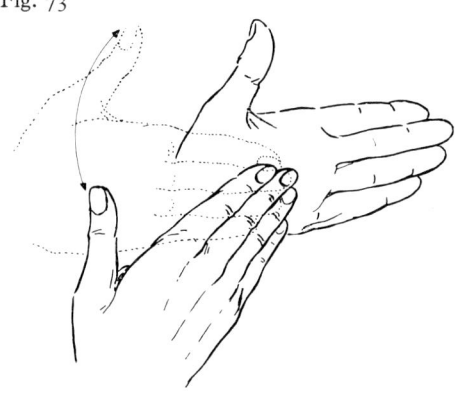

22. The same exercise as No. 21, but with the difference that the edge of the right hand instead of the palm is turned downwards. In this way, the wrist, on account of the vertical motion of the forearm, carries out a passive lateral movement. Both this and the previous exercises should be practised alternately with the right and left hands (5 to 10 flexions).

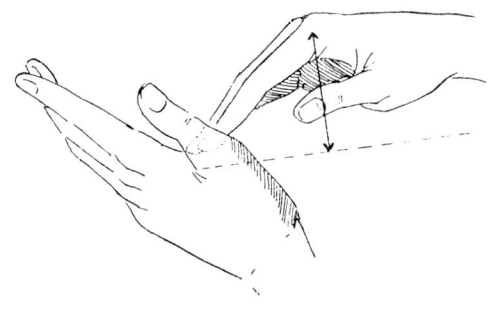

Fig. 74

23. Hold the extended left hand with the palm turned inwards, as in Ex. No. 22. The middle finger of the downward-turned right hand lightly touches the palm of the left hand, and keeping this touching-point we move the forearm in a way that the first joint executes a passive movement. Thus both the second and third finger joints and the wrist are immobile, only the elbow executes active, and the knuckles passive movements.

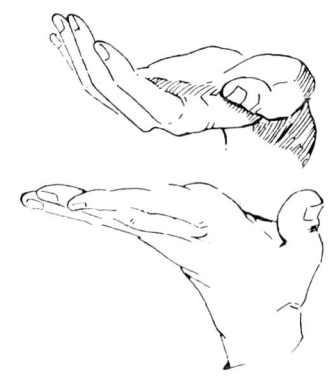

Fig. 75

24. The palms are turned upwards with softly bent fingers (to the extent compatible with a comfortable position). Starting from this position, stretch the fingers tautly backwards — moving the thumb a little away from the palm — so that the first joints are lifted as high as possible.

25. The same exercise as No. 24, combined with rotation of the forearm. Slowly rotate the forearm between the two extreme positions of pronation and supination, while the first finger joints execute quick, uninterrupted movements.

26. Clench both fists lightly (with thumbs folded inwards but without being squeezed by the other fingers), then throw the hands vigorously open by tautening the fingers backwards. Repeat this ten times at first, then on subsequent occasions more and more often, but making sure that the fists are always opened and closed with equal energy.

The exercise may also be carried out in such a way that the actual swinging motion is directed outwards, the inward movement consequently being a mere preparation of the former.

The contrary process is the inward swinging motion, whereby the opening of the fingers prepares the clenching of the fist. It is important that the movement should have continuous momentum and not be cut in two. (In the case of similar exercises having three modes of execution we shall henceforth use the term: triple mode of practising.) To be practised only with both hands. Having acquired proficiency in this exercise, it should be practised in combination with exercise No. 2 (synthesizing circle).

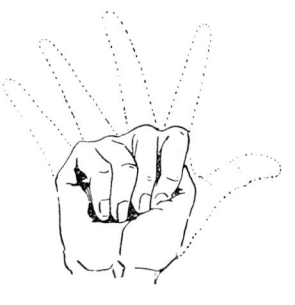

Fig. 76

The use of synthesizing circles in finger gymnastics constitutes a preparation for the legato, since in legato playing, too, we carry out active finger strokes within large synthesizing arm movements. In addition, it ensures the synchrony and naturalness of the movements.

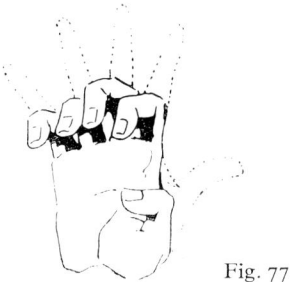

Fig. 77

27. Stretch the fingers, spreading them well apart and tautening them a little backwards. Bend the first and second joints of the thumb and the second and third joints of the other fingers until they form a right angle. Triple mode of practising. To be carried out also with both hands simultaneously, as well as in combination with synthesizing circles.

Fig. 78

28. Strike the fleshy part of the first joint with the finger-ends, next strike the centre of the palm, then its lower part, and finally again the centre, after which begin all over again. The fingers must not be squeezed against each other, but also not be spread too far apart. They should be lifted only as far as is necessary for the next stroke. Practise this exercise also with both hands, while simultaneously performing synthesizing circles.

29. Stretch the fifth finger, moving its tip down the palm's surface, as near as possible to the wrist. Then draw the finger-end back towards the first finger joint as if caressing the palm. Do the same successively with the other fingers.

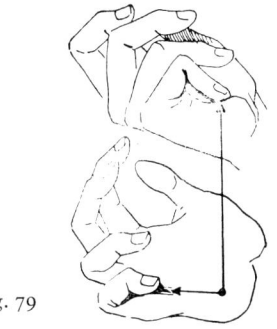

Fig. 79

30(a). Extend the fingers of the left hand pressed tightly one against the other, with the thumb held somewhat apart (abducted). Slide the third and fifth fingers of the right hand over the left hand and the second and the fourth fingers under it. Now, pull back the right hand and move the second and fourth fingers over the left hand and the third and fifth finger under it. Make sure that the thumb of the right hand does not get over the left thumb, because this would hinder quick change. When practising the exercises with the left hand, the left thumb must, of course, be below. The fingers must not be tautened, slide them lightly on the other (closed) hand and the change of the fingers must be made together even in the air. Thus the fingers must slide to their place not one by one but all at once.

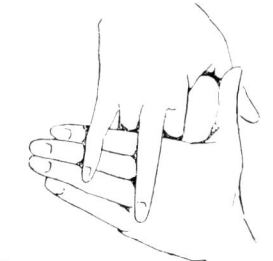

Fig. 80

The exercise should be carried out at first slowly and only once or twice. When you have acquired greater skill, it may be repeated 40 to 50 times with both hands. This is an excellent preparatory exercise for playing thirds.

30(b). The above exercise is very suitable also for the technical preparation of beginners. Children may learn it in a playful way. The left hand is a plank and the thumb is a proud nail and it must be pulled aside in order not to hurt somebody. The five fingers of the right hand are five lions. (This is an excellent occasion also to learn the order of succession of the fingers.) The thumb is an old lion, we don't make him work, but with the others we are going to practise for a difficult show. The tamer (the child) gives the command: number 2 and 4 over the plank and number 3 and 5 under the plank. The lions are somewhat lazy and clumsy in the beginning, but they will obey gradually.

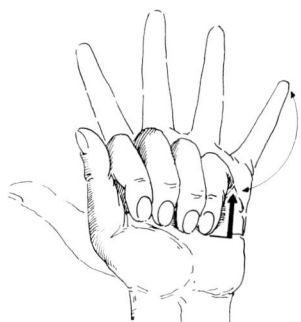

Fig. 81

31. The fingers first glide upwards over the palm and are then swung into a spread-out position. The movement must have full momentum and stop only when the spread-out position has been reached. To be practised also in combination with synthesizing circles.

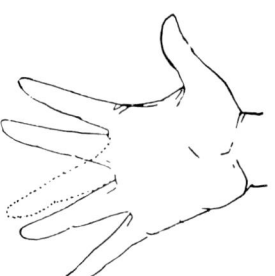

Fig. 82

32. Carry out lateral movements with each finger separately as far as the joint allows. Practise this exercise several times successively but never to the point of exhaustion. (The lateral movement is the most important means of the strengthening the interossei, the muscles of velocity. If the exercises, containing lateral movements, are practised several times daily and with endurance, the ability, "productive capacity" of our fingers will develop rapidly.)

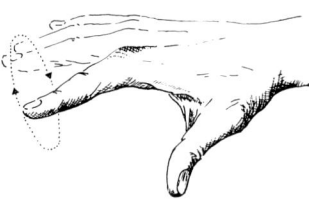

Fig. 83

33. Each finger should describe 8 to 10 circles successively, first all in one direction, then in the opposite direction. Make large circles but only as large as to execute them comfortably. One must have the feeling of agreeably stretching himself. Our whole attention must be concentrated on the tip of the finger being exercised (imaginarily lengthened) while the other fingers are allowed to move freely.

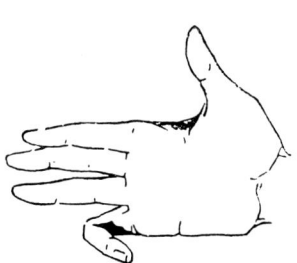

Fig. 84

34. Bend the second joint of each finger one after another, up to the point of forming a right angle.

The aim of this exercise is not the strengthening of muscles. It is to learn to concentrate (direct one's motion-command) on the second joint. Therefore bend it only to the right angle because continuing the bending beyond this point will scatter the attention over too wide a territory. If one concentrates fully on the second joint, it will be hard as steel while the third is so relaxed that the finger-end — after being struck with the other hand — will resume its resting position only after two or three vibrations.

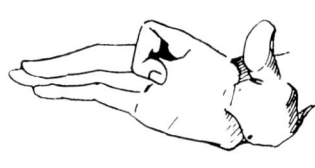

Fig. 85

35. Bend each finger successively at the third joint. The bending of the third joint can be carried out by correct innervation only if the second joint is simultaneously flexed because there is no extensor insertion which would hold the second phalanx extended. (See on page 128.) The bending must not be more than 50–60 degrees because beyond this it is impossible to concentrate fully on the third joint and one will rather begin to "feel" the second joint.

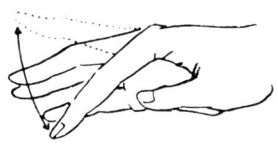

Fig. 86

36. Slowly raise each completely relaxed finger successively at the first joint. One should feel as if the finger were being drawn by a thread attached to its end. The finger must be a complete entity: during the process of raising, the joint must, therefore, be neither completely extended nor bent. The movement should be carried out in such a way that one concentrates only on the finger-end while the finger is completely relaxed at the first joint. Do not let the lifted finger remain in raised position — because then it will become stiff — but let it fall immediately as if the thread pulling it up had snapped. If we were to wait, we could not let the stiffened finger drop freely but, instead, would have to propel it.

The purpose of the exercise is not dropping the finger but the full concentration on the finger-ends in order to learn to raise the finger as a whole. If the dropping is easily executed, it shows that the concentration on the finger-ends was successful. After dropping one finger, rest for some seconds in order to prepare for concentrating on the next raising.

As a preparation for dropping it is advisable to practise exercises Nos. 34, 35, and after that, 33. By their aid the equilibrium of the muscle and a relaxed position will be restored. Those with very strongly flexed — almost cramped — fingers have to execute more circling, while those with unstable, hyperextended fingers have to execute more bendings from the second and third joints.

37. Bend the thumb at the first joint. The joint will in many cases permit only a slight movement but this is no disadvantage. Our object is not the extent but rather the awareness of the movement.

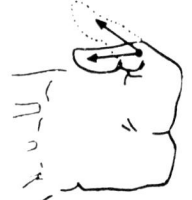

Fig. 87

38. Bend the second joint of the thumb.

Fig. 88

39. Turn the palm inwards, then raise and let drop the thumb at its base (carpo-metacarpal) joint, as the other fingers in exercise No. 36. The thumb must be perfectly united and free of any tension. The fleshy part of the thumb (thenar eminence) should remain completely relaxed.

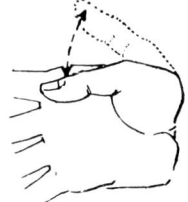

Fig. 89

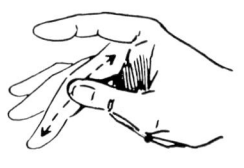

40. The thumb glides successively along the other fingers (caressing).

Fig. 90

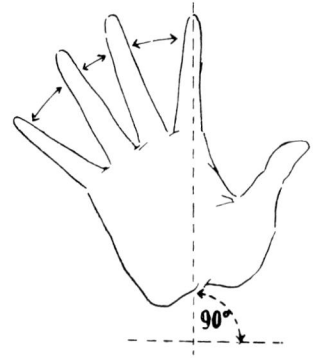

Fig. 91

41. Open the hand widely, then close the fingers successively towards the second finger, which remains motionless. Inversely: First open (abduct) the fifth finger, then move the others successively towards it.

42. Open and close the fingers (even the thumb) in fan-like fashion but with the second finger held motionless. Practise the same with motionless third of fourth fingers.

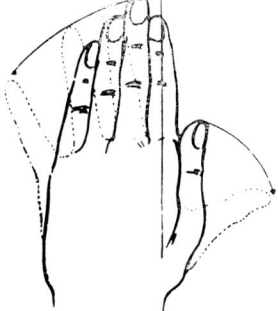

Fig. 92

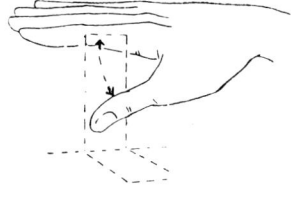

Fig. 93

43. Move the thumb back and forth (abducting and adducting it at the base) at right angles to the palm. Triple mode of practising.

44. The second and fourth fingers touch each other alternately above and below the third one. Then, the third and fifth fingers do the same above and below the fourth one.

Fig. 94

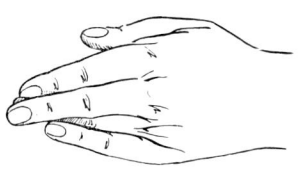

Fig. 95

45. Fingers 2 and 4 and fingers 3 and 5, respectively, touch each other simultaneously, with the first pair alternately above and below the second. Also with synthesizing circles.

46. Shut the fingers close together, then open them between the third and fourth fingers.

47. Perform the same exercise as No. 46 but now opening the hand between fingers 2–3 and 4–5 while fingers 3–4 are held closed.

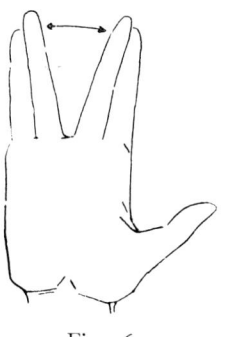

Fig. 96

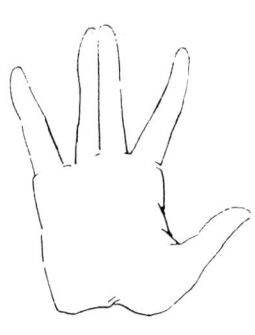

Fig. 97

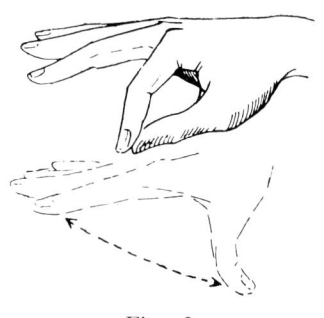

Fig. 98

48. The tips of the thumb and the second finger touch each other and then suddenly spring apart along an imaginary arc. Perform the same movement with the thumb and fingers 3–4–5, successively. Later also with synthesizing circles. The springing apart of the fingers must occur quickly. This exercise is the most useful when executed simultaneously with synthesizing circles. The arm carries out calm, even movements. The most advisable order of succession for the fingers is 2–3–4–5 4–3–2–3, etc.

49. Describe with the imaginarily elongated end of the thumb a triangle and then a square in the air. Execute the same exercise successively with the other fingers with the palm held downwards.

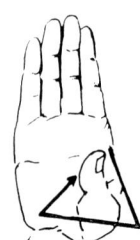

Fig. 99

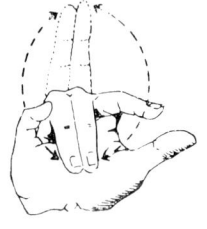

Fig. 100

50. Describe successively circles with each finger pair (the fingers of each pair moving in opposite directions and describing a semicircle). The hand and the arm should give no aid: the movement must be executed by the fingers exclusively.

51. Each finger should strike the thumb successively. The lateral movement is carried out by the thumb. To be practised also with synthesizing circles as in exercise No. 48. The fingers must just tap and not touch the thumb longer than a split second. After that they prepare for the next stroke.

Fig. 101

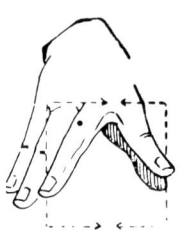

Fig. 102

52. Draw a square with two fingers. Open the fingers in extended position, bend them parallel at the first joint, then close them in lowered position.

263

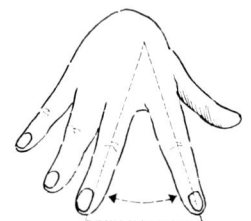

Fig. 103

53. Draw a triangle with two fingers. Open the closed fingers gradually and bend them simultaneously at the first joint. Close them again below.

54. Describe circles with the second and third fingers simultaneously but in opposite directions. Practise the same in the following combinations: 3–4, 4–5, 2–4, 3–5.

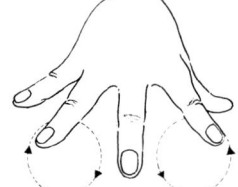

Fig. 104

Fig. 105

55. Strike each finger-tip successively with the thumb. Do not hold the other fingers stiffly or allow them to help the thumb by much movement but rather concentrate on the full and energetic movements of the thumb.

56. Raise and lower the fingers one after another in a continuous and entirely even motion. The finger-ends are moved from the first joint, consequently the fingers are felt as an entity. The movements should not be too wide because otherwise a stiffening of the fingers becomes unavoidable.

57. Execute slow trill motions with each pair of fingers. (The most expedient order of succession is 2–3, 3–4, 4–5 and 1–2.) The fingers have to strike firmly and energetically, but the whole movement should be a thoroughly controlled one. The motion of the fingers taking part in the trill should be absolutely simultaneous. (While one rises, the other sinks.) As we have to maintain control over the movement, we cannot allow it to develop to its fullest possible scope. The movement should be continuous; neither of the fingers should stand still at the top or the bottom of its course.

As soon as the exercise can be carried out faultlessly in an even rhythm, it should also be practised in the following manner:

Example 126

58. Describe synthesizing circles at varying speeds (two quick circles and one slow one).

RECOMMENDATIONS CONCERNING RATIONAL UTILIZATION OF THE GYMNASTIC EXERCISES

If fatigue develops while playing the piano, the execution of several synthesizing circles in a calm tempo will refresh the tired fingers as well as the wrist in a short time. (Massaging or rubbing the wrist will only increase the irritability of the tissues which may easily result in disability.)

The synthesizing circle intensifies the blood circulation not only of the upper arm but also of the arm as a whole, including the fingers, and will thus refresh exhausted muscles.

As long as the individual exercises are not yet perfectly mastered, the whole material should be gone through, as far as possible, in the given order. The upper-arm exercises should, nevertheless, be repeated between the finger gymnastics, too.

The work should as far as possible be distributed over the whole day, only a few exercises should be carried out at one time. This will lead to a better and quicker result both by developing the muscles and innervating the correct movements.

Although steady training in all exercises is needed only at certain periods (e.g. during the summer holidays or when preparing for some technical re-adaptation), work at the piano should be supplemented daily by the exercises Nos. 2, 5, 29, 33, 34, 35, 36, 37, 38, 39, 40, 57.

The daily practising of these exercises should not take more than 10 minutes' time at the most.

This series may be extended – if necessary – by the addition of special exercises. In the case of passivity of the upper arm, for instance, one should add Nos. 2, 3a, 3b, 4, 5, 6, 7, 11.

For the preparation and development of the technique of octaves, chords, and skips, take Nos. 9, 10, 12, 13, 14a, 14b, 15, and to attain a sure mutual co-ordination of the fingers all the gymnastic finger exercises should be practised alternately.

To increase finger velocity turn to Nos. 32 – 39.

To warm cold hands, exercises Nos. 26, 27, 28, 29, 31, 40, 48, 51 should be practised with synthesizing circles.

To supplement or (in case of necessity) replace warming-up at the piano, use Nos. 2, 5, 29, 34, 35, 36, 37, 38, 39, 40, 57, 58.

First gymnastic exercises of beginners: Nos. 2 (connected with singing), 30, 32, 33, 46, 47.

Other combinations should be employed according to the individual needs and disposition. Selection of the appropriate gymnastic exercises will be facilitated by a thorough study of the chapter on anatomy.

NOTES ON TEACHING THE TECHNICAL PROBLEMS OF BEGINNERS

In the preceding chapters it was stated that the most important technical task in piano playing is the production of tones corresponding to our musical concept. (Tones of different volume, tones with and without noise-effect, etc.) Piano technique in its entirety thus depends directly on the musical concept.

PREPARATORY SCHOOLING

The first requirement in the teaching of beginners and also from the point of view of the mechanics of piano playing, is to develop the musical imaginative capacity of the child even before he begins to play the piano.[1] This aim is attained by preparatory teaching, with its songs and games which serve to develop the musical faculties.

The mechanical work needed in piano playing places a complex task before the pupil even in the earliest stages of study. He has to concentrate on his arm and fingers without detriment to his musical concept, and all this must be done under considerably more difficult circumstances than those faced by adults, because the dimensions of the piano – the size and weight of the keys – are built for adult proportions. In connection with piano playing, many tasks, therefore, have to be solved by preparatory teaching. On the one hand, the pupils's sense of polyphony and a certain skill in simultaneously concentrating on a number of things have to be developed; on the other hand, some of the mechanical difficulties faced by the beginner must, if possible, be overcome, already at this stage.

Preparatory teaching aims at developing reading notes to a level enabling the pupil to read two-voice pieces effortlessly. (It must be emphasized that, later on, note-reading has also to be practised hand in hand with piano playing, if the pupil is to become a good sight-reader.)

The task of the preparatory teaching is also to enable the pupil to develop as much freedom of movement as possible. It is a most difficult task to correct stiff movements during the piano playing. By practising playful movement exercises even pupils with cramped, jerky movements will almost imperceptibly acquire relaxed, loose and light movements.

Although the material of the preparatory teaching does not belong strictly to the material of piano technique dealt with in this book, a short description of the movement exercises is nevertheless given here, on account of their special importance. If – for some reason – the pupil is unable to visit the preparatory school, the greater part of the movement exercises must be made during the piano lessons. No trouble must be spared in carrying on these exercises because the naturalness and freedom of the movements of the pupil can be assured for years by the aid of them.

The three main groups of the movement exercises are the following:
walking exercises, rhythmical hand movements, synthesizing movements.

[1] In the preparatory school the teacher has to provide opportunities for the pupil to familiarize himself not only with the piano but also with stringed and wind instruments. The problem of choosing the instrument to be studied by the pupil must not be decided by whatever instrument he has at home already but rather by the expressive possibilities of whichever instrument is most attractive to the pupil.

Walking exercises

1. In the "melody-walking" the pupil (child) executes a step on each tone of some well-known folk-song.

2. In the so-called "character-walking" the child shows – by listening to music with different tempo and different emotional content – how the soldier walks, how the old woman walks when carrying brush-wood, how the bunny runs, how the turtle creeps, etc.

3. In the walking exercises – aiming at the development of attention – the pupil starts walking and stops at short commands (the best one is Dalcroze's "Hopp"). Later on the exercise can be made somewhat more complicated by the child's turning on the command "Hipp" and crouching down on the command "Hepp."

4. In the "ostinato-walking" the pupils walk in an ostinato rhythm by singing a folk-song.

5. "Canon (catch) walking." There are four kinds:

a. The teacher plays a rhythmical series of chords and the pupils clap or step on each chord with a delay of one bar.

b. The pupils sing the folk-song and step to the rhythm of a catch.

c. The teacher plays a well-known folk-song and the pupils clap the rhythm with the delay of one bar, and step on the rhythm with the delay of two bars.

d. The teacher improvises rhythmical chords, the pupils clap a bar later and step two bars later.

Rhythmical hand movements

1. Imitation of the flying of birds, e.g., when imitating the flying of the eagle the arms are to be moved in half notes (the arms are moved as a unit, as if they were wings), the pigeons "fly" in quarter notes, the sparrows in quavers, etc.

2. Work movements. The teacher fits up a carpenter's shop. One of the children "works" with a hammer, another with a plane, another with a saw, etc., i.e. they imitate the movements as lifelike as possible to the rhythm of a folk-song.

The most important thing is to keep perfect freedom and easiness when clapping the rhythms. If the pupil claps with cramped, clenched hands or moves them too stiffly (or even opens them too suddenly) – i. e. if the preparing of the clapping and the clapping itself is not executed as one single unit – it will be most harmful for the beginner's piano playing. (Equally harmful is to make the pupils mark the rests by active movements because this, too, may cause stiffness.)

PREPARATION OF TECHNICAL WORK

The first task in the direct preparation of technical work is the teaching of the synthesizing movements. The simplest method is to make the pupil describe synthesizing movements and afterwards let him conduct to the playing of the teacher.

The practising of the synthesizing circles (see on page 250) on singing melodies enables the pupil to learn to divide continuous, unbroken arm movements into the units of the music. The teacher plays a melody (which he wants the pupil to learn to play later on the piano) – the best ones are pentachord folk-songs – and the pupil describes synthesizing circles with his arms, first one circle to half of the melody, later one to the whole of the melody. If there are two or more pupils present, the exercise must be executed in the form of a contest: the winner is the one who is the best in describing the circle by the most even movement throughout the exercise and ending it exactly at the end of the melody. The practising of the synthesizing circles must be made systematically (more or less often according to necessity) in the first months of learning the piano playing.

Equally important is to make the pupil conduct even before beginning piano playing. He also must get the experience of creating music by movements, and has to learn that one movement may unite a whole series of tones. He need not execute regular conducting movements, but only truly spontaneously felt movements. The ideal solution for the teacher is to improvise music according to the movements of the pupil. However, playing pentachord folk-songs, too, renders good services just as in the case of the synthesizing movements.

The mechanical preparation of the finger action is made through gymnastic exercises and slow trill movements carried out in the air. The gymnastic exercises will enable the pupil to begin piano playing immediately with melodies. This is very important because even beginners should be taught from the start — on the basis of musical experience — real music. It would be entirely wrong to start the very first lessons with finger exercises executed on the piano. The beginner would then concentrate merely on the fingers instead of on tone producing, and this would render proper innervation difficult when playing real compositions. Even if the only aim is a purely mechanical one, it is more serviceable to practise the finger movements without dependence on the keys and only afterwards to require them to adapt themselves to the keyboard.

The pupil is to be led to feel even before playing the first melody that he has to play on the strings by the aid of the keys. The curious fact that the player only sees the keyboard almost always misleads the beginner and he plays as if the tone were produced by the key. (The noise-effect is really added to the tone colour by the key, and thus the piano really has the double character that both the strings and the keys are tone-producing parts. This may cause serious harm even with more advanced players when a considerable noise-effect is needed to produce the desired tone colour. In such cases it is the searching for the appropriate tone colour which leads to the "key-playing.")

Even adults run the risk of striking the keys as if they produced the tone. But the danger is even more serious with children for whom even the bringing into motion of the heavy keys is a great task which might be easily considered by them as the final aim. Therefore the teacher must indefatigably lead the pupil again and again to the right way of tone producing, which means that the key must be felt as a mere tool at his disposition. (See page 82.)

Some pupils — and mainly the skilful ones — may run the risk of becoming detached from the instrument. The movements of such pupils are in themselves correct and sure, but they are not used in the service of making music. This may be avoided by teaching the pupil right at the beginning to make the piano sing. And this is the truth, for after all, the piano is to be taught to reproduce the composition according to our musical conception. Our task is only to find the movements by which the piano can be compelled to do so. This approach to the problem is to be applied often even by very advanced pianists if they forget that the movement is only a means toward producing the appropriate tone.

One has to make the pupil understand the character of the key in its functioning as a two-armed lever. This is first demonstrated by a stick or ruler (see page 84), then on the piano by sounding tones. Learning the first melody should be started only after the pupil has found out the great difference between "playing on the keys" and "playing, by the aid of the keys, on the strings."

First a pentachord melody is to be taught which is so familiar to the child that he can sing it. Then encourage him to find the tones of the melody on the piano. The next step is to practise the melody — motif by motif — on the instrument and also playing them in the air in order to join exactly the finger movements with each other.

Practising without the piano facilitates the teaching of even finger movements. We thereby also ensure that the movement of the fingers will not be carried out in a haphazard manner and the fingers, instead of striking as deeply as the key permits, descend only as deeply as we desire.

We transform the musical concept into movements, a process which is considerably facilitated by practising without the piano. If the pupil practises immediately and exclusively at the piano, faulty innervations will very soon establish themselves, because the beginner has to master an excessively complex task. Whatever is possible to learn without the piano — e.g., the synthesizing movements of the arm and the finger movements – must be taught before any piano playing, because it will make the first experiments of the beginner at the piano much easier.

The synthesizing has already been prepared by the synthesizing circles and the conducting. Now we also have to prepare the more delicate nuances of the synthesizing by making the pupil feel as if he moved his fingers from his heart, from his chest, as if the tone flowed through his whole body and fingers and through the keys and strings into the air. If this streaming of the energy is made perceptible to the pupil, we have already obtained the functioning of the whole body as an elastic support.

The finger work has to be expedient and exact even during the first attempts at piano playing. If the pupil concentrates on the work to be executed, if the finger-ends strive for grasping the keys as one grasps the handle of a hammer, the "giving" on the part of the third joint and superfluous movements of the second joint will be avoided.

Initial and final tones are always to be struck from the shoulder. At the beginner's stage this also applies to repeated and staccato tones. However, much worry is caused to the beginner – and even to the advanced pianist – by the apparently twofold function of the upper arm. In the synthesizing, the upper arm is apparently unmoved when sounding the single tones. Why is it required then, in other cases, to move the whole arm in the sounding of each tone? To the pupil a much simpler solution will seem, to strike each tone also with the forearm, thus "sparing" the fingers (and the upper arm) from the great work of moving the keys. This is strongly motivated for the beginner because the thin fingers of the child only overcome the weight of the key with difficulty, suited to an adult hand.

Thus a choice must be made between two ways. Either we choose the erroneous way followed by the greater part of the disciples of the "weight-technique school," i.e. making the beginner play for a long time only with the whole arm, or the opposite way: to choose a material for the beginners where strokes with the upper arm are rarely needed. This applies mainly to 4–5 melodies played in the first lessons and even afterwards we may introduce only gradually repeated tones and staccatos.

The forearm staccato – i.e. the rapid staccato – should be avoided in the first years, because its perfect execution already requires an absolute sureness in the synthesizing movements of the upper arm.

This sureness will be attained comparatively early if the pianist sees to it that precise finger action and synthesizing arm movements have an equal part in legato playing. This co-operation must not be disturbed either by any shaking of the forearm or overburdening of the fingers (the latter is usually a consequence of a wrong body position). The fingers should execute conscious striking movements in legato playing (that is, the pupil should concentrate on the stroke and not on the lifting process) and that, in the staccato, the fingers, as elongations of the arm, only make movements which are absolutely necessary.

LEGATO

The basic task of teaching technique to the beginner is teaching legato playing. This is rendered difficult by the fact that the child faces an unsolvable situation of being expected to sound keys, whose size and weight are made for the hand of an adult. The child will "shake" with his forearm instead of playing with intently controlled finger swing-strokes, because his fingers are unable to sound the tones with such slowed-down and small movements.

Thus when demonstrating legato playing for children, the teacher's finger movements should be larger than usual, especially during the first months of the lessons. The legato tone of a child beginner will become satisfactory only if he applies somewhat more finger work and strikes from somewhat higher than an adult would need to do. But legato playing must not be taught only through demonstrating the movements. The teacher has to show the pupil the tone colour required for this legato. It corresponds approximately to the clear and resolute legato of the Bach style, but similar service is rendered also by folk-songs. A folk-song where we can almost hear the words when playing it on the piano requires precisely the type of legato which is the most useful to the child. When playing melodies without any words we have to think of the above legato of the Bach style.

Thus, in teaching children we must not begin with romantic legato, where the tones melt one into another, because this type of legato requires only slight finger movement, while the role of the arm becomes more prominent on account of the strongly surging dynamic current.

For a good legato execution one has to encourage the pupil to practise gymnastic exercises aimed at overcoming the special difficulties of legato playing. (See exercises Nos. 26, 27, 48, 51, 55.)

PLAYING TO THE PUPIL

The pupil should be accustomed from the beginning to place maximum demands on his own playing. It follows that the teacher has to be equally demanding as regards his own performance when playing to the pupil.

Good playing by the teacher is not only helpful in developing the musical conception, but also an important sign-post towards attaining the proper mechanical balance on the part of the pupil.

The movements of a pupil in his teens have to be rectified in almost every lesson. The arms, grown long "overnight'" are liable to become passive, and the teacher has to show and explain patiently again and again how much more beautiful the tone becomes by the use of an active swing-stroke, by the synthesizing movements of the upper arm and by never letting the arm only "hang down." It must be shown again and again how great the difference is if the upper arm executes free accommodating movements instead of extending the elbows or pressing them tightly to the trunk. The pupil must be taught that each tone is important and that each slightest detail requires perfect elaboration.

Special attention must be paid to the utmost importance of working on details. Not only does the pupil have to play the difficult parts with separate hands but the teacher, too, has to play for the pupil with separate hands every melody with a somewhat difficult solution. In this way more opportunity is given to the pupil to observe every detail of the melody and find almost involuntarily the most appropriate movements for the correct solution.

Playing to the pupil must entirely be adjusted to his momentary physical possibilities. In the same way as we enter musically into the child's inner world, we also have to apply more simple mechanical solutions. Technical solutions, remote from childish mentality, involved or excessively passionate interpretations, will give rise to faulty innervation and make it difficult for the pupil to unfold his own means of expression. (This does not, of course, mean some sort of special style marked "for children only" but just simple, direct, pure playing.)

In playing to adult beginners, the problem of adjustment will be an easier one, but even here account must be taken of the past musical experience of the pupil. Playing to the pupil has to help children and adults to solve both their *musical* and their *technical* problems.

The aim of playing to the pupil is not to give some pattern to be imitated by him. But rather we have to display an indefatigable work, even from the beginning, to encourage the pupil to express his own musical conception. Even the apparently less talented pupil may have his own concept if he is fascinated by music. Maybe this concept is not a remarkable one, but it is his own anyhow and thus of more value for his future development than any perfect imitation of a pattern.

IMPROVISATION

Improvisation is a most important means of developing the child's ability to express his own musical concept. Improvisation on the instrument is to be prepared by vocal melody improvisations already during the preparatory teaching. With little children one has to request just a finishing tone or a motif but the teacher may let them improvise a half period also. The teacher sings the first part of the melody and lets the pupil finish it.

In piano teaching, too, the improvisation must be begun in this way, by choosing first pentachord melodies. The pupil will soon play his own little improvisations more freely than anything learned from notes. Of course, in order to attain this the teacher has to give encouragement to him, he has to make it clear to him that one can talk also through the piano. Most probably these little melodies will not be always masterpieces! But are our own sentences used in everyday life always masterpieces? And still, we are able to express ourselves with our own words. It is not enough to know a lot of beautiful poems by heart, we could not get on with them in life, without having also our own words and sentences. One could hardly purchase anything by using quotations from Longfellow. But could anybody recite Longfellow if he were unable to form two sentences with his own words? In the same way, in order to give a good "recital" of Bach or Beethoven one should first be able to talk with his own words and sentences on the piano. Thus the pupil will not lose his head at the slightest lapse of memory because improvising will aid him toward a better understanding of the musical content of the composition and he will be able to reproduce it with the same ease as if they were his own "words".

Improvisation may also be an aid in learning technique. If, e.g., the teacher wants the pupil to practise some difficult technical formula, he may "sneak" it into the melody. (This is of particular importance in trills and similar movements requiring a great freedom.) The pupil, when improvising, plays in a free and easy way and cannot be depressed by the thought (as usually occurs) that he has to overcome some particularly difficult technical task.

RESTS, COUNTING

An almost universal fault with beginners is the fact that they do not sustain the rests exactly. After the muscle activity the inactivity of the pause seems to be too long to the child and so he wants to cease it as quickly as possible. What is the remedy here? By no means the solution applied in some preparatory schools, to make him mark the pauses also by active movements. Instead we have to make him understand even during the first rhythmical exercises that the pause marks an increase of intensity. Pauses are also component parts of the music and a good expression will be possible only by "playing" them exactly. They do not mean any interruption – not even from the point of view of motion – but rather a preparation for the sounding of the next tones. The synthesizing movement continues even during the pauses.

Counting is a very valuable help to the pupil in his striving for a sure rhythm. In the rhythmical exercises executed in the preparatory and solfeggio lessons counting must be applied systematically. The counting should always apply to the meter, i.e. to the most frequently occurring metric values. When, e.g., playing in 2/4 time, the pianist should count in quavers ("one-and two-and") only if dotted quavers occur frequently. Otherwise only crotchets should be counted ("one-two").

Continual counting when playing the piano merely diverts attention from the musical contour-shaping, because it keeps the pupil from concentrating on sounding the tones. However, as a means of control, counting is very serviceable when playing a rhythmically complicated part, in which case it is to be considered as a sort of polyphonic problem. (Even when playing the Bach Two-Part Inventions counting will sometimes serve as a good means of checking: in the case of the Invention in E major, the pianist should count in quavers, while each hand practises its parts separately.)

TONE VOLUME

The most delicate problem of playing for a pupil is to try to compensate for the difference between the child's small, light hand[2] and the heavy keys.

When we play to the pupil, the volume tone must also be adjusted to the physical capacities of the child. The teacher should be careful not to force the pupil to wrong solutions by demanding an excessive tone volume. In the initial stage of learning the tone volume depends entirely on the size of the hand and the weight of the arm; consequently the pupil will only gradually find the tone corresponding both to his musical concept and to the level of his intellectual and physical development.

A correctly chosen tone volume organically links up with the musical concept of the pupil but never transgresses the limits set by this physical development. It is obvious that the natural tone volume of which an eight-year-old child is capable does not equal that of an adult; indeed, in most cases it does not even reach that of a child with similar hand- and arm-build, but four or five years older. Thus it would be a great mistake to fix the tone volume by some general standard and to demand the same tone volume from a child of slight build as from an adult with a hand weighing three times as much. We repeat: the weight of the key is suited to an adult hand.

It would be just as great an error, however, to demand of the beginner a small tone volume at any price. This is why we often find adolescents with powerful extremities timidly playing with a thin tone as if afraid of breaking their fingers. Generally speaking, the same importance should be attributed to the tone conception as to the physical endowments. Pupils of the same physical structure but differing as to their intelligence and musical development may have different conceptions of tone volume, just as their faculty for musical shading may differ, too.

Phot. 360
CHANGEABLE GOLDHAMMER KEYBOARDS

[2] This antagonism is almost entirely eliminated by Dr. Otto Goldhammer's uprights with exchangeable keyboards. On account of their very simple structure the keyboards can be exchanged in a few minutes even by a layman and so there is no obstacle in the music schools because every pupil plays on a keyboard fitted to his hands. The keyboards of different size also have a graduated range of key resistance and so they optimally fulfil the requirements.

A very frequent fault is to express intense emotions by straining the muscles. Instead of making the piano work, of making it sing, the pupil will work, and the simplest solution of this is to press down the keys jerkily to the key-bed. This is harmful not only from the technical point of view, but it also weakens the shaping of the dynamic contours because it breaks up the unity of the movements and with it also the dynamic unity.

The straining of the muscles and the pressing down of the keys most frequently result from the fact that the pupil does not obtain expected tone volume from the instrument. It is not an easy task to make him discover that greater tone volume may be attained by more expedient movements instead of more strained ones. (See page 82.) The pianist should always avoid pressing down the keys even if it seems to give a sense of muscular stability in learning a piece, because this pressing will very soon cause a passivity of the fingers and forearm and will render impossible the delicate accommodating movements of the upper arm. Wrong technical solutions for obtaining the required tone volume must not be tolerated even temporarily.

TECHNICAL EXERCISES

A large number of wrong innervations may arise if the beginner is allowed to get musical experience only through hundreds of technical exercises. Music must be taught starting only from the music. In this way much better and more perfect technical solutions may be obtained than by solving *l'art pour l'art* technical tasks. However, it would be a grave fault to reject technical exercises entirely. They, too, are required but always in direct connection with the solving of some musical task.

Even when beginning to play the very first melodies, certain parts may cause difficulties. When this happens, the pupil should construct little finger exercises and variants under the guidance of the teacher. Such finger exercises will be linked directly with the music and thus the pupil will yield less easily to the temptation of playing mechanically and indifferently. The fact that he will soon succeed in inventing these exercises all by himself will teach him self-reliance, so that, in learning to apply this method step by step, his work will become more and more reliable.

At the same time, however, the teacher cannot protest sufficiently against all kinds of finger exercises having an end only in themselves. If these "musicless" finger exercises are continued systematically and over an extended period (a whole hour is no rarity, sometimes even an hour and a half), the pupil is practically forced to play inattentively and mechanically, because neither the music nor the movements are interesting enough to engage his attention.

Independent technical work is permissible only in one case: the practising of the basic playing forms.

PRACTISING OF FUNDAMENTAL PLAYING FORMS

The most important playing forms are scales, chords, octaves and passages. The practising of these playing forms should not begin until the pupil has developed enough physically to be able to solve the task both mechanically and musically.

If the pupil has already mastered small pentachord pieces to the point of sight-reading them, he may begin to practise scales. Only when the use of the arms has become free and easy and the work of the fingers firm and reliable, with the finger-ends transferring the received energy with as little loss as possible, only then may the pupil undertake to practise both the complicated act of passing the thumb under the palm and the no less complicated synthesizing movements of the arm required in scale playing.

Scale playing in the first years may be slower or faster, according to necessity, but the pupil should never use slow practising. The aim here is, first of all, to automatize the "feeling" for the proper order of succession of the keys. The most difficult – and at the same time the most important – task for the beginner in scale practising is to play the scales by means of a single, wide synthesizing movement. It is hardly possible to begin practising this before the middle of the second year of study. Frequently the pupil will succeed in executing this kind of wide synthesizing movement, simultaneously with energetic and expedient finger action only toward the end of the second year.

If we wait until the fingers have already learned to carry out their work reliably and the arms have acquired some experience in performing smooth synthesizing movements, it will be unnecessary to increase the range of the scale gradually octave by octave. From the first, scale exercises should be practised over a range of two octaves, and when the pupil has mastered this, he may pass onto scales spanning four octaves. This will at the same time afford new possibilities for synthesizing arm movements. If the scales are played with synthesizing movements and pure finger work, the playing of four octaves will prove no more difficult than that of three, and scarcely more difficult than the playing of two octaves. On the other hand, the scale of four octaves will direct his attention to the most important factor: the synthesizing of the whole scale.

It would also be inappropriate to teach scale playing at an earlier stage of development because this would require familiarity with intervals. If, however, the pupil has learned to construct the scale consciously in all of its transpositions, his self-reliance will be greatly furthered, provided that the teacher does not impose artificial and complicated rules of fingering upon him, but lets him determine the fingering of the scale by himself.

The teacher must discuss with the pupil the necessity of not placing the first and fifth fingers on the black keys owing to their inconvenience, and of using the same fingering when playing in the same position when the tones recur in successive octaves.

The pupil may be led to construct the fingering of, say, the C major scale in the following way:

Let him begin an ascending scale with the left hand, the five fingers striking in succession. Now the question will arise which fingers to use up to the next D, since the pupil already knows that the fourth finger will come on the D. (The fifth finger cannot be used during the course of the scale because it is inconvenient to pass it over.) If the fourth finger is placed on the A, the first finger will come on to the D, yet he wants to strike the D with the fourth finger. Thus it is the third finger which should strike the A, and this now gives him the complete C major fingering!

The fingering of the right hand will be built up in the same way. However, as the right hand is a mirror-like reflection of the left one, the pupil has to commence a descending scale, because the proper fingering can be found only in this way.

What will happen with regard to the transpositions? There, too, the same method applies. In trying to find the correct fingering of the A flat major scale for the right hand, the following comments may be useful:

Since the fifth finger – in view of its shortness – cannot be put on the A flat, try to do it with the fourth finger. This, too, will not prove expedient, for now the first finger will come on the E flat. Thus we are compelled to begin with the third finger. Now let us try to use the fourth finger on the E flat. The pupil will notice that this, too, is inappropriate, because again the first finger will come on a black key, i.e. on the B flat. The E flat will consequently be struck by the third finger and the fourth one will be placed on the B flat in order that the A flat can be sounded by the third finger – as in the beginning of the scale.

This manner of learning the scales is at first somewhat tedious, but it has the advantage of inducing the pupil to take his first independent steps in the science of fingering. The procedure should be accompanied by a clear explanation of the fingerings employed in the pieces which the pupil is asked to study. The teacher has to accustom the pupil gradually to construct his fingerings independently.

In general, special practising of chords becomes necessary only in the third or fourth year. If a chord occasionally occurs earlier, practise it divided into two notes at a time just as later when practising the chords systematically. (The systematic practising of broken chords is unnecessary.)

The playing of passages should not be begun before the fifth year, because passages are employed only in pieces already requiring a rather advanced technique.

Octave playing must already be prepared for in the third or fourth year, by means of exercises in sixths. Systematic octave exercises will be needed only simultaneously with the passages, but at the same time a thorough, steady training in octave playing is required.

THE USE OF THE PEDAL

No general rule can be established as to the level of development at which the use of the pedal should begin. It depends, first of all, on whether the pupil is tall enough to be able to dispense with a footstool. If the pedal can be used only through a wrong sitting position, it will be advisable to postpone teaching the use of the pedal, because an incorrect body posture, acquired in the course of the first years of study, may seriously endanger the success of the whole course of study.

The main function of the pedal is to embellish the tone; this is attained by the resonance of the undampened strings. The pedal may also be used to sustain the tone if there is no possibility of holding down the keys with the hand.

The pupil must become accustomed to deciding, after careful reflection, whether there is any necessity for using the pedal in a certain musical item. With our assistance, the pupil should more and more frequently determine himself which notes require the use of the pedal.

Do not leave learning to use the pedal entirely to instinct, because the result will be that the pedal will be used by the pupil as a veil for covering up his uncertainty and even wrong tones or rhythms.

The pupil must be taught, above all, not to jump about on the pedal but rather to keep his foot on it continually in order to be able to depress it noiselessly. He must also be reminded that he must not place his whole sole on the pedal but merely touch it to the extent required to depress it lightly. The association of the musical concept with the use of the pedal can be attained only by the simplest movements.

As our aim is to make the tone more beautiful, we must try to reduce the noise-effects to a minimum. For this reason the pedal must, if possible, be pressed down after the sounding of the tone, because then the noise-effects will not be amplified by resonance. This way of employing the pedal also has the advantage of making the tone volume more even, because its natural tendency to decrease is counteracted by the amplifying effect of the resonances.

The use of the pedal is more difficult in fast tempo since there is not enough time for delay and the pedal must be depressed simultaneously with the sounding of the tone. It is very important not to place the pupil before such a difficult task until delayed depression of the pedal has become automatic, otherwise he may simply beat the time with the pedal instead of using it musically.

The teacher has to show the pupil convincingly how much the beauty of the tone will be enhanced by depressing the pedal at the proper moment and with due carefulness, rather than by thoughtless use of the pedal. The pupil should try to determine for himself several times in succession which way of using the pedal will assure the most beautiful tone effect.

The teacher should show him how each style requires a different kind and extent of pedal use. He should prove by examples that the harmonic interrelation will stand out more clearly through the correct use of the pedal, while its wrong application confuses even the clearest musical structure. By analysing in detail — and with the co-operation of the pupil — the errors committed in using the pedal, we can gradually convert the pedal into an easy and serviceable means of improving tone quality.[3]

[3] Very appropriate for the first attempts at using the pedal are Bartók's little pieces "For Children" because here the principles of aesthetic use of the pedal may be easily applied; moreover, these pieces do not require much use of the pedal.

COMBINING MUSICAL AND TECHNICAL DEVELOPMENT

An absolutely indispensable prerequisite of successful teaching is the all-round musical development of the pupil.

Let him do sight-reading (mainly of unfamiliar material) in order to link the visual and motor elements. Insist on his playing melodies by ear (to link aural and motor elements) and also on his improvising an accompaniment for them (even if it be a mere "bagpipe-bass"). Depending upon the theoretical level attained by the pupil, there should always be a thorough analysis of the pieces he is learning, thus helping him to appreciate how greatly the technical solutions are strengthened by such analysis.

Special attention must be devoted to avoiding a one-sided development of the pupil. If he has difficulty in note-reading, he should read a lot; if he is weak in memorizing, he must memorize the details consciously; and so forth. The teacher should never resign himself to the pupil's backwardness in any field of technique. On the contrary, some solution must always be found to ensure a harmonious development both musically and technically.

Once the mechanical aspect has been mastered by the pupil, the technical work will take up comparatively little time. Every tone resulting from expedient movements will be useful and will help to develop his technique. Everything he plays will assist him in creating movement associations corresponding to the musical interrelations and in acquiring mastery over his arms and fingers.

Even during the first lessons the pupils must be taught to find out that the piano can be made to sing. Even while playing the first folk-songs he must become aware that keys are nothing else than handles, by the aid of which the piano can be induced to sing.

The pupil must never be given tasks beyond the technical level he has arrived at.

The important thing is that he should perform his piece beautifully and naturally and that he should play as freely as if he were improvising the composition in question.

Every true music-lover has something personal to express in sound (even if it is not always of great importance). It is the teacher's task to ensure that developing the musical conception should occupy a central position in his teaching.

This does not mean, of course, that the teacher should attach no weight to technique. However, the road to the acquisition of good technique does not lead through a dense thicket of finger exercises but through a profound living of the music itself in the course of re-creating it with a full sense of responsibility for each single tone produced.

Anyone who is fond of poetry may learn to recite poems intelligently and beautifully – although this will not yet make him a great reciter. But what would we think of somebody's trying to improve his reciting by practising an ever louder and swifter enunciation of the syllables or lines of a verse or by rattling off a whole verse in one breath? It is just as silly for a pianist to try to gain access to Beethoven's or Mozart's world of musical concepts by a mere abundance of finger exercise or scales or by a mere thumping of the piano for hours on end in the name of "slow practising".

Technique is within everybody's reach. If a pianist finds himself unable to acquire a reliable technique, it is usually the result of his trying to attain it independently from the music.

But even the best musical concepts are in vain if we are unable to realize them at the piano through appropriate movements. Therefore, the pupil should from the start apply only such movements as are capable of further development.

The teacher must not be led astray by the fact that a child beginner will sometimes achieve a good musical effect with the aid of wrong movements (e.g., by "shaking"). Only those solutions are acceptable which may be considered as final and which fit into the perspective of the pupil's musical and technical development.

INDEX

Names	Figuring in the text	Photos of hands	Sitting at the piano	Filmstrips	Musical Examples
D'Albert, Eugen		24, 133			
Ammerbach, Nicolaus	239				
Antal, István		138		64, 151	
Arias, E.		202			
Bach, C. Ph. E.	9, 77, 86, 94, 193, 239, 245				167
Bach, J. S.	9, 36, 73, 77, 82, 104, 110, 237, 270, 271				237, 239, 240, 243
Bach, W. Fr.	240				
Backhaus, H.	12				
Backhaus, Wilhelm	56	207	74		
Bartók, Béla	16, 78, 232, 275		95		231
Beethoven, Ludwig van	9, 73, 77, 82, 110, 271, 276				33, 34, 71, 172, 182, 229, 231, 232, 235, 237, 238, 239, 244, 245
Brahms, Johannes	97				183
Brailowski, Alexander			199		
Bruchollerie, Monique de la			91		
Buchmann, G.	13, 14				
Busoni, Ferruccio	228, 232		59		
Bülow, Hans von		133			
Cabezon, Antonio de	239				
Carreño, Theresa	132	130			
Casadesus, Robert		187	108		
Chopin, Frédéric	9, 36, 110, 125, 129, 143, 145, 150, 156, 193–194, 209, 235–236, 240, 246	132			60, 63, 65, 111–112, 156, 169, 182, 218, 246–248
Clementi, Muzio	235				
Cortot, Alfred					112
Couperin, François	58, 193, 225, 235, 239, 249				167, 240
Cramer, J. B.	235				
Curzon, Clifford			100		
Czerny, Carl	235				234
Delezenne, Ch. E. G.	17				
Diruta, Girolamo					240
Ekier, Jan			140		
Ferber, Albert			116		
Fétis, Fr. J.	145				226

279

Names	Figuring in the text	Photos of hands	Sitting at the piano	Filmstrips	Musical Examples
Fischer, Annie	56, 132	53, 130, 208	52	60–61, 152–153, 184–185, 194–195, 220–221	
Fischer, Joseph, Dr.	249				
Fuller, M. V.	11				
Gáti, István	77				
Gieseking, Walter			113		
Gilels, Emil		133	72		
Goldenweiser, A. B.	80				
Goldhammer, Otto, Dr.	147, 169, 272				
Gosh, R. N.	13				
Haas, Monique			106		
Hanon, Ch. L.					202
Hart, H. C.	11				
Haskill, Clara		129			
Haydn, Joseph	214				
Händel, G. Fr.	16				
Helmholtz, Hermann von	12, 16–17				
Horowitz, Vladimir		145			
Jackson, Edwin W.	249–250				
Joachim, József	17				
Johnen, Kurt	90				
Kalkbrenner, Fr. W. M.	21				
Karsai-Szemes, Márta	13, 97				
Kentner, Louis			57		
Kerer, Rudolf		137	88		
Kodály, Zoltán					186–187
Kraus, Lili		67	66		
Lange, W.	12				
Liszt, Franz	9, 56, 77, 125, 143, 150, 156, 169, 177, 180, 235, 242	134	22, 30		155, 156, 168, 177, 179, 184, 186, 230, 231, 236, 237, 238, 244, 246
Longfellow	271				
Lukács-Schuk, Anna	249–250				
Lusby, W. S.	11				
MacDowell, E. A.	135				
Marx, A. B.	82				
Martienssen, C. A.	12, 20				
Matthay, Tobias	56, 82				

Names	Figuring in the text	Photos of hands	Sitting at the piano	Filmstrips	Musical Examples
Mendelssohn, Felix		133			
Meyer, E.	13–14				
Moór, Emánuel	150				
Moscheles, Ignaz	145				226
Mozart, Leopold	226				226
Mozart, W. A.	9, 31, 77, 110, 129, 197, 214, 235, 276				32, 33, 34, 35, 228
Neuhaus, H. G.	80				
Nikolaev, A. A.	80				
Oborin, Lev		137			
Obraztsov, S.	76				
Paganini, Niccolò	99, 156, 168, 186				
Pavlov, I. P.	91, 99				
Piccirilli, E.	250				
Planck, Max	11				
Prentice, R.	250				
Purcell, Henry					240
Quantz, J. J.	226				
Rachmaninoff, Sergei			58		
Richter, Sviatoslav	38, 56, 132	133, 136	37, 115	39–47, 62, 166	
Riemann, Hugo	126				
Riemann, Ludwig	14				
Rubinstein, Anton	132	137	55		
Rubinstein, Artur			146		
Rubinstein, Nicolaus	103				
Sándor, György		137			
Sauer, Emil	56, 103, 156	49, 142	48		
Schlesinger, H.	13				
Schubert, Franz					38, 64, 155, 208, 242
Schumann, Robert	99				62, 155, 166, 172
Sorel, Claudette		168			
Stanislavsky, K. S.	75, 77, 85, 99, 101, 102				
Tchaikovsky, P. I.	125				
Tetzel, Eugen	11, 20				
Thalberg, Sigismund	80, 82				
Tonassi, Pietro	250				

Names	Figuring in the text	Photos of hands	Sitting at the piano	Filmstrips	Musical Examples
Toscanini, Arturo	97				
Türk, D. G.	77				
Ungár, Imre	56	138	93	63	
Urbach, F.	13				
Vásáry, Tamás				65, 180–181	
Vierling, O.	13				
Weber, C. M.					234
Weissenberg, Alexis		209			
Zak, Jakov		136	144		
Zecchi, Carlo		137			

Photos without the indication of any name represent the author

Figure 1 has been taken over from an article of R. N. Gosh (T. A. S. A. 7, 127, 1935)

Figure 5 from an article of F. Trendelenburg, E. Thienhaus and E. Franz (Akustische Zeitschrift XII. 1940)

Figures 24, 38–39, 41 from the Anatomical Atlas by Sobotta (Lehmann, München)

Figures 27, 28, 31–36 from the Anatomical Atlas by Toldt (Urban and Schwarzenberg)

Photos 3, 97, 157, 159, 160, 170, 171, 179 from Breithaupt's "Die natürliche Klaviertechnik" (1912, C. F. Kahnt Nachfolger, Leipzig)

Phot. 100 from Bie's "Das Clavier" (Cassierer, Berlin)

Phot. 142 from R. Hauert (Kister Verlag, Genf)

Photos 181, 313 from Nouneberg's work "Les secrets de la technique du piano" (Max Eschig, Paris)

LIST OF FILMSTRIPS

Sviatoslav Richter playing the middle part of Schubert's Impromptu in E flat major	39–47
Annie Fischer playing the middle portion of Chopin's Fantaisie Impromptu	60–61
Sviatoslav Richter playing Schumann's "Warum?"	62
Imre Ungár playing Chopin's Nocturne in F major	63
István Antal plays the slow movement of Schubert's Sonata in A minor	64
Tamás Vásáry plays Chopin's Ballad in F minor	65
Fast octave-playing with complementary wrist action	151
Chord-progression with complementary wrist motion	152–153
Chord-exercise	161
Sixth-repetitions	162–163
Fast chord playing	166
Skips executed by even motion	180–181
The octave-skip	184–185
Beginning of Chopin's Fantaisie Impromptu	194–195
Touch exercise with the fourth finger	200–201
Progressive touch exercise	204–205
The action of the thumb in fast playing of the B major scale. Lateral view	211
Slow practising of fast scale	212–213
Fast playing of B major passage	220–221
Thumb stroke in B major passage played in outward direction	222–223